Peggy Guggenheim

Also by Mary V. Dearborn

Pocahontas's Daughters:
Gender and Ethnicity in American Culture

Love in the Promised Land:
The Story of Anzia Yezierska and John Dewey

The Happiest Man Alive:
A Biography of Henry Miller

Queen of Bohemia:
The Lkife of Louise Bryant

Mailer: A Biography

Mistress of Modernism:
The Life of Peggy Guggenheim

Peggy Guggenheim

Mistress of Modernism

MARY V. DEARBORN

Virago

VIRAGO

First published in Great Britain in September 2005 by Virago Press
First published in the United States in 2004 by Houghton Mifflin

Copyright © Mary V. Dearborn 2004

The moral right of the author has been asserted.

A CIP catalogue record for this book
is available from the British Library.

ISBN 1 86049 973 2

Typeset in Goudy by M Rules
Printed and bound in Great Britain
by Mackays of Chatham plc, Chatham, Kent

Virago Press
An imprint of
Time Warner Book Group UK
Brettenham House
Lancaster Place
London WC2E 7EN

www.virago.co.uk

For Meryl Altman and Mary B. Campbell

ACKNOWLEDGMENTS

I have been working on this book for a long five years, mostly because I have enjoyed the work so thoroughly that I did not want it to end. It was the people who made writing the life of Peggy Guggenheim such an interesting and congenial project. The list of those to thank is long, and inevitably I have left people out; my apologies to those I've overlooked.

I made new friends: John Hohnsbeen, an indispensable source, a kindred soul, and a believer in Peggy; Anne Dunn; Charles and Lenore Seliger; the extraordinary Francis V. O'Connor; the late David Gascoyne and his wife, Judy; Sara Havelock-Allen; Domingo de la Cueva (who introduced me to prosecco); and the incomparable Lyle Bongé of Biloxi. Relatives of Peggy whom I have interviewed include John King-Farlow, Nicolas Hélion, and Barbara Benita Shukman. Pegeen Vail's second husband, Ralph Rumney (1934–2002), was a dear and unforgettable resource. His son, Sandro Rumney, and Karole Vail, Sindbad Vail's daughter, were both extremely helpful and always gracious and insightful about my project; I am particularly grateful to them for their generosity in supplying or authorizing the use of photographs, and for granting me permission to quote from their grandmother's unpublished writing.

Art historians who helped me include Avis Berman, Ingrid Schaffner, Roger Conover, Francis Nauman, Mel Lader, Francis V. O'Connor, Helen Harrison, Roberta Tarbell, and Dore Ashton. Artists whom I have interviewed, some of whom showed at or visited Peggy's New York gallery, include Paul Resika, Charles Seliger, Peter Ruta, David Loeffler-Smith, Al Kroesch, and Philip Pavia. Thanks also to Ethel Baziotes, the late Lillian Kiesler, Suzanne Ruta, and Natalie Pavia. I owe a great debt to other biographers, many of whom are or have become friends: Calvin Tomkins (Marcel Duchamp); Carolyn Burke (Mina Loy and Lee Miller); Marion Meade; Ken Silverman; Brenda Wineapple; John Szwed (Miles Davis); Julia Van Haafeten (Berenice Abbott); Jane Dunn (Antonia White); Cressida Connolly (the Garman sisters); Valerie Grove (Dodie Smith); Florence Rubenfeld (Clement

Greenberg); Joan Mellen (Kay Boyle); William Feaver (Lucian Freud); Richard Greene (Edith Sitwell); Karl Orend (Henry Miller), and, especially, Noël Riley Fitch (Julia Child).

I am very grateful to those who knew Peggy and shared what they knew (many of whom I've mentioned above): Peter Lauritzen, Fred Licht, Tom Messer, Margot Waldman, Giselle Waldman, Colin Webster-Watson, Jacqueline Ventadour Hélion, Edmund White, David and Marian Porter, Jock Stockwell, Baroness Maria Theresá Rubin de Cervin, the late Charles Henri Ford (with the help of Indra B. Tanang), James Lord, John Loring, Eileen Finletter, Manina, Joan Fitzgerald, Alan Ansen, Marc Dachy, Yasmin David, Judith Malina and Hanon Reznikov, Iris Owens, Yoko Ono (with the help of John Hendricks), Philip Johnson, Donald Windham, and Marilyn Sorrel.

Those who helped me with questions, untangled knots for me, or gave me good press and/or information include the late Billy Klüver and Julie Martin; Jonathan Bayer; Chris Busa; Sandra Chait; Pierluigi Consagra; Ron Hogan; Laura Kuhn (and Rita Putnam); Mimi Roberts; Ron Stocker, Helen Harrison; Judith (Kiki) Malin (and Rebecca Lieb); Ben Heller; Sylvie Mettetal; Steven Beyer; Sigrid Falton; Sandra Kraskin; Judith Gutman; Kathleen Raine; Timothy Baum; Dierdre Connolly; James Mayor; Kathleen Flanagan, Richard Kostelanetz, Mary Wesley, Michael C. D. Macdonald, and Lyndall Passerini Hopkinson. Freda Hamric has been an excellent researcher at the University of Texas in Austin.

The Peggy Guggenheim Collection (PGC) in Venice has been more than helpful. I especially want to thank Philip Rylands and his wife, Jane Turner Rylands, who have been wonderful hosts; both also provided memories of Peggy that have been essential. The PGC mounted a show in September 2003 about Peggy Guggenheim and Frederick Kiesler, the visionary designer of Art of This Century (Peggy's New York gallery during World War II), which was extremely revelatory. My deepest thanks go to two curators who put the show together, at different Guggenheims, Jasper Sharp (of Venice) and Susan Davidson (of New York); as well as the designer who brilliantly reconstructed the gallery in models and an accomplished essay, Don Quaintance; and Dieter Bogner of the Frederick Kiesler Foundation.

Through Barbara Loeb Kennedy, in a felicitous turn, I found that I am related to the Guggenheims (by marriage only, so not at all). Barbara led me to the wonderful Susan Sandberg, who is the daughter of the gifted photographer Marjorie Content, my grandmother's first cousin. Content, part owner of Sunwise Turn, the innovative bookstore that employed Peggy in

1919, was married to Peggy's cousin Harold Loeb, Barbara Loeb Kennedy's uncle.

I happily thank some archivists: L. Rebecca Melvin Johnson in Special Collections, University of Delaware Library; Beth Alvarez in Special Collections, University of Maryland Libraries; David Koch and Katy Salzman at Southern Illinois University; Judy Throm at the Archives of American Art, Smithsonian Institution; Christa Aube at the Art Institute of Chicago; Wim de Wit at the Getty Research Institute; Ruth Long at Cambridge University; Sara Hodson at the Huntington Library; Margaret M. Sherry at Princeton University Library; Chris Petter at the University of Victoria; and Tara Wengler at the Harry Ransom Center for the Humanities Research Center, University of Texas, Austin. For help with photographs, I want to thank Carolyn McMahon from AP/Wide World Photos, Sydona Barrett from the University of Oklahoma, Lara Adler from Bettmann/Corbis, Dean Rogers of Vassar, Rona Tuccillo of Getty Images, Beth Krieger from the Calhoun School, Tara Schindler at Yale, Natalie Evans, and, most especially, Cindy Johnson at Commerce Graphics, the Berenice Abbott archive.

I was fortunate to rent, for a week in May 2003, a vacation cottage that was an outbuilding of Hayford Hall, the estate in Devon that Peggy and John Holms took for two summers in 1931 and 1932, where they held an idyllic, very literate house party, on the edge of Dartmoor. My thanks to Carol and Clive Richardson, my hosts; the Hayford Hall groundskeeper, David Wright; and Malcolm Dunstan and his wife, Kate, the current owners of Hayford Hall.

I am very grateful to those who read the manuscript or parts of it and offered comments: Meryl Altman, Dick and Tommy Dearborn, Tina Ruyter, Anne Dunn, David Gratt, John Hohnsbeen, Francis V. O'Connor, Charles Seliger, and Philip Rylands, as well as those who organized the 2003–2004 Frederick Kiesler show at the PGC. Erik La Prade, the authority on Charles Henri Ford, added a new dimension to my research and has generally aided and enriched my efforts. Also I must thank those friends who put up with me: Ruah Donnelly, Meryl Altman, Mary B. Campbell, Shirley King, Keith Nightenhelser, Warren Johnson, Tina Ruyter, Martin Hurwitz, Joe Markulin, Dan Rosenblatt and James Pritchard, Jay Gertzman, Val Clark, Mark SaFranko, and Lisa Greenwald.

I am, as always, grateful to my peerless agent, Georges Borchardt; and I thank Janet Silver, who believed in this book; Deanne Urmy, my very talented and resourceful editor; Walter Vatter, the book's excellent publicist; and Jayne Yaffe Kemp, who cleaned everything up and helped me say what I meant to say. Melissa Grella was efficient and smart throughout and deserves kudos.

My greatest debt is to Eric Laursen, my dear companion of nineteen years and the keenest of editors.

Mary V. Dearborn
New York City, March 2004

CONTENTS

LIST OF ILLUSTRATIONS

Peggy's maternal grandfather, James Seligman (*Bass Collection, University of Oklahoma Libraries*)

Peggy's paternal grandfather, Meyer Guggenheim (© *Bettmann/Corbis*)

Peggy's parents, Benjamin and Florette Guggenheim, circa 1910 (*Private collection*)

Peggy and her two sisters, Hazel and Benita (*Private collection*)

Peggy as a geisha girl, circa 1908 (*Private collection*)

Peggy with a ribbon on her forehead, with the Jacobi School class of 1915 (*Courtesy of The Calhoun School*)

Peggy with her pug, circa 1915, the first in a long parade of canine pets (*Private collection*)

Peggy Waldman, Peggy's friend and adviser (*Courtesy of Gisele Waldman*)

Berenice Abbott's portrait of Peggy, circa 1926 (© *Berenice Abbott/Commerce Graphics Ltd., Inc., NYC*)

Peggy's friend, the writer Djuna Barnes, circa 1922 (© *Oscar White/Corbis*)

Peggy and her friend, the British artist Mina Loy (© *Underwood & Underwood/Corbis*)

Emma Goldman with her secretary, Emily Coleman, Saint-Tropez, 1928 (© *Bettmann/Corbis*)

Robert McAlmon, Kiki, Louis Aragon, Peggy, and Clotilde Vail (*Yale Collection of American Literature, Beinecke Rare Book and Manuscript Library*)

John Holms, Djuna Barnes, Antonia White, and Peggy in an idle moment at Hayford Hall (*Special Collections, University of Maryland Libraries*)

Peggy at Hayford Hall. Dartmoor lies beyond (*Private collection*)

Emily Coleman, one of Peggy's closest friends, mid-1930s (*Special Collections, University of Delaware Library*)

Laurence, Kay Boyle, Sindbad, and Peggy, mid-1930s (*Private collection*)

Douglas Garman's daughter, Debbie, Pegeen, and Samuel Beckett, Yew Tree Cottage, 1938 (*Private collection*)

Yves Tanguy and Peggy, at the height of their affair, July 1938 (*Private collection*)

A Portrait of Peggy, circa 1938, the year she opened her London gallery, Guggenheim Jeune (*Private collection*)

Sindbad and Pegeen with their mother, circa 1939 (*Private collection*)

Peggy with Jacqueline, Aube, and André Breton, Chateau Air-Bel, outside Marseilles, 1941 (*Private collection*)

The Vail family in 1941: Apple, Laurence, Pegeen, Kay Boyle, Clover, Bobby, Kathe, and Sindbad

Max Ernst, 1946, with a detail from *The Temptation of St. Anthony* (© 2002 *AP Wide World Photos*)

Group portrait, New York City, 1941: Jimmy Ernst, Peggy, John Ferren, Marcel Duchamp, Piet Mondrian, Max Ernst, Amédée Ozenfant, André Breton, Fernand Léger, Berenice Abbott, Stanley William Hayter, Leonora Carrington, Frederick Kiesler, Kurt Seligmann (*Marcel Duchamp Archives. Courtesy of the Philadelphia Museum of Art*)

Peggy on a piece of Frederick Kiesler's correalist furniture in her Art of This Century gallery, 1942 (© 2002 *AP Wide World Photos*)

Peggy's autobiography: front jacket art by Max Ernst, back by Jackson Pollock. The Dial Press, New York, 1946 (*Private collection*)

Pegeen, around the time of her marriage to the artist Jean Hélion, circa 1943 (*Private collection*)

Jacqueline Ventadour with her husband, Sindbad, and Jean Hélion with his wife, Pegeen, circa 1946 (*Private collection*)

Peggy sunbathing on the roof of her palazzo on the Grand Canal, Venice, 1953 (*Frank Scherschel/Time Life Pictures, Getty Images*)

Peggy's friend, the writer Mary McCarthy, Venice, early 1950s (*Special Collections, Vassar College Library*)

Raoul Gregorich, Peggy's last love, early 1950s (*Private collection*)

Peggy with her much-married sister Hazel, at a London party in January 1965 (© 2002 *AP Wide World Photos*)

Peggy with her Calder sculpture at an exhibition of her collection in the Tate Gallery, December 31, 1965 (© 2002 *AP Wide World Photos*)

A lifetime in passport photos (*Private collection*)

Peggy Guggenheim

I

Fortunes and Family

Peggy Guggenheim viewed the Seligmans, her mother's side of her family, as 'peculiar, if not mad.' Her ancestors displayed unconventional sexual practices (and an openness about them) and remarkably eccentric behavior that suggested a streak of downright lunacy. By the time of Peggy's birth in 1898, however, this budding merchant banking dynasty had established itself as a pillar of the German-Jewish community in New York City, whose Edwardian and august members of the aristocracy have been given the soubriquet 'our crowd' by the popular historian Stephen Birmingham in his book of the same name. Characterized by ambitious and at the same time philanthropic patriarchs with many children and large extended families and by women who dedicated themselves to pursuits of the most *haut bourgeois* (teas, family gatherings, European tours, attention to their children's rearing), the German-Jewish circle was slightly inbred and exclusive to the point of a distinct suspicion of outsiders. Young men were expected to marry well and join the family business – usually banking or the law. For young women, who grew up in mansions on Fifth Avenue and, decades later, the Upper West Side, the future was even more rigidly prescribed: to be scantily educated in academic subjects but deeply immersed in French, needlework, and music, exposed to the arts but exclusively old masters, perhaps broadened (though that word would never be used) by a grand tour. They made their debuts and a few years after married Jewish men of the same community, if not of a related family, who would install them in establishments identical to their mothers', in order to devote themselves to their children and the smooth running of their very large households. The affluent German-Jewish woman's fate was one that Peggy Guggenheim, from a very early age, determined to escape.

Seligman means 'blessed one' in German, but the Seligmans of Baiersdorf, a small town on the Regnitz River just north of Nürnberg in

Bavaria, were generally poor tradespeople. David Seligman, a weaver and later a merchant selling woolens and sealing wax, was no exception. Conditions for Jews in Bavaria in the first half of the nineteenth century were constrained indeed; they could own no property other than the land on which their houses stood, marry only as permitted by law (which sought to limit the number of Jewish families), had to pay a toll whenever they left their settlements, and had to submit to random and extortionary taxes. As factories began springing up in cities, peasants from ghettos like Baiersdorf's were migrating to cities, making country life even more financially straitened.

In 1818, David Seligman married Fanny Steinhardt, from the nearby village of Sulzbach, who brought with her a small stock of linens, bolts of cloth, and other dry goods (her father was probably a merchant), enough to set up a modest shop in David's small attached house in Baiersdorf's Judengasse (Jew Street). Between 1819 and 1839, Fanny gave birth to eleven children. The eldest, Joseph, worked at his mother's side in her shop. Fascinated by the differences among coins paid in exchange for goods, he began converting out-of-town money into local currency and vice versa, charging a small fee for each transaction, excellent training for a future banker. Fanny was determined that Joseph get a good education, and she used her life savings to send him for two years to the University of Erlangen, where he excelled.

It was clear that a future in Baiersdorf held no promise for such a talented young man. Germans had already begun to emigrate, in growing numbers, to America, where opportunities were said to be unlimited. In 1837, Joseph set off for the port of Bremen in a wagon with eighteen other neighborhood boys. He had $100 sewn into his clothing by his mother and the $40 necessary for steerage in his pocket. Crossing the Atlantic on board the *Telegraph* took just over two weeks, a grim voyage indeed. Steerage passengers received one meal a day – water, beans, and pork – the latter, of course, proscribed by Jewish dietary laws. Joseph had no choice but to eat the fare.

Landing in New York, Joseph, then seventeen, made his way, as planned, to the Pennsylvania town of Mauch Chunk, where he had the address of his mother's cousin, and where German was spoken, thereby easing barriers for German-speaking immigrants. He worked for a year in Mauch Chunk as a clerk and cashier for a Yankee boatbuilder, Asa Packer, but he wanted to make money himself, not work for another man, and he outfitted himself with enough goods – first jewelry and watches, soon sewing equipment, bolts of cloth, shawls, table linens, and such items as eyeglasses and shoehorns – to take to the road with a pack on his back, traveling through the countryside and sleeping in fields at night. He soon had enough money to send for his younger brothers William and James, who also proved themselves successful enough at peddling that the three brothers could open a shop in Lancaster, Pennsylvania, and send for the fourth-oldest Seligman, Jesse.

James, Peggy's grandfather, the best-looking of the Seligman brothers, was known for his ability to sell. Eager to try his fortunes in the South, whose economy was booming, he wanted to buy a horse and wagon to haul more goods around the countryside than he could carry on his back. But Joseph put his foot down. Family lore has it that James and Joseph were arguing in the shop on a hot summer day when a customer walked in. James said under his breath to his brother, 'If I can sell her a pair of galoshes, will you let me go?' Joseph said yes. Though the shop had not a pair of them in stock, James, turning on the charm – he had a way with the ladies – managed to sell the customer a pair, telling her he would have them for her the next time she came in. In later years, James is said to have pronounced, 'To sell something you have to someone who wants it – that is not business. But to sell something you don't have to someone who doesn't want it – *that* is business!' Joseph did indeed set James up with a horse and wagon, and James went south, returning very soon with $1,000 in profit. Impressed, the brothers sold their store in Lancaster and moved to Mobile, Alabama.

There a letter reached them from Bavaria, telling them that their mother had died and that business was going so badly that David could not support the remaining seven children. The four sons raised $2,000 to bring Babette, twenty, Rosalie, fifteen, Leopold, ten, Abraham, eight, Isaac, seven, and two-year-old Sarah to the United States. David kept thirteen-year-old Henry to help him. Soon after, however, David wrote to say that his business had failed completely. Joseph wrote his father's creditors that he would make good on David's debts, and in 1843 David and Henry made the trip to America. The elder sons set up the family in a flat on New York's Lower East Side, with Babette running the household. The patriarch, David, died just two years after arriving.

In the South, Joseph rented three buildings outside Selma and opened dry goods stores in them, and the brothers became employers for the first time. When Babette and Rosalie wrote that they were marrying, Joseph insisted that they divide the remaining children and take them into their new families. James went up to New York for Babette's wedding and opened J. Seligman and Brothers, Merchants, on William Street; the brothers also opened stores in St. Louis, Missouri, and Watertown in upstate New York, with the new brothers-in-law participating. When gold fever struck in California, Jesse and Leopold made their way by ship through Panama to San Francisco, where they rented a brick building and opened a store, hoping for their share of that abundant wealth. (Their selection of one of the city's few brick buildings for their business paid off during the 1851 fire.) The store's markups were high, but not higher than the considerable market could bear, and soon Jesse and Leopold were sending shipments of gold back to New York, where the other brothers traded it on the commodities market or took it to Europe on the buying trips they had begun to make. The Seligmans were now officially in the banking business, just in time for a huge upsurge in the economy. (One blip was the panic of 1857, of which Joseph heard rumors beforehand, liquidating all the Seligman holdings, thereby remaining unaffected.) In 1857, Joseph, who in 1848 had married Babet Steinhardt, a Baiersdorf girl and his first cousin, moved into a brownstone in the Murray Hill district of New York City. By then, most of the brothers were married, and big family dinners became a Sunday tradition at Joseph's house.

The Seligman brothers in 1857 had joint capital of over $500,000, but the real family fortune was amassed during the Civil War. In 1860, William Seligman reasoned that it would be more profitable to make clothing than to sell it and started to open clothing mills. It did not take a visionary to deduce that the government would need uniforms in the coming war, and William positioned Isaac to be in the right place at the right time to obtain government contracts – something other businesspeople found too risky a proposition, the government being less than stable at the time. The venture was indeed risky, as the brothers were paid almost entirely in Union Treasury bonds, almost unsalable in the United States but which Joseph was able to sell abroad at a steep profit. Upon hearing of Lee's surrender in 1865, Joseph Seligman set up J. and W. Seligman & Company as an international bank. Soon the brothers established offices in Paris (run by William), Frankfurt (Henry), and London (Isaac). The Seligman brothers had thirty-six sons and their sisters eight more. The family became known as 'the American Rothschilds' and were close advisers to presidents; Joseph was offered the post of secretary of the Treasury under Grant, but reluctantly declined. Few American fortunes have been made so quickly and from such humble beginnings.

The Seligmans were among the first generation of American immigrants who made good in spectacular fashion, but other German-Jewish families were doing well themselves; among their number were the Lehmans, the Warburgs, and the Schiffs. The Seligmans belonged to the generation that rose to great wealth during the Civil War and the economic expansion that followed; in this respect their peers were the Vanderbilts, the Rockefellers, the Morgans – parvenus who within two generations would buy and marry their way into the American upper class.

The Seligmans also, perhaps more significantly, were among the first generation of Jewish businesspeople who benefited from the opening of the European ghettos and enjoyed the opportunity to prove their mettle in the wider world. These immigrants felt a constant tension between the desire to assimilate and enjoy the comforts familiar to gentiles, and a protective instinct based on centuries of persecution. The way they chose to negotiate the situation was to bond very closely within their families (participation in the family business was mandatory, not optional) and to create a distinct subset of New York high society – a sort of Jewish microcosm of the old Manhattan elite. They were socially conservative, but persistently Jewish (despite their tendency to patronize the newly arriving eastern European Jews), and they distinguished themselves by contributions to the arts – Otto Kahn would be the moving force behind the Metropolitan Opera, for instance – and in philanthropic reform efforts. Members of this community may have felt the strictures of their bourgeois world, but there were no bars to what they could achieve.

James Seligman, who had worked as a roofer in Bethlehem, Pennsylvania, before joining Joseph and William in the first Lancaster store, was interviewed at eighty-eight in 1912 by the New York Times, as his yellow canary, Billiken, sat on his shoulder. Told by a nurse that Seligman, while in possession of his other faculties, was totally deaf, the reporter asked him several questions with the help of a pad of paper. James related that as a boy he had trained as a weaver, arriving in the United States at fifteen with some small savings from that trade; he had contracted smallpox on the boat. By the time of this interview, James Seligman was the oldest banker in the city, the third-oldest member of the New York Stock Exchange, 'an old gentleman clad in black, with snow-white, flowing locks and a long, spare, white beard, deeply immersed in the contents of a newspaper, his slippered feet extended before him upon a velvet hassock.'

James had married Rosa Content in 1851, when he was twenty-seven and she seventeen. She was from a Dutch New York family that predated the Revolution in America and looked down on the Seligmans as 'peddlers.' Rosa had dark eyes and an olive complexion; she was thought 'handsome but erratic.' She loved material things, and James bought them for her, despite being somewhat miserly himself. She had an English butler named James and liked to say to him, 'James, tell Jim that dinner is served.' Rosa, a 'very beautiful, strongly tempestuous, unaccountable woman,' knew early on that her husband had taken a mistress, and she used to ask salesclerks, leaning confidentially across the counter, 'When do you think my husband last slept with me?' Rosa's several eccentricities, according to family legend, included a fear of the newly invented telephone; she would allow only the servants to use it. 'Bearing philosophically the hectoring of his impatient wife,' according to a family historian, James fathered eight children, five boys and three girls, though Peggy would mistakenly say in her autobiography that these grandparents had eleven children, perhaps counting siblings who had died in childhood.

The eldest of the girls, Frances, known as Fanny, was, according to Peggy, 'an incurable soprano.' She wore feather boas and a rose in her hair and was an excellent cook, but nevertheless was given to wiping household surfaces down with Lysol, the German disinfectant first sold in 1889. The family story had it that after quarreling with her for thirty years, her husband tried to kill her and one of their sons with a golf club, failed, and threw himself in a reservoir with weights on his feet. Another aunt, Adelaide, was enormously fat and late in life deluded herself into thinking that she was having an adulterous affair with a druggist named Balch; though her family tried to convince her that Balch did not exist, she remained so guilty and remorseful that they eventually put her in a nursing home. A third daughter, Florette, was Peggy's mother.

To educate his sons, James's brother Joseph had called in no less than Horatio Alger, the author of such enormously popular books as *Tattered Tom* and *Ragged Dick*, in which poor boys make good through 'luck and pluck.' Alger tutored Joseph's five boys, and James's five sons joined them. The slight, mild-mannered, and effeminate schoolmaster could barely control his charges and was the butt of many family jokes, which he took in good humor. The grateful Joseph and James opened an account for him at their firm and deposited his literary earnings there, investing them so wisely that Alger became rich himself, just like his heroes. He was long a fixture at Seligman family dinners.

James and Rosa's two eldest sons, DeWitt and Samuel, were 'nearly normal,' according to their niece. Peggy's favorite, DeWitt (named for New York governor DeWitt Clinton), earned a law degree and joined the family firm. An inveterate writer of plays, he could never figure out how to finish them, ending each one with a fantastic explosion. He produced a weekly magazine, *Epoch*. Samuel Seligman, the next eldest, was obsessed, like Rosa, with cleanliness and bathed several times a day.

The best-looking son was Jefferson, who married a rich girl but lived in two small rooms in an East Side hotel, which he filled with dresses from Klein's department store to give away to his mistresses. His sister Florette, visiting, took away an armful for herself, saying, 'I don't see why I shouldn't have some, too.' Jefferson became a member of J. and W. Seligman & Company, winning a reputation for handing out fruit and ginger – remedies, he thought, for every ill.

Another brother, Washington, never married and did not join the family firm. He was troubled with indigestion and nervousness, and tried to kill himself in 1903 by gashing his throat with a razor blade. An investor, he lost heavily on Wall Street. He had a habit of chewing charcoal, which gave him black teeth, and had a suit made with special pockets for the charcoal and for the ice that he also chewed. At fifty-six, leaving a note that read, 'I am tired of being sick all my life,' he shot himself to death in his rooms at the Hotel Gerard on West 44th Street.

Eugene was, Peggy said, the 'notably miserly' Seligman, who enrolled at Columbia Law School at the age of fourteen (after being admitted at eleven) and four years later graduated with the highest honors in his class. He never married either, and was a constant freeloader at his brothers' and sisters', where he amused his nieces and nephews by playing 'the snake,' wriggling his body's length atop a row of chairs.

Florette, Peggy's mother, had her eccentricities as well. She too used Lysol detergent on all surfaces. And she had a habit of saying everything three times. Her nephew describes a scene in which a policeman in Rome stopped her as she drove the wrong way down a one-way street. 'More hurt than flustered, Aunt Florette had answered, "But I'm goin' one way, goin' one way, goin' one way."' In another story, she went to a milliner for a hat with a feather. After her request of 'a feather, a feather, a feather,' she was given a hat with three.

Florette had a great deal to bear in her marriage to the handsome Benjamin Guggenheim. He was the fifth son of Meyer Guggenheim, who came to the United States in 1848 with his father, Simon, a tailor, and the family of the woman who would become his stepmother, Rachel Meyer, from the northwestern Swiss town of Lengnau. His first identifiable ancestor was 'der jud Maran Guggenheim von Lengnau,' mentioned in official documents of the duchy of Baden in 1696. On the voyage to Philadelphia, Meyer Guggenheim, twenty, fell in love with the daughter of Rachel Meyer from her prior marriage, Barbara, then fifteen, whom he married in 1852. Although trained as a tailor like his father, Meyer began his life in America, much as the Seligmans had done more than ten years before, by peddling in coal country in northeastern Pennsylvania. Seeing that most of his profits went to pay his suppliers, Meyer became a manufacturer himself – of stove polish, a product that he had heard his clients complain about. He hired a scientist to study the existing stove polish and create a product that would not sting or stain. Very soon, Meyer had a personal fortune of $800,000 and housed the family in a Philadelphia townhouse, maintaining a stable nearby whose horses pulled the business's wagons on weekdays and the family's carriages on weekends.

By the 1880s Meyer and his seven sons owned lace-making factories in Switzerland and the stove polish company, which expanded to sell coffee essence (a substitute for high-priced coffee). Meyer's goal was to bequeath to each of his sons – Isaac, Daniel, Murry, Solomon, Benjamin, Simon, and William – a million dollars.

In settling a business debt in 1881, Meyer, for $5,000, bought a one-third share in two lead and silver mines, the A.Y. and the Minnie, near Leadville, Colorado; it marked a turning point in his fortunes. Meyer pumped out the two mines, which had been flooded with water from the nearby Arkansas River, and before long, back in Philadelphia, he received a telegram that read 'Struck rich ore in A.Y. shaft number one.' The A.Y. was yielding fifteen ounces of silver per ton, along with considerable copper ore. He sent sons Benjamin and William to Leadville to learn metallurgy while he and his other sons turned themselves to the business of smelting the copper ore in economic fashion. Smelting and refining were to become Meyer and his sons' specialty; eventually they would even sell ownership of the mines while retaining the right to smelt the ore found there. In 1882 Meyer formed the company M. Guggenheim's Sons, with each of the sons an equal partner; they bought their first smelting operation in nearby Pueblo (where Benjamin was put to work as manager, having first served as bookkeeper for the A.Y.) and then one in Mexico. In 1890, the Minnie mine, only one of their operations, was worth $14.5 million. The next year they formed a trust called the Colorado Smelting & Refining Company. By 1895 the Guggenheim smelters were earning $1 million a year in cash.

Meyer had moved his family to New York City in 1888, settling in a brownstone on West 77th Street opposite the Museum of Natural History. In 1895 Benjamin, 'as near a black sheep as existed among the Guggenheims,' according to one family historian, was called back east to run a metal refinery that the family had just bought in Perth Amboy, New Jersey. During this time, he met Florette Seligman and proposed, to create what his daughter Peggy would call a 'mésalliance.' The Seligmans far surpassed the Guggenheims socially, though the latter had amassed the greater fortune. The Seligmans are said to have cabled their families in Europe that Florette was marrying into the great smelting family; the wire was garbled and read, 'Florette engaged Guggenheim smelt her.'

In 1899, the Guggenheim brothers formed the Guggenheim Exploration Company, known as Guggenex, which bought copper and silver mines in

Nevada, Utah, and New Mexico; copper mines in Alaska; tin mines in Bolivia; and a variety of metal mines in Mexico and Chile, the latter the great Chuquicamata copper mine. A rival trust, controlled by the copper miner Henry H. Rogers and backed by William Rockefeller and Adolph Lewisohn, sprang up. Called ASARCO (American Smelting and Refining Company), this trust appeared to be a threat, but the Guggenheims took advantage of a labor strike in 1900 to flood the metals market, driving down ASARCO's share price. Daniel Guggenheim, acting as leader for his brothers, began buying up shares in ASARCO until the Rockefeller interests offered to buy him out. Daniel made it a condition that the new ASARCO trust would include Guggenex only if all the brothers were to serve on its board. Thus the Guggenheims wrested control of ASARCO, going on to become the mining leaders of the world. By the time the First World War broke out, they controlled 75 to 80 percent of the world's silver, copper, and lead. But William and Benjamin lost interest in this battle, both of them dropping out of the family business in 1901. Benjamin, Peggy's father, retired on $250,000 per year from the interest he still held in the company.

Marguerite Guggenheim was born to Benjamin Guggenheim and the former Florette Seligman at home on August 26, 1898, in the family's rented rooms at the Hotel Majestic, on East 69th Street. She joined a sister, Benita, born in 1895, and in 1903 another sister would follow, Barbara Hazel (known as Hazel), of whom Peggy would be 'fiendishly jealous.' Her father called the newborn Maggie; she wouldn't be known as Peggy until she was about twenty, when the nickname came into national favor. He bought her a little bracelet made of pearls and diamonds in the shape of a chain of marguerite daisies, henceforth Peggy's flower.

    Before Peggy was a year old Benjamin installed his family in a renovated limestone mansion on East 72nd Street, just steps from the East Side entrance to Central Park. The grand old house was typical of the Gilded Age palaces favored by the status-conscious rich of the era. To a child, it was immense and spooky. One entered it through a little vestibule dominated by a stuffed eagle that Benjamin had shot at a family camp in the Adirondacks. Beyond was a sweeping marble staircase and what must have been one of the first elevators to be installed in a private home. It all made a big impression on the little girl, just as it did on her sixteen-year-old daughter when they visited Peggy's childhood home in 1941. 'Mama, you lived in this house when you were a little girl?' her daughter asked her as they rode up in the tiny elevator. When Peggy said she had, Pegeen replied, 'Mama, how you have come down in the world.'

Beyond the elevator and staircase was a high-ceilinged dining room, hung with panels and tapestries, and beyond that a conservatory filled with plants. A reception room was dominated by a tapestry of Alexander the Great and a silver tea set at which Peggy's mother sat once a week, pouring tea for other East Side matrons.

In the front of the house on the next floor was the parlor, decorated according to Louis Seize style, with huge mirrors and more tapestries. It had a bearskin rug and a grand piano, under which Peggy remembered taking refuge from punishment when she had misbehaved. On the third floor, where her parents had their rooms, was a red velvet-paneled library with a tiger-skin rug and four portraits of the girls' grandparents. Peggy remembered sitting at a Louis Quinze table in this room and being fed by a nurse. Her appetite was never good, and when the nurse forced her to eat, sometimes Peggy vomited in rebellion.

The daughters had the fourth floor to themselves. But what Peggy best remembered of this floor was the 'steep and dark' staircase leading up to the servants' rooms, chambers that seemed to her cramped and miserable, especially in contrast to those in which the family resided. She was especially horrified by the quarters for the male servants, 'in the back of the house on queer little landings along the . . . back stairs.'

Peggy was a pretty child, with an oval face and animated blue eyes. Benita was thought to be the beauty of the family, with her mother's heavy-lidded, deep blue eyes. Family photos give the lie to this, however: Benita was indeed a soulful beauty, but Peggy was the more conventionally pretty daughter, apart from her large nose, which would become more prominent in adolescence; she was terribly self-conscious of it. The two sisters sat for a painting by the German painter Franz von Lenbach, known for his portrait of Bismarck; he also painted five-year-old Peggy alone. In these portraits, Peggy's hair is unaccountably blond (though perhaps it was quite light when she was very young) and her blue eyes rendered brown.

The lodestar of Peggy's childhood was Benita. Hazel was a despised interloper, and she indeed felt left out of things. Peggy and Benita formed a close bond. 'I don't remember my mother at all at this age,' Peggy would later comment, referring to the time when she was between eight and puberty. She had no friends, it seemed. She thought vaguely that she might have had friends if she had been allowed to go to school, but the girls were tutored instead. Their father saw to their artistic upbringing, hiring a Mrs. Hartman, who accompanied the girls on their yearly trips to Europe, shepherding them in and out of museums, teaching them French history, and reading British novels with them. Peggy remembered Rene Gimpel, of the grand E. Gimpel and Wildenstein Gallery on Fifth Avenue, coming in at teatime on Saturdays to sell her father old masters. Peggy herself showed hints of a sense of style at a young age. She had a collection of 'elegant little wax models' for which she designed clothes based on the fashions she saw on the ladies and courtesans at Trouville, where the Guggenheim girls and their mother spent a summer. (Peggy was mortified there by the crosses the porters had chalked on the family luggage to advertise Florette's reputation for giving poor tips.) A dollhouse in the nursery was the source of much nostalgia later in her life; she tried without success to recreate it for her own daughter. She remembered its contents especially: elaborate crystal chandeliers and bearskin rugs. Someone noticed how she loved a glass cabinet filled with tiny ivory and silver furniture and gave her the key, which she guarded zealously.

The girls all worshipped their handsome father, a romantic figure. Benjamin Guggenheim had quite a career as a lady's man, according to family legend. Benjamin told his nephew Harold Loeb, 'Never make love before breakfast. One, it's tiring. Two, you may meet someone else during the day that you like better.' Loeb observed, 'Of all the brothers he was the most extravagant in his amorous divagations, even introducing them into his own home.' Benjamin came by his reputation honestly. When his mother, Barbara, died in 1902, a certain Hannah McNamara brought suit against Benjamin's father, Meyer, for $25,000, claiming that during twenty-five years as a domestic in the Guggenheim household she had been intimate with Meyer. The outraged old man promised to give anyone who would say he had seen the two of them together $10,000, and McNamara dropped the suit. But Peggy believed he was 'looked after by his cook. She must have been his mistress. I remember seeing her weep copious tears because my grandfather vomited.'

Among Peggy's earliest memories was the awareness of another woman in her father's life. Florette nearly left Benjamin over Amy Goldsmith, the sister of a Guggenheim daughter's brother-in-law; Peggy had a dim memory of various Guggenheims traipsing through the house, bent on convincing Florette not to leave her husband. The next source of trouble was a trained, live-in nurse, Benjamin's red-headed masseuse, as Florette told her daughters. Her mother too often let Peggy know the details of her father's extramarital pursuits, so that Peggy was given to inserting herself into the conjugal drama, taking her father to task for making Florette unhappy. One night when Peggy was seven she was banished from the family table for saying, 'Papa, you must have a mistress as you stay out so many nights.'

While Peggy was having tea at Rumpelmeyer's in Paris with Benita and their governess one afternoon, a fashionable woman caught the little girl's eye, a woman who seemed to acknowledge her presence in some mysterious way. Weeks later, when she was importuning the governess to reveal the identity of Benjamin's latest amour, the governess told Peggy she already knew her. Peggy was delighted to figure out that it had been the woman having tea at Rumpelmeyer's, a woman their father called the Countess Taverny. Peggy never forgot being with her mother when she encountered the 'Countess' in the fitting rooms at Lanvin; the staff discreetly gave Florette a room of her own. The 'Countess' was succeeded by a young blond singer, Léontine Aubart, known as Ninette.

To Peggy and Benita, all of this intrigue was incredibly romantic, an escapist fantasy. Otherwise, these were dreary years, punctuated by child-hood illnesses. Peggy was thought delicate, and her parents tried out one cure or another on her, including, at the age of ten, a series of 'colonic irrigations' that she associated with an attack of appendicitis and an emergency appen-dectomy. One terrible winter she was separated from Benita, who had whooping cough. Florette took a house in New Jersey and nursed Benita while sending Peggy to a hotel with a trained nurse. Peggy could see Benita only on the street from a great distance. It was one of her first experiences of loss.

Central Park was the scene of many of Peggy's childhood experiences, not all of them happy. When she was very young her mother used to drive her through the park in an early electric carriage. She had a foot-pedaled toy car that she rode in the Mall. She remembered climbing in the hilly and wild West Side section of the park known as the Ramble, her governess watching her from below. Ice skating there was a bad memory; weak ankles and feet haunted Peggy all her life, and the defect became more troublesome as she tried to skate. She also had an accident riding sidesaddle on horseback that resulted in a broken jaw and extensive dental work. She remounted the horse, however, as one is told to do, and learned to ride astride: horseback riding continued to be a pleasure to her later in life.

Florette's ownership of an electric brougham indicates how rarefied was the air the Guggenheims breathed. The family's mining fortune gave them access to new developments of which the rest of the world only dreamed. By 1910, for instance, only 500,000 (of about 92 million) Americans owned an automobile; the Guggenheims owned several. But some areas were com-pletely closed to Peggy. About the development of motion pictures, for example, she knew nothing; there was no one who could or would take her to a moving picture show, generally a pastime of the working classes. While she often listened to Wagner – a favorite of her grandfather's – on records, or pos-sibly in recitals at her home, she knew nothing of the explosive popularity of jazz in the first two decades of the century. Moving as she did between the city's Upper East Side and Upper West Side across the terrain of Central Park, she barely saw the skyscrapers that were refashioning the urban landscape farther south; needless to say, she probably did not even know of the existence of the Lower East Side, with its impoverished population of eastern European Jews. Her life was as circumscribed as that of a child a century before; the only difference was, perhaps, that she had more playthings. And few adults, beyond nurses and governesses, peopled her world.

She remembered distinctly the notes her father whistled upon entering the front door; an excited Peggy would run headlong down flights of stairs to welcome him. But Benjamin Guggenheim receded as Peggy grew. Describing her father's presence in her life in her memoirs, Peggy wrote, 'In 1911 my father more or less freed himself from us.' It must have felt that way to the thirteen-year-old. By this time, Benjamin had taken an apartment in Paris and spent most of the year there, having invested in the International Steam Pump Company, which had bid on a contract to replace the elevator in the northern 'leg' of the Eiffel Tower. By April 1912, Benjamin had not been home for eight months. On April 9, he had dinner with his nephew Harry Guggenheim in Paris; he told Harry that he was on his way to Cherbourg to catch a boat for New York City in time for Hazel's ninth birthday, which he did not want to miss. On arriving at Cherbourg, he learned that the stokers of the ship on which he had booked passage had gone on strike and that passage was delayed. Instead, he boarded the *Titanic*, the White Star Line's new ship. Said to be the fastest and safest vessel yet built, the *Titanic* was also the world's most luxurious ocean liner. Peggy's father bought a first-class cabin for himself and one for his valet and secretary, Victor Giglio, and a second-class cabin for his driver, René Pernot. He also bought a first-class ticket for his current mistress, Ninette, who was traveling with her maid, Emma Sägesser.

Peggy remembered that her family, on hearing that the ship had sunk, wired the captain of the S.S. *Carpathia*, which carried the liner's survivors, to see if Benjamin was on board. The captain wired back 'no.' For some reason Peggy learned of this while (in her memory) her mother remained ignorant. An early report said 'Mr. and Mrs. Guggenheim' had been on board the *Carpathia*; indeed, when two of Peggy's cousins went to meet the ship, they saw Benjamin's mistress (and her maid) come down the gangplank. Florette, in the company of her brother DeWitt and his wife, went to the steamship office to see the lists of survivors herself.

James Etches, assistant steward in the first cabin of the ship, arrived at the St. Regis on April 19 with a note for Florette from Benjamin that read, 'If anything should happen to me, tell my wife in New York that I've done my best in doing my duty.' The story Etches told was this: When he first got word that the ship had hit an iceberg, he woke up Benjamin and his valet, putting a life preserver on Benjamin. The older man complained that it hurt him and the steward adjusted it. He then put a heavy sweater on Benjamin, and the two men went out on deck. Etches said that he saw Guggenheim assisting at the lifeboats. But forty-five minutes later, he saw Guggenheim and his secretary, Giglio, in their evening clothes, without preservers. 'We've dressed in our best,' Guggenheim told Etches, 'and are prepared to go down like gentlemen.' The last Etches saw of him he was on the sinking liner as Etches's boat pulled away.

The Guggenheim brothers must have done some fast thinking in the hours after news of the tragedy reached them. No doubt Ninette was sent back to Paris on the very next boat. (She had wired her family in Paris, 'Moi sauvée mais Ben perdu.') But that was not the last the family would hear from her. Mistresses were something of a Guggenheim tradition, and the clan took pains to see that they were treated well. Ben's older brother Solomon was said to have held forth in his club about their care and feeding, saying sonorously that 'when the time came to part, it is of the utmost importance to provide generously for the lady in question.' Benjamin had provided for Ninette as he had her predecessors, by setting up a trust. Ninette, about whom little further is known beyond a cryptic citation that she 'held parties during the twenties that were ended by the police,' lived until the age of seventy-seven, when she died in 1964 in the south of France. Peggy later told a reporter, referring to yet another of Benjamin's mistresses, 'I still inherit little bits here and there from my father's old mistresses. He set up trust funds for them which revert to me when they die. There's one still alive in the south of France. She must be 100.'

But these matters were beyond what Peggy, at thirteen, could take in. Surely the description of her father, in evening clothes, going down with the ship would resonate with any young girl in Peggy's place; she was an impressionable and imaginative person, who – all romance aside – must also have visualized the horror of his watery death. Her father's body was never found. In any event, she went through a religious phase, attending services and saying kaddish at Temple Emanu-El, the synagogue of which her grandfather was a trustee. 'I suppose, if Father had lived, Peggy would have married bourgeois men and stayed married to them,' her sister Hazel later speculated. As it was, Peggy was heartbroken, writing later, 'It took me months to get over the terrible nightmare of the *Titanic*, and years to get over the loss of my father.' She added, with hindsight made possible by familiarity with popular psychology, 'In a sense I have never recovered, as I suppose I have been searching for a father ever since.'

That summer Peggy and her mother and sisters did not go to Europe for the summer, since Florette had a new distrust of ships. Instead, they went to the New Jersey shore, to the stretch of coast around Allenhurst – near Deal, Elberon, and West End – where other German-Jewish families summered. Their homes, like those of other very rich families of the pre-World War I era, were a riot of fantasized European styles. A Guggenheim uncle with an Alsatian wife had built a house that was an exact copy of Le Petit Trianon, while another one had an Italian villa with formal gardens and marble courts. In contrast, Peggy's grandfather Seligman's house in West End was a Victorian affair, surrounded by porches on which relatives rocked the days away. To Peggy's relief, her mother allowed her to put aside the black clothes she had been wearing since her father's death in April and to wear white, but still she mourned. Despite the fact that they 'bathed in the Atlantic in the wild breakers and played tennis and rode horses,' Peggy hated West End. 'It was the ugliest place in the world,' she said. It seemed to her barren. She had clearly sunk into depression. The only flowers she saw were rambler roses, nasturtiums, and hydrangeas, and she conceived a lifelong hatred for these flowers on the spot. In Allenhurst that summer a hotel that did not admit Jews got out of control of the firefighters and burned to the ground, and Peggy and her cousins watched with some relish.

2

Changes, Taking Leave

For Peggy, life changed profoundly after her father's death. At the time, she and her mother and sisters were living in rooms in the St. Regis Hotel, which was something of a Guggenheim fortress, with Daniel Guggenheim and his family occupying the floor below. But soon after Benjamin's death the brothers found that his estate was in complete disarray. Not only was it sadly diminished by his secession from the family firm, but the $8 million or so he had put into his elevator venture was mostly lost. The securities in his portfolio yielded little interest and the share price of most of them was too low to consider selling. For a time Florette was unaware of her finances and continued living in the same comfort she had enjoyed while her husband was alive. The Guggenheim uncles 'gallantly' – Peggy's word – paid the considerable bills, keeping the real situation from her.

But Benjamin's widow learned, eventually, the sorry state of her fortunes. To her credit, she immediately cut her spending drastically, moving the family to smaller rooms in the Plaza Hotel. She let most of the servants go and sold many of the furnishings of the 72nd Street house – now rented to a relative – as well as some of her jewelry and personal effects. This comedown cannot have been easy for her, and her children picked up on the general indignity. Peggy would say that from this period dated her feeling that she was a 'poor relation' and her sense of humiliation in family circles. Four years later Florette's father died, leaving his daughter a considerable sum, and the Guggenheim brothers invested what remained of Benjamin's estate wisely, so that when Peggy came of age in 1919 and received her inheritance it was worth $450,000, about $5 million today. However, the fact that Peggy and her sisters were to be heiresses, but modest ones, created for Peggy a problem that would last to the end of her life. Strangers as well as friends assumed the Guggenheim name meant that Peggy had unlimited funds at her disposal.

The writer Djuna Barnes, a lifelong friend of Peggy's, told Charles Henri Ford in 1931 what she conceived to be the extent of Peggy's fortune; as Ford wrote in a letter to his father, 'When we got home Djuna said, would you think just looking at her that she had 70 million dollars?' Peggy was to support Djuna and others financially for most of her life, according to an uneasy mix of impulses – generosity, obligation, a need for connection – and these relationships would prove to be highly fraught. She suffered embarrassments when she was forced to make clear that she did not have the kind of money her recipients thought she had, and she was, in fact, personally penny-pinching, a shortcoming that was even more damning in this context (why should she check restaurant bills when she has $70 million? the thinking would run). Her friends sometimes felt resentment when she limited the amounts she provided them. In general, others perceived of her as stingy – quite at odds with her proven generosity.

Peggy's isolation in her adolescence eased somewhat when she enrolled, briefly, in school. She went to a small academy that was the precursor of one of today's most prestigious Manhattan private schools, Calhoun. Founded in 1896 as the Jacobi School, it was run by Laura Jacobi, a German immigrant who was the niece of an eminent professor of pediatrics, Abraham Jacobi, and of the reformer Mary Putnam Jacobi. She was from a distinctly progressive family, committed to women's rights and community service. Jacobi originally opened what was known as a 'brother-and-sister' school in a townhouse on West 80th Street; among her first students were the children of the eminent anthropologist Franz Boas. Soon it became a girls' school, attracting the daughters of the German-Jewish rich. 'All the girls from "Our Crowd" came here,' said a trustee, 'from Peggy Guggenheim to the Morgenthaus to the Strausses.' The school was academically strong, especially in languages and history, and taught the students that they must help the less fortunate. Far from being merely a finishing school, at a time when women were not expected to work the school turned out well-educated graduates, many of whom went on to professional careers or engaged in settlement or other volunteer work.

It was extremely unlikely that Florette Guggenheim chose the school for its progressive agenda (if she understood it). No doubt she sent her daughter there because her relatives as well as her friends had done so. Unfortunately, Peggy's first year at the Jacobi School was foreshortened by her own bad case of whooping cough, which obliged her to spend the winter in bed. It was a lonely year, because her mother was much preoccupied with Benita's debut. Peggy managed to keep up with her class at home, doing the required homework and passing the exams, but these studies did not fill her days, and she spent her additional time reading. Peggy was always a prodigious reader, but the list of authors with whom she said she became acquainted in these early years is impressive nonetheless and notably progressive for the time: Ibsen, Hardy, Chekhov, Wilde, Tolstoy, Strindberg, Meredith, and Shaw.

After her recovery, Peggy enjoyed a full year at the Jacobi School interrupted only by a short bout at home with the measles. Encouraged by a drama teacher, she played the role of Amy in the graduation play, *Little Women*, and seems to have thrown herself into the production. Peggy also made some friends among her classmates, remembering later a Fay Lewisohn on whom she had a schoolgirl crush. She and the other girls planned a monthly ball, for which they drew up lists of desirable young Jewish boys. Before the ball, Peggy auctioned off these 'bachelors'; the highest bidder then invited the young man. Talking about the suitability of young Jewish men was good preparation for a life of bourgeois respectability, but Peggy, perhaps because no adults were involved, found this and similar parties 'gay and really not at all stuffy.'

Peggy later recalled in her memoirs all sorts of childhood and adolescent crushes, some more serious than others. Many of the candidates were inappropriate indeed. When she was eleven, Peggy met a friend of her father's close to him in age, named Rudi, and wrote him passionate letters about nailing her body to the fire of the cross. Later, she described him as 'a typical roué'; he can't have been too unacceptable because Peggy's mother arranged a marriage between him and a Guggenheim cousin, which made Peggy cry 'bitter tears.'

Like other urban, Edwardian children, Peggy probably received almost no sex education, remaining innocent of such elementary matters as where babies come from; this area had seen little progress from the Victorian era. Peggy did have some selective sexual knowledge that could even be quite technical. One of her earliest memories was of a nurse calling Florette away from the table because she had heard a kitchen maid's cry. In her room they found 'a newly born infant hidden in a trunk, strangled in its navel cord.' The kitchen maid had come to the Guggenheim house only a few days before, hiding her condition Peggy was given to understand that '[s]he had given birth alone and then murdered her illegitimate offspring.' No doubt the information was relayed to her by a servant, from whom Peggy elicited the details. From this particular incident, she learned something of the mechanics of birth (the detail about the umbilical cord), as well as the horror of having an illegitimate child, even for a servant. Because the Guggenheim family doctor declared the housemaid 'insane to save her from prison,' Peggy also may have concluded that in the Guggenheim world, with enough money, actions did not have to have consequences. It was a lot of information for a young girl to take in.

But the Guggenheim household was strangely sexualized, as we have seen, given the common knowledge of the patriarch's adventures. As a little girl in the throes of love for her father she took great interest in his romantic affairs, and Peggy did indeed know something about Benjamin Guggenheim's sex life at a very early age – after all, she convinced a governess to identify his latest mistress. She also knew something of the dramas of adulterous love, having witnessed her mother's early attempt to leave her father over an affair and Florette's dismissal of the redheaded live-in nurse. It was not necessarily that she understood her parents' behavior as hypocritical. There is no indication that she received any moral or ethical guidance, except perhaps at school, though she certainly learned plenty about manners. Behavior like her father's was beyond morality for the little girl; for men to take mistresses and for women to countenance such activity was simply the natural order of things. Peggy seems to have taken away the message that a Guggenheim was above and beyond rules of sexual decorum, and later in life she would recreate just such a sexualized household surrounding her own children.

Benita, meanwhile, had made her debut and was receiving no end of male attention, further feeding Peggy's romantic fantasies. In 1914, the older sister fell in love with a dashing Russian baron she had met in Europe. He visited her frequently during the war, when he was attached to his country's American legation, and seemed to be in love with her as well. There is no indication that her family disapproved of the suitor, but for some reason the Russian never proposed. Peggy was vicariously disappointed, regarding Benita's other suitors as far too pedestrian.

Peggy's younger sister, Hazel, felt extremely left out of these exciting activities. She and Peggy had been great rivals for their father's affection, each believing herself his favorite, and they would continue to be rivals as adults. Hazel, of course, had suffered horribly as well when her father died on the *Titanic*, and indeed bore a special burden of guilt. Florette seems to have told Hazel, perhaps in a fit of grief-stricken fury, that her father had booked passage on the ship because he wanted to make it home for her birthday, April 28. Peggy – and perhaps Benita – picked up on this, accusing Hazel, in children's singularly cruel way, of causing her father's death. However irrational the accusation, Hazel had to bear its burden.

Peggy graduated from the Jacobi School, but afterward, at sixteen, she was not sure what to do. She considered college, which would have been a real departure for a girl from her background, though perhaps not for a person of her abilities. In any case, no one in her immediate circle would have supported such a decision, and, in fact, Benita counseled her not to go. Later, however, Benita claimed that Peggy had talked her out of college, leaving the impression that she had never told her sister she should not pursue her education. Not doing so was a decision Peggy later said she regretted.

Instead, she continued to work with tutors, pursuing study in history, economics, and Italian. One remarkable woman had a powerful effect on her: 'I had one teacher called Lucille Kohn,' Peggy later wrote, 'who had a stronger influence over me than any other woman has ever had. In fact, because of her, my life took a completely new turn . . . She had a passion for bettering the world. I became radical and finally emerged from the stifling atmosphere in which I had been raised. It took me a long time to liberate myself, and although it was not for years that anything occurred, the seeds that she sowed sprouted, branching out in directions that even she never dreamed of.'

Lucille Kohn had earned a doctorate in classics from Columbia University in 1909, a highly unusual achievement for a woman of that day. Officially, she taught Peggy economics and political science, but she was also an avid follower of current events, and had been, in 1912, a supporter of the 'New Freedom' reform platform upon which Woodrow Wilson ran successfully against President William Howard Taft. '[Kohn] had complete faith in Woodrow Wilson,' Peggy wrote. 'But when she was disappointed by his inability to carry through his program she joined the labor movement.' After his election, Wilson did carry through on several measures backed by progressives, including the institution of a progressive federal income tax and new brakes on monopolies. But many felt he had betrayed his stated principles. He gave no help to labor and initially opposed many social welfare programs, even coming out against a child labor law (which did eventually pass). He had promised a banking system over which the people would have more control, but the Federal Reserve Act that he signed into law in 1914 created a system dominated by big bankers.

Kohn was one of those disappointed, which led her into a lifetime of labor reform work, especially with the American Labor Education Service. All these matters she discussed with Peggy at some length. Kohn later told a biographer of Peggy's, '[W]e learned and felt together that people like the Guggenheims had an obligation to improve the world.' Peggy and Kohn corresponded many times over the years, Peggy slipping into her letters, said Kohn, 'countless 100s' for labor causes.

As Peggy admitted, not everything Kohn taught her would sink in for some time. It was impossible, for example, for her to throw everything over and work among the poor, or to work for labor reform herself. Peggy's situation was so anomalous, the demands and strictures of her upbringing so great, that she could not decide where, outside a proper marriage to an appropriate young man, she fit in. In the war years in the United States and the United Kingdom, work for women, especially if it was patriotic, was accepted for the time being; Peggy may have felt comfortable with this, though her family did not. In 1919 she enrolled in a business school to learn stenography and typing with a view to getting a war-related job, but she found the subjects difficult to master; also, 'the girls . . . were all of the working class and . . . made me feel like a rank outsider.'

Similarly, she had to temper a developing worldview sympathetic to outcasts and outsiders with the fact that she too was an outsider, herself discriminated against. Anti-Semitism was rife in American society in the early years of the last century. Peggy was protected from most of this discrimination by the spectacular insularity of her milieu, but, like other Jewish Americans, she inevitably came up against it. Her great-uncle Joseph Seligman, the patriarch of the banking clan, had been involved in an infamous 1877 incident of anti-Semitism: after summering in Saratoga for years, he made reservations at the sumptuous new Grand Union hotel there, only to be turned away because the manager, Judge Henry Hilton (who was also, perhaps not incidentally, a political foe), informed him that 'Israelites' were not allowed. The subsequent uproar in the newspapers was one of the first high-profile revelations of anti-Semitism among 'society' people in the United States, but ironically the affair led more hotels to prohibit Jews.

A subsequent New York state law forbade hoteliers to refuse overnight lodgings to anyone, but informal policies against Jews remained in place for years. During the first summer of the war, when they could not travel to Europe, Florette and her daughters went on a motoring trip to Canada. On their way back they stopped at a Vermont hotel, where they were explicitly told Jews were not welcome. Because Vermont had a law similar to that of New York, the party was allowed to stay overnight, but the next day they were told their rooms were rented and they had to leave.

Peggy's response was distinctive: 'This gave me a new inferiority complex,' she wrote in her memoirs. Later, when the phrase came into popular usage, she would be very fond of saying she had such a complex (and her friends often said it of her – even going so far as to suggest that it was valid, that she was somehow inferior). Rather than feeling anger at such blatant discrimination, not to mention outrage, Peggy internalized the rejection – even though it was by definition not personal. It contributed to her feeling that she did not fit in. She did not feel at home in the insular German-Jewish New York her family inhabited, but she could see no place for herself outside it either.

Her debut, on February 19, 1916, in the Ritz Tent Room, only increased her feelings of alienation. Following it, Peggy went out with a string of appropriate young Jewish men. Though she loved dancing, 'I found this sort of life idiotic,' she later said flatly. 'The whole thing seemed to me artificial and I never met anyone I could talk to seriously.'

The pressures soon grew intolerable. After briefly taking a war job as a clerk for a supplier of military uniforms in the fall of 1918 (in a strange echo of the history of the Seligmans, who made a fortune in Civil War uniforms), Peggy had a nervous collapse. At first, she could not sleep, and then gave up trying to sleep completely. She stopped eating, growing thinner every day. She worried she was losing her mind. She developed a strange compulsion: picking up burned matches everywhere – in ashtrays, on floors, in the gutters. She wanted to be sure that there were no unburned matches left unattended, which, in a clear delusion, she thought liable to start a fire. She lay awake nights worrying that she might miss a stray match. (Again, this obsession echoed a Seligman uncle's penchant for chewing charcoal.)

At one point Peggy saw a psychologist, but he did not take her problems seriously. Finally Florette noticed how thin and nervous her daughter had become and hired the nurse who had attended the late James Seligman to watch her. The nurse's duty was to accompany Peggy everywhere, talk her through some of her delusions, and, presumably, make sure she ate. Gradually, Peggy's obsessive thinking eased and then disappeared, as did her sleeping problems. She does not say so in her memoirs, but presumably she began eating again. She never had a robust appetite, preferring to pick at her food, and she remained very slim into her middle age. At various later periods of upset, she again would find herself unable to eat, as would her daughter at similar junctures.

Peggy recovered throughout the summer of 1919 and became engaged to Harold Wessel, an aviator who had not yet shipped out to war. She had, in fact, had several such 'engagements' – a common enough phenomenon when men are rushing off to war. Once they were overseas, these arrangements were forgotten. Peggy was devastated, however, when Benita married. Barely recovered from her love affair with the Russian baron, Benita impulsively agreed, without telling her mother, to marry Edward Mayer, another aviator, who had just returned from Italy. Peggy believed that Benita agreed to marry Mayer because he threatened to kill himself if she didn't. Benita had asked her sister Peggy and Peggy David, a close friend of the Guggenheims, to serve as witnesses at the city hall ceremony. When Florette learned of the marriage she tried to have it annulled, to which Benita at first agreed. But she then decided to go off on her honeymoon and thus remained married. Peggy found Mayer distinctly unromantic. Worse, she was left alone with her mother, who had sent Hazel off to boarding school.

'My mother's one idea was to sacrifice her life to her children and she had done nothing else since the death of my father,' Peggy wrote. The children hoped she would remarry, and when she did not Peggy felt stifled and constrained by her mother's constant, controlling attention. No doubt this vigilance had contributed to her breakdown the winter before.

All seemed to be well, however, when, that summer, Peggy at last came into her inheritance. Each Guggenheim daughter received her $450,000, and their mother slightly more. Florette's father, James Seligman, had died in 1916, leaving Florette 'a small fortune,' again $450,000, part of which would come to Peggy at her mother's death.

As Peggy later said, coming of age made her independent. Florette's reaction? 'My mother was greatly upset. She could no longer control me,' Peggy wrote with evident satisfaction twenty-five years later. Her determination to escape the bourgeois fate her upbringing decreed for her was now set; all that had been holding her back was her subjection to her mother's will.

She explored her options. After a cross-country trip (she stopped to see her fiancé Harold Wessel in Chicago, where they broke off their engagement), Peggy made another journey, in the winter of 1920, to Cincinnati, to see a surgeon who specialized in plastic surgery. She wanted a new nose, and the high price – $1,000 – was no impediment to her. Plastic surgery was not a new field, but it had been performed in the United States largely for reconstructive purposes, mainly on war casualties. Elective plastic surgery to improve one's looks was relatively new, and few doctors specialized in it. It was also still fairly rudimentary, as Peggy's experience suggests. The Cincinnati specialist had her choose from among some plaster models the nose that she wanted, and she chose one 'tip-tilted like a flower,' a phrase from Tennyson that she remembered. During the operation, performed under local anesthetic so that Peggy was quite uncomfortable, the doctor said that he could not give her the nose she wanted and asked her to choose another type. By this time in considerable pain, Peggy pleaded with him to leave her nose as it was. 'It was ugly,' she wrote, 'but after the operation it was undoubtedly worse.' In the aftermath, it was swollen for some time, and Peggy dallied in the Midwest, not wanting to face anyone at home. When her nose settled down, it was more potato-ish than ever; and whatever the doctor had done made it susceptible to shifts in the weather, reddening and swelling with any change. It undeniably marred her looks, and Peggy was well aware that many people could not see past it to admire her distinct attributes. The question remains why she did not later have another operation, especially after plastic surgery techniques improved. The answer must be that the pain had been so severe, the humiliation of the whole experience so great, and the trauma of coming out of it looking worse than when she went in so extreme, that she developed an aversion to the very subject. Her nose was something she did not talk about.

After her return to New York, Peggy was at the dentist one day when his nurse was ill and absent; Peggy offered to replace her until she was well enough to return. Oddly enough, she viewed this experience as a turning point, calling it, in her autobiography, her 'actual liberation.' She discovered with pleasure that she could perform simple tasks with alacrity and that she liked working with people. She may have seen it as a sign that she might have some place in human society after all.

Immediately after, she took a job that really did liberate her, opening her mind to new ideas and introducing her to creative people of accomplishment. Harold Loeb and his wife, Marjorie Content, both Peggy's cousins, owned a part interest in a very unusual bookstore called the Sunwise Turn. The shop was founded by two remarkable women, Mary Mowbray Clarke and Madge Jenison. In 1916 it was a unique place; one observer said, 'They did everything [in the store]: James Joyce, Peruvian fabrics, color-influenced studies, Gurdjieff, handwriting analysis.' Madge Jenison described the idea behind the enterprise: 'Why doesn't some woman open a real bookshop, I thought, that would pick up all that is related to modern life that would flow in and out of the doors of such a shop and make them available; and bring to it the tradition of the professional spirit which puts its knowledge and integrity at the disposal of the community, and what it does not know, finds out, as a physician does.' The store, first located on East 31st Street at Fifth Avenue, around the corner from Alfred Stieglitz's gallery, 291, had burnt orange walls; it moved, in 1920, to the Yale Club building on Vanderbilt Avenue, across from the recently built Grand Central Station.

The two women hired unpaid volunteers in the winter of 1919 to 1920, eight young women, all 'with a good deal of background.' Peggy went to work at the store in the fall of 1920; Jenison remembered her 'in a moleskin coat to her heels and lined with pink chiffon, going out for electric-light bulbs and tacks and pickup orders at the publishers, and returning with a package large enough to make any footman shudder and a careful statement of moneys disbursed.'

Peggy's mother had disapproved of her taking a job in the first place and was not impressed by the bookstore either; she came in often to see what her daughter was doing and, embarrassingly, to bring her rubbers when it rained. Her aunts came and bought books by the yard for decorative purposes. Peggy ran errands but also worked as a clerk in the second-floor offices, coming down to the bookselling floor only at lunchtime, when she filled in for the absent booksellers.

Peggy began to absorb avant-garde culture through Sunwise Turn. At the store she met the poet Margaret Anderson, who was seeking to raise money for the literary magazine *The Little Review*. Started in March 1914 – the first issue carried stories by Floyd Dell and Sherwood Anderson – the magazine, though a critical success and the harbinger of a modernist literary awakening in America, was always at the point of financial disaster. Supported by Margaret Anderson's lover, Jane Heap, and by Ezra Pound and John Quinn, it was currently serializing Joyce's *Ulysses* (which would bring about the arrest of Heap and Anderson and a sensational trial, which the magazine lost). Anderson, in one of her many appeals for money, won Peggy's attention; she argued that if one wanted to prevent future wars, the best thing to do was to invest in the arts. Persuaded, Peggy gave her $500 and an introduction to her uncle Jefferson, thinking he might help her as well. It was an important moment – Peggy's first decision to subsidize artists and writers.

Harold Loeb later remembered how Peggy had won her employers over by her willingness to perform lowly duties and her joy in being among creative people: 'Coming under Mary Clarke's spell, Peggy gradually discarded many traditional taboos and adopted a whole set of new ones. Feeling guilty, no doubt, for having inherited wealth, she came to deny herself some of the luxuries to which she was accustomed. In compensation she collected the latest in experimental painting and gave money and meals to poor artists and writers.' Though Loeb was conflating Peggy's entire career in this statement, he correctly marked her early experience at Sunwise Turn as the first step in what would become her life's work. Peggy was beginning to move in a definite direction: artists and writers would constitute her world.

The Sunwise Turn not only sold books; it exhibited and sold unusual art, including works by William Zorach, Hugo Robus, and Martha Ryther, and several artists working in batik, then an experimental medium (the owners had a special interest in fabrics). Mary Mowbray Clarke's husband, John, was a sculptor who had been vice president of the Association of American Painters and Sculptors, the group behind the controversial Armory Show of 1913. In 1920, the year Peggy worked there, the shop had on view reproductions of works by Cézanne, Gauguin, Monet, Picasso, Redon, van Gogh, Matisse, and Renoir, among others. It sponsored cultural events, including a series on Tuesday evenings, at which Amy Lowell discussed free verse and Theodore Dreiser's plays were produced; Alfred Kreymborg read his play *Lima Beans* (1916), soon to be performed by the Provincetown Players. Sunwise Turn staged discussions among such intellectuals as Lytton Strachey, Thorstein Veblen, and Arthur B. Davies.

Marjorie Content noted the interconnection of various 'scenes' around the Sunwise Turn: 'The writers, painters and sculptors of that area and around New York were such a small group relative to those of today that most everybody in the arts seemed to know everybody else.' Peggy observed, but her shyness kept her from joining in at first. She came to recognize Marsden Hartley, the painter whom Alfred Kreymborg called 'the long lean eagle from the hills of Maine' and the poet and novelist Gilbert Cannan, who ran off with the Scottish playwright James M. Barrie's wife, but both intimidated her. Her real introduction to the avant-garde world came when she met Leon and Helen Fleischman at Sunwise Turn.

Leon Fleischman was devilishly handsome and Peggy fell quite in love with him; the Fleischman marriage, in its fourth year, was an open one, so Helen looked the other way, though Peggy and Leon did not get past a flirtation. A would-be poet, Leon was a vice president of the prestigious publisher Boni and Liveright, then publishing Sigmund Freud, Sherwood Anderson, Eugene O'Neill, and Waldo Frank, among others. The publisher Horace Liveright created the vice president's position for talented and wealthy young men who wanted to learn about publishing. Essentially a vanity position, it would be filled by some who went on to distinguished publishing careers, including Bennett Cerf and Donald Friede. Because of his work, Leon knew most of the cutting-edge writers of the day. Helen, three years older than Peggy, was from her milieu – her maiden name was Kastor, and her father was a manufacturer of cutlery – but, as her open marriage indicates, she had broken free of her staid, bourgeois background; each party in the marriage felt free to pursue other lovers. Peggy practically moved in with the couple and their young son, David, she later said. They helped fill the void left when Benita moved away from the city with her new husband.

The Fleischmans brought Peggy to visit Alfred Stieglitz, whose gallery, although recently closed, had handled such modern American artists as Hartley, John Marin, and Arthur Dove. She saw her first work of modern art at Stieglitz's: a painting by Georgia O'Keeffe, which she turned around and around because she could not decide which way was up. 'They were delighted,' Peggy wrote about her audience. Indeed, part of what drew people to Peggy was her curiosity, a certain naivete, and her willingness to admit ignorance and laugh at herself.

Through the Fleischmans, Peggy also met Laurence Vail, a young play-wright who had just written a one-act for the Provincetown Players, *What D'You Want*. Vail had a flowing mane of hair and 'never seemed to care what people thought,' Peggy later said. He had grown up in France, was on his way back there, and spoke of America with disdain. Vail and the Fleischmans represented to Peggy the possibility of a life outside hidebound social conventions, one deeply involved in the arts.

Late in 1920 Peggy made another trip to Europe. It was meant to be a kind of grand tour; Florette's motivation in arranging it may have been a desire to pry her daughter loose from the new people she was seeing in New York. This time, with her new, intense cultural interests, Peggy enthusiasti-cally sought out all the art she could see. She had a friend, Armand Lowengrad, who was the nephew of Sir Joseph (later Lord) Duveen, the London dealer whose chief adviser was the eminent art historian Bernard Berenson. Lowengrad was a great enthusiast for Italian art and convinced Peggy to study art systematically, beginning with Berenson's writings, which he challenged her to read, saying she probably wouldn't understand them. She plowed through all of Berenson's four volumes on Italian painting and went looking at art with a new vocabulary altogether, seeking out 'tactile values,' for instance, one of the seven points for looking at art spelled out in Berenson's *Florentine Painters of the Renaissance* (1896).

Eventually Peggy moved into the Crillon in Paris with a Russian girl-friend, where she entertained suitors and discovered French fashions. Slowly, she was coming to realize that living in Europe could give her heretofore unallowed freedoms. Europeans were famously more sophisticated and toler-ant than Americans, and, while Parisian society included a distinguished circle of expatriate American matrons and their husbands, this was a much easier atmosphere from which to break free.

Peggy had no idea, she said, that when she left for Europe in 1920 she would remain there for twenty-three years, with minor exceptions. On her first brief visit to the United States, in June 1921, she attended Hazel's wed-ding to Sigmund Kempner. While in New York she sounded out the Fleischmans. How could they bear America? she asked them. Did they not realize how free life in Europe was? And Paris – how could they resist Paris? And in accord with Peggy's overtures, Leon had become convinced after a year at Boni and Liveright that a lot of good writing was turning up abroad, and convinced Horace Liveright that '[Paris] was the place to be then for young Americans.' He resigned his position after Liveright agreed that he could work as the firm's scout in Europe.

Peggy was delighted that her friends were willing to make such a jump; it confirmed her sense of their freedom as well as her belief that Europe was the best place for the unconventional and the creative. Peggy shook the dust of America from her heels. An ocean separated her from the stifling world of her upbringing, and that was the way she wanted it.

3

The King of Bohemia

When Peggy met him, Laurence Vail was on a distinctly upward trajectory. A poet, playwright, artist, and *bon vivant*, he displayed an appetite for life the likes of which Peggy had known only in her father. He was vital to the point of exhaustion, and Peggy would spend the next seven years trying to keep up with him.

Laurence's father, Eugene, was born in France of American parents. Vails had lived in Europe for at least three generations; Laurence's great-grandfather, Aaron Vail, had been chargé d'affaires to Great Britain and Spain and had died in France. Eugene was a painter in the academic style, given to *crises de nerfs* and tantrums and of a somber and gloomy disposition; his nickname was Le Maître Noir. A grandson remembers Laurence describing how Eugene periodically put on elaborate death scenes, staging his own last rites in flickering candlelight. Though Laurence knew better, he believed the scenes every time and was somewhat morbid as a result. Laurence's mother, the former Gertrude Mauran of Providence, Rhode Island, was a Daughter of the American Revolution, and distinguished herself as the first woman to climb Mont Blanc, which she reputedly did in blackface to save her skin from sun damage; Laurence shared her love of mountaineering, having climbed the Matterhorn when he was eight and Mont Blanc a year later. The family was also devoted to skiing, then a very expensive and demanding sport.

Born in 1891 and raised partly in France, partly in the United States, Laurence had gone to Pomfret School in Connecticut and later to Oxford. He spent several years in Greenwich Village, where he bedded the female writers and artists of the day and associated himself with the local theater group, the Provincetown Players. The Players produced his *What D'You Want* in December 1920 and January 1921; the play was set in a drugstore, and customers were given not only their orders but fulfillment of their dearest wish.

It was a quasi-nonsensical production, parodying American consumerism and the new popularity of Freud – rather typical fare for the Players. Throughout the decade Laurence would publish stories and poems in *transition*, *Broom*, *Poetry*, and the *Smart Set*.

He was also writing a novel when he met Peggy: *Piri and I*, which was published by the not very distinguished New York firm of Lieber and Lewis in 1923. (Communications between publisher and author may have been sketchy, as Laurence's first name was misspelled.) Light and comic, *Piri and I* is a humorous society novel about Michael Lafosse, a self-described 'brilliant and versatile poseur,' 'a blond lad with large and uncertain blue eyes, and a slightly irregular mouth,' who, Vail reveals, 'happens to be no other than the writer of these pages.' The novel reveals Laurence's self-knowledge (or lack of it); the narrator, like Laurence, 'learnt to idle – to idle deliciously . . . I learnt to be a meager dilettante, an average snob, a passable dude, and elaborate poseur.' These are qualities Laurence evidently believed were charming; it is the novel of a man who has accomplished little but thinks very highly of himself.

Laurence was a local sensation in 1920s expatriate Paris; it was his hometown, and his position in the artistic community earned him the nickname 'King of Bohemia.' It was natural that he gravitated back to Paris in 1921. His mother gave him an allowance of $100 a month, a sum that went far in 1920s Paris, when a dollar was worth twelve francs.

As a second-generation expatriate, Laurence would have seemed a true exotic to Peggy, and unlike any man she was expected to marry. For one thing, he was not Jewish, and had absolutely nothing in common with the scions whom Peggy's family would have deemed acceptable. While he did not hold an ordinary job, Laurence dabbled not only in literature but in art, having learned a fairly competent technique, either from his father or from lessons at school or elsewhere. Mostly, though, he was a *boulevardier*. Matthew Josephson, a fellow bohemian, describes Vail in the early 1920s: 'With his long mane always uncovered, his red or pink shirts, his trousers of blue sailcloth, he made an eye-filling figure in the quarter. Moreover, he was young, handsome, and for all his wild talk, a prince of a fellow; whenever he came riding in, usually with a flock of charming women in his train, he would set all the cafés of Montparnasse agog.'

Another observer, John Glassco, wrote a memoir of his years in Paris in which Laurence appears as Terence Marr, of whom he writes, 'He was not only the best-looking man I had ever seen, but he seemed quite unaware of it.'

In Montparnasse, Laurence was usually with his younger sister, Clotilde, to whom he was uncommonly close. With similar yellow hair and the same beaky but aristocratic-looking nose, Clotilde cut a striking figure, and the two served as models for the poet William Carlos Williams's portrait of an incestuous brother and sister in his 1928 novel, A Voyage to Pagany. In it, he described Laurence and Clotilde, the models for his Dev and Bess: 'The thing which had always kept them together was the total lack of constraint they felt in each other's company – a confidence which had never, so far, been equally shared by them with anyone else.' Bess tells her brother, 'I shall never love anyone as I love you.' Nobody really believed that brother and sister had slept together, but their closeness was well known.

When Peggy first met him in New York City early in 1921, however, Laurence was having a fling with Helen Fleischman, Leon having egged his wife on. The Fleischmans invited Peggy and Laurence to dinner, and Peggy was impressed by Laurence's looks and his attitude. At twenty-eight to Peggy's twenty-three, he looked 'like someone out of another world.' He was the first man she had met who didn't wear a hat, a distinguishing habit in the days when a hat was almost required dress. Peggy described the impact he had on her at the time: 'His beautiful, streaky golden hair streamed all over as the wind caught it. I was shocked by his freedom but fascinated at the same time. He had lived all his life in France and he had a French accent and rolled his r's. He was like a wild creature. He never seemed to care what people thought. I felt when I walked down the street with him that he might suddenly fly away – he had so little connection with ordinary behavior.'

There is no record of Laurence's impression of Peggy, which is a shame. At the time she was entirely caught up in French fashion. She sported a twenty-inch-long cigarette holder and painted her lips with 'Eternal Wound,' a brilliant red. At one point she shaved her eyebrows and penciled in black half-moons. She visited all the couturiers – Paul Poiret, Jean Patou, Lucien Lelong, Worth – but Poiret was a favorite. Her figure was flattered by the new 'flapper' fashions; the shorter dresses showed off her shapely legs and slim figure to great advantage. With her gleaming chignon of chestnut hair, she cut an impressive figure.

Evidently Laurence did find her attractive and interesting, though she was shy at this first meeting. When they met again in Paris in December 1921 he came to see her at the suite she shared with her mother at the Plaza-Athénée Hôtel at 25 avenue Montaigne. They went out for a walk, passing the Tomb of the Unknown Soldier and continuing along the Seine. At a bistro, Peggy ordered a porto flip, an unlikely request in a simple French bistro, a setting unfamiliar to her. She was used to grand hotel restaurants, at which a request for a frivolous frozen drink involving port, two eggs, sugar, and nutmeg would not have been out of place. She was overdressed, too, wearing an elegant costume trimmed with Russian weasel skins that she had designed herself. Clearly, though, Laurence's attentions emboldened her enough that when at that first meeting he said he wanted to get an apartment rather than continue to live with his parents in what was, according to Peggy, 'a very bourgeois apartment near the Bois,' she offered to share it with him.

At the time, Peggy was fixated on a collection of photographs she had seen of frescoes taken at Pompeii depicting couples in outlandish sexual positions. Determined to lose her virginity, she somewhat startled Laurence by acquiescing completely the next time he made advances to her. Unfortunately they were in her hotel suite, and her mother was bound to return soon. Laurence, who had taken a room at a hotel in the Latin Quarter, said that they could go there sometime. Peggy took this to mean they should go there now, and she rushed to put on her hat, and they were off. She later commented dryly, 'I think Laurence had a pretty tough time because I demanded everything I had seen depicted in the Pompeii frescoes.'

But Laurence was mercurial, and Peggy was convinced he wanted to back out of his engagement to her from the very moment he proposed at the Eiffel Tower at Christmastime in 1921. (Had they remarked on Benjamin Guggenheim's contribution to the tower's elevator system?) When Laurence impetuously suggested, in March 1922, that they get married the following day, she bought a new hat, feeling too uncertain of the outcome to buy a wedding dress. On March 10, they were married in the office of the *mairie* of the Sixth Arrondissement; Florette, who had threatened to investigate Laurence's past, gave the couple a wedding reception with lots of champagne at the Plaza-Athénée. But the more memorable party commenced after the reception, an all-night celebration at Le Boeuf sur le Toit (The Ox on the Roof), the nightclub of the moment, named after a Cocteau opéra bouffe and decorated with dadaist drawings. A 1925 guidebook said, 'At the Boeuf, one encounters the artistic trend of the moment, the literary trend of the moment, and, briefly, the *trend* of the moment, whatever it may be.' (Proust is said to have pleaded in 1923, just before he died, 'If I could only be well enough to go to the cinema, and Le Boeuf sur le Toit.')

Three days after the wedding, the new couple left for Rome (but not before Florette, perhaps having noted Laurence's temper and his roving eye, managed to get Peggy a new passport under her married name, in case she wanted to run back to America). There they visited Peggy's cousin Harold Loeb, who was publishing the literary magazine *Broom*, which had recently printed a poem of Laurence's. Peggy was 'bare-legged and be-sandaled,' Loeb later wrote, and commented on Laurence's 'pink face and bright blue eyes.' From Rome they went on to Capri, where Clotilde joined them. (Laurence was already worried that his marriage would drive a wedge between him and his sister.) But from the beginning, the married state rather disappointed Peggy. 'As soon as I found myself married,' she would later write, 'I felt extremely let down. Then, for the first time, I had a moment to think whether I really desired the marriage. Up to the last minute Laurence had been in such a state of uncertainty that I had been in suspense and never questioned my own feelings. Now that I had achieved what I thought so desirable, I no longer valued it so much.'

The presence of Laurence's sister didn't help. Older than Peggy, Clotilde seemed immensely more sophisticated and mature; she had an endless string of lovers, each of whom made Laurence wildly jealous. The honeymoon distinctly fizzled at the Vails' last stop, Saint-Moritz, where Laurence's mother and Florette joined them. Laurence made no secret of his contempt for the Guggenheims; when particularly displeased he could resort to making anti-Semitic remarks about them. (In his 1931 novel, *Murder, Murder!*, the autobiographical hero confesses about a scene with his wife, 'I continued in this [hectoring] strain for upward of four hours, including in my torrent of attack her nephews, her aunts, her uncles, in short, a considerable part of the Jewish people.') In his autobiographical manuscript, 'Here Goes,' he dubbed the Peggy figure 'Pigeon Peggenheim.' Peggy had overcome tremendous obstacles (the objections of her family, for instance) in marrying a gentile, and it must have been unnerving, to say the least, to find that her husband had such prejudices, however common they may have been at the time.

But Laurence introduced her to a new world, one that she had seen little of from the suite she shared with her mother in the Plaza-Athénée. Laurence's stamping grounds were the cafés of 1920s Paris, particularly in the Latin Quarter and Montparnasse. His favorite was the Dôme, where he would while away the afternoon, talking to other Americans – scores were around, drawn to France by the tremendously devalued franc – and letting the saucers pile up at his table. He hated the other café most frequented by the expatriates, the Rotonde, across the road from the Dôme. One evening at the Dôme with Peggy, he was joined by Harold Loeb, the American midwestern writer Robert McAlmon, the French surrealist Louis Aragon, the expatriate newspaperman Harold Stearns, and the dadaist Tristan Tzara, 'with monocle in place.' The American writer Malcolm Cowley hinted that the owner of the Rotonde was a *mouchard*, a police informant. For some reason this particularly infuriated Laurence, and he stormed across the avenue, his companions in tow, demanding to see the proprietor. The Rotonde waiters threw out Laurence and his pack; they reorganized at the Dôme and decided to make another attack. Back at the Rotonde, Louis Aragon addressed the crowd, 'spitting insults.' Cowley then hit the proprietor, whereupon he and his friends were thrown out and Cowley was taken into police custody. The following day, Harold Loeb observed, Peggy 'had gone to court with a group of elegantly dressed women' and testified loyally that Malcolm Cowley had not even been in the café the night before.

Cowley remembered the occasion somewhat differently, believing that Laurence, in the middle of a conversation about something else, said, 'Let's go over and assault the proprietor of the Rotonde.' This would ally Laurence with the ranks of the dadaists, precursors of surrealism who favored the absurd over everything else and were given to disrupting social occasions, as well as producing artwork that would reshape the art world. But Laurence was never so organized; though he and Peggy knew many of the dadaists and admired their actions, he (and she) failed at this point to see the deeper potential of their message.

Laurence, as Peggy learned very early in her marriage, was given to tantrums. He was apt to drink too much and get into fights – a habit that would render Peggy's time with him often hellish. Yet he could be charming beyond measure and was well liked by all the expatriates and a boon companion to some. The parties he threw at his parents' apartment were legendary. At the first one Peggy attended, homosexuals were thick on the ground – Laurence's father, Eugene, came upon boys whispering together in the bathroom, and Peggy received a proposal ('I can hardly say of marriage,' she clarified) from a supplicant young woman kneeling at her feet. It is an understatement to say that alcohol fueled many of these parties; in fact, it seemed at times that liquor was the lifeblood of 1920s Paris. As William Carlos Williams wrote, 'Whisky is to the imagination of Paris of that time as milk was to a baby.' Prohibition, of course, was in force in America, and freedom from its reach no doubt encouraged many American visitors to overdo. But Laurence, by any standard, had a special talent for getting noisily drunk.

Through Laurence, Peggy would form some of the most important friendships of her life. In the early 1920s, she met two women who would become lasting friends, both of whom had been mistresses of Laurence in Greenwich Village in the late teens. The first was Mary Reynolds, the widow of an American soldier killed in the Great War, who came to Paris to avoid the bourgeois remarriage her midwestern parents expected of her. A beautiful woman with strawberry blond hair and a slim carriage, Mary was soon to become the lifelong mistress of the French artist Marcel Duchamp, whom she had earlier met in Greenwich Village. A highly original woman, she papered her apartment with striking maps and hung one wall with her prodigious collection of dangling earrings (Peggy would take up a similar collection and also display hers on her walls); Duchamp would paint one wall dark blue and pound tacks into it at different angles, connecting the tacks with white string. Mary would take up bookbinding, sheathing volumes in all manner of strange fabrics and animal and reptile skins, stitching them together in remarkable fashion.

Peggy's second new friend was the writer Djuna Barnes, also a former lover of Laurence's. Born in 1892 to rural New York parents, Djuna had a chaotic upbringing, bonding most strongly with her grandmother Zadel, a writer and believer in free love. Djuna's father, an impecunious dilettante, had a mistress with whom he had children and who lived with Djuna's immediate family; Djuna had to support her mother and four brothers after her father decamped with his second family for good. She became an enterprising newspaperwoman, writing idiosyncratic features about extraordinary phenomena and personalities in the distinctly bohemian world she frequented; for one of the most memorable, a feature about the hunger-striking suffragettes published in the New York World in 1914, she subjected herself to force-feeding for the sake of a story. In 1921 McCall's magazine sent her to Paris, which she made her base for the next twenty years. A striking, auburn-haired beauty with an ample bust, Djuna was known for her biting wit and markedly eccentric turns of phrase. While supporting herself with journalism, Djuna was trying her hand at fiction; she had published a strange volume, A Book of Repulsive Women, in 1915. Peggy was highly impressed by this arresting woman, noting that Djuna, like Mary, had a lovely nose, 'the kind of nose [she] had gone all the way to Cincinnati for in vain.' After giving Djuna some secondhand lingerie, Peggy learned that Djuna resented the gesture, but she discovered her sitting at her typewriter wearing it, which greatly embarrassed Djuna. Peggy then gave her new friend an entirely new set, a russet cape, and her favorite hat; Djuna would be the lifelong recipient of Peggy's generosity – not an easy relationship for either woman.

Peggy evidently did not mind that Mary and Djuna had been Laurence's lovers before she came on the scene. But other surprises confronted her in the early weeks of her marriage. She had had one fight with Laurence before they were married, which had prompted him to stalk out in a fury. However, Peggy laconically relates in her autobiography, '[I]t never dawned on me that was a sample of what I might expect perpetually in the future.' She had not been around Laurence long enough to witness his violent behavior; it is possible, as well, that the constraints of marriage made him more violent.

Laurence, Peggy discovered, was not only violent but exhibitionistic. He liked to create scenes with her in front of servants or in cafés, which she of course found doubly humiliating. In her memoirs, Peggy cites his habit of rubbing jam in her hair and observed, '[W]hat I hated most was being knocked down in the streets, or having things thrown in restaurants.' She continued, matter-of-factly, 'Once he held me down under water in the bathtub until I felt I was going to drown.'

Peggy speculated that the scenes could be averted if someone simply told Laurence not to be an ass; Djuna had done so in a Paris restaurant with great success. Yet Peggy couldn't put him in his place that way, she said, fearing it would only further enrage him. Although she would come to see the balance of power differently later, for the time being his scenes mortified her and undermined her confidence; she noted that he 'always made [her] feel inferior.'

But perhaps Peggy's self-esteem, never her strong suit, made her feel she couldn't stand up to it – made her feel, quite possibly, that she deserved Laurence's abuse. Just as anti-Semitic slights in her adolescence gave her 'a new inferiority complex,' so too did she internalize Laurence's criticisms of her. Two admirers of Peggy's later in life commented on this key aspect of her personality. Eileen Finletter, her daughter's close friend, said there was always something 'off' about Peggy. 'Maybe if she'd – I don't know, had a better nose job – that would have kept her from this fundamental insecurity.' Anne Dunn, a great admirer, saw early on that Peggy was unjustly maligned and discredited, venturing, 'Her lack of self-regard was picked up by others,' who perhaps found it easy to denigrate her.

Shortly after her wedding, on a quick visit to New York to see Benita, Peggy realized she was pregnant and wired Laurence about her condition; she was so thoroughly stricken by morning sickness that her aunt Irene, Solomon's wife, took her back to Europe in her stateroom, Peggy making most of the trip in bed. (When up and about, she ran into some 'Jewish ladies' on board, who endeavored to learn just what family she belonged to. 'Vail, née . . . Vail, née . . .?' they asked. To which Peggy replied, 'Yay, yay.') Reunited with Laurence, she determined to have the baby in London, for the French could claim military service from a son. But for the winter of 1922 to 1923, Peggy and Laurence took a villa on the French Riviera in the town of Le Trayas. Peggy had bought what would be the first in a long line of luxury automobiles, a Gaubron convertible whose top they left off whenever they could. Laurence learned how to drive and was on his way to becoming a reckless driver indeed, hurtling along with empty wine bottles, the contents consumed en route, rattling about his and his passenger's feet.

Peggy, still feeling sick, consumed volume after volume of Dostoyevsky. She was learning fast that a drunk Laurence was a dangerous Laurence, given to throwing her shoes out the window and breaking crockery, mirrors, and furniture. Yet there was no one to whom she could turn. Florette would likely have counseled Peggy that she had made her bed and now must lie in it, and she also hated to confirm that her mother had been right in her initial distrust of Laurence. Similarly, she hated to disillusion Benita, her other likely confidante. Hazel, recently divorced and remarried to Milton Waldman, a writer, may have seen her sister fairly frequently in these years, but Peggy never felt she could share intimacies with her. Suffering Laurence's scenes in public, Peggy lost whatever privacy she had had, and, perversely, was very much alone with her problem.

The birth of a son, in London on May 15, 1923, barely slowed Peggy and Laurence down; indeed, they threw a party the night before with Mary Reynolds and her current boyfriend, Tommy Earp, the English translator and art critic, and Earp's wife (old friends of Laurence's); and Bob McAlmon, the expatriate who had acquired a considerable fortune through a *mariage blanc* to the heiress Winifred Ellerman, a lesbian writer known as Bryher. Peggy's water broke when one of Laurence's friends threw a pillow at her. The party-goers had a hand in selecting the new baby's name. While Peggy labored, Mary Reynolds, the painter Cedric Morris, and Lett Haynes, also a friend of Laurence's, were playing bridge with their host. Laurence told them they could each suggest a name. Mary, momentarily smitten with Cedric Morris, suggested Cedric. Someone else suggested the name of an old friend, Michael Carr (Michael was Peggy's choice for a name, perhaps because it was the name of the narrator in Laurence's first novel, *Piri and I*), and Haynes suggested Sinbad, though Peggy remembered later that Laurence had chosen the name out of the *Arabian Nights*. The chosen name was Michael Cedric Sindbad Vail, and the boy would not find it easy to grow up with the evil-sounding name of Sindbad (spelled, unaccountably, with an additional *d*), or even worse, with the nickname Sindy, which came from Djuna Barnes.

Dr. Hadley, Peggy's obstetrician, insisted that she stay in bed for three weeks after giving birth. As if in answer to prayers, her old schoolmate Peggy David appeared on the scene to stay with the Vails. A friend since childhood, Peggy David had joined the family, so to speak, in marrying Edwin Loeb, a Guggenheim cousin (and Harold's brother). 'The most intelligent woman I ever met,' as Peggy Guggenheim called her, Peggy David would surface at a number of critical junctures, always a rock of dependability for her friend. Her daughter believes that her mother 'understood' Peggy. 'They were from the same background, and they both broke free from it,' Peggy David doing so when she divorced Loeb.

This ménage – Laurence, Sindbad, the two Peggys, and a baby nurse –

returned to Paris in July for Bastille Day, an occasion Laurence traditionally celebrated by dancing in the streets for three days and nights. From there they went to the town of Villerville, in Normandy – the Channel beaches were a fashionable vacation spot for wealthy Parisians – for the rest of the summer, renting a big villa with a garden where everyone painted, Peggy trying it for what would be the only time in her life. Among the Vails' guests was Mina Loy, a talented poet and artist sixteen years older than Peggy. Jewish and English, Mina was a friend of Gertrude Stein's, a collaborator of Marcel Duchamp's, and a lover, in the preceding decade, most of it spent in Florence, of the futurist artist Marinetti. A much-photographed beauty, Mina had been in Greenwich Village in 1917, where she played the role of a spinster who decides she wants a bohemian husband in *What D'You Want*, Laurence's play with the Provincetown Players. After her first marriage produced three children – only one, Joella, another noted beauty, survived – Mina took as a lover Arthur Cravan, the legendary poet and boxer who claimed to be Oscar Wilde's nephew. After impregnating Mina with a daughter, Fabienne, Cravan vanished off the Pacific coast in Mexico and was never found. This story only embellished Mina's considerable legend. While she was not particularly forthcoming in personal relations and later became a near recluse, she nonetheless was an important friend to Peggy.

Other friends of the Vails in Paris included Peggy's cousin Harold Loeb and his current girlfriend, Kitty Cannell. Harold would very soon become, in Ernest Hemingway's 1926 novel *The Sun Also Rises*, the model for the much-maligned literary dabbler Robert Cohn, on whom Hemingway vents his anti-Semitic spleen. Kitty, an American fashion writer and Parisian fixture, would become the model for Hemingway's unfortunate Frances Clyne. (Peggy's friend Leon Fleischman had arranged for Hemingway's first book, *In Our Time*, to be published by Boni and Liveright, his first American publisher, the year before.) The American-born photographer and artist Man Ray was in Paris with his model, the fabled Kiki of Montparnasse, said (incorrectly) to have no pubic hair. One day James and Nora Joyce made an appearance; they were visiting their daughter, Lucia, at boarding school nearby. While never a close friend, Joyce would become an important presence in Peggy's life, and Peggy liked Nora immoderately, instantly seeing the woman's charm. Clotilde's current boyfriend, Louis Aragon, rounded out the group.

The pace was relentless. From Normandy, the Vails went to Capri again for several weeks, where they hired Lilly, a baby nurse recommended by Peggy's cousin Eleanor Castle Stewart (her uncle Solomon's daughter Eleanor had married into the family of Earl Castle Stewart). Capri was a cheerful refuge, an island perched on cliffs, where visitors reputedly lost all the inhibitions that plagued them on the mainland. There, in an incident that could have appeared in Norman Douglas's popular comic novel *South Wind* (1917), Laurence fought with a suitor of Clotilde's. In the fight, a policeman's thumb was broken, and Laurence had to spend ten days in jail until, through some connections supplied by a lawyer in thrall to Mary Reynolds, he was released. Peggy was ashamed that her husband had been in jail and always rushed to explain, though explanations did little to mitigate the circum-stances. Peggy and Laurence had no doubt devoured *South Wind* by this time, the author much later becoming a friend of Peggy's.

From Capri they continued on to Amalfi (on a yacht supplied by Mary Reynolds's lawyer friend) and then to Egypt; Peggy David, Mary Reynolds, and Clotilde went back to Paris. Peggy and Laurence amused themselves in the souks of Cairo, she buying fantastic dangling earrings and he bolts of Egyptian cloth to be made into colorful shirts; John Glassco's Terence Marr, modeled on Laurence, wears a suit made of pale green Egyptian linen. They ripped open a rag doll and filled it with four hundred cheap Egyptian cigar-ettes to bring back into France without paying a duty on them. When they returned to Paris they gave cocktail parties at which they showed the guests their Arab treasures.

Matthew Josephson remembered that in Paris, 'Laurence and Peggy Vail . . . ruled as informal social leaders of the "American quarter" . . . In those days Peggy was very much the young matron, somewhat shy in manner and plain in appearance, but beautifully dressed.' She and Laurence took rooms in the Hôtel Lutétia on the boulevard Raspail, where they had lived before Sindbad's birth. With the baby and Lilly it was crowded, and they soon took a six-month lease on an apartment on the boulevard Saint-Germain. Peggy never forgot the bohemian parties they gave in this flat. Laurence went with her to Paul Poiret's showrooms, where he encouraged her to buy a cloth-of-gold evening dress with a dramatically embroidered blue and white top made of crêpe de Chine. With it she wore a headdress, a tight net gold band. Photographed by Man Ray in this outfit, she looked the picture of Parisian sophistication. Yet she was often bored at these parties; she drank hardly at all and found her guests' drunken antics tiresome; she also didn't like people making love on her bed, an event that happened more than once.

The Vails occasionally presented another image during this time. The doctor and poet William Carlos Williams remembered a party they gave that Laurence's mother attended. At the Vails', he wrote, 'we had a suburban sort of party that was really amusing. At table, Peggy (née Guggenheim) and her pink ice cream about which Mrs. Vail was very insistent. At each place the *petits pains* had been hidden in the napkin to keep them warm. Floss and I and Mrs. Vail spilled them out on the floor.' For all their bohemian cachet, Laurence and Peggy had to labor mightily to remove themselves from their parents' shadow. Peggy hoped to distance herself from her mother, who embarrassed her with her solicitude; Florette telephoned her daughter every morning to tell her how to dress for the day's weather, called women who had lovers 'N.G.,' for 'no good,' and, as always, repeated phrases three times. When Laurence, who made flirting with her a habit, kicked her under the table meaningfully, she said, 'Shush, Peggy will see, Peggy will see, Peggy will see.' (This behavior was decidedly odd; why would Florette call attention to her son-in-law's action rather than ignoring it or telling him to stop? Furthermore, why would she leave open the interpretation that Laurence did this sort of thing in Peggy's absence?)

That winter, Peggy bobbed her mane of dark brown hair. Long and wavy, it was a 'headache' to her, she said. Clotilde, too, had her long hair cut. Laurence did not react well; according to Peggy, he threw her under the dressing table. When spring came, she was off to Venice, only to find on her return that Laurence had had an affair with an American woman. Peggy affected not to care, but the incident marked another not-so-petty humiliation at her husband's hands.

In the summer of 1924 the Vails left for Saint-Moritz to spend some time with Benita and her husband, and then went on to Lake Como and other Italian resorts. While they loitered, with Mary Reynolds and Clotilde and sometimes Eugene and Gertrude Vail, Peggy and Laurence bought lots of antique furniture, never considering that they had no home to put it in. Spending the following winter in Venice, a city Laurence knew well because his father often made trips there to paint, Peggy got to know it in a way she hadn't on previous visits, discovering that all parishes in Venice – not just San Marco – had their own piazzas. From Venice they went on to Rapallo, where they visited the American poet Ezra Pound and played a lot of tennis. On New Year's Eve 1924 in Rapallo, a man asked Peggy to dance. Laurence flew into a fit and 'hurled' Peggy against the wall in the presence of an audience. During another fight in the same town, Laurence smashed a tortoiseshell dressing-table set she had bought that day after months of bargaining; when she later told Pound how much she had hated Rapallo, he replied, mildly, 'Maybe you have unpleasant personal memories of it.'

Laurence, according to Peggy, hadn't wanted a child, although he was 'crazy about' Sindbad. What he really wanted, he told her, was a daughter, and she promised to give him one. Within three months Peggy was pregnant again. As soon as spring came, she and Laurence went by automobile to the south of France, where they entertained the idea of buying property. The Riviera was not then a fashionable vacation spot for Parisians. By the end of the nineteenth century, Russian, German, and French aristocrats visited the little fishing towns along the coast, but only in the winter, and they seldom ventured inland.

Peggy and Laurence found an inn near Le Canadel, a little town midway between Saint-Raphael and Toulon on the Côtes des Maures (named after the Moors who had once peopled the coast), where Jean Cocteau had once lived with his lover Raymond Radiguet. A white plaster building in the Provençal manner, the house had a wing that, according to Peggy, 'made the place not only possible but attractive.' The wing consisted of one oversized room with a large fireplace and French doors opening onto a terrace planted with orange trees and palms; though the house had but one toilet and no telephone or electric lights, it did boast a private beach, a double garage with three servants' rooms, and a little green wooden cabin in a pine grove. A friend would later describe the house as 'standing on a rock overlooking the sea.' After negotiating a cheaper price by saying they would never operate a hotel there or use the inn's name, La Croix Fleurie, the Vails bought it and ordered a studio to be built on the premises before they returned to the place after the birth of their child in August.

In March 1925 they cut short their stay in France, embarking for New York, Peggy to see Benita, and Laurence to take a break from writing his novel. They took with them some creations of Mina Loy's. Mina had cut leaf and petal shapes out of colored paper, making 'bouquets' of them, which she arranged in marvelously painted bowls and vases. Others she placed in antique frames. These inventions, according to Loy's biographer, 'crossed the still life with Cubist collage.' Laurence cleverly called them 'Faded Blossoms,' and he and Peggy (with a hugely swollen belly) successfully peddled them to department stores and galleries all over New York City.

On their return to Europe, they went to Switzerland, to the enormous Beau Rivage Hôtel in Ouchy on Lake Geneva, to await the birth of their child. Just as Sindbad was born in London, this child was to be born in Switzerland rather than France. One night in mid-August, Laurence dumped a plate of beans in Peggy's lap in their hotel's dining room and then made a scene in their suite, 'throwing all the furniture about and breaking a chair,' which brought on labor. Peggy delivered a black-haired girl on August 18. Since the child was the girl she had promised Laurence, she decided her childbearing days were over. Peggy nursed the child for a month, as she had Sindbad. Shortly after the birth, Alan Macdougall, a writer friend, wired, 'Congratulations: call her Jezebel.' Jezebel it was, with the middle name

Margaret, after Peggy's given name, Marguerite. Perhaps following the lead of their friend Polly (aka Caresse) Crosby, wife of Harry, who named her daughter Polleen, Peggy called the child Pegeen. (The Crosbys ran the Black Sun press, which published, among other things, Harry's poetry.)

With the new child, Sindbad, and baby nurse Lilly, the Vails returned to their new home. The nearest railroad stop to it was Pramousquier, and Peggy gave that name to the house. (Florette insisted on calling it 'Promiscuous.') They took the little train to go to the nearby village of Cavalière, which had a small shop, or to Le Canadel, where they drank Pernod at an establishment known as Mme. Octobon's. They had three luxury cars by this time: a Lorraine Dietrich, a Hispano Suiza, and a Citroën. Peggy raced the Citroën all over the coast to buy food – particularly milk, in short supply because there were few cows in the area – avoiding the dangerous railroad crossings that had killed residents, including their housepainter's son. They acquired a sheepdog named Lola that the painter Francis Picabia's wife, Gabrielle, had left behind. Lola gave birth to puppies, which the Vails kept (one named Lulu became a favorite), though the dogs tore up the gardens Laurence had laid out and roamed about the countryside, often killing neighbors' chickens.

Mina Loy was one of their first guests with her daughters, Joella and Fabienne; she painted a fresco of lobsters and mermaids in the spare bedroom. (An inheritance from the place's former occupants, murals by Cocteau of Raymond Radiguet suggestively decorated other walls in the old inn.) Peggy had furnished Pramousquier with the Venetian antiques she had bought with Laurence, and she converted the servants' rooms over the garage into a studio for Clotilde. To accommodate their friends Bob and Elsa Coates – he was a literary critic for The New Yorker, later its art critic – they built another house at the end of their property; later, the French surrealist playwright and poet Roger Vitrac, the new boyfriend of Kitty Cannell, replaced the Coateses. Peggy came to feel that Laurence, a Frenchman by birth, really belonged to the country and that Pramousquier rooted the two of them.

As little Pegeen grew into a bouncing toddler, golden curls replacing her black hair, Peggy was smitten by her family. In Paris later the next year she would ask the photographer Berenice Abbott, once Man Ray's assistant and an ambitious photographer herself, to make a portrait of her and the children. Peggy had effectively launched Abbott's career, lending her 5,000 francs to buy her first camera and commissioning Abbott to photograph her naked and pregnant with Pegeen, a distinctly outrageous move. In the photographs Abbott took of the children, Pegeen and Sindbad positively radiate light, though Pegeen already wears the lost and pensive expression that would come to characterize her appearance.

The winter of 1925 and 1926 was one of the rockiest times in Peggy's eventful marriage. The family went skiing in Wengen, in the Jungfrau region of Switzerland. Peggy avoided the sport because of her weak ankles, and she cracked a rib while taking Sindbad out on a sled. She decided to leave Laurence in Wengen, and took Pegeen, Sindbad, and Doris, the baby nurse who replaced Lilly, to Paris with her. There she took advantage of Laurence's vacant studio in an alley off the avenue du Maine to throw a big party, the first bohemian occasion that was all her own and not Laurence's. There, as she says cryptically, 'I found what I wanted,' presumably a man whom she bedded, under drunken circumstances. Somehow Laurence got wind of what was going on and rushed to Paris, surprising Peggy at the Sélect café. She was clearly drunk, with two red crosses lipsticked on her cheeks, and surrounded by a crowd of repellent businessmen. According to Laurence's autobiography, she said she had been awake for forty-nine and a half hours, spending most of the time drinking and shopping. 'You get drunk all the time,' she told Laurence. 'All your friends get drunk. I thought I'd get drunk too.' But Laurence suspected that she had been unfaithful and was floridly jealous. After Peggy slept off her escapade, Laurence lost control. He threw furniture about and then tossed her shoes out the window. He tried to get into Sindbad and Pegeen's room, but the new nurse had locked herself in with the children. He rushed out, only to return a few hours later to resume the scene.

The fight continued for several days. Dining at Pirelli's, a little bar in Montparnasse, Laurence again began lamenting Peggy's infidelity and proceeded to throw a bottle of vermouth and a bottle of Amer Picon over the heads of five diners. The police came and Peggy fainted; when she came to, the police had taken Laurence in a wheelbarrow to the station house. According to Peggy, Clotilde stepped in at this point and asked Marcel Duchamp for advice. Duchamp recommended that Peggy and Clotilde turn on the charm and get the diners to withdraw the complaint that had landed Laurence in custody. (The charm evidently worked, as one of the plaintiffs, Alain Lemerdy, a captain from an old French military family, would eventually marry Clotilde.) By the next morning Clotilde had got the last of the plaintiffs to withdraw, and Laurence was released and given an official warning.

Money was a big factor in the Vails' quarrels. Laurence, who had only a small amount of his own, inevitably resented Peggy's largesse, or the absence of it. In his 1931 novel *Murder! Murder!*, Laurence would portray her as being 'too busy with the laundry prices of five countries.' Later, Peggy said frankly, 'Because of my money I enjoyed a certain superiority over Laurence and I used it in a dreadful way, by telling him it was mine and he couldn't have it to dispose of freely.' Laurence in turn told her that she was accepted in bohemian circles only because of her money and generally belittled her savagely. These were the days of armchair Freudianism, and Laurence began to talk about Peggy's 'inferiority complex.' Peggy really did seem to suffer from one, but Laurence used the term only to indicate that she was inferior to him, not in reference to her feelings. His constant scorn began to wear on her, and their shared good times no longer compensated.

Clearly, Laurence played the leading role in the marriage. Their reckless and footloose life, he felt, was terribly unconventional and therefore greatly to be admired. He also seems to have felt that he was doing Peggy a favor in introducing her to this world. He encouraged her to have sexual encounters but at the same time was plagued by fierce jealousy. Peggy seems to have enjoyed traveling in bohemian circles, but Laurence's pace was relentless, as was his verbal and physical abuse.

Later in 1925 Peggy found diversion herself in a new business venture with her friend Mina Loy. Mina had devised some marvels: three new kinds of lamps. One was a globe of the world, with the light inside; one had a shade decorated with boats whose sails were in relief; the third had a double shade of cellophane with paper cutouts in between, which cast wonderful shadows. Peggy put Joella Loy in charge of a workshop that she set up next to Laurence's studio, while Peggy herself would run a shop she rented on the rue du Colisée. Hoping to make some money, Peggy allowed her mother to invite her lingère to sew some underwear to sell at the shop's opening; Mina was so offended that she stayed away on opening day. The future gallery owner Julien Levy recalled the rue du Colisée shop in his Memoir of an Art Gallery (1977), in which he described Mina's lampshades as féerique (fairylike). The shop expanded its offerings to include slippers painted by Clotilde Vail; Peggy and Mina also organized a show of Laurence's paintings. According to Peggy, the best one was called Women and Children, in which factory women nursed their babies while smug factory owners looked on, cigars in their mouths. But the shop was not a financial success, and eventually Edgar Levy, Julien's father, gave Mina $10,000 to buy Peggy out.

Peggy and Laurence were showing the stirrings of class consciousness during 1926, as Laurence's Women and Children indicates. In May, Peggy was moved to donate $10,000 to the relief fund for the General Strike in England. She cabled her bank to sell the last stocks left from her grandfather's legacy; her uncle Jefferson objected, asking the bank if she thought she was the prince of Wales. The delay in getting the funds meant that the miners received the money in mid-May, just after the strike was over. 'Never mind,'

Laurence consoled her. 'There will be just enough for every miner to have a glass of beer.'

In general, Laurence did not share Peggy's political sympathies. Their friend Matthew Josephson commented, 'Peggy used to observe, frankly enough, that she considered her inheritance an accident and felt strong sympathies for the Socialists . . . Her husband disapproved of her Socialist tendencies, holding that all political movements, and especially those of the Left, were "so boring."' (The remark is vintage Laurence: boredom was his great enemy.) But Laurence did not intervene, and Peggy continued her support of labor causes, regularly sending her old teacher Lucille Kohn, now a labor activist, generous checks.

The Vails lived a very simple life at Pramousquier (though they maintained a retinue of servants), where they retreated in the warm months, occasionally fleeing the mistral that plagued the region and always arranging to travel in August, when the heat of the Midi was overwhelming. The perpetual sun of southern France meant that they did not need to heat their house, and only on cooler evenings burned a large log in the living room fireplace. They would swim in the ocean upon waking and once again as evening neared. They took all their meals out of doors, in the summertime having lunch on a second terrace that was protected from the sun and received cool ocean breezes. They customarily drank so much wine at lunch that siestas were in order. In colder weather they ate on their large terrace overlooking the sea, surrounded by palm trees and orange trees that bloomed in the early winter and sent forth a marvelous fragrance. The countryside was covered with mimosas. In the evening Laurence would lead visitors on a long walk. There were two common routes, which Peggy and Laurence dubbed 'du côté de chez Swann' and the other 'le côté de Guermantes,' after Proust, according to Peggy. They grew their own tomatoes, delicious when eaten raw and hot from the sun, and once butchered a pig of whom they had grown fond.

In the winter of 1926 to 1927 Laurence and Peggy embarked for America again, Peggy bringing with her more Mina Loy creations, this time fifty lamps and lampshades. The lamps were decorated with peacocks, butterflies, clowns, and such figures as Bacchus, Napoleon, and Lafayette. An art world admirer spoke of Mina's 'lampshades of her own design, of spun glass and frosted cellophane, mappemondes and arum lilies, cherubs, flowers, and passepartouts.' Peggy was tremendously proud of the fact that they had used old wine bottles, which cost a few cents each, as lamp bases and that she was able to then sell the lamps for $25 each. Mina had instructed her to sell only to boutiques and galleries, fearing that having her wares in department stores might cheapen them, but Peggy, flush with success, sold them to all the big stores, eventually sending Mina a check for $500. Mina was not pleased, however, when she learned of Peggy's disregard of her instructions, and the venture ended their collaboration once and for all.

From New York, Peggy and Laurence retreated to Connecticut in early 1927 so Laurence could finish *Murder! Murder!* Peggy, bored with the countryside, in April hurried to Benita's side in New York, but Laurence took her away again, back to France. Benita was once more pregnant, after five miscarriages, and her pregnancy was now in its fourth month – past the mark at which the miscarriages had occurred. Peggy wanted to be with her sister at the birth of her first child and would always blame Laurence for not letting her stay.

In Paris that fall Peggy met Isadora Duncan, the forty-nine-year-old modern dance pioneer, who had fallen on hard times. Duncan received them at the Hôtel Lutetia, offering them champagne. Isadora may have hoped Peggy would help her out financially, but if so, Peggy disappointed her. Peggy did, however, give Isadora a party, in the apartment she and Laurence had taken on the boulevard Saint-Germain across from the Café de Flore. At the party, Isadora lounged on a divan, as admirers surrounded her. In attendance were Cocteau, Hemingway, Pound, Gide, Janet Flanner, Natalie Barney, and Jules Pacsin, among others. Marcel Duchamp – now involved with Mary Reynolds and thus well known to the Vails – brought Julien Levy to the party, where he first saw Joella, the daughter of Mina Loy and Stephen Haweis. He fell in love with her on the spot; they would marry later that year.

In 1926, *The Sun Also Rises* had just come out, and readers were still guessing about the real identities of Hemingway's thinly disguised characters. One evening Laurence, meeting Matthew Josephson at the Dôme with Lady Duff Twysden (Brett Ashley in the novel), her English friend Pat Guthrie (Mike Campbell), and Harold Loeb (Robert Cohn), said, 'Well now, all we need is to have Ernest drop in to make it a quorum.' Peggy took in this information with great glee, fueling the gossip mills.

That summer, Isadora Duncan visited the Vails at Pramousquier, arriving in the little Bugatti in which she was soon to meet her dramatic end. Peggy remembered her as wearing a purple and rose costume, in vivid contrast to her red hair. She told Peggy, 'Never use the word wife,' and mock-christened her Guggie Peggleheim. Peggy was willing to hear and remember that advice, and it may well have influenced the decisions she would make in the next few years. At this point, however, she was incapable of action.

The English writer Mary Butts was another visitor in the summer of 1927, along with her daughter, Camilla. Mary was unfortunately addicted to opium, and Peggy noted that she went through a whole bottle of aspirin one day when her opium ran out. Mary passed the time reading Wyndham Lewis, Trollope, and Forster's *Passage to India* (1924), and writing 'The House Party,' one of her best stories. In a letter to a friend she said that she was 'désintoxiquée,' but that didn't stop her from asking Peggy for money. She expected a 'cheque of deliverance' from her hostess, but was disappointed.

In the middle of Mary Butts's visit, Peggy received dreadful news. By mistake, she opened a cable addressed to Laurence, asking him to break the news to her gently: Benita had died in childbirth, as had her baby. At once Peggy dissolved into abject grief. Benita was the one person in her life whom she loved unequivocally, and who loved her the same way. She would write in her autobiography that she 'developed a great love for her' in part because her sister had been her only companion as a child. She and Benita had shared governesses, while Hazel was left behind with the baby nurse. Peggy had no memories of her mother when she was a small child, only of Benita. Now she cried nonstop for weeks; Clotilde and Laurence kept the house filled with flowers, which seemed to bring her some comfort. Clotilde for once knew the right things to say because of her own closeness to her brother. Laurence was jealous of Peggy's suffering and kept saying that after all, she still had *him*. But Peggy was seething at Laurence for what she saw as his efforts to keep her away from Benita for years. Peggy David, now divorced and remarried to Antoine Deutschbein, a Dutchman, came to visit with her daughter Gisele, who was six weeks younger than Pegeen and would become Pegeen's close friend, and she and her daughter went on a trip with the Vails to the mountains in late July to escape the heat of the Midi. Once again Peggy David knew what was best for her grieving friend and saw to it that she got it.

In the fall of 1927, on a visit to Toulon, Laurence threw Peggy to the ground on the boulevard de Strasbourg and then burned a 100-franc note. The police agreed with Peggy that being beaten by her husband was her own business but declared that burning the 100-franc note was an insult to the Banque de France. They soon released Laurence, but this did little to check him. Peggy had filled her room with blown-up snapshots taken of Benita years before and Laurence, in a jealous rage, tore them up. When he went off in the winter of 1927 to 1928 to ski, she was glad to be rid of him. A fortuneteller she consulted had told her that she would meet a man in the south of France who would become her next husband. Ever a believer in crystal balls, Peggy hoped for some kind of deliverance.

4

The Heiress and the Anarchist

By 1928, Peggy had become very close to an unlikely person, the anarchist and feminist Emma Goldman. The date of their first meeting is impossible to place, but as early as March 1925, before Pegeen's birth, Emma wrote to a friend that she was staying at Pramousquier on a trip to the south of France. The following summer Emma, with her lover Alexander Berkman, rented a cottage in nearby Saint-Tropez, then a rustic fishing village, found for her by her friends Nellie and Frank Harris, the author of My Life and Loves (1922–1927). She enjoyed herself basking in the sun, tending her little garden, and working on a book about Russian drama. Laurence and Peggy were frequent visitors, particularly fond of the meals she cooked over an ancient charcoal stove, especially her gefilte fish. By the spring of 1927 Peggy had spearheaded a committee to raise funds for Emma to write her autobiography free of material cares.

In 1925, Emma was fifty-six to Peggy's twenty-seven. Born in a Jewish ghetto in Lithuania in 1869 to parents who ran a small inn, Emma immigrated to America in 1885. She was radicalized the next year by the Haymarket tragedy in Chicago, when a bomb thrown into a crowd of police at a rally of workers agitating for the eight-hour day led to a trial – on little physical evidence – of eight anarchists, five of whom were executed by hanging. At the trial, the judge stated frankly that the defendants were on trial not for their actions but for their political beliefs: 'Not because you caused the Haymarket bomb, but because you are anarchists, you are on trial.'

In New York City, Emma was drawn to the anarchist Johann Most, who sent her on speaking tours, ostensibly to promote the eight-hour day but really to urge the necessity of overthrowing the state and the capitalist system. In 1906 she and Sasha Berkman started the journal Mother Earth. By this time Emma had become one of the best-known and most influential radical journalists and polemicists in America – introducing the country to the advanced drama of Ibsen and Strindberg, advocating free love and equality between the sexes, free speech, and union organization. With Berkman, she planned to assassinate the robber baron Henry Clay Frick, who had called in armed guards to suppress a strike at his Homestead, Pennsylvania, mill in 1892. The attempt failed, and Berkman received a twenty-two-year prison sentence (he was released after fourteen). In 1893, Emma was put in jail for a year for urging the unemployed to steal bread. In 1917, Berkman joined Emma in agitating against mandatory conscription in the First World War; arrested again, Emma spent two years in jail. Released in 1919, she and Berkman were deported to Russia amidst the wave of political persecution known as the Red Scare. Traveling with Berkman to Russia, Emma joyfully witnessed the revolution, but gradually became disenchanted with the ensuing bureaucracy and repression of political dissidents, culminating in the Kronstadt mutiny of 1921, when sailors and soldiers stationed on an island in the harbor of Petrograd rebelled and were in turn crushed by Trotsky's Red Army. Denied a return to the United States, Emma spent the next two decades in exile, usually in Britain and Canada but in the mid-1920s in Paris and the south of France.

At Saint-Tropez and Pramousquier, Emma met the poet Edna St. Vincent Millay's sister, Kathleen, and her husband, the playwright Howard Young. Young was adamant that Emma write her autobiography, raising a fund for her to do so without material concerns. 'A woman of your past!' Young exclaimed. 'Just think what you could make of it.' Peggy seconded the proposal (Emma said she 'added a few more bottles of wine to those already opened at dinner'), and in spring 1927, evidently having not heard more from Emma on the topic, wrote a note asking her to take up Young's offer. To get the campaign going, she donated the first sum, $500, to subsidize Emma's writing. By January 1928 the committee, nominally headed by Edna (who seems otherwise to have had nothing to do with it), could report that it had raised nearly $1,000, and by the time Emma arrived, from Canada, in France in March 1928 she had $2,500. Peggy, however, quickly became the aging anarchist's chief financial support, giving her another $1,500 over the next three years. *Living My Life* (1931) would prove to be an important (and best-selling) account representing the anarchist's very open feelings about sexuality along with incisive political commentary about anarchism, feminism, and the state of affairs in America at the turn of the twentieth century.

Eleanor Fitzgerald, an old friend of both Peggy and Emma's from the Greenwich Village days, suffered a serious bout of pneumonia in the winter of 1927 to 1928, and Peggy and Emma arranged for her to come to the south of

France for the summer, with Peggy donating the cost of the ticket and Fitzie's travel expenses. She asked Emma to arrange for the purchase of the ticket, as she and Laurence were off to North Africa for three weeks. On their return in June, they went to Paris for an exhibition of Laurence's paintings and hoped to spend the summer with Fitzie in July, then send her to Emma while they went off to escape the August heat. (Fitzie would be one of many whom Peggy supported with a monthly check; she sent her $50 on the eleventh of every month until Fitzie's death in 1955.)

At this point, Peggy's friendship with Emma was cordial but a little distant; it would soon become much closer and considerably more complicated due to the many differences between the younger and the older woman. Peggy's upper-class German-Jewish upbringing contrasted sharply with Emma's lower-middle-class Russian-Jewish origins. Peggy was a young wife who thus far had allowed her image to be molded by a charismatic but unstable husband; Emma Goldman had spent an entire lifetime shaping her own image and identity as an independent woman at the forefront of a political movement that questioned the authority not just of the state but of the family – including, of course, husbands. Peggy was the privileged offspring of an affluent family; Emma had become famous and influential but never wealthy, often dependent on the help of comrades and admirers, never free of certain working-class resentments of the rich and privileged.

Peggy had known independent, politically committed women before – her teacher in adolescence, Lucille Kohn, for instance. And, like Emma, who became an expert on contemporary European theater without formal schooling, she would largely educate herself, eventually becoming a cultural force by cultivating her own tastes and experiences. If her life was not like Emma's, there remained a remarkable affinity between the two women. Peggy's generous, sweetly naive nature touched chords in Emma, and the older woman responded warmly. And, given that Emma was a passionate feminist, she was exactly the sort of friend Peggy needed in 1928. That summer would be a major turning point in Peggy's life, with Emma playing a pivotal role.

In the spring of 1928 Emma Goldman rode down to the south of France with Peggy and Laurence in their new silver Hispano Suiza, a gift from Florette; it was a rather harrowing trip, as the car could reach very high speeds but was plagued with mechanical problems. In Saint-Tropez, only thirty kilometers from Pramousquier, Emma arranged to spend the months of June through December in Bon Espirit, the little cottage she and Berkman had occupied in 1926. Goldman thus described her 'enchanted' little house: 'a little villa of three rooms from which one caught a view of the snow-covered Maritime alps, with a garden of magnificent roses, pink and red geraniums, fruit-trees, and a large vineyard, all for fifteen dollars a month.' Some had a hard time picturing the aging anarchist in such a venue, but Emma was quick to set them straight. When a New York friend came upon Emma at a Riviera watering hole clad in an embroidered mandarin robe over a summer evening dress, she remarked on the anomaly. 'But that's what the fight's been for,' Emma replied. 'So that everyone can play and be happy.'

With Emma Goldman was her secretary, Emily Coleman, known to Emma as Demi. Emily, who would also become a key figure in Peggy's life, was born in Oakland, California, just six months after Peggy, to an upper-middle-class family. Attending private boarding schools and graduating from Wellesley in 1920, Emily, who had light brown hair, a very wide mouth, and an unusually expressive face, married the psychologist Lloyd Ring Coleman, known as Deak, in 1921. She bore him a son, John. They migrated to France in 1926, where she was the society editor of the *Paris Tribune* and a foreign correspondent to the *Chicago Tribune*. A contributor to the prestigious *transition* and other literary magazines, she aspired to be a poet and novelist and wrote voluminous diaries and letters. She had been corresponding with Emma since 1925, when she had written her future employer a fan letter. Deak Coleman and Emma's nephew, Saxe Commins, a medically trained book editor, had collaborated on a 1927 book called *Psychology: A Simplification*. Impulsive, ebullient (she was constitutionally unable to keep a secret), and rather tempestuous in nature, Emily, who had sought work in the south of France for health reasons, having temporarily separated from Deak and left her son in his care, staged a surprise birthday party for Emma just three weeks after she arrived in Saint-Tropez. The party featured champagne and cake and a trip to a village café to dance; it's likely that Peggy and Laurence attended.

Emily encouraged Emma to write, taking dictation and doing typing and filing. She wrestled Emma's reminiscences into readable form. Emily 'not only thinks while I dictate but she corrects me every time I say something she doesn't agree with,' Emma said in a letter to the writer Evelyn Scott, a friend who was also an admirer of Peggy's. 'You can see she follows my train of thought, in fact, so much so that she calls me a god-damned liar and yet we have been together only three weeks.' At one point Emily lost her temper so badly that she wrote Emma a letter saying that she would go away if Emma wanted her to; she was, she realized, 'just like a baby – the moment there seems to be the least misunderstanding of me, I begin to yell at the moon.'

Emily was still in Emma's orbit in the summer of 1928; she had made

Peggy's acquaintance by this time, but their relationship was cordial and nothing more. All that was to change when Emily fell in love with John Holms. She met the red-haired Englishman, a would-be writer, at a Saint-Tropez café. He was traveling through Europe with his girlfriend, a woman who believed so fiercely that she was married to him that she used his last name. Peggy wrote that Emily 'produced [John and Dorothy] in the way she always produced everything that she had discovered – with the delight a magician manifests in bringing something out of a hat.' Dorothy Holms, thirty-seven to John's thirty, was an attractive redhead with catlike green eyes. She was an amateur astrologer and writer, then working on a book about the man who preceded Holms in her affections. John Holms did not reciprocate Emily's feelings, but he appreciated her as an eager audience, and would talk about literature and ideas into the small hours of the morning, emptying wine bottles but seldom seeming drunk.

On July 21, the one-year anniversary of Benita's death, Laurence insisted that Peggy go with him to the cafés in Saint-Tropez to dance. Peggy later wrote, 'My melancholy turned into a kind of desperation and I remember getting quite wild and dancing on the table.' They ran into Emily, who in turn introduced them to John and Dorothy Holms. All Peggy remembered was that John Holms took her to a nearby tower and kissed her.

All this came at a time of especially erratic behavior on Laurence's part. Peggy could see that he was becoming more violent, and she was frightened. The language she uses to describe his behavior in her memoirs conveys the real fear she had felt in his presence. She remembered him hurling her against the wall in January 1925, when she was pregnant with Pegeen. Laurence's action was 'more than painful' to her, she wrote, going on to say that he dragged her down to the sea and went in the water with all his clothes on, then insisted on taking her to the cinema, shivering in his wet clothes. His behavior was to her more than painful indeed; it was downright terrifying. She feared that she was married to a violent madman. She remembered as well Laurence trying to get into the children's room during a fight in their quarters at the Hôtel Lutétia in Paris, a new wrinkle.

In response, Peggy had thought about taking the children and leaving Laurence, but it was not something she discussed openly. By now she was telling Emma about what was happening to her, however, and Emma asked her how she could lead such a life. Peggy said she could not leave the children. But, as Peggy would have told Emma, on one occasion in the spring of 1928, Laurence threw her down the steps of his Paris studio, then burned a sweater of hers, and walked on her stomach four times in the same evening. (Walking on her stomach – an act it is rather difficult to imagine, but which

Peggy said he commonly did – always had a particular appeal to Laurence, perhaps an indication of his hostility to women and their biology.)

In the middle of the tempestuous summer that followed, she and Laurence packed up the children and fled the heat of the Midi for Maloja in the Swiss Alps, taking Fitzie, Clotilde, Hazel, and Hazel's husband, Milton Waldman. Hazel's marriage had entered a rocky phase. About this period Peggy wrote: 'I could not live with Laurence any more as our scenes were becoming more horrible. In Maloja we had another dreadful evening in a café, when he had thrown everything about, and in St. Tropez, after we got back, he had tried one night in a bistro to tear off all my clothes because he was upset by Clotilde's making a spectacle of herself dancing with her skirts up to her thighs, and because he was suspicious of John [Holms].'

The difference this time was that Laurence's violence showed itself before concerned friends who felt they had to intervene. Emma Goldman and Sasha Berkman were present that evening; in fact, Berkman stepped in and prevented Laurence from stripping Peggy completely. But even that was not the end of the scene: '[T]hen Laurence slapped me so hard in the face, that, although I must have been quite drunk, I became sober,' Peggy would later write. Emma and Berkman were appalled.

Peggy recognized that in her attraction to John Holms she was looking for a means of escape. Over the summer, as the two contrived ways to be together, Laurence's violence escalated still further. Once, Emma lent Bon Espirit to Peggy and John for a tryst, but John, who suffered from a paralysis of will and could seldom take action, was reluctant to upset Dorothy by running off with Peggy. And Peggy also had developed a close friendship with Dorothy, who didn't know of Peggy's infatuation but did know of her troubled marriage. So at first Peggy and John shared a few stolen nights, but that was all.

Then Peggy brought matters to a head by visiting John in the guesthouse at Pramousquier at a time when she knew Laurence was nearby. Sure enough, Laurence walked in on them, and a battle royal ensued, on a scale Peggy had not dreamed of. Only the arrival of the gardener, at the point when John was about to knock out Laurence, who was trying to hit him with a heavy pewter candlestick, averted disaster. Peggy smuggled the Holmses out of Pramousquier in secret, arranging to meet them at a later date in Avignon.

At this point, Peggy left a note for Laurence, telling him she was leaving to see Peggy David, now Peggy Deutschbein, in London and that she wanted a month to think about the marriage and whether she wanted to return to him. She then joined the Holmses briefly in Avignon. A few days later, in Dijon, she called her lawyer – the only one she could think of was employed by Laurence's mother, which would have its own consequences later – and gave him another note to give Laurence, explaining that she wanted a divorce and custody of the children. The lawyer did not deliver the letter, and instead told Laurence by telephone of Peggy's intentions. He then told Peggy to return home at once lest she endanger her case for custody, offering to send armed guards with her, an offer that she declined.

Laurence had decamped by the time she returned. The children, who had been lost in the shuffle for some weeks and left in the care of the baby nurse Doris, now drew his and Peggy's attention. He had taken Sindbad with him to Paris, afterward wiring for Pegeen and the servants to join him. Doris knew better than to answer him and stayed home awaiting Peggy. On the night Peggy returned she left again immediately for Saint-Tropez, where she collected Emma and Emily and went overnight with them to a nearby town, where they discussed the upcoming divorce. It was then that Emily learned for the first time of the attraction between Peggy and John Holms, something that Emily, with rare discretion, decided to keep to herself.

For the next two weeks Emma drove back and forth many times over the rough road between Saint-Tropez and Pramousquier. Emma was a bulwark; more than a friend now, she was involving herself in Peggy and Laurence's relationship, although with some trepidation. 'Peggy gave me to understand,' she told their mutual friend Fitzie, 'that Lawrence [sic] did not wish her to come under my influence because of my ideas regarding women's independence. I was therefore afraid he would resent my mixing in the business.' She had straight off sent a letter to Laurence on December 7. She had not wanted to interfere, she wrote, '[B]ut when I saw Peggy's desperate condition, I felt that nothing mattered so much as the need she had of a friend.' She apologized profusely for Peggy's having called in lawyers; the only reason she had done so, Emma said, was 'because you seem to have frightened and terrorized her into silence and the need of seeking legal release.' She urged him to be 'big' and 'brave' and to '[l]et Peggy go in a friendly way.' Laurence may well have regretted the summer, which had exposed Peggy not so much to Emma's feminism but to her belief that every individual had fundamental rights, including wives who literally had been beaten by their husbands.

At virtually the same time, Peggy received news of a terrible tragedy in New York. Peggy's sister Hazel, then in Paris, had learned that her husband, Milton, was seeking a divorce. She hastily packed up her two young sons, Terrence, aged four and a half, and Benjamin, aged fourteen months, and sailed with Florette for New York. Once there, Hazel went with the boys to visit a cousin, Audrey Love, who lived in the penthouse on the sixteenth floor of the Surrey, an apartment-hotel on East 76th Street. When Hazel arrived she found her cousin out, but the servant showed her and the boys to the apartment's terrace. Hazel said later that she had gone over to sit down on the parapet. What exactly happened never became clear to anyone, but minutes later Hazel started to scream: the boys had somehow fallen off the roof, and their lifeless bodies were lying on the roof of a three-story building below. There were no eyewitnesses, and after two police investigations, the deaths were declared to be accidental. The chief medical examiner interrogated Hazel, now under the care of the family physician at the Park West Sanitarium on the West Side. She stated that she had sat on the parapet to rest while holding the younger boy. His brother began to climb up in her lap as well, she said, and in the scuffle that followed they went over the edge. Hazel was said by family spokespeople to be in a state of nervous collapse. In subsequent months she would go to Europe to recover.

Cables with the news of this tragedy reached Peggy just as her marriage was breaking up. She and Laurence both reacted in horror and disbelief. Hazel had always seemed rather dim and vacant, but no one had thought she was capable of such perhaps psychotic irrationality. Coming on the heels of Benita's death, the tragedy shook Peggy and her small circle. Though none of them spoke of it directly in letters, Laurence alluded to it when he wrote back to Emma Goldman after receiving her first note. 'It is fair that I should have [Sindbad]. I think a boy is better brought up by a man . . . I can not bear for my son to be brought up by the Guggenheim women.' It was not the last time Laurence would attempt to enlist the tragic deaths of Hazel's sons against Peggy.

Peggy may have expected Laurence to use Hazel's tragedy as leverage. She conveyed that she was willing to let Laurence have Sindbad with him most of the year, going along with the idea that a boy needs his father. But she wanted to retain legal guardianship of both Pegeen *and* Sindbad. Emma, who was becoming the person whose advice both Peggy and Laurence sought before communicating with each other, explained to Laurence that his wife had explicitly told her she had no plans to 'snatch' his children away from him: 'If she nevertheless insists on the guardianship of the two children it is because you have terrorized her and she fears that in certain moments you may also scare Sinbad [sic], or terrorize him. It is this fear which impels her to insist that she retain guardianship – not because you do not love Sinbad.'

In another letter to Laurence written later on December 7, Emma reiterated that Peggy had not for a moment thought 'to turn Sinbad over to her family,' explaining, 'she knows her relatives too well to let any one of them have Sinbad.' Peggy's insistence on being guardian was only due, wrote Emma, typing in all capitals, to 'HER FEAR THAT IN MOMENTS OF

VIOLENCE YOU MAY DO TO HIM WHAT YOU HAVE DONE TO HER.'

Emma introduced a new note in this letter: Peggy's frail condition. Laurence in his earlier letter had spoken of his concern for her; he feared that she was obsessed with the divorce and, most likely, 'growing thinner every day.' (The previous summer, after Benita's death, she had also lost a lot of weight, being unable to eat or sleep, and Doris had had to oversee her eating habits.) Emma acknowledged that she was not bearing up very well: 'Peggy is keeping on her feet by sheer nervous energy.' That was yet another reason for not letting the whole matter drag on and on or bog down in 'recriminations.' Peggy's eating difficulties had surfaced again.

Laurence admitted that he had 'not been as careful of Peggy as I should have been. I know that I have been violent & possessive & jealous – & that I have frightened her.' He may have had 'bad tempers,' he wrote, but he was worried about her. 'I may get wild at times,' he admitted, 'but I have more fundamental stability than Peggy.' He reiterated that he was only concerned for her welfare and that he wanted to have custody of Sindbad. At times he seemed to be laying the groundwork for a case that Peggy was insane and should never see the children; Peggy would have been horrified at even the suggestion. It is notable that Laurence, even with a history of violence and unpredictability, anticipated having considerable say over his children's disposition. It seems likely that he understood that mothers had much less say in such matters before the courts at the time.

To Fitzie, who had returned to New York in September, Emma wrote that she felt she had been instrumental in convincing Peggy not to bring charges of cruelty against Laurence. 'Heaven knows Peggy has the goods on him,' she added, letting Fitzie know just how humiliating Laurence's behavior toward Peggy had been – as if Fitzie hadn't herself witnessed it earlier that summer. '[A]ll the servants and I do not know how many café owners in Toulon, St. Tropez and god knows where know that Lawrence made quite a practice of beating Peggy up and kicking her about.' She also referred to the Holmses, only to let Fitzie know that John Holms had little to do with the breakup. Dorothy and John 'have goaded Peggy on to a divorce that is only the hair that broke the camel's back,' she wrote. The Holmses had 'merely strengthened her backbone.'

Emma also made a crucial point in her letter to Fitzie: Laurence's drinking was not at issue. 'Mark you Peggy insists Lawrence's violence has nothing to do with drink, he has kicked her about when he was perfectly sober.' Though it might seem that Peggy and Laurence, like many of their expatriate counterparts, were seldom sober, in fact Peggy was not drinking to excess.

Laurence certainly was, and liquor doubtless fired many of his scenes, but he had beaten her in the most mundane settings and in the most everyday situations without drinking at all.

At the end of December, Peggy wrote Emma another note. Emma had gone off for a two-week visit to Spain – having spent nearly the entire fall on Peggy's affairs – and received a note from Peggy on her return. By then Peggy could report that Pegeen was 'developing wonderfully away from Sindbad's tyranny,' and that she herself was 'getting fat as a pig,' trying to reassure her friend that she was eating normally. She lamented that her divorce was going to cost an 'insane price,' in part 'because of the expensive name Guggenheim.' She remembered Emma making her way over the terrible road between Saint-Tropez and Pramousquier and said she did appreciate and would never forget it, adding, 'Also how you gave me back my lost self-respect!!'

Laurence did not take very long to recover from the dissolution of his marriage. Almost as soon as he got to Paris, he met the woman who would become his second wife. Out with Clotilde just before Christmas, brother and sister stopped into La Coupole, where they spotted Bob McAlmon, who was greeting a dark-haired beauty with sexy eyes and a regal profile, and called him over to their table. The woman was the writer Kay Boyle, divorced from her first husband, a Frenchman, and the mother of a little girl, Sharon (known as Bobby), by the recently deceased American writer Ernest Walsh. At La Coupole, she had with her a bunch of mistletoe; Laurence grabbed it and held it over her head, kissing her nose, eyelids, and mouth. She was charmed. They spent New Year's Eve together, and from there retreated into the countryside. Boyle's biographer Joan Mellen says that Laurence intended to stop drinking and to take his art seriously. He still stubbornly wanted to keep Sindbad, and the settlement that would make the arrangement legal was not really valid until the divorce was complete.

Kay was able to dominate Laurence as Peggy had not been able to do; she limited his contact with Clotilde and his access to alcohol. 'Whenever she sensed he was about to make a scene,' writes Mellen, 'she made one herself instead.' Kay Boyle was a mistress of scene-making, as Laurence was to learn over the years. When Peggy told her mother about Kay's treatment of Laurence, Florette responded, 'too bad he wasn't frightened of you, frightened of you, frightened of you,' indicating that Peggy had eventually confided Laurence's behavior to her mother (and, possibly, that her mother hadn't been very helpful about it). In fact, Kay's taming of Laurence proved to be a wonderful development for him, as over time it permitted the best side of him to triumph.

Nothing was to resolve quite so easily for Peggy. While she had 'used' John Holms to make her escape from the marriage to Laurence, she had at the same time begun to think she might be in love with him. In her autobiography she says she knew it when John disappeared one night at Pramousquier for an hour and she became frantic. By the time Laurence left for Paris, John and Dorothy Holms were still a couple, yet Dorothy knew that John and Peggy were involved. By December, Dorothy had agreed to go to Paris for six months and let John and Peggy see whether their relationship would last. According to Peggy, Dorothy did not take her seriously, but in fact Dorothy would become a rather towering nemesis over the next year.

And John Holms did very much take Peggy seriously. He 'realized what he could do to me and he was fascinated by the idea of remolding me,' Peggy wrote. 'He knew I was half trivial and half extremely passionate, and he hoped to be able to eliminate my trivial side.' Peggy found herself, in the aftermath of the breakup with Laurence, thoroughly in love with Holms – and, it seems, he with her. The relationship was in part an educational one: he directed her to certain books and encouraged her as she tackled D. H. Lawrence. 'When I first met John,' she later wrote, 'not only was I ignorant of all human motives, but, worst of all, completely ignorant of myself . . . In five years he taught me what life was all about. He interpreted my dreams and analyzed me and made me realize that I was good and evil and made me overcome the evil.' For better or worse, she had found her next Svengali.

British men of letters – many of them barely remembered today – have waxed eloquent on the subject of John Holms, leaving the impression that he was a legendary figure, a singular intellect, perhaps one of the great talkers of all time. Yet the man remains somewhat shadowy. He was born in 1897 to a civil servant in India and his Irish-born wife; he had a talented sister, Beatrix, who, among other achievements, would later publish the poem 'The Zodiac,' which would greatly impress Peggy and John's circle. When World War I broke out, John was at Sandhurst Military College. He joined the army in France, subsequently earning a Military Cross. Then during a big retreat at the Somme in March 1918, he was captured by the Germans and spent seven months in the citadel at Mainz, among a remarkable group of men that included Alec Waugh; Hugh Lunn (later to be called Hugh Kingsmill), who was working on a novel called The Will to Love (1919); Milton Hayes, a music hall artist; and Gerald Hopkins, the novelist and translator of François Mauriac. Surrounded by a high barbed-wire fence guarded by sentries, the men, students of what Waugh called the 'University of Mainz,' had no duties or jobs and spent most of their days, armed with paper and pen and books, in a narrow book-lined room off the dining hall that they nicknamed the

'Alcove.' Fortified by cigarettes and 'a sour, casual hock' that cost a pound a bottle, to which they had unlimited access, they talked as they wrote, consulted a thesaurus, and read out passages from their work. Waugh dryly added, 'Holms in particular provided interruptions.' Holms carried with him a notebook filled with 'illegible pencil-inspired sentences' that he refused to read to anyone but was never seen without. He was known for taking up a book, snorting, and saying to one of the others, 'Listen to this, old man, isn't it revolting?'

John Holms would, in fact, prove himself to be one of the most singularly unproductive men of letters that literary England may ever have known. Yet the men around him found something in this to admire, taking it as evidence of his genius. A later friend, the novelist and critic William Gerhardie, invoked Goethe, saying, 'In every age . . . there are men who while achieving nothing give an impression of greater genius than the acknowledged masters of the day.' Waugh commented, 'He was how I expected a genius to look before he had found his medium.' Willa Muir remembered him talking about an epic poem he projected, about the evolution of animals, but nothing ever came of it. Peggy would acknowledge, 'John had written only one poem in all the years he was with me. I had done nothing but complain about his indolent life.'

At the time he met Peggy, John Holms had produced one story, 'A Death,' printed in the June 1925 number of *The Calendar of Modern Letters*, a literary journal edited by Edgell Rickford and Douglas Garman (which published Holms's sister's much-admired poem 'The Zodiac'), a competitor of *The Criterion* and a forerunner of *Scrutiny*. 'A Death' is a portrait of the last days of a man conscious only of the extreme pain and anger he feels – sensations that portend his death, which occurs as the story closes. It is a fine effort, but there is nothing to suggest the genius his contemporaries said they found in him. He published one or two longish review essays as well, including one on H. G. Wells, and he wrote several reviews for *The Calendar*, most of them dismissive: he admitted, for example, to finding *Mrs. Dalloway* to be Virginia Woolf's best book thus far, but rejected it as 'aesthetically worthless,' and in another review he found David Garnett's *The Sailor's Return* 'without aesthetic life.'

But being involved with *The Calendar* meant that Holms was on the cutting edge of English letters. Like *The Criterion* and *Scrutiny*, it was anti-academic and classical, rather than romantic, and published poetry by the Americans Allen Tate, John Crowe Ransom, and Hart Crane, and fiction by D. H. Lawrence, Chekhov, Pirandello, and Babel. In its pages readers found Arthur Waley on Japanese literature, Samuel Hoare on French literature, and criticism by E. M. Forster, Aldous Huxley, and Robert Graves. *The Calendar's* 'obsessive theme,' writes a scholar of Scrutiny, was 'the disruption of cultural life brought about by the spread of scientific thought and the consequent dissolution of religious belief.' The journal tried to celebrate (though just as often bemoaned) the modernist response to this massive shift.

John's friend Edwin Muir, an Orkney Islands-born writer and translator and himself a contributor to *The Calendar*, devoted many pages in his autobiography to discussion of John Holms and his attributes, declaring him 'the most remarkable man I ever met.' Wrote Muir, 'His mind had a majestic clarity and order.' Muir also wrote with passion about Holms's failure to follow through: 'Though his sole ambition was to be a writer, the mere act of writing was another enormous obstacle to him: it was as if the technique of action were beyond his grasp, a simple, banal, but incomprehensible mystery. He knew his weakness, and it filled him with the fear that, in spite of the gifts which he knew he had, he would never be able to express them; the knowledge and the fear finally reached a stationary condition and reduced him to impotence.' Emily Coleman, in her voluminous diaries, spoke of his 'incapacity to shoulder responsibility through some inexplicable paralysis of the will.'

Women did not always see John Holms in a charitable light. Edwin Muir's wife, Willa, in *her* memoirs, recalls a man who ignored her presence and talked only to her husband, and who questioned her housekeeping; she complains about 'Holms's monopolizing personality.' Eventually she told her husband she would 'rather die than sit at the same table with [Holms] again.' Djuna Barnes told John, whom she otherwise liked, that his behavior reminded her of 'God come down for the weekend.' He rejoined, 'What a weekend!' Emma Goldman, though she tried, did not much like him. She thought him a snob, and, over time, she complained that he was making Peggy into an Englishwoman.

Physical descriptions of John Holms vary as well. He had a short pointed beard; to Alec Waugh's eyes, he 'looked like a Spanish grandee,' and Waugh added, 'People stared at him when he came into a room.' Peggy noted his 'elastic quality' and his resemblance to images of Jesus Christ, something other observers mentioned too. Muir described him as 'tall and lean, with a fine Elizabethan brow and auburn, curly hair, brown eyes with an animal sadness in them, a large, somewhat sensual mouth, and a little pointed beard which he twirled when he was searching for a word.' Muir noted that his friend was known as a fine athlete at Rugby, but commented on his somewhat odd physical presence: 'In his movements he was like a powerful cat; he loved . . . trees or anything that could be climbed, and he had all sorts of odd accomplishments: he could scuttle along on all fours at a great speed without bending his knees; walking, on the other hand, bored him. He had the immobility of a cat too, and could sit for long stretches without stirring.' Several observers noted a generally unkempt Holms; Waugh said that by 1919 he 'was wearing pre-war shabby clothes,' noting also, however, 'he wore them with an air.' When Holms visited William Gerhardie in London in the thirties, he arrived in a Rolls-Royce, but he wore 'a very old soiled mackintosh.' Gerhardie, who would directly portray Peggy and John in his 1936 novel *Of Mortal Love*, continued, 'We went for a long drive together, and the immaculate chauffeur took his peremptory orders from his red-bearded, dilapidated, shabby master with faint distaste.' Peggy, however, notes in her memoirs that she converted him to dressing well, sending him to London tailors.

Peggy experienced the full blast of Holms's character at an extremely difficult time of her life. She had barely recovered from the tragedy of losing Benita and the emotional turmoil of her break with Laurence. Next came Hazel's tragedy, and on top of that the massive embarrassment of having it talked about – by Laurence, for instance. (It is remarkable, however, how seldom her contemporaries *did* comment on Hazel's tragedy, on the record. Emily Coleman – the not-very-surprising exception – would record that she asked Peggy about it once: 'Peggy told me the horrible truth about Hazel, that she probably did throw her children over the balcony.') After coming, as she did, out of an abusive marriage – still recovering from the humiliation of the experience, still reeling from the intense two weeks when Emma Goldman made sure she stuck to her guns – Holms's personality must have seemed overwhelming.

It would have been one thing if John had simply swept her off in knightly fashion. But his lack of will made it impossible for him to take action. Shortly before Peggy's marriage ended, John had asked her to suspend having sexual relations with Laurence. This she found hard to do – she and Laurence evidently had an active sex life – and she was at her wits' end. 'It was all getting too much,' she wrote, 'and I wanted John to take me away, but he couldn't make up his mind. He lived in a perpetual state of paralysis of will, and he hated to give up Dorothy.' He also wanted to keep on an even keel with his family, who supplied him with a modest allowance, and he didn't want to have to explain new developments. Emma Goldman was a little more blunt about John's inability to act. As she wrote to Emily in January 1929, 'The main trouble is that John is weak and ineffectual, a drifter unable to make one single decisive step. He wants to eat the pie and keep it at the same time.'

Peggy and John may have sent Dorothy Holms away to Paris, but she remained a constant presence in their lives. Emily and Emma reported to each other and to Peggy the horrible things Dorothy had said she would do; in May, Emily wrote Emma that Dorothy was convinced that John was going to marry Peggy and that if he did, '[Dorothy] will get a revolver and kill her.' At another point, Dorothy, calling Peggy a 'little shit,' was convinced that Peggy would have a baby to hang on to John, and was frantic as a result. Once, when Peggy and John were in Paris, John told Dorothy where he was staying but neglected to tell her Peggy was with him; Dorothy burst in one morning, beat Peggy on the feet, called her a wicked woman, and had to be removed by the valet de chambre. At one point, when John did not reply to some cables, Dorothy sent a wire to Peggy at the Guaranty Bank in Paris, the Guggenheims' bank, saying, 'Advise you permit my husband to communicate with me at once.' A Seligman relative had to give Peggy the message, a great embarrassment for everyone concerned. Moreover, Dorothy constantly complained that she needed money. John and Peggy sent it to her regularly, and Peggy would continue to send Dorothy monthly payments even after John's death. John finally told his family about the situation, evidently suggesting that he should not depend on Peggy but rather support himself, for his allowance from the family was nearly doubled.

Then Dorothy started to sound a new note. When the six-month period she had agreed on was almost up, she began to insist that John marry her. Dorothy argued that they had long presented themselves as husband and wife and that it would humiliate her to return to England unmarried and without John, especially as she felt herself to have been deserted. John's feeling of guilt was immense – and as a result he agreed to the proposition and married Dorothy quickly in Paris in May, although with no intention of a continuing relationship, other than financial, with her. Of course, this decision would only complicate the lives of all three, but it temporarily (and perversely) gave Peggy and John some relief.

Another impediment to Peggy and John's life together was, of course, Peggy's upcoming divorce. (It could not have been lost on her that she was not free when John decided to marry Dorothy; perhaps he would have married her had she been divorced.) In January she and Laurence had to appear before a judge for a conciliation, a ceremony at which they would again state that they would not live together. It was difficult for Peggy to see Laurence on this occasion; oddly, they exchanged presents, with Laurence giving her a pair of earrings and Peggy giving him a sweater she had knit for him. Afterward they went to a café to have a drink, where they both wept.

Peggy and John then discovered a new problem: Peggy had learned that she was pregnant. With Emma's help, Peggy arranged to have an abortion in Berlin. She sought out Emma's friend Therese and went into a convent hospital. A Russian doctor called Popoff administered the abortion; he specialized in these cases and was said to have been the *accoucheur* of a Romanov grand duchess. Peggy would heretofore refer to abortions as 'Popoffs.' She reports in her autobiography the story that he once said, in the middle of a curettage, *'Tiens, tiens, cette femme est enceinte!'* Vacuum aspirations were not available then, and a dilation and curettage involved the literal scraping out of the uterus, which doctors at that time performed under general anesthesia, a procedure that had aftereffects comparable almost to those of childbirth. Though Peggy could tell Emma, 'The thing in Berlin went off very well,' the operation left her weak and drained, and she spent most of her time in Berlin in bed.

Yet soon after, Peggy recovered quickly, as she had done so many times in her marriage to Laurence, springing back even after gross humiliations, and buoyantly bought a new car, a Citroën, with a view to future travel. (She always bought the latest and most fashionable cars, which were then two-seaters, in spite of the fact that she would have at least one child, the dog Lola, and Pegeen's nurse to transport.) But by this point, in the summer of 1930, it was time for Doris's annual vacation, and Peggy returned to Pramousquier to mind the two-year-old Pegeen, who, remarkably, hadn't seen her mother in six months. Pegeen had developed a fierce attachment to Doris, her primary caregiver while Peggy was away, and the nurse's leaving must have been very hard. The little girl shifted her dependency to Peggy, and clung to her 'like ivy to the oak,' Peggy said. Peggy found her daughter unbelievably beautiful, with her platinum hair and blue eyes; her skin was 'like fresh fruit,' she remarked. Pegeen liked John perfectly well, though Peggy thought her daughter was surprised to see him again.

In Paris, in July, Peggy saw Sindbad, for the first time since December. Then five, Sindbad was living with Laurence's mother, as Kay and Laurence were not yet settled. Laurence would not let Peggy see their son alone and came along for the visit in a Paris park. Sindbad was wearing a sailor suit and long pants and Peggy thought he looked very strangely grown up. It nearly tore her heart out to see him. She reported to Emma that Laurence suggested they not see the child in each other's custody, or see them as little as possible, for the next two years, 'for the children's sake, so as to give them a chance to get used to the new arrangement & not get muddled up & nervous by visits.' This was, she confessed, 'an awful blow,' making her feel 'more hopeless than ever' about Sindbad, but she agreed to it, thinking Laurence right. The decision was of course in large part a result of Laurence and Peggy's emotional incompetencies as parents, but it is important to remember that divorce was rare in their day and shared custody not a familiar arrangement.

Indeed, separate custody may well have seemed beneficial for all concerned – but especially for the parents, who as a result need not have much contact with each other – for the short term. But in the long run it would prove disastrous. The children's young lives were disrupted all the more. Pegeen had probably established some bond with Laurence before an entirely new person took his place (only to have her mother go off with him for nearly six months): it is hardly surprising that she clung to Peggy. Sindbad would see his mother only briefly over the next two years, during which period Laurence and Kay would plot continually to get Peggy out of their lives completely. (Kay wrote Caresse Crosby, in a letter from this time, that she and Laurence were 'nervy and peculiar and worried about his Guggenheim wife and whether she'll throw the babies off the roof as her sister did . . . We want to get them back.') The wobbly family structure had completely collapsed, and Pegeen and Sindbad were left adrift, with the rubble of the family all about them.

5

Mr. and Mrs. Bonzo

Peggy and John did not linger in Pramousquier but set out on a prolonged tour of Germany, Austria, and Scandinavia, with Pegeen, Doris, and Lola the dog packed in 'like sardines' in the back, as Peggy reported to Emma Goldman in a September letter. The dog was not allowed in Norway, Sweden, or Denmark, so they had to smuggle her in 'with the greatest care.' Peggy said she liked crossing borders: 'I feel as though I am getting away with something really important.' The summer had been 'beastly,' raining continually. Peggy and John spent their days sightseeing, reading, or, when the weather allowed, playing tennis.

In September 1929 Emma asked Peggy for a loan of $500, and Peggy agreed to it, adding a second $500 to the original $500 she had given Emma for her to work on her memoirs two years earlier. But this time the money was to be a loan, and Peggy sent it to Emma in installments, saying that she needed every penny to pay for her divorce. She also told Emma she'd received an appeal from the jailed anarchist and labor agitator Tom Mooney, who had been framed and sent to prison as a perpetrator of the bombing of a Preparedness Day march in San Francisco in 1916. Over the years Mooney had become a cause célèbre on the order of Sacco and Vanzetti, and Peggy told Emma she had 'always wanted to do something for that innocent victim of society.' She was now giving monthly sums to Dorothy Holms, Djuna Barnes, Eleanor Fitzgerald, and Laurence, besides making frequent loans to others and giving to labor causes – including, as a 1932 letter to Matthew Josephson's wife, Hannah, indicates, relief funds for coal miners in West Virginia – and it was hard for her to raise the money she needed to pay her lawyers.

Why Peggy should have paid Laurence a monthly sum is unclear. It is doubtful that it was required by law, but was more likely an informal arrangement, probably instigated by Peggy. She likely wanted him to have enough money to provide for Sindbad, but why she supported the Vail-Boyle ménage at this contentious stage in their relations is another matter. Kay Boyle made a certain amount of money writing potboilers in addition to her serious fiction, but the family relied heavily on Peggy's stipend. Over time, Peggy and Laurence became fast friends, and she was happy to send him monthly sums.

Fall found Peggy and her entourage in Paris, where they stayed in a rented flat on the rue Campagne-Première. Emily Coleman was now in Paris as well and, judging from the prolix daily entries in her diary, almost always in their company. That year Emily published her first novel, A *Shutter of Snow*, the story of a woman who experiences postpartum psychosis after bearing a son and develops the *idée fixe* that she is God; it was based on Emily's own experience.

Emily's diary contains pages analyzing John and Peggy and their interactions; Emily dubs the couple, unaccountably, Agamemnon and Wendy. Sometimes her observations are shrewd, although she sometimes overinterprets trivial gestures. She provides an excellent physical picture of Peggy, which conveys a genuine affection for her: 'She is a quick sprite, she moves suddenly and like a bird she looks around. She is shaped perfectly, thinly, her bones might break. She turns her head upon her neck and snaps her hand. Her shoulders are narrow and she walks with assurance which she has not, but so she walks.'

In November 1929, Emily wrote, 'Wendy is a courageous little person,' Peggy evidently having confided her insecurities. Often, it seems, Peggy felt less than equal to joining in Emily's marathon talks with John. 'Wendy said she could not tackle abstract ideas, that she was a little jealous when we talked intellectually.' Peggy talked constantly about her inferiority complex, once joking that she had 'pretensions to inferiority.' In December, Emily, noting John's return from a quick family trip to England, recorded that 'Agamemnon has done nothing but quarrel with Wendy since he returned,' and she described one such quarrel: 'He told her things that hurt her pride – he told her she knew nothing when she met him . . . He said she lived in other people's opinions and thought nothing of herself, that she lived in reaction, like all Americans.' Peggy's drive to attach herself to men she felt could reinvent her, and her attendant strain of masochism, were coming into play again.

Peggy had her own withering view of Emily's attachment to her household, writing, 'I both loved and hated having Emily with us . . . Emily was always staying with us or going on trips with us. She was like our child.' John and Peggy were indeed traveling constantly, with Emily in tow. The summer of 1930 found them in Saint-Jean-de-Luz, where they visited Peggy's old friend from the Sunwise Turn bookstore days, Helen Fleischman. Helen had left her husband and was living with Giorgio Joyce, the writer's son, whom she would marry in December. Peggy, John, and Emily rented a stone house outside of town and moved in for the summer. Because they were settled, if only temporarily, Peggy petitioned Laurence to send her Sindbad for two weeks. (She had run into Laurence in December at the Sélect. Emily recorded the incident, commenting about Laurence, 'He is a fool and a jackass, but he loves Wendy underneath.') As on many occasions when her son came for a visit, the arrangements were an elaborate cat-and-mouse game between Peggy on the one side and on the other, Laurence and Kay. Peggy offered to send Pegeen, with Doris, 'as a hostage.' Emily, in her diary, reported Peggy's diffi-culty in convincing Laurence to allow the mother-and-son reunion, adding, 'I think Laurence underestimates her feeling for the child.' But Laurence eventually agreed, and they exchanged the two children in Sainte-Maxime. Shortly after, Peggy found herself in the rumble seat on a car trip with Sindbad, 'and by degrees renewed my acquaintance with him,' she wrote. Laurence had impressed upon the boy that Peggy might try to run away with him and he must not let her. He had also warned Sindbad not to go to Spain, which was very close by, evidently suspecting that Peggy might try to get cus-tody of him in another country. When they visited some subterranean grottos on the border, Sindbad insisted that they leave when he learned that they were partly on Spanish soil. In fact, Kay and Laurence were still exploring ways to keep Sindbad from seeing Peggy, and even to get Pegeen. Before Sindbad's visit to his mother, Kay told Caresse Crosby that they were think-ing of fleeing Europe, perhaps even going to Russia, in order to evade Peggy: 'We can't fight her,' she wrote, 'but we can clear out.' The visit with Sindbad was successful, however, and Laurence was reassured that Peggy meant to behave reasonably.

  In the fall, Peggy, John, and Pegeen returned to Paris and found a house to lease on the avenue Reille in the Fourteenth Arrondissement, a working-class quarter almost at the Porte d'Orleans. It had been built by the painter Georges Braque and was, as Peggy described it, 'like a little skyscraper with one or two rooms on each of its five floors.' The view of Paris from the top floor was extraordinary. Peggy also rented a studio for John, lining it with cork because he was extremely sensitive to noise. Emily wrote to Emma in a letter dated March 17, 1931, 'Peggy and John are established at 55 avenue Reille and I believe are planning to remain some time. They seem to be quite con-tented – Peggy is never happy, and John can't forget Dorothy, but they love each other, and I think grow closer as time goes on.' (Emily was adept at, but sometimes mistaken in, seeing difficulties in almost every situation.)

Peggy and John leased the Paris house for three years, but because they traveled so much they were seldom in residence except for a couple of months in the winter. In the winter of 1930 to 1931 they saw a lot of Peggy's cousin Harold Loeb, who had since given up his literary journal, *Broom*. He and John were very fond of Jean Gorman, whose husband, Herbert, was writing a book about Joyce. John would stay late into the night at the Gormans'; Jean Gorman eventually complained in front of Joyce, who wrote her the following poem, which Peggy reprints in her memoirs:

> Go ca' canny with the cognac and of the wine fight shy
> Keep a watch on the hourglass but leave the beaker dry
> Guest friendliness to callers is your surest thief of time
> They're so much at Holms when with you, they can't dream of Guggenheim.

Their days slipped into a routine. John got up late and read all day, seldom using his cork-lined studio. Pegeen attended a bilingual day school in Neuilly run by Maria Jolas, whose husband, Eugene, edited *transition*, the literary magazine to which both Laurence and Emily contributed. Peggy or John usually picked her up from school in a little Peugeot that Peggy had bought to use around town. At about six, they sent Pegeen down to the floor she shared with Doris for her supper and bed, and John and Peggy would usually go out in search of company. Sometimes they returned for dinner, bringing unexpected guests. The cook, who was 'marvelous,' always managed to serve them, however many they were. John often wanted to stay out later than Peggy, in which case she went home early, but not without some resentment, and some days he irritated her by simply staying in bed with a hangover.

The writer Charles Henri Ford, who was at the time having an affair with Djuna Barnes (both were bisexual), described in a letter to his father a typical evening with Peggy and John.

> Djuna and I were taken to dinner the other night by Peggy Guggenheim, a millionairess: she has 30 million dollars in her own name and will have 70 million when her mother dies. Others in the party were Eugene MacCown, Mary Reynolds who lives with Marcel Duchamp, and John Holms, an Englishman with a red beard that Peggy is in love with. Had huge dinners, wines, three rounds of liqueurs. Afterwards John suggested we go to Le Boeuf sur le Toit in Peggy's little car with rumble seat – Had drinks there, I drank Pernods and at 2:00 went to Montmartre, the

original artists quarter on a monstrous hill overlooking Paris. First stop was Florence's, good negro orchestra, then on to Brick Top's . . . Had something to eat there, got home 4 or 5, Peggy having paid for the whole party, spending something like 1700 francs (65 or 70 dollars).

Given Ford's understanding that Peggy had $30 million and expected more than twice that, it is not surprising that he and the rest of the party accepted her largesse. But that such companions would later harp on her stinginess suggests at the very least a certain heartless entitlement on their part.

Managing the children's visits had become a lot easier; Sindbad now stayed with Peggy at Christmas and Easter plus one month in the summer, and Pegeen went to Kay and Laurence for equal lengths of time. Yet Peggy still felt that Laurence and Kay tried to turn her son against her. On one visit Sindbad complained that Laurence and Kay had to work so hard (translating, or, in Kay's case, writing) while Peggy and John lived so well. Peggy did not tell him, evidently to salvage Laurence's pride, that she gave his father several hundred dollars a month.

In the fall of 1931, Emma Goldman sent a copy of her just published *Living My Life* to Peggy with a pleasant note. In the finished book, issued in two volumes, she thanked Peggy in the preface and in the narrative; in both places, she described how Peggy had set up a fund for her and offered its first donation. 'The first to start the fund to secure me from material anxiety was Peggy Guggenheim,' wrote Emma in an opening section headed 'In Appreciation.' Peggy responded with a letter saying it hadn't been necessary to send the book as she already had bought it and had read it, exclaiming how much she had learned from it and wishing Emma the success she deserved. But at a dinner Emma gave, a contretemps developed. Peggy had earlier asked Emma to inscribe the first volume of *Living My Life*, and now Emma offered to do so. Peggy replied, 'Not necessary. You have already said enough about me in the preface.'

Somehow Emma took Peggy's remark to mean that Peggy resented not being given more space and thanked publicly with more warmth. Evidently something in Peggy's manner gave this impression, and, indeed, it is possible that her remarks, as Emma recorded them, were meant sarcastically. Peggy let other friends like Emily Coleman know that she was unhappy about her place in Emma's story. Laurence had in fact told Emma that he thought her 'tribute to Peggy was on the thin and mild side.' Peggy may well have felt that the events of the summer and fall of 1928, when Emma helped her to leave Laurence, were an important part of Emma's life and implied an important connection between the two women that should have had a place in the book. Perhaps because that time was so important in Peggy's life – Emma herself said it was the 'most critical period of [Peggy's] life' – she expected it to be of equal importance in Emma's.

Emma took this reaction as resentment, and felt stung. She had never been comfortable on the subject of Peggy and money. In January 1929 Peggy had given her 30,000 francs to buy Bon Espirit, the Saint-Tropez cottage, but she felt that in turn Peggy wanted her to report all she knew about Laurence. She considered returning the money to Peggy, but did not. Perhaps Peggy did something to reassure her. In describing her discomfort in a letter to Berkman, Emma wrote, 'Don't think Peggy was not just as decent in the way she gave me the check as she has always been. Nobody could have been nicer about it.' But she feared Peggy's charity was affecting their friendship.

In response to another note from Peggy praising her memoirs, Emma wrote a very curt letter, starting by saying she was glad Peggy's resentment hadn't clouded her judgment in reading the book. She went on to say that she had expected more from Peggy. She was used to the rich wanting something in return when they gave, and that was why she had steered clear of being subsidized in any way. 'But you were so different. You gave me the impression you found joy in giving. It was this faith in you which made it easy to come for help either for myself or for others.'

Peggy evidently did not know what to make of this. She was not comfortable giving Emma money. It was a loaded subject for her, and she did indeed sometimes think that she had not been thanked sufficiently. But in this case it seems that Emma for the most part misread her, with ramifications that were disastrous for the friendship. Emma might well have thought, as Charles Henri Ford did, that Peggy had untold millions, in which case the amount she expended on Emma was but a drop in the bucket. It was probably difficult – and embarrassing – for Peggy to set her friends straight as to just how much discretionary money she had. To have such a frank discussion may well have helped to sort out these confusions, but evidently this was beyond Peggy, shy about such matters, and not a conversation that Emma, who was very set in her mind, would have elicited.

Almost immediately Emma, to whom the friendship was extremely important despite her ambivalences, began backpedaling. Sasha Berkman (to whom she had described the dinner, omitting Peggy's remarks), when he heard of Peggy's resentment, advised Emma to drop her. Emma responded, 'Speaking of giving up . . . how glibly you suggest it in the case of Peggy. I just could not throw her over. I am too fond of her in the first place and I can not easily forget her help or her interest.' In late November, Emma saw Peggy at a party held by an American couple, and Peggy embraced her with what seemed to Emma the old warmth. She reported to her niece that she supposed she would see Peggy in the future.

> But the friendship is cracked. If I starved to death it would be impossible for me to ask Peggy for anything again. I have always known that there could be no real, lasting friendship between those who have lots and those who must fret for every sou. For a time Peggy made me waver in this. Now I know that she is like the rest. Yes, she gives, more readily than others of her class. She gives cordially to those she cares about . . . She has an awful inferiority complex . . . She can not imagine one would care for her if she had no money. My experience with Peggy is one more proof of the gulf which must always remain between the haves and the have nots.

Nevertheless, Emma bought toys for Sindbad and Pegeen for Christmas, and in Peggy's note of thanks she invited Emma to spend Christmas with them. In the coming year, Emily Coleman would continue to make mischief between the two, harping to Emma on the hurt Peggy felt when Emma took her response the wrong way.

Emma would drive past Pramousquier in the fall of 1933 and write a friendly letter to Peggy, saying that she remembered 'all the gay times under your hospitable roof, your visits to me in St. Tropez, our drives back and forth from Pramousquier over the bumpy road during your difficult experience.' The memory made the landscape 'poignantly alive.' But she still blamed Peggy:

> How little one knows in advance what fate has in store for one. Never had it occurred to me then that we would drift so far apart, that you would change towards me to the extent of complete indifference. I suppose life consists of a process of elimination. Perhaps it is natural you should have eliminated me from your life. I know I will never be able to eliminate you. You had meant too much for me, you always will whether you know it or not. I realized this yesterday more than I had thought since our unfortunate break. Your break, really.

Peggy did not respond. No doubt Emma's persistent accusation that an unbridgeable gulf existed between them and her portrayal of Peggy as a typical rich person who could not give without strings would have profoundly hurt Peggy. The events of the summer and fall of 1928 – the turning point of her life, when she gave up the charade of happily married life and began to devise her own way of living – would now be colored in her memory by their seeming insignificance to Emma. The loss of Emma Goldman she added to the list of those she loved now gone: her father and Benita.

In the spring of 1932, Emily Coleman wrote John Holms that she was excited over Peggy and John's getting a house in Devonshire or Cornwall. The night before, she said, she had had an elaborate dream about the house. The idea seemed filled with possibility.

John and Peggy were tired of traveling. They wanted to spend the summer and fall in a fixed abode, preferably a house in the English country-side. Though it was nearly impossible for Peggy to get John to agree to take a house – his indecision was so great – he too was eager to spend the summer in England. With the Depression – which had not really affected Peggy, so conservative were her uncles' investments of her trust funds – the expatriates had fled Paris in droves, and life there was much changed. In a different set-ting, Laurence grumbled that by 1930 the Dôme was overrun with 'barbarians, happy German families in ulsters, Scandinavian raw-fish eaters' who sat on the *terrasses* and took hours to finish two beers, a 'morose contrast to the old days, when, in less than two hours, Flossie Martin and other nota-bles could pile towers of saucers half a meter high.' Two visitors to Peggy and John in England noted, 'Awful tales of France from Peggy and John . . . Say it is so dead – art galleries, cafés, everything. London much more alive. And Paris is so expensive.'

Renting a car, Peggy and John traveled all through Devon, Dorset, and Cornwall, with John still unable to make up his mind on a house. After they returned to Paris, however, he wrote to the owners of a place they had seen on the edge of Dartmoor, taking a two-month lease. After collecting Pegeen and Sindbad, they set out in the Peugeot with Doris, their cook, and Djuna Barnes in tow and made the journey to Hayford Hall in southwest England. Emily Coleman would join them there with her son, John.

Near the small village of Buckfastleigh on the edge of Dartmoor, this was no bucolic country retreat. Isolated and remote – almost two hundred miles from London and twenty-five miles from Exeter, the nearest decent-sized town – it bordered the wild and inhospitable moors, rugged terrain indeed. Many believe that Hayford Hall is the model for Baskerville Hall, the eerie locale of Arthur Conan Doyle's *Hound of the Baskervilles* (1902). The text would be well known to Peggy and her party, and some of the tale's bleakness and mystery indeed surrounded the house. It would not have been hard to imagine, for instance, the unearthly distant screams of a moorland pony per-ishing in quicksand late in the night as the wind howled about the hall.

Emily Coleman, whom John and Peggy immediately summoned,

described the manor house itself: 'The house is low and white, in Tudor style, surrounded by enormous beeches and evergreens. A brook runs through the garden, making a fall at the side of the house.' Inside, she continued, she found 'a great ugly comic living room, like a raftered barn . . . full of ancestral portraits, generals.' John gave them a tour of the grounds: 'The beeches covered with lichen, mountain ash here grows like hawthorn. Tennis court and swimming pool, the latter pleasant and rustic.' The children had their own wing and a schoolroom downstairs and generally lived quite apart from the adults. The house had eleven bedrooms; Emily took a pleasant one with a writing desk in an alcove, and they all agreed that Djuna should take a bedroom done up in rococo style, as they felt it suited her.

The garden was quite beautiful, half wild, but beyond was Dartmoor – vast, rolling, mostly barren, hundreds of acres square, and, except for wild ponies, uninhabited. All that grew there were bracken and heather and, in treacherous swampy parts, a feathery white flower. Once a year the neighbors rounded up the ponies and the children learned to ride them in a paddock. Peggy and John kept about six horses, though the only one that was any good was a hunter called Katie, which John would usually claim for himself.

Throughout that summer Emily was smitten by nature. She was reading W. H. Hudson's *Birds and Man* (1915), and it was making a great impression. Djuna, who had weathered a most intense love affair in the 1920s with a woman named Thelma Woods, was recovering from her experience and working on the bizarre and brilliant manuscript that would become *Nightwood* (1936), which she would dedicate to John and Peggy. She often kept to her room the entire day, only to emerge to cut a rose in the garden, which she would give to Peggy. For their part, John and Peggy, often with the children, rode, swam, puttered in the garden, and played tennis; John would often drive to nearby coves, usually deserted, where they could bathe in the ocean.

But in the evenings all would convene: first, for a perfunctory (but delicious – Peggy and John's French cook, Marie, was excellent) meal in a 'very dreary' dining room and then to the great hall, of which Peggy wrote, 'I am sure so much conversation was never made in this hall before or since.' The talk was the kind at which John excelled, ranging over such authors as Strindberg, Ibsen, Dostoyevsky, Tolstoy, and the Greek philosopher Zeno. But these conversations usually turned into a comparative examination of the participants' own personalities and talents; it was a common topic, for example, that Djuna had enthusiasms in literature but no critical faculty to discuss it. Another was John's comparison of Djuna to Emily Brontë. (Djuna, who, as Emily Coleman related, 'said she was more conceited about her work than I could imagine,' resisted the comparison, saying Brontë was like Shakespeare.)

Much discussion turned on the residents' sexuality, Djuna's in particular. Emily once asked Djuna if she was 'really lesbian,' and Djuna responded, 'I might be anything. If a horse loved me, I might be that.' Another time Emily asked her whether she hated men; Djuna laughed and said of course not, though later in the evening a man came up in conversation, and she said, 'But, my dear, I hold no brief for men. I'd just as soon stick one of them with a poker as another.'

The game of Truth was another favorite activity. The players would put down on paper comments on the feature of a chosen person in the room, a feature determined beforehand – looks, faults, or sex appeal, and then one of them, usually Djuna, would read the results; what made it fun was trying to guess who had written what. One evening Djuna came down for something after the others had gone to bed and found Emily pawing through the contents of a wastebasket, muttering, 'Garter [sic] see who gave me a zero for sex appeal.'

Emily's diary recounts every conversation of any significance (and many of none). Though she describes fights with Peggy – at one point Emily's criticisms inspired Peggy to ask her to leave – and though they had their differences (during a particularly bad period Emily wrote, 'Our relation is so complicated with love and hate that it's easier for her to pretend it's hate'), in the main Emily reports every nuance of Peggy's character with fondness. She recounts that one evening John and she 'talked about Djuna's lack of subtlety, . . . and also why she does not know Peggy's wit. I said I could not laugh at Djuna's kind of wit, not laugh with all my soul, whereas Peggy makes me feel delighted through and through. Peggy is witty because she isn't trying, she has the gift, and does not think of any audience.' Another time, when Emily took extra servings at dinner (she was known for her appetite and bad table manners), she apologized, saying, 'I don't want to be a pig.' Peggy said, 'What are you going to do instead?' Citing another unfunny witticism, Emily acknowledged, 'This is an example of her kind of wit, she plays on words, and at the moment it is amusing, often not repeatable.'

But sometimes the games of Truth took a darker turn; indeed, Emily writes that when one 'said a little truth,' devastating remarks often followed. One night the women turned on John: 'Djuna said a little truth, goaded by me. She was sitting on the couch. Peggy was by John. Peggy said, "What do I care what his genius is, it does me no good? He doesn't use it." She said my diary [the one Emily had read from] had shown him up. I said, "It isn't that he's an encyclopedia, it's the sense of life he gives one." Peggy said, "He gives me a sense of death." Djuna said he did her too.' The conversation continued, with Emily concluding, 'John with three women fighting about him, an ideal moment for him, except that both P. and Djuna thought he was a fool.' Peggy could be, as this exchange suggests, tough on John. In this light, it should be noted that a strong possibility exists that Peggy invited others to Hayford Hall, and attached Emily to her household, because, for whatever reason, she did not want to be alone with him.

Life at the hall could be a pressure cooker, with John surrounded by a veritable seraglio of women: a blonde, a brunette, and a redhead. Emily (the blonde) had of course been in love with John back in 1928, and sometimes admitted that she still was. Djuna, the auburn-haired beauty of the three, was also an accomplished writer and had the meanest tongue; John in particular must have been ambivalent about her presence. Although she could equal anyone in verbal sparring, Peggy found it difficult to keep up with some of the more intellectual conversations (though she had read widely, Emily and John had read nearly everything, it seemed). Like Djuna, Peggy did not go in for lengthy discussions about abstract concepts, and she must have suffered her share of jealousy, as John often stayed up far into the night talking to Emily long after Peggy went upstairs. Certainly a lot of sexual tension was in the air, no less so than for Emily's continually pointing out and analyzing it. One night Djuna said to John, 'Why, I wouldn't touch you with a ten-foot pole.' Peggy, overhearing, said that John could touch Djuna with one – a little off-color compliment meant for John. Another night Djuna joined Peggy and John after washing her red hair. Peggy was languorous and fell asleep listening to John and the other women talk. When she awoke she saw that John was playing with Djuna's soft, fluffy hair. 'If you rise, the dollar will fall,' Peggy admonished John with witty innuendo.

When alcohol was added to the mix – as it almost always was, in great quantity – the potential for real trouble escalated. A new expression of the 1930s was 'plastered,' and Emily records many occasions when all four were plastered. A common morning drink was a prairie oyster, a hangover remedy containing an egg yolk, brandy, Worcestershire sauce, cayenne, and Tabasco; a later guest was to dub the house Hangover Hall.

Indeed, a lot of nastiness went on behind closed doors. Emily overheard John entering the bedroom that he and Peggy shared after a late night downstairs talking with her and Djuna. Emily writes,

> I shut my door, then heard screams from Peggy's room. I heard 'You dirty little bitch, you falsify everything. You lie and lie, like a serpent.' He kept on talking and talking, and she did not reply, after the screams died down. He said he could not stand her malice and venom.

I knew she had probably accused him when he came up, and probably said it was later than it was, and he had hit her.

Emily clearly was not perspicacious on all matters, however, for she
added, 'This was a clearing of the air, putting his woman in her place.
Tomorrow she would be more humane.' Evidently Emily hero-worshipped
John to such a degree that she could see nothing wrong with his behavior and
took it as run-of-the-mill. And though she records moments when John said
thoughtless things to Peggy, she mentions no other such incident in a two-
month-long diary that is seemingly all-inclusive.

Was Peggy again in an abusive relationship? Certainly her mother, mindful of the abuse Peggy had received from Laurence, suspected as much. Once,
Peggy made a number of malicious comments about an Italian boyfriend of
Emily's and enraged her so much that Emily gave her a black eye. Florette,
who called John 'Mr. Holms' and refused to stay in the unmarried couple's
house when she visited, believed that John had given her the black eye and
was convinced otherwise only with much effort. There would be other occasions when John was physically violent to Peggy, although not so often as in
Laurence's case and never in front of servants or friends.

For their first two years together, Peggy later wrote, she loved John as a
man and he loved her as a woman, which was her way of saying that the relationship was very successful sexually. At first, she said, she refused to listen to
him talk, for she wanted to keep the relationship intensely physical. But
'Little by little I opened my ears, and gradually, during the five years that I
lived with him, I began to learn everything I know today.' He encouraged her
to broaden her reading, recommending D. H. Lawrence and other moderns,
and to keep a diary – advice her letters indicate she took, though no diary survives. But this mentorship had its negative side: she wrote in the next breath,
'He held me in the palm of his hand and from the time I once belonged to
him to the day he died he directed my every move, my every thought.' Later,
after John's death, she had trouble making decisions by herself about such
matters as renting places for summers, inviting guests, handling the staff,
directing the children: 'I had been completely dependent on [John]; I was
incapable of thinking for myself. He had always decided everything and as he
was so brilliant it was much simpler to accept his judgments than make my
own. He told me that when I tried to think I looked like a puzzled monkey.
No wonder I avoided it whenever I could!'

Still, Peggy believed that she was happy with John, and the relationship
had a sexual, emotional and intellectual intensity that she welcomed: she
must have felt, after the frivolous – and painful – years with Laurence, that

she was really living for the first time. John (usually) took her seriously – a feat that Laurence, who took nothing seriously, could never achieve. An evening at Hayford Hall is rather delightful to contemplate (if somewhat exhausting): delicious food and fine wines, great talk in lovely surroundings. Whatever the tensions between them, the adults interacted and talked as equals. John, definitely heterosexual but hardly what we would today call an alpha male, was on the same footing with the women, despite a seeming need to dominate discussion. The participants could envision a whole new way for men and women to live together, a new footing for personal relations. For Peggy, this dynamic must have been a revelation; the communally lived summer made her feel that she was a person to be taken seriously, not just as an appendage to a man about town like Laurence.

At Hayford Hall she thrived. A steady stream of guests made for a relentless pace, to which Peggy responded with vivacity. Edwin Muir, one of John's prison camp friends, and his wife, Willa (whom Peggy and Emily adored), came frequently, as did Sir Samuel Hoare, known as Peter, who was a member of the same set of writers and poets and also an M.P. since 1910 and secretary of state for India. Emily pursued Hoare for years, but even after divorcing his wife he stubbornly refused to marry her. Inevitably, Peggy misspelled *whoring* as *hoaring*, to mean sleeping around, and the group took the term up with relish. Among the female guests were the novelist Antonia White, known as Tony, who was then married to Tom Hopkinson, and her friend Phyllis Jones, a kind redhead who devoted most of her life to caring for her sick mother. Another guest was Silas Glossop, a mining engineer who fathered Antonia White's first child and would later have an affair with Djuna, though nothing sparked between them that summer. Because so many of the guests had literary connections, talk was often about their modernist contemporaries, D. H. Lawrence especially, but also Aldous Huxley, H. G. Wells, and E. M. Forster, as well as past literary lights. They did not talk much about politics, except perhaps to glean some gossip from Peter Hoare. (John sometimes scolded Peggy for not reading newspapers.)

A repeat guest was William Gerhardie, with his married mistress, the writer Vera Boyse. Gerhardie too had served time in prison camp with John and considered him a great friend. That would not prevent him from writing about John and Peggy as Mr. and Mrs. Bonzo in his 1936 satirical novel, *Of Mortal Love*. In the novel, Bonzo and his wife live in what is clearly Hayford Hall: '[The Bonzos] had rented a roomy house lost on many acres of gardens, woodland, and meadows, on the very edge of Dartmoor, with no dwellings for miles around them.' Emily Coleman figures in the novel, 'an American poetess and worshipper of Bonzo.' And Bonzo himself is 'a shy, sultry lone wolf in his middle thirties, who wore a little red beard, hardly visible at the sides but tapering down to a point which he fingered with an air of fastidious indulgence, and a smile of cautious benevolence.' Molly is his rich American wife; the portrayal is a fond one and amazingly true to life.

Life seemed effortless. Doris went every day to market in Buckfastleigh with Marie. On Thursdays they and the French maid, Madeleine, had their holiday; on that day, an English maid came in and served English specialties such as steak and kidney pie and cottage pie; over the whole ménage presided a housekeeper-maid and assistant who came with Hayford Hall. Sindbad and Pegeen, and Emily's son, John, who was Sindbad's age, thrived as well. The children had lunch with the adults and swam, rode, and played tennis with the residents and guests. They had a favorite horse called Starlight. Two dogs had the run of the place: a little one named Jane, and a black dog named Michael that Djuna described as effervescent, as he farted all the time, often disrupting lunch.

Peggy, at thirty-four, was blooming. Though her relationship with John Holms was complicated, she believed, and others observed, that they were very much in love. And hers was not a stuffy, English country house existence. Because of Dartmoor's remoteness, Peggy and John went practically the whole summer without seeing anyone (except for each other, the guests, and the servants and children). The countryside was not cultivated, a home to farm animals, or given over to crops; it was wild, rugged, elemental. And life within the walls of Hayford Hall was never dull. Antonia White's daughter by Silas Glossop would call it 'a version of Boccaccio, with an all-female cast,' and the description is fairly apt. The women sported, flirted, made endless conversation, and put John at their center, not as a figure to be worshipped or looked up to but to be sported with, to spend hours with in stimulating repartee. One of them was writing a modernist masterwork, while John as usual threatened all sorts of epics; Peggy may have felt herself a muse.

On the other hand, it would be misleading to describe the Hayford Hall period entirely as an idyll, however much its inhabitants thought of it as such. Surely weeks of drinking, gossip, and baring of souls, complete with sexual tensions both subterranean and acted upon, made at times for a harrowing, hardly restful experience. Emily Coleman, with her nosiness, egotism, and general obnoxiousness, often must have made daily life excruciating. But the inhabitants loved having this wonderful country home at their disposal, with refreshments and amusements provided by generous hosts, and the atmosphere of romance was persuasive. Peggy, too, enjoyed her own largesse, perhaps for once feeling she was appreciated rather than resented.

Whether Peggy was, indeed, 'happy' at this stage of her life is another question. She can't be said to have accomplished much – beyond continuing her education – but she had at least succeeded in carving out an existence far from the life of an 'our crowd' German-Jewish matron that her mother and the extended Guggenheim family would have chosen for her. Her tempestuous marriage to Laurence and her relationship with the creatively paralyzed John Holms may have been difficult, but they had aligned her firmly with a bohemian, literary-artistic milieu in which she felt at home and alive. This life was more creative and better suited to her temperament and aspirations than the only other one she could imagine, and it placed her squarely in the world of artists and writers she would cultivate and often support for the rest of her life.

6

Endings and Beginnings

In the spring of 1932, just before the Hayford Hall interlude, Peggy marked the effective end to her first marriage when Laurence Vail married Kay Boyle. Peggy's divorce, awarded on grounds of cruelty, had come through in January. Doris the baby nurse; Peggy Deutschbein (now Waldman, having married Milton Waldman, Hazel's second husband, as it happened – rather a bizarre wrinkle); and a Saint-Tropez café owner all gave testimony, in what must have been a humiliating experience for everyone concerned. The divorce cost Peggy. As she had forecast, 'the Guggenheim name' made for an expensive outcome: she had to pay her lawyers $10,000 and was ordered by the court to pay Laurence's lawyers $2,000. She struck an informal agreement with Laurence as well, under which she would send him a certain sum of money each month, at first $300. The agreement reflected her wish that Sindbad be properly cared for, but by the time Sindbad was grown up she would be so fond of Laurence and accustomed to the arrangement that she would keep paying the monthly sums right up to his death. Laurence still received an allowance from his mother, and this sum, on top of the income from Kay's writing, allowed his family to live fairly well.

The regular exchanges of the children were going more smoothly and communications between Laurence and Peggy had improved, but their parenting was not without hitches, partly because of Kay's extreme antipathy to Peggy. Once, when Peggy came to take Sindbad for a weekend, Kay complained dramatically that without her stepson she was looking for somewhere to go 'for consolation.' Another time, when Peggy was due to arrive to retrieve Pegeen, Kay wrote a friend, 'I'm afraid Laurence won't get over this week.' And Kay used to tell others that Peggy resented it keenly when Kay made money from her writing that she could then use to support Sindbad.

Kay even complained that John Holms had made a pass at her, when he followed her into a ladies' room in a café.

Kay bore Laurence a daughter, Apple, in December 1929, and Laurence was elated, feeling that he now had a daughter to replace the one he had lost. (No evidence exists that he considered how this may have made Pegeen feel.) Boyle's biographer relates a story of Kay washing her daughter Bobby's mouth out with soap when she used bad language. Afterward, she found Pegeen crying quietly: 'You never wash my mouth out with soap,' the little girl mourned. 'I'm only your stepdaughter, so you don't.' The Vail family otherwise was a very tight one. After the birth of another daughter, Kathe, in 1935, they would buy a skiing villa in the town of Megève in the Swiss Alps and call it Cinq Enfants, for Bobby, Apple, Kathe, Pegeen, and Sindbad; there was even a Vail family newspaper, produced at regular intervals. But Sindbad and Pegeen couldn't help feeling a little left out – Pegeen especially so, as she was there only on vacations.

Laurence and Kay had chosen to be married in late March at the city hall in Nice. Peggy later wrote that 'for some morbid reason' Laurence invited her and John Holms to the wedding. Perhaps because they were then passing through Nice and perhaps for the sake of the children, Peggy and John attended, taking with them Emily Coleman and her son, John. Their presence, Peggy later wrote, with uncharacteristic cynicism, 'gave the impression to the outside world that we were excessively friendly.' Somehow, after the ceremony, Sindbad, then eleven, got hold of a pistol, and wedding photos captured him brandishing it, to the nervous laughter of the bride and groom and their guests.

After decamping from Hayford Hall in the fall of 1932, Djuna Barnes accompanied Sindbad back to Paris, where Laurence reclaimed him. Peggy and John sent Pegeen and Doris off to visit Milton and Peggy Waldman and their children outside London, while they toured Bath and saw the cathedral at Glastonbury with Emily. Then they drove north to Cheltenham in Gloucestershire, where John visited his parents. He left Peggy at a hotel, but his sister Beatrix slipped off to visit her there, which Peggy found touching.

In November, Peggy, John, and Pegeen (and their retinue, including Emily Coleman) were back in Paris at 55 avenue Reille. Emily, as usual, kept a bursting diary, detailing Peggy and John's comings and goings and Pegeen's behavior. On December 14 she noted that Peggy and John talked a good deal on the telephone with their insurance agent because John had collided with a funeral procession early one morning when he was drunk. She made no mention of Peggy's reaction to the accident. Emily found Peggy and John irritating, she confessed, citing 'Peggy's avarice and fussing, John's repeating everything he has said to me for five years,' yet she added, 'But I don't like anyone but them.'

Emily also described a downright grim night out with the couple that came to a distinctly odd end. They were at the well-known Prunier's, where Emily had oysters and 'dressed crab,' and then went on to Le Boeuf sur le Toit, no longer the most of-the-moment nightspot, where Peggy got 'very tight' and berated John with his many failings, which unaccountably caused Emily to laugh 'terrifically.' Next they went to La Coupole, where Peggy threw her pocketbook at John and missed. When they arrived home, they had a disagreement about the key to the garage, John called Peggy 'stupid,' and Peggy became 'really angry with him.' Peggy refused to go up to their bedroom and instead climbed in bed with Emily. According to Emily, Peggy went into 'a frenzy,' going on about her 1929 abortion and how 'she had had it because he was an inhuman man and she couldn't live with him, or bear children by him, that he stifled all her true womanly feelings.' John, evidently in the room and listening, was very hurt. Peggy still refused to go up to her bed, so John too climbed into Emily's bed, 'and we slept that way for the rest of the night.' (The next day, Emily wrote that Peggy was 'feeling happy today, purged of her furies. They seem to love each other, and it's a pleasure to be with them.') A week later, they slept three to the bed again. Emily described it, making clear that these occasions were not sexual: 'We all slept together again, but though it makes us like each other and promotes intimacy, John & I talk, and no one gets any sleep. He sits between us and drinks, and Peggy complains.'

In London in March, the Waldmans lent them their house in Trevor Square, which meant that John and Peggy could install Pegeen, her nurse, and Marie the cook. Here Peggy first crossed paths with another man who would become important in her life, Douglas Garman. Five years younger than she, Garman was a friend of John's from *The Calendar of Modern Letters* days and was now an editor at the left-wing publishing house Wishart and Company; John contacted him because he was trying to find a British publisher for Djuna Barnes's first novel, *Ryder*, which had been published in the United States in 1928 to scant notice. Garman was no help, but Peggy extended an invitation to him to visit them at Easter in their Paris house. There she conceived a violent attraction to him, which he seemed to reciprocate. Garman was dashingly handsome. Peggy later commented, 'I imagine I felt Garman was a real man, and John was more like Christ or a ghost.' John sensed enough of what was going on to become jealous, and Peggy already thought that Garman might be part of her future, but nobody acted at this juncture and Garman left without incident. Back in London, Garman came to tea with his daughter, Debbie, who was just Pegeen's age and even looked like her, having the same sturdy but not heavy carriage.

In July, Peggy and John took up residence at Hayford Hall again. As second-year tenants, they were trusted enough that they could bring all their own servants without oversight by the staff who had helped them the year before, and to Doris and Marie (the maid, Madeleine, they had left behind at the avenue Reille house) they added a cockney butler, Albert (who drank), and his Belgian wife, Louise. Once again Emily and her son were with them, as well as Djuna Barnes. Antonia White, who had had a complete breakdown in 1923 and still suffered from depression, came down early in the summer, where she made a special hit with Emily. Emily recorded in her diary a loving scene between Tony and Djuna, 'Djuna lapping and little Tony grooming her.' But Emily felt Djuna was being dishonest with Tony, whose autobiographical novel, *Frost in May* (1939), based on her convent-school upbringing Djuna was trying to read in manuscript. Sexual tensions were surfacing as they had the previous summer, perhaps with more urgency.

According to a curious diary entry that Emily made for July 23, Djuna, while being especially loving to John one night and 'kissing him passionately on the neck,' suddenly began to 'pound' Peggy 'in the bottom.' Peggy's response was 'My God, how this woman hates me.' Then Djuna, in Emily's words, 'began to pound me. She hadn't hit me four times before I had an orgasm' and later 'pounded and massaged me thoroughly.' John turned down the lights and left them alone.

Despite difficulties with Emily, Peter Hoare came to visit several times. William Gerhardie came once with Vera Boyse, whose husband was divorcing her (the Hayford Hall butler, Albert, would be forced to testify that Gerhardie had visited the house with Boyse). A visit from Florette coincided with the arrival of the French-American painter Louis Bouché, his wife, Marian, and their daughter Jane (who was Sindbad's age); Bouché had received one of the prestigious John Simon Guggenheim Fellowships, which Peggy's uncle had instituted in 1925. Bouché was an old friend of Djuna's and an enthusiastic drinker who could hold his own with John Holms; Marian Bouché kept a spirited diary for the summer and autumn of 1933. Their experience at Hayford Hall was, in retrospect, not happy: Marian wrote in September, 'Rather glad we won't be going back to the Guggenheim Hangover Hall once more as they are leaving – Djuna going to Venice. Too drunken, too hectic. Seems an unhappy household underneath.' Clearly, Bouché picked up on the downside of the seeming idyll.

Nevertheless, the Bouchés saw a lot of Peggy and John that November and December. Marian's entry for December 12 reads, 'Peggy and John moved into their London house. Called us up . . . and took us to dinner at the Café Royal. Hardly out of their sight since. We had lots of fun with Peter Hoare who was along. Such good wine.' Shortly after, she described going to the British Museum with their children, coming back to tea with Peggy, then staying for cocktails, and staying on still further for dinner: 'John got me tight again and off I went, enjoying the applause.' The Bouchés were taking an ocean liner back to the United States; Peggy and John drove them down to Southampton, where they were picking up a new Delage automobile shipped from France. 'All the way to Southampton,' wrote Marian, 'we took swigs of whiskey from a flask. (Also they gave us a present of two bottles.)' At the end of the diary, Marian toted up the trip, and Peggy came under the heading 'Nicest person we met.'

Peggy and John had been making plans to go to Ireland and Spain over the winter, but their plans hit a snag in the third week of August, when John suffered an accident. He had been horseback riding in the rain and his glasses kept misting up; he didn't see an upcoming rabbit hole, and his mare, Katie, stumbled into it. The doctor from nearby Totnes found that John had broken his wrist. He set the wrist but evidently botched the job, for it continued to hurt over the weeks following, despite being encased in a plaster cast. John and Peggy returned to Paris and the avenue Reille, where a doctor at the American Hospital again X-rayed John's wrist and said that a small piece of bone had chipped off, recommending salt baths and massage. The massages brought him only worse pain.

They returned to London in November, staying with the Waldmans at Orchard Poyle, their house in Buckinghamshire, while they looked for a house of their own. Wyn Henderson, a plump woman who worked as a typographer, traveled in artistic circles, and was a good friend of Antonia White's (though White wrote that she was 'really a *bad* woman . . . She will procure you any drug or distraction at a price'), and whom Peggy had met in the last year, was able to find them a house in Woburn Square in the heart of Bloomsbury. Peggy described the house as 'very English eighteenth-century, [but] really quite nice by the time we made it a little less formal.' John took up with his friends Hugh Kingsmill, William Gerhardie, Edwin Muir, and Peter Hoare, while Peggy enjoyed seeing Emily, Antonia White, and her friend Phyllis Jones, as well as the Waldmans.

Peggy had told a horrified Emily of her attraction to Douglas Garman, and Emily counseled her to put it out of her mind, but one cold December night Peggy told John of her feelings. He reacted violently, forcing her to stand, naked, in front of an open window and throwing whiskey into her eyes. According to Peggy, he said, 'I would like to beat your face so that no man will ever look at it again.' Peggy was so terrified that she made Emily spend the night with her for protection. Again, the chief relationship in her life was turning violent, and Peggy's masochism was such that she did not contemplate leaving John because of it.

At the same time, John was talking about getting a divorce from Dorothy and marrying his lover. Peggy insisted he make out a will in her favor, reasoning that otherwise Dorothy would be his legal heir. Peggy had already signed an agreement that she would give Dorothy 360 pounds a year. In retrospect, Peggy saw that she had become preoccupied by the possibility of John's death. She worried morbidly that she would have no say in his burial but that Dorothy and John's family would take charge.

John's wrist stubbornly would not heal. A Harley Street doctor said that he needed to have a simple operation to break the extra growth in his wrist. He would need to have anesthesia, but the operation could be done at home and would take only a matter of minutes. John and Peggy scheduled the surgery, but John came down with the flu and they had to set a new date.

Christmas intervened, and Sindbad came to stay for the holidays. Afterward, Peggy took him on the train to Zurich to meet Laurence, who would take his son back to Austria. On her return, pulling into Victoria Station, she blamed John for causing her separation from Sindbad and swore 'a terrible oath' that she never wanted to see him again. But she found that Emily had scheduled John's surgery for the following morning. (Why Emily had intervened in this way is not clear.)

John stayed up late on the night of January 18, 1934, talking and drinking with friends, including Gerhardie, who was then writing a book about 'the Astral,' according to Peggy (presumably his 1934 *Resurrection*). Gerhardie told John that he would be leaving his body while under the anesthesia. John asked, 'What if I never come back?'

The next morning John had a hangover, and Peggy felt it would be best to call off the surgery again, but she was too embarrassed to do so, and both she and John wanted to get it over with. She held John's hand while he was put to sleep and acquiesced when John's doctors – a general practitioner, a surgeon, and an anesthetist – asked her to leave the room. When they had not emerged after half an hour, she went up and listened outside the bedroom door. Hearing nothing, she crept downstairs again. Minutes later one of the doctors appeared in the front hall to get a small bag. He disappeared again and, after seemingly hours passed, the doctors appeared downstairs and told her what had happened. After the operation, when the three had moved off to the side, the physician looked over and noticed that Holms was failing. The men cut open his chest and injected adrenaline into his heart, but no measures they took revived him. The physician, who was also Milton Waldman's, called the Waldmans and asked them to come in and be with Peggy. After the three men left and before the Waldmans arrived, Peggy was left alone with the body. 'He was so far away it was hopeless,' she later wrote. 'I knew that I would never be happy again.'

When the Waldmans arrived they sent for Emily, who would remain at Peggy's side for the next two months. As undertakers carried John's body down the stairs, Peggy remembered the oath she had sworn at Victoria Station – that she never wanted to see John Holms again – and 'let out a terrible scream.' She sent for Beatrix Holms and Dorothy – still John's legal wife – and made plans for a cremation. First she had to appear at an autopsy and inquest. The coroner read the autopsy report, which indicated that alcohol had affected all of John's organs and that his death had not been the doctors' fault. The prospect of the cremation was too much for Peggy, and she stayed home with Peggy Waldman. Only Edwin Muir, Hugh Kingsmill, Milton Waldman, Dorothy, Emily, and Beatrix attended the service. Peggy, with Peggy Waldman, lit a candle in a Soho Catholic church in John's memory. When she was listening to a recording of Beethoven's Tenth Quartet in her bedroom afterward, Beatrix came in to say goodbye, taking Peggy by surprise saying, 'Whatever your life is to be, I hope it will be happy.'

Dorothy stayed on, as did Emily. Pegeen remained ignorant of John's death; she had recently suffered a loss that was, to her, much worse: the baby nurse Doris, who had cared for Pegeen since she was born, had left over Christmas to be married. Doris was willing to come back and resume work, but Peggy was so jealous of her superior place in Pegeen's affections, under-lined for her by Pegeen's negative reaction to Doris's marriage, that she would not allow Doris to return. In a bookstore one day, shopping with her mother, Pegeen asked when John would be coming home from the nursing home where she believed him to be. 'Never,' said Peggy. 'He is in heaven with the angels.' A few days later Pegeen came home from school early and said she was never going back, having been brutally informed by a classmate of the reality of John's death; Peggy found her a new school in Hampstead.

Before Dorothy left, she and Peggy came to a new agreement, tearing up the old one. Peggy gave her all of John's books and money. His estate, approx-imately 5,000 pounds, would render Dorothy about 200 pounds a year. On top of that, Peggy agreed to send Dorothy 160 pounds annually – a total match-ing the earlier sum to which Peggy had agreed. This time Dorothy trusted her and did not consider a new legal document necessary. Again, it is not clear why Peggy agreed to this arrangement, when Dorothy had been such a thorn in her side. Perhaps she still felt guilty for what Dorothy saw as Peggy 'stealing' her man.

On the heels of John's death, Peggy had to see to the Paris house. She and John had sublet it, but the term was up and she had to discuss with the landlord some alterations she and John had made to the ground floor. She put all the furniture into storage and closed the house up, glad that nothing remained there of her life with John. 'Now that John is dead,' she told Emily, 'we are running into eternal danger.' Every day she looked in the mirror 'and watched my mouth sag more and more.' She believed she had lost her very soul. For years to come she would, with Emily's enthusiastic support, speculate about the afterlife and John's presence among them, but she put an abrupt stop to this thinking when Emily, in a religious fervor, began to speak of 'channeling' John's spirit.

Back in Woburn Square, the mail brought many condolence letters, among them one from Douglas Garman. Peggy found herself thinking about him more and more until he became an obsession. Somehow she convinced Emily – who probably relished the intrigue – to ask him out for a drink, and to probe him to see if her attraction was reciprocated. Emily brought back good news: he seemed interested, and, better yet, he had separated from his wife. Peggy invited Garman – no one in her circle called him Douglas – to a dinner at the Woburn Square house to which Emily invited Peter Hoare. The dinner was a success, and Peggy went home with Garman that night. Not eight weeks had passed since John's death.

Peggy had not lived without a 'husband' since she was twenty-four, and now, at thirty-six, may not have felt that she had the emotional resources to contemplate a life alone. As she thought about her sagging chin and the beginnings of gray in her hair – though her slim figure had not failed her yet – she may well have felt anxious about her ability to attract a man. Then, too, she felt John's absence had left her without direction or any clear plan for a future. She knew that she wanted to make her way among writers and artists, but she had no idea how she might do so. She had tried writing and she had tried painting – a decade ago, during a summer in Brittany – and she seemed to think she had no talent for either (why friends like Emma and Djuna never encouraged her writing is not clear – Peggy wrote an excellent letter, witty, irreverent, with interesting, well-told narratives). Though she was by no means over her mourning for John – that would take several years, and she would never really recover from the loss – the only course open to her seemed to have been taking on another 'husband.' Though sexual attraction was part of it, she didn't desire Garman only physically; she looked to him almost as a savior.

Douglas Garman was not a bad choice, if security and devotion were what she sought. Born in 1903 to a wealthy doctor and his wife (she was said to be half-Gypsy), he grew up in an Elizabethan manor house called Oakeswell Hall in Wednesbury, near Birmingham in Staffordshire. Garman had a brother, Mavin, a farmer in Hampshire, and seven remarkable sisters, several of whom would figure in Peggy's life in the future. The beautiful Garman girls carried on a dizzying, decades-spanning roundelay of marriages and affairs with prominent men that would have left Alma Mahler envious. They included Mary, who married the fascist South African poet Roy Campbell and had an affair with Vita Sackville-West; Sylvia, who was said to have had an affair with the elusive T. E. Lawrence; Kathleen, the muse and mistress of Sir Jacob Epstein, the sculptor, who became his wife only after bearing him three children; Rosalind, who prosaically married a garage owner and had two children; Helen, who married a half-Norwegian fisherman in France and had a daughter; Kathy, who married the much-loved poet and memoirist Laurie Lee (whose *Cider with Rosie* was published in 1959); Ruth, who lived in Herefordshire and had several children by different men; and Lorna, perhaps the most beautiful of all, who married Ernest Wishart, the publisher who employed Douglas Garman, and bore him a child at seventeen, later had an illegitimate daughter with Laurie Lee (afterward her niece Kathy's husband), and later still had an affair with the painter Lucian Freud (who, in turn, later married and had a child with Kitty Epstein, another of Lorna's nieces, the daughter of Kathleen). Peggy was to consider all these Garmans as a kind of honorary family.

Douglas Garman had gone to Cambridge but then veered from a conventional course, announcing to his grandfather, also a doctor, that he wanted to be a writer. The grandfather, livid, brushed his wishes aside and told him there were four professions open to a gentleman: the church, the army, law, and medicine. When Garman ignored this advice, his grandfather cut him out of his will.

Garman was an agreeable man by all accounts, but increasingly drawn to Communism. On a trip to Russia he had fallen in love, which had occasioned his break from his wife. But his Russian lover could not come to England. Garman was ready for a great love, and Peggy was very available. Though he had worked on *The Calendar of Modern Letters* with John Holms, he had not had close ties to him and initially did not feel constrained by her history with him. According to Peggy, he quoted Shakespeare to her, especially about Cleopatra ('Age cannot wither her, nor custom stale her infinite variety') and wrote a poem celebrating 'the gift between your thighs.' The sexual attraction between them was considerable. But Peggy found it impossible not to cry over John, which Garman eventually found annoying.

At Easter she took Pegeen off to Kitzbühel to visit the Vails for ten days, leaving Garman behind. Kay was pregnant again, and, Peggy wrote Emily, 'Laurence feels he's the great patriarch with two wives & four children & one inside.' Sindbad, while happy to see his mother, didn't want to talk about John Holms, and Peggy felt she couldn't talk about him with anyone else there. Her outlook was bleak: 'I feel life is Bloodier & Bloodier . . . No one will ever take care of me again. John held me in the hollow of his hand.' Emily, she said, had saved her life by being with her since John's death, and she would never forget it. And she was able to report that she felt closer to Pegeen, who clung to her leg the first day, crying inconsolably, but then, as she slowly understood that this time her mother would not just be dropping her off, improved greatly and gladly played with the Vail children.

Upon her return to London, Peggy stayed in the Woburn Square house until June, when the lease ran out, spending nights with Garman but always making it back home for breakfast. With relief, she rented a place in Hampstead, near Pegeen's school, where she was able to report that her daughter seemed happy for the first time since Doris left. Garman visited often and was finally allowed to stay the night in Hampstead; Peggy had not wanted to have him in the house where John had died. She was happy then with Garman: he had a good sense of humor and was a talented mimic. He was smart and could talk about literature without being intimidating, and Peggy soon began to formulate and tackle her own reading lists. She felt self-conscious about the five-year age difference between them, so Garman advised her to update her wardrobe and to do something about the gray in her hair, both of which she did.

Garman had installed his mother in a house called Vine Cottage in South Harting in Sussex; he urged Peggy to rent a house nearby for the summer, enabling him to live at his mother's house with his daughter, Debbie, while editing a book for Wishart and visit Peggy at the same time. Peggy found a place called Warblington Castle, about a mile from Havant, which was not a castle at all but a farmhouse partly surrounded by a moat; in the garden was a tall brick Tudor tower, the remains of a castle. Compared to Hayford Hall, wrote Emily, '[T]he house is far nicer, more comfortable, and more agreeable, and the place more wide open and sunny – just the place for a practical summer, with children, and society.' Emily came with her son, John, Garman brought Debbie as a companion for Pegeen, and later his niece Kitty, who also lived with his mother. Sindbad came as well, traveling alone across Europe for the first time. Peggy hired Antonia White's friend

Phyllis Jones to look after the children, but treated Phyllis otherwise as another guest. A male Sealyham terrier, Robin, given to Peggy and her children by Milton and Peggy Waldman, was the dog of the house and was joined, in mid-July, by a female whom Sindbad, an extremely zealous sports fan, named Borotra after the Basque tennis star.

'Anybody can ask anybody they want,' Peggy told her guests, 'if they'll sleep with them.' The Waldmans visited, as did Peggy's cousin Willard Loeb and his wife, Mary, and their two children; Mary had been a great friend of Benita's, so Peggy was especially glad to see her. Antonia White also visited, on the edge of another nervous breakdown. Later, Dorothy Holms came briefly, her visit for once uneventful. Peter Hoare came for a visit, and Emily managed to get him into bed several times. Garman was not always in residence, and Peggy tried to keep secret her affair with him, though she told Emily and she was obliged to tell Sindbad because Garman insisted on disciplining the boy. Pegeen already knew.

Activities included tennis on the court that came with the house, riding – though the Downs, the rolling, cultivated or wooded fields around Havant, were a far cry from Dartmoor – and swimming in the sea at Hayling Island, ten miles away. The evenings were as rollicking as ever, though the talk was not on the intellectual plane that had characterized Hayford Hall earlier in the decade. Emily described a typical night: 'Very witty conversation going on the whole time . . . I long for a dictaphone in the living room. Tony is witty, Peggy's ga-ga comments are perfection, Phyllis makes dry rejoinders. I am naïve in my best way and Garman says a good thing in the general heat.'

But Emily could be critical of Peggy, more so than ever. She was especially critical of Peggy's children, finding them far too aware of sexuality. This was an old complaint on the part of Peggy's friends. Of the Vails, Mina Loy had remarked in the 1920s, 'They are scandalizing the most outré of the Bohemians, and their children are being brought up in a manner that frightens me – on Fabi's [her daughter's] account.' Emily complained in a July 12 diary entry, 'Both her children have been brought up . . . to think of sex, and falling in love, until it's dreadful.' Peggy asked one of the Loebs' daughters, who was thirteen, if she had a sweetheart yet, in what Emily said was 'a vulgar Jewish American way. The child was embarrassed . . . [Peggy] is absolutely revolting about sex. Delicacy is unknown to her.'

Sexually precocious or not, Pegeen was beginning to show artistic talent, which the others recognized. One day Emily brought her some colored papers and Pegeen cut shapes out of them, creating flowers, which she then hung on the wall – 'like an exhibition,' Emily said, 'and we all bought them. She made about a dozen, and there wasn't one that wasn't beautiful.' No doubt her mother had told her that artists hung their pictures on the wall, in art galleries, and it was not lost on young Pegeen that her mother respected artists. On another occasion, Antonia White bought a painting by Pegeen of three girls with daisy chains on their heads for 2 shillings 6 pence and hung it in her children's playroom; her daughter Lyndall didn't like it.

The frenetic level of activity had an oddly agreeable effect on Tony's mental state: she felt better. 'Without John to control us,' she wrote her husband,

> Emotions run high and there are Pretty Doings. The only male here is my old enemy Douglas Garman & we had a really frightful scene at dinner last night when Emily flung a full wine glass all over the table, completely lost her temper & screamed at Garman . . . & slammed out of the room . . . It's even madder than Hangover Hall but it takes your mind off yourself & though it's exasperating & you can't get any breakfast or tea or get your shoes or find a match or hear yourself speak, I rather enjoy it.

In such a context she felt relatively sane.

At the end of the five-week period for which the house had been rented, the guests dispersed and Peggy and Garman drove Pegeen and Sindbad to Dover, where the children, then eleven and nine, embarked on a cross-Channel boat together; the children would then take the train across Europe to Kitzbühel. (It seems the children were awfully young to be traveling such a distance on their own; Peggy must have tipped crew members and porters to keep an eye on them, but such supervision would have covered only the initial stage of the trip.) Peggy and Garman then went to his mother's empty cottage for a few weeks. Garman was working hard on his book and Peggy looked after Debbie and Kitty, while rereading Dostoyevsky's *The Possessed*, which she didn't understand any better the second time around.

By the time Garman finished his editing job, his mother had returned and Peggy and he went on a short holiday to South Wales, staying in a little boarding house on a river in Pembrokeshire where room and a generous board could be had for 15 shillings a week, then about 'three dollars and seventy-five cents,' Peggy explained. Their landlady was once the kitchen maid to Consuelo Yznagas, one of Edward VII's American mistresses and later the duchess of Manchester (which would have delighted Peggy), and their landlord was a 'half-mad' sea captain who built his house to resemble a ship. In the inlet in front of the house were the derelict ships that remained of his fleet. Though the countryside was beautiful, Peggy still mourned John;

Garman would later complain that she cried on his shoulder for a year and a half. She was not sure she loved Garman, but she felt less alone, and their sexual bond was strong. She was still reluctant to let John's friends know that she was with Garman, fearing they would think badly of her, but gradually she let Tony White, Peter Hoare, and Djuna in on the fact; Phyllis, Dorothy, Emily, and the children already knew. She had been traumatized and still had many bad moments, but she had managed to stave off a real depression. She was getting stronger.

7

An Idea

In the fall of 1934, with Pegeen once again in the small school near South Hartley with Debbie Garman and Debbie's cousin Kitty, Douglas Garman suggested to Peggy that she find a nearby house. It was difficult for Peggy to make a decision – she seems to have inherited John's hesitancy about settling on domestic arrangements – but Garman found her a house called Yew Tree Cottage, so named because an enormous yew fronted it, in Petersfield, a small town in Hampshire. It was a beautiful, though small house with exposed beams and rafters, and two living rooms, one with a fireplace so large that several people could fit into it. There was only one bathroom, and four bedrooms upstairs. Only an acre of land came with the house, but countryside surrounded it. The house was built on a slope in a valley, and a stream flowed through the property. Garman at once hired a gardener with whom he worked closely. They put in a swimming pool and leveled ground for a tennis court. Peggy's 'honorary nephew,' Michael Wishart, the son of Garman's boss, Ernest Wishart, and Ernest's wife, Lorna (Garman's youngest sister), remembers that as a child he was impressed by the 'Marxist heated swimming pool' (referring to his uncle's political views).

Peggy shared the cottage with Pegeen and their Italian maid, Beppo, who taught her how to cook several Italian dishes. Garman, as secretive about their affair as Peggy, still refused to move in with her openly, though he visited often. Soon after moving to Yew Tree, Peggy quarreled with Emily, then living in London on Oakley Street. Emily had asked Peggy to make an allowance for Phyllis Jones, and Peggy somewhat grudgingly agreed to provide $85 every month. She also arranged to send Phyllis to America for a visit, as her friend's spirits had been low. But to Emily's mind, the ship on which Peggy booked Phyllis's passage was not expensive enough, and she evidently told Phyllis to turn down the offer. Peggy wrote Emily an angry letter: 'Having botched up all this for Phyllis you vent your anger on me . . . [Y]ou turn on me & give me hell for not giving her more and ruining her trip. A bit thick. One expects a little more sense from a woman your age & a friend.'

The backdrop to this contretemps was the unfurling of a great drama that had commenced about a year before and would keep on for several years hence: Emily's insistence that Peggy grant Djuna Barnes a stipend. Peggy would always do so, except for a brief period in 1939 when she believed that she was simply encouraging Djuna to continue on a course of suicidal drinking. But to Emily, Peggy's contributions were always wanting: either not enough, or given erratically, or not given in the right spirit. When Emily traveled to America for an extended trip in the beginning of 1935, Peggy was not unhappy about the respite.

Emily was particularly passionate about both Djuna and Emma Goldman, which partly explains why she so often interceded for them with Peggy. But she also seems, consciously or not, to have been testing Peggy for selfishness. In the years before World War II, anti-Semitism ran rampant in genteel circles like those in which Emily Coleman and Laurence Vail's family moved. A common feature was the assumption that Jews were greedy and close-fisted, and Emily, however enlightened she may have been in other areas, often subscribed to this notion. Perhaps agreeing with Emma that Peggy gave money only with strings attached, she undertook to open up Peggy's purse. Peggy's generosity was ambivalent, as Peggy herself recognized. She told Emily that Sindbad had two sayings about money, 'you can't live without it' and 'you can't take it with you,' adding, 'The latter he got from me. When I feel mean I always say it to untighten my purse strings.' It was evidently something she joked about with the children. According to Emily, Peggy once said to Sindbad, 'Let's play the Guggenheim game; do you know that?' and he replied, 'What's that? Swindling people?'

After the angry exchange between Emily and Peggy regarding Phyllis, Peggy waited more than a month before responding to a 1935 cable from Emily commemorating January 19, the first anniversary of John's death, which would forever be a dark day for both women. When she finally wrote, Peggy had been in Kitzbühel at the Vails' for five weeks with Garman and Pegeen. On the first day there, Garman, who had never skied before, fell and broke three of his fingers; a doctor who exchanged quotations from Dante with the multilingual Garman put the injured hand and forearm in a plaster cast, which distressed Peggy because it reminded her of John's cast the previous year and the horrible outcome. The Vails, however, whom the doctor called 'Vail and Company,' treated them well; Peggy wrote, 'Laurence accepts me as his oldest daughter with a young too young husband.' Laurence loved his role as paterfamilias.

The coming of spring to Yew Tree Cottage affected Peggy wonderfully. She marveled at how indifferent she had been to nature with an enthusiastic John; now she responded to it completely. She was no longer taking her cue from the man of the hour but rather coming to rely on her own instincts. Yet she was aware of a potential problem in her domestic arrangements with Garman: she was terribly isolated. 'I think one reason I like things better is that I so rarely see anything or go anywhere. It is much more of a treat when I do.' Garman had finally moved in with her, bringing Debbie, and Peggy found that she liked living with him, although for the first time she also had come to like being alone as well. (Garman often spent the week in London, where he kept a flat while 'Wisharting,' as Peggy referred to his editorial work.) At the end of March she wrote to Emily, 'I have at last found an inner self to fall back on. I no longer mind being alone. In fact I love it . . . I feel I could write if I had enough peace . . . It is a handicap not to be able to get something out, because I feel it would [be a] fine release to my spirit.' (Next to this last comment, she added 'Balls!')

One obstacle to her happiness was that Garman did not want another child. He told her when he brought Debbie to live with them that he was doing so only if Peggy would promise not to get pregnant. If she became pregnant, she told Emily, 'Garman would rush me off to be Popoffed,' using her old term for abortions. Two months later she would report, 'I seem to be on the verge of my 6th Popoff,' and she added, 'I never do anything about repopulation.' These are rather remarkable statements. In letters, she mentions only the one abortion she had had in Berlin in 1929, and later, when she fought with John in Paris in 1932 in Emily's presence she had referred again to this same abortion. She may have had several abortions while married to Laurence, and she may have had abortions during her time with John between 1932 and his death in 1934, though it is not clear why she would not have referred to any of these in her memoirs. But she would have told Emily about her history, and Emily makes no reference to this remark about five previous abortions. It is possible that she had had curettages for other reasons, and that as the procedure was the same as an abortion, she regarded them as such. Or this may simply have been her way of being dramatic.

Remarkably, Peggy also claimed not to have used any birth control. Several kinds were available then (though none was very reliable), as she would have known well, surrounding herself as she did with women who led active sexual lives. In fact, as the same letter indicates, she rather enjoyed being pregnant, even if it meant an abortion would follow. 'I like being

pregnant,' she wrote, 'even if only for three months. It is better than nothing – maybe Garman will relent.' She added, 'I have at last proved I am still
competent.' Perhaps pregnancy enhanced her sense of femininity and, by
extension, her feelings of attractiveness and sexual desirability. Perhaps it
gave her a sense of power, something she seldom experienced in her relations
with men. But it seems distinctly odd to enjoy being pregnant when an abortion will almost surely follow.

She was mistaken, in any event. She did not get pregnant with Garman,
despite overlooking birth control. Eventually, Garman softening a little on
the matter, they would consult a doctor and determine, 'It was Garman's
fault and not mine that I do not have a baby,' she wrote Emily. The news
upset Garman, who was generally not in the best of health and worried that
this inadequacy was another symptom. Peggy did not very much mind, she
said – she seldom felt a longing for a child and the few times she did she 'sup-
pressed' it. But the years to come would prove that she was indeed still fertile.

Otherwise Peggy was in fine spirits. The amount of reading she plowed
through in 1935 is remarkable. She read Henry Miller's *Tropic of Cancer*
(1934), which, she said, 'speaks for itself,' and called it 'terrifying' and told
Emily to get Djuna to read it. In June she reread *War and Peace* (1886); in the
evening Garman often translated aloud for her from the Russian. She read
seventeenth-century poetry and a lot of Blake, which she was eager to discuss
with Emily, a Blake fanatic. She read a Defoe novel and Jonathan Swift's
Correspondence (1910). She read Frieda Lawrence's memoirs of her life with
D. H. Lawrence, *Not I, But the Wind and Other Autobiographical Writings*
(1934), which inspired her, as she felt that she too had lived with a genius in
John Holms. Most impressively, she read all of Proust's *A la recherche du temps
perdu* (1913–1927) in French. 'Proust gives me great joy,' she wrote Emily.
She also read Céline's *Voyage au bout de la nuit* (1932), again in French. In the
evenings she also enjoyed reading *Ivanhoe* (1819) to the children.

Peggy wanted more and more to write – inevitably, surrounded as she was
by writers and would-be writers. She knew she was creative and sought some
outlet for her energies. In a letter to Emily in which she discussed mostly
household matters, Peggy wrote, 'Of course I never write & with all these
domesticities I never will. But when I think of John I feel I must or I will die.'
Emily had written a new novel to be called 'Tygon,' which Peggy read in
manuscript (it was never published), and in May she wrote a review of it,
attached to a letter. It was meant to be a serious review; Peggy had read
many reviews, and picked up the idiom with ease. She confided, 'This is my
first attempt at reviewing. I never thought I could before. You have inspired
me. I hope you won't find it too smarty-smarty. Reviewing always is.' Months

later when Emily finally commented on it, Peggy wrote back, 'I am glad you like the review. I feel it was very inadequate & superficial & smarty-smarty.'

Writing the 'review' brought a new development: 'Anyhow it has started me off writing. I now keep a diary & rush to put in it every word that is spoken. It seems to write itself.' She had been inspired to begin the diary by an upsetting dream about John on the night of her birthday, August 26, and originally the diary was solely about John, only later becoming a true daily journal. On September 28 she noted she had thus far written eighty-seven pages.

Peggy read parts of her diary aloud to Emily, Antonia White, and other friends, which was not at all unusual. Their immediate circle constantly read one another's diaries, covertly or openly; it was often how they communicated, however cruel the process may sometimes have been. The diaries, especially Emily's, provided an evening's entertainment when read aloud. In other situations, they constituted emotional capital that the writer could employ to great effect. Because a lot of Peggy's diary was about John, the group fretted about whether she should let Garman read it. In fact, Garman had no desire to. 'I thus feel,' Emily wrote, 'that [Garman] is sensible not to want to see the diary; and [Peggy] intelligent in that she kept it from him.' But, Emily continues, '[S]he teased him with the diary, which he did not want to see, and goaded him.'

Peggy may have tormented Garman with her diary, but it is not very likely. She had come to accept the fact that Garman did not like to hear about John, that talking about John only made matters worse in their relationship, and that it was best to hide any evidence indicating that she had been thinking about her dead lover. In any event, perhaps because of this tension but more likely because of Emily's inexplicable near hysteria on the subject, Peggy burned the diary sometime in November. Djuna had the wisest response: 'Why did you burn your journal, why not have hidden it from Garman?' If he did not like reading about John Holms, that was tough, she said. Peggy began a new journal, this time saying little about it to anybody. Nothing of the new diary survives either, but we do have a report from Emily about it: on April 11, 1936, she writes, '[Peggy] read me a diary the other day which she wrote last winter, which was simple and moving and extraordinarily interesting as a document, because of its honesty and sympathy.'

Peggy had referred in a letter to the 'domesticities' that kept her from writing more often. In 1935, she had a house to run and two young girls on her hands and Sindbad for holidays. Sindbad was something of a worry; he had contracted what doctors thought was bronchitis while on a ski holiday in Kitzbühel early in the year. In fact, it turned out to be pleurisy, which was thought in those days to lead to tuberculosis. Because of his condition, Kay and Laurence would move to Devon the next year because that climate was better for the boy.

'I still shop for food every day & do domestic turns,' Peggy wrote Emily in June. Once she reflected, rather extraordinarily, that she might be a good role model for Pegeen: 'I think my life is admirable to Pegeen & very good for me to be a simple woman & do normal domestic things for a change.' In early December she wrote that she was making the little girls costumes for a Christmas pageant about the Pied Piper, with Pegeen in the starring role.

But at other times Peggy felt hemmed in by responsibilities: 'My life has been so strange you would not believe it,' she wrote to Emily in November. 'It is going to sound like complaints but it isn't meant to. I think I have gone quite mad not to have found a better thing to do than to live in the country & look after two little girls (really looking after them like a governess, mending included, & only one night off a week).'

And despite her newfound awareness that she welcomed being alone, for other reasons she found that Garman's priorities – first working for Wishart, a left-wing press, and later for the Communist Party – were also a problem. Laurence Vail and John Holms had each logged many hours with Peggy. But with Garman, Peggy was often left alone, often overwhelmed with domestic chores. Several times she decided to end the relationship but found that she could not. 'If I followed my instinct I would leave him,' she wrote Emily. 'Though I do love him I don't think we should be together. But I haven't the courage to go.' She did not have the emotional resources to live alone, she feared, calling the prospect 'Eternal Danger.' She was forced by circumstances – Garman's ties to London and his work for the cause – to shift for herself, though, and along the way she began to see that she did have the wherewithal, and that she wanted to find some meaningful occupation.

Also troubling Peggy and Garman was Garman's divorce. His wife wanted to marry again. All Debbie's related grownups wanted her to live with them at term time, but they finally decided that Garman and Peggy would have the ten-year-old until the summer of 1936; her mother would then have her during term time, and Peggy and Garman for holidays. Peggy felt guilty, picturing herself in the role that Kay Boyle had played with Pegeen and Sindbad and keeping her so-called stepdaughter from her mother. 'It is awful to think of making another woman suffer as I did about Sindbad,' she wrote Emily. Garman had the upper hand, she went on, as his wife had left him: 'A divorce is difficult because we are all living in sin.' Eventually Garman gave his wife what she wanted, allowing Peggy to be named as a correspondent and saving his wife the ignominy of being caught with her new friend in a compromising position. At the same time Kay managed to get under Peggy's skin by questioning her ability to take responsibility for another child; Peggy responded that Debbie was responsible enough to take care of all of them.

Gradually, Peggy was getting over John Holms. In March she wrote thanking Emily 'for reminding me that I was not happy with John, or confirming it rather.' This was a new tack. With time Peggy was growing more suspicious of her great love, more analytical about the time she had spent with him. On another occasion, when Emily wrote her a letter filled with thoughts about John, she could hardly bear to read it. 'Of course that life is over. It is death & agony to admit it,' she wrote. 'But on the other hand it has left us two different women.' Emily recorded in a January 1936 journal entry that Peggy had said 'that she knew she would never be able to live again with John's drinking should he come back again.' The quotidian domesticity she shared with Garman no doubt contributed to her growing distance from John's memory. Then, too, her life with Garman wasn't balanced. As Peggy wrote to Emily, 'All my excess energy goes into [domestic tasks] or all my excess love because Garman doesn't want me the way John did & there is so much left over that I don't know what to do with & he thinks I'm not enough interested in him & what he does.' Emily noticed this unevenness too, and wrote to Djuna, 'She is madly in love with him. She wants him far more than he does her; this is the first time that's happened to Peggy.' No doubt Garman's indifference frightened Peggy and made her unhappy. Over time, however, it would galvanize her.

News reached her in London in late November 1935 that Clotilde, Laurence's sister and Peggy's rival for his attentions, had died under anesthesia during an appendectomy, in much the same way John had. She marveled that someone she had been 'so passionately connected with and someone so alive as Clotilde' could be dead. The news made her worry about Laurence, who had left Devon with Kay and who was now in Paris. Laurence had two other losses that year: his father and his uncle George, who left him enough money to buy the Megève chalet.

In the same year, Sindbad went to school at Bedales, an English boarding school conveniently in Petersfield. Already an avid sports follower, at Bedales Sindbad became a cricket fanatic. Pegeen continued at the dame school. Understandable confusion developed as to what Peggy's surname should be. They were about to settle on Garman (of which the elder Mrs. Garman approved) when Garman suggested that Peggy consult the woman who ran the school. This woman, herself unmarried, did not know how to advise her, and Peggy never forgave Garman for sending her on this ridiculous interview. She went back to using Guggenheim as her name.

Peggy and Garman spent Christmas in the south of France with Garman's sister Helen and her husband, leaving the children with Laurence and Kay. But they were quarreling frequently and the trip was not a success. Emily's diary indicates that Peggy and Garman were spending as much time apart as they were together. On January 16 she wrote, 'They are not suited and cant [sic] stay together. Ive [sic] never said this, but I did say it this time. They have nothing in common but sex. She has done her best, it only makes things worse, and she really ought to leave him.'

Peggy wrote Emily in February describing a horrible weekend she and Garman spent in Dorset for his birthday. One of the major obstacles between them was Garman's increasing commitment to Communism. He had read all of Marx in a studio he had built on the Yew Tree Cottage property. 'I think now,' she wrote Emily, 'that at last we might live peaceably as far as John goes, but we can't because of Communism and for this I feel I ought to leave.' Peggy feigned interest in politics for a while, but she found being dishonest too difficult. They bickered about party politics and fought over Stalin. Garman and the party had an answer for everything. Moreover, Garman gave up all pleasures, including his horse, for Communism, and he insisted that they have only Communists, mostly laborers, for houseguests. He went around the country in Peggy's expensive Hispano giving lectures and recruiting party members, clearly unaware of the incongruous figure he cut. He wanted Peggy to join but told her she would first have to do 'a job' for the party. Eventually Peggy wrote to Harry Pollitt, the general secretary of the British Communist Party, and said she wanted to join but had to care for two girls and had no free time. The party accepted her anyway. (She learned to be quiet about her affiliation, perhaps coming to see that the press might have a field day if they were to hear of it. She would be frank about it in her memoirs.)

Evidently Peggy was vaguely sympathetic to many of the goals of the Communist Party, but she did not want to apply herself intellectually to it, which Garman seems to have demanded. It was becoming clear that from their different starting points Communism was not something they could share.

In the meantime, Emily, still living at 7 Oakley Street (Peter Hoare had the flat below and Antonia White lived at 105 Oakley), was very busy on Djuna's behalf, pestering T. S. Eliot at Faber and Faber to publish Nightwood. In January 1936 Eliot wrote her to say he was taking the novel. Djuna, back in the States, was in great financial difficulty, and, at Emily's urging, Peggy agreed to send her the new sum of $100 each month. Emily would work on Peggy until she agreed to pay for Djuna's passage over in the late spring, whereupon Djuna moved in with Emily and made several trips down to Yew Tree Cottage to see Peggy. In June, Emily remarked in her diary, 'Djuna said the English looked like they would never die. Peggy said they never die because they never live.'

In the summer Peggy took a ten-day trip to Venice, taking Sindbad and her great friend from her early Paris days, Mary Reynolds, along for the first few days. After they left, Sindbad for Megève and Mary back to Paris, Peggy was by herself there – and she found she not only tolerated it but thrived. In a letter to Emily written at about the same time, she engaged in some sober stocktaking. 'Garman has given me many things I want to talk to you about,' she wrote. 'I don't know if he is responsible or if it comes from living alone so much or suffering so much . . . I feel now I have more poise and better manners. I am less vulgar and much more at home in England. This latter comes from being here so long I suppose, also John made me feel terribly inferior. That way he was so snobbish.'

Peggy's relationship with Garman, despite their persistent sexual attraction, had deteriorated: 'Garman and I seem to drift further and further apart spiritually & mentally though the physical is overwhelming still,' she wrote Emily in August. One night that summer, she got drunk and goaded Garman: 'I was so miserable I didn't care. I was complaining because I had no life, no joy. He said he tried to share all his with me & I would not let him. Of course this is true. But is no good to me.' Then, surprising her, he hit her 'over & over.' Strangely, she didn't mind: 'I liked his hitting me. I knew it was my fault. It was a great relief after so much intellectualizing balls. We had spent days in a frozen death with nothing between us. Now we are better.' No doubt making up after a physical row can make two people feel closer, but for Peggy to believe that she deserved it is evidence that her self-esteem was still shaky, her masochistic tendency still ascendant.

The year 1936 was marked by Edward VIII's ascension to the English throne in January and his abdication in December. Peggy and her friends followed the subject avidly, Peggy something of an insider because of her subscription to *Time*, which provided details not available in the English press. Djuna had interviewed the king (but had not published the result, for unknown reasons) and told her friends how he had 'chased her around the palace.' Dorothy wrote Peggy a letter analyzing 'Mrs. SIMP and King Sweetie Bugs' astrologically. Peggy and Garman rather cynically entered into a bargain that if the rumors were true and the king were to marry the American divorcée Wallis Simpson, then Garman would marry Peggy. When it seemed inevitable that the king would abdicate and marry, Garman wired Peggy at Yew Tree Cottage. But he refused to marry her. In a rage, Peggy dug up one of his meticulously planted flower beds. She was able to replant most of it the next morning, but hereafter they would call that flower bed 'Mrs. Simpson's Bed.'

Peggy spent Christmas 1936 in Paris at the Hôtel Royal Condé, an establishment that she and John had patronized back in 1929. In a letter from there she asked Emily Coleman about Emily's latest lover, the Welsh poet Dylan Thomas. Peggy reported that she had spent a 'wild night' with Mary Reynolds, one that 'ended up in action instead of talk,' presumably a lesbian encounter. It had not gone well – 'but did it only as idea so of course did not enjoy it' – and she feared (unnecessarily, it would turn out) for their future as friends.

But Peggy clearly knew that an old phase of her life was ending and another not-yet-defined one was about to begin. In a letter from the same period, she wrote, 'I can't bear to think of a new life & my old one obviously is broken now, though I still love Garman.' By March they had decided that their life together was over. Garman had met a working-class woman who shared his enthusiasm for Communism. Yet he and Peggy would spend their holiday that summer as they always had, taking a trip to Wales; Garman insisted that they all be together because of the children. Throughout the spring they spent several weekends together at Yew Tree Cottage. They were still physically in thrall to each other: rows and bad times did not change that.

But the troubles escalated at several points. On June 8 Peggy wrote Emily and Djuna that she could not come to London for a few days as she was not presentable: Garman had deliberately hurled a tennis ball at her stomach, which caused her to slip and fall on her face, losing a great deal of blood. Phyllis Jones, who still took care of the children from time to time, told her to 'end this idiotic life' and never see Garman again. Peggy wanted to continue seeing him as a friend, though she admitted, 'if we are going to resort to blood it won't do any good.' Later in the month, after spending a deadly dull weekend in the country, she and Garman had it out in a pub where 'a marvelous woman like a Hardy heroine' served at the bar. Peggy wrote in late June, 'G said he did not wish to depress me, but he wanted me to realize that he still wanted this other life with someone who shared Com—— with him.' Peggy agreed, though this conversation took place just before their holiday together with the children in Wales.

Yet that same letter (to Emily) has an interesting footnote that suggests new developments: 'He also gave me lots of useless advice about how to lead my life not to have an art gallery etc but I won't let him undermine me now.' This is the first indication that Peggy was hatching a plan.

Talking with Peggy Waldman had given her the idea. 'I am so sorry that you're so upset and unhappy,' Peggy Waldman wrote on May 11, 1937,

[A]nd I wish you'd do some serious work – the art gallery, book agency – anything that would be engrossing yet impersonal – if you were doing something helpful for good painters or writers, or better still, a novel yourself. I think you'd be so much better off than waiting around for G. to come weekends and tear you to bits . . . I mean that you'd have a more painless perspective if you had another active interest besides, and particularly one that brought you in contact with stimulating people.

On June 21, Emily noted in a letter to Djuna that Peggy wanted to open an 'anti-chi chi gallery' and to live in rooms above it. By July, Peggy was busy making concrete plans.

It was that simple. Peggy knew she wanted to be around creative people and she was used to acting as patron to such people – Laurence Vail, Djuna Barnes, Eleanor 'Fitzie' Fitzgerald, and Emma Goldman among them. She later told a reporter that she was 'wildly enthusiastic' about the 'madly egotistical artists' she traveled with: 'They're full of wonderful ideas and fantasies, they are so much more alive than stockbrokers and lawyers.'

Peggy had also not forgotten her old tutor's injunction that she must do something constructive with her fortune. She was done with her third 'husband' and it had been an unpleasant, dragged-out affair that left her reluctant to enter into a new long-term relationship. She had found it difficult to envision her life without a man, but the promise of a future given over to supporting artists – an activity that she had been engaged in, in a sense, for more than a decade – and running a business of her own was a challenge, and a promise of independence.

Peggy Waldman's suggestion that the best alternative for her friend was to write a novel was compelling. But Peggy Guggenheim evidently believed she would flounder as a writer, cursed with an unscheduled life and drawing on inner resources she was not sure she had to work at a craft she had not previously developed, except in letters. (Even her diary started off with John Holms as the subject.) It is not clear what Peggy Waldman meant by 'book agency' – becoming a literary agent or starting a publishing company. But a publishing venture would require too much money; in any case, either alternative demanded a knowledge of the book world that she did not have. Her future did not appear to be literary.

Art, on the other hand, had immediate appeal. Here she had an inspiration near at hand, even a ready blueprint. Her uncle Solomon, the fourth of the Guggenheim brothers, with his wife, Irene, who had a good eye for art, had by the mid-1920s assembled a fine collection of old masters, Italian and Flemish paintings, some Dutch paintings of the Barbizon School, and Watteaus. But in 1927 he met the redoubtable Baroness Hilla Rebay von Ehrenweisen, a German painter and collagist who painted portraits for a living but was an ardent proponent of what she called nonobjective art, by which she meant abstract rather than representational art. She also clung to the conviction that this kind of art was necessarily spiritual. Solomon and, initially, Irene were taken by Rebay (as the baroness was known) and hired her to paint Sol's portrait. Over many sittings, Rebay won his love (she became his mistress) and also his commitment – after showing him the work of the Polish-born painter Rudolph Bauer – to collect modern art. On buying trips to Europe, Hilla and Sol began amassing a collection that included Kandinsky, Klee, Delaunay, Chagall, Léger, and Mondrian, among others. Unfortunately, Bauer, a love interest of Rebay's, dominated the collection; Irene hated him, and the paintings were substandard. At first, Solomon's object had been to assemble a collection and leave it to the Metropolitan, but by 1930 Hilla Rebay had visions of a 'temple' of 'nonobjective art,' and in 1937 the Solomon R. Guggenheim Foundation was formed and a museum projected to open in 1939. By that time the collection was so large that Solomon had had to rent rooms at Carnegie Hall, where Hilla had her lodgings, to show it to friends. His eight-room suite at the Plaza Hotel was already filled with the collection, and the old masters were relegated to Irene's bedroom – she loved them – and eventually sold.

Though Peggy steered clear of her family for the most part, she had inevitably seen some family members on her visits to New York in the twenties, and it is likely that she saw her aunt and uncle's artworks at their Carnegie Hall apartment. Her aunt Irene was also one of the few relatives with whom Peggy maintained contact. By 1937, newspapers and magazines trumpeted the upcoming museum.

Collecting art and opening museums was almost a competitive sport for the rich in the twenties and thirties. Abby Aldrich Rockefeller, with Lillie P. Bliss (patron of the artist Arthur B. Davies) and Mary Quinn Sullivan (a collector), founded the Museum of Modern Art in 1929, appointing the young Alfred Barr, Jr., as director. Dedicated exclusively to modern art, this museum sought works similar to those that Peggy would pursue, and she would become keenly interested in its doings and indebted to Barr for his guidance in the years to come. Abby Aldrich Rockefeller, the wife of the Standard Oil scion, had donated to the Museum of Modern Art her collection of nearly two hundred works of art in 1935; her son Nelson was another generous contributor. Gertrude Vanderbilt Whitney founded the museum that bore her name in 1931, based on a collection of more than seven hundred pieces, most of them given by her; she leaned toward Ashcan School artists, among them John Sloan and George Luks, and the American realist painters Edward Hopper and Thomas Hart Benton. The Whitney's common practice of acquiring art for its biennial exhibitions of American art, begun in 1932, ensured that the collection remained strongest in American art.

Financially speaking, Peggy was not in the same league as the Rockefellers and Mrs. Whitney, nor did she share their temperament, which held itself aloof from the actual creative realm. Peggy wanted to know artists, to live among them, to work with them, to be part of their activities. In this sense her project was a lot more democratic than that of her contemporaries, and, especially, her uncle Solomon's. Solomon Guggenheim, like many other successful German Jews, sought, as soon as he made his fortune, to place himself above commerce by turning toward aesthetics. Nonobjective art was the ultimate in aestheticism, as it was abstracted from any sort of grimy reality.

If Peggy had company in her desire to build a collection, this is not to say that what she was setting out to do was in any way regarded by the general public as respectable. Though the other Guggenheim brothers and their off-spring were known for their philanthropy, Sol was initially thought eccentric for his collecting. Moreover, it was one thing to collect and another thing entirely to deal art, as Peggy was proposing to do. Guggenheim women were not supposed to go to work, and the art-dealing world was rough-and-tumble, sometimes not entirely reputable. No doubt Peggy enjoyed upsetting these assumptions; her bohemian existence had been hard-won, and she loved to tweak her elders with it when she could. Furthermore, Peggy would be interested not only in the abstract art that drew her uncle but in surrealism, which constantly referenced sex and power relations in an often blasphemous way that to her uncle would likely seem vulgar.

Just before Christmas 1937 Peggy wrote to Emily, 'My life has taken such a strange turn – I just can't believe it. To live without love & a man & to be happy is almost too good to be true.' This was a future she had never dared to envisage. Though she had sought out interesting and talented men, she had conducted herself in her twenties and thirties rather respectably, in the sense that she had been serially monogamous, with the sole exception of the man she had slept with in Paris in 1925, when she left Laurence skiing in Switzerland. Escaping her seeming destiny – bourgeois marriage and the life of an aristocratic matron – had heretofore been her greatest achievement.

She had surrounded herself with creative artists and writers but was also dragged down by domestic responsibilities. She could assemble a country house and create seemingly idyllic salons like Hayford Hall, but she had nothing really to show for it. Her fortieth birthday was approaching. There was a time when that prospect would have filled her with horror. Now she saw nothing but possibility.

8

A New Life

Peggy's mother arrived in London in the summer of 1937 in the company of a trained nurse. Peggy learned to her great dismay that Florette had lung cancer and was not expected to live more than six months. Peggy made plans to go to New York at Christmas, but for the time being Florette went to Paris and took a suite at the Hôtel Crillon, where Peggy visited her in August and September, with the children joining her from Megève. At the time, Peggy suspected that her mother did not know how serious her condition was; Florette returned to New York at the end of September and died on November 15 after two days in a coma in an oxygen tent. 'It was a bad blow,' Peggy wrote Emily. 'I think now she knew everything all the time. That is the worst.' Peggy would eventually receive another $450,000 from Florette's estate, which would serve her new project well.

Her mother's death marked the beginning of an intense period in Peggy's life, months in which she had two more affairs – one with a man who would steer her into an entirely new field of interest, the other a thoroughly irregular romance with a man who would make a great name for himself. She came into her own, emotionally speaking, during this time, discovering new freedoms that allowed her to do pretty much whatever she pleased. Most important, she discovered her *raison d'être*, professionally and temperamentally: to further the cause of modern art, start an exemplary collection of the same, and live among artists.

Emily Coleman had recently had an affair with a remarkable man whose tenure in her affections overlapped with Dylan Thomas's. Humphrey Jennings was a decidedly odd but extremely talented man. Peggy said he looked like Donald Duck, while in Djuna's more telling description 'he looks like a denuded giraff [sic], ill and thin, red-eyed and as large as to ears as necessary.' But, she added, 'quite sweet, something nice about him.' He came down to Yew Tree Cottage, which Peggy was now renting from Garman, as Peggy relates in her memoirs: 'Emily was there, and as she was now finished with him, she offered him to me as though he were a strange object she no longer required, and I went in his room and took him in the same spirit.' A six-week, rather tumultuous affair followed.

Humphrey Jennings was a crucial factor in turning Peggy's attention to surrealism and to the concrete business of opening a gallery. Born in Suffolk in 1907 to an architect and a painter, Jennings graduated from Cambridge. He was a surrealist painter and poet who also worked for John Grierson's General Post Office (GPO) unit, making cutting-edge documentaries; he came to be known as one of England's top directors of the thirties and forties and would go on to direct a series of visually arresting, and much renowned, wartime documentaries (and would then meet an untimely death in Greece, scouting locations – walking backward to frame a shot, he fell off a cliff).

Jennings had been instrumental in setting up the 1936 International Surrealist Exhibition at the New Burlington galleries, serving on the selection committee with the painter Roland Penrose and the eminent art historian Herbert Read. (In Paris, the surrealist 'pope,' André Breton, selected European exhibits for the show, with Paul Eluard.) British surrealism was a somewhat tamer version of the European variety, tending to drain politics from the Continental approach. The British artists had, however, a keen understanding of their European counterparts, and they helped point Peggy in a definite direction as an art collector. Herbert Read, called by Penrose 'the angel of anarchy,' dubbed his country's surrealists the 'children of Alice,' after *Alice in Wonderland*. The British surrealists included Jennings, Henry Moore, Paul Nash, Eileen Agar, Hugh Sykes-Davies, Conroy Maddox, and the poet and *wunderkind* David Gascoyne. A center of their activities was the London Gallery on Cork Street, owned by Roland Penrose and run by E.L.T. Mesens, the Belgian-born surrealist friend of René Magritte and a proponent of his art. The 1936 exhibition drew 25,000 guests. At its opening Breton gave a speech, Eluard read the French surrealist poets, and Gascoyne and Jennings read their own poems. The exhibition aroused much controversy; many felt that not all the artists exhibiting were true surrealists. Peggy did not attend, though Garman urged her and Djuna to go. Peggy later wrote, dryly, 'We were both blasé and refused, saying Surrealism was over long ago, and that we had had enough of it in the twenties.' She had indeed 'lived through' surrealism in the twenties; Laurence Vail, as readers of *Murder! Murder!* (1931) could detect, was an early follower of dadaist, absurdist trends that were to develop into full-blown surrealism. Peggy added, 'In view of future events this was a most strange coincidence.'

In 1937, Jennings was trying to help Peggy open an art gallery in London, preferably one near the Mayor Gallery. Freddy Mayor's gallery was located on Cork Street, at the back of Bond Street and at the end of the Burlington Arcade, which had once been home to moneylenders and later to tailors; it was reputed to have been the scene of some wild Edwardian parties. Mayor, described as a 'short, rubicund, cigar-smoking, bowler-hatted bon viveur, whose admirable taste in pictures was equalled by his enthusiasm for the race course,' had opened the Redfern Gallery in 1925 in a space behind a cigar shop; in 1933 he reopened it as the Mayor Gallery, with the art collector Douglas Cooper as his partner. The gallery, then at 18 Cork Street, showed such artists as Fernand Léger and Juan Gris (in 1926), Joan Miró (in 1933), and Paul Klee (in 1934). Nearby, at number 28, was the London Gallery, also known for its emphasis on modern art. It was a welcoming environment to anyone looking for gallery space and interested in surrealism. Peggy looked up the plump, well-connected Wyn Henderson, her erstwhile neighbor in Woburn Square in the John Holms years, and promised to make her manager of the gallery. She sent Wyn out to look for a place, ideally on Cork Street.

Peggy did not yet have a gallery when she went off to Paris to stay at the Hôtel Crillon with her mother in September. Humphrey Jennings followed her there; Peggy took a room in a Rive Gauche hotel, and the two spent the weekend in bed. He came to Paris another weekend as well, but Peggy, now that the initial attraction had faded, made him take his own room in another hotel while she stayed at the Crillon. Humphrey wanted to meet Marcel Duchamp, and Peggy, an acquaintance of the artist through Mary Reynolds, obliged. They also went to meet Breton in his gallery, Gradiva; Humphrey already knew him, but Peggy did not, and she found that 'he looked like a lion pacing up and down in his cage.' Another time she and Humphrey approached the painter Yves Tanguy about exhibiting his work in Peggy's (not yet existent) gallery: Tanguy agreed, although Humphrey had strange ideas about how the pictures should be hung. (Peggy didn't reveal these, but they may have informed her innovative installations with the architect Frederick Kiesler in her future New York gallery, Art of This Century.) Although in July Peggy had told Emily that Humphrey's 'art is divine – he is a genius I feel,' by December she was saying she was happy she had 'got rid of him.' In November she confided to Emily that she had gone 'hoaring' once, and that 'it was a great improvement on H.J. but it was a real hoaring and anonymous and I think a mistake to repeat it.' She added in a handwritten afterthought, 'I mean this particular one,' indicating that she hadn't liked her partner but was not forswearing 'hoaring.'

She was glad she had put Humphrey behind her, Peggy told Emily, for 'I would have had no fun with my gallery. Now I am the patronne it is much pleasanter.' Humphrey had served his purpose – getting her on the right track, educating her on surrealism and the British art scene, introducing her to such figures as Penrose, Mesens, and Read. Now, with her inheritance from her mother on its way, she was launched. On her first day shopping, Wyn reported that she had found a place on Cork Street at number 30 and signed a bargain eighteen-month lease beginning January 1, 1938. It was a second-floor space that had once been a pawnshop; Djuna remarked on how much misery must have passed through these rooms over the years, but Peggy thought of all the misery that might pass through in the future because of disappointed artists.

Peggy's friends greeted her venture with a blast of condescension. Never very supportive, they denounced her enterprise with seeming glee. Djuna confided to Emily that she had her doubts about Peggy's opening a gallery, mainly because, '[Peggy] has no settled mind of her own, poor darling, does not know what she wants or if what she does think she wants is the right thing.' Her first 'idiotic mistake,' said Djuna, was to install 'that baggage' Wyn Henderson, implying that her size would put off 'prospective picture buyer[s].' The shipping heiress Nancy Cunard described Wyn as 'a fat, very fat, rollicking redhead.' Wyn had two sons still living with her, Nigel and Ian. Nigel, a picture restorer, was twenty, and Ian was older; Antonia White, now thirty-eight, had affairs with both of them before deciding on Ian. Peggy may well have slept with one or the other or both, though she denied sleeping with Nigel to Emily. Like Djuna, Tony White disapproved of Wyn, but Wyn was extremely competent. One of her first acts was to design a distinctive letterhead, one that Peggy would use as a template for all future addresses; she also suggested the name, Guggenheim Jeune, partly in reference to the eminent gallery Bernheim Jeune in Paris and partly to serve notice that this was not the Museum of Non-Objective Painting run by the elderly Solomon Guggenheim, but something quite different, presided over by a younger model. By now, also, the Guggenheim name was well known in the art world, and many artists were grateful to Peggy's uncle for buying their art. Those who had not drawn his attention were no doubt hoping that Peggy would. (It should be remembered that the public did not know that she was one of the 'poor' Guggenheims.)

The first thing Peggy did for the gallery was to go to Paris to line up exhibitions. For advice she turned to Mary Reynolds's paramour, Marcel Duchamp, possibly the most influential Western artist of the twentieth century. Duchamp was now supposedly retired from producing art, having replaced it with chess, at which he was a master, but he could not resist dipping his hand in now and then. He also played an important role in guiding collectors, from Walter Arensberg to Katherine Dreier, and in so doing he had a great hand in building the canon of twentieth-century art.

Born in 1887 in provincial France, Duchamp arrived in Paris in 1904, where he became part of the Golden Section, a group of painters that included Léger, Gris, Picabia, and others. In 1912 he produced the cubist masterpiece *Nude Descending a Staircase*, which depicted female forms on a series of planes. The painting caused a maelstrom of controversy at the well-known Armory show in New York City in 1913. In that same year he produced the first of what he called 'Ready-Mades' – found art, everyday items such as a bicycle wheel, a bottle dryer, and a snow shovel. Léger once told a story about Duchamp and Constantin Brancusi at an exhibit on aviation: 'Marcel, who was a dry type with something inscrutable about him, walked around the motors and propellers without saying a word. Suddenly he turned to Brancusi: "Painting is finished, Who can do anything better than this propeller? Can you?"' Duchamp, taking great pleasure in simply being alive in the twentieth century, had come to question the whole idea of art. From 1915 to 1923 he worked on his monumental *The Bride Stripped Bare by Her Bachelors, Even (The Large Glass)*, a mammoth assemblage of images on glass. The piece remains unfinished.

In 1917 Duchamp made another statement: to the New York Independents Show (mounted by the Society of Independent Artists) he sent a urinal that he called *Fountain*; it was signed 'R. Mutt' and again aroused great controversy. In 1915 he had left Paris for New York City and was the center of a group watched over by Walter Arensberg, which included Man Ray, Mina Loy, William Carlos Williams, Francis Picabia and his wife, and the composer Edgard Varèse, among others. Called 'a loner' by his biographer, Duchamp was also called 'king of the bachelors' because of his success with women. The epitome of elegance, he was also inordinately charming.

Rejecting what he called 'retinal art,' which simply produced an effect on the viewer's eye, Duchamp asserted that the mind of the artist was what was important. While he was by temperament closer to dadaism, such views allowed him to appreciate certain surrealist artists and to advise Peggy on showing them. In this vein, he had Man Ray take a photograph of him dressed as a woman, which he signed 'Rrose Selavy' (*eros, c'est la vie*); he signed this name to several of the contributions he made to the art world, even after he gave up producing art for good in 1923. A connoisseur of art, he was not above dealing in art himself. Djuna Barnes conveyed a sense of his benign detachment and his considerable charm when she wrote to Peggy in Venice in 1965 that in New York 'Marcel skims ever overhead, the bird that nobody as yet has shot down.'

In 1937 Duchamp was still advising the formidable German-American patron Katherine Dreier about her significant collection, which she called the Société Anonyme. Man Ray, visiting her with Duchamp, had seen the French phrase in a magazine; Duchamp said it was the equivalent of 'Incorporated' and thus a very good name for the collection; when legal papers were drawn up it became, effectively, 'Société Anonyme, Inc.,' or 'Inc., Inc.,' which must have pleased Duchamp no end. (Interestingly, Dreier was one of the Independents who had voted to reject, with great ambivalence, his *Fountain* in 1917, which caused her considerable anguish.)

Peggy would have been well aware of Duchamp's reputation. The sheer good humor (or was it that?) of many of his actions would have appealed to her sensibility. She later wrote that at the time her London gallery opened, 'I couldn't distinguish one thing in art from another. Marcel tried to educate me.' She went on, 'I don't know what I would have done without him. To begin with, he taught me the difference between Abstract and Surrealist art. Then he introduced me to all the artists. They all adored him, and I was well received wherever I went. He planned shows for me and gave me lots of advice. I have him to thank for my introduction to the modern art world.' Note that Peggy was careful to thank Duchamp publicly for introducing her to the *modern* art world. She was proud of the education she had already acquired in art history. She had pored over Bernard Berenson's books and absorbed his lessons about the seven points to look for in works of art.

When Peggy first went to Paris for art to show in her gallery, she initially planned to contact Constantin Brancusi, the sculptor she had met in the twenties, but he was out of town. Instead, Duchamp recommended that she call on the writer Jean Cocteau, who had designed some wonderful sets for a production of his recent play, *Les Chevaliers de la table ronde* (1937). Peggy visited Cocteau in his hotel on the rue Cambon, where he received her at bedside, smoking opium all the while; another night he took her to dinner, mesmerizing her by looking at his own reflection in a mirror opposite the whole time. They completed their negotiation: he agreed to write a preface for a catalogue, but Peggy would have to find someone to translate it. She arranged to borrow some furniture and plates he had designed for the set, as well as some thirty original ink sketches, many of hands, and two bed sheets on which he had drawn, especially for the show, an allegorical picture called *La Peur donnant ailes au courage* (1937) of the actor Jean Marais and others in the nude; he had drawn in their pubic hair and then pinned leaves over the area.

British customs was not amused by these creations and threatened to hold up the whole show. Peggy appeared at the customs office with Duchamp

Peggy's maternal grandfather,
James Seligman

Peggy's paternal grandfather,
Meyer Guggenheim

Peggy's parents, Benjamin and
Florette Guggenheim, circa 1910

Peggy (left) and her two sisters,
Hazel and Benita

Peggy as a geisha girl,
circa 1908

Peggy, far left in top row, with a ribbon on her forehead, with
the Jacobi School class of 1915

Peggy with her pug, circa 1915,
the first in a long parade of
canine pets

Peggy's first husband,
Laurence Vail, circa 1920

Peggy Waldman,
Peggy's friend and
adviser

Peggy and her friend, the British artist Mina Loy

Peggy's friend, the writer Djuna Barnes, circa 1922

Berenice Abbott's portrait of Peggy, circa 1926

Emma Goldman with her secretary, Emily Coleman,
Saint-Tropez, 1928

Left to right: Robert McAlmon, Kiki, Louis Aragon,
Peggy, and Clotilde Vail

John Holms, Djuna Barnes, Antonia White, and
Peggy in an idle moment at Hayford Hall

Peggy at Hayford Hall.
Dartmoor lies beyond

Emily Coleman, one of Peggy's
closest friends, mid-1930s

Laurence, Kay Boyle, Sindbad, and Peggy, mid-1930s

Douglas Garman's daughter, Debbie, Pegeen, and Samuel Beckett, Yew Tree Cottage, 1938

and argued the point, finally agreeing not to exhibit the drawings to the general public but to show them only in her office. To spare Cocteau a long explanation, Peggy bought the bed sheets from him, one of the first pieces of modern art she owned. (Later Pegeen hung them in her bedroom and lip-sticked phone numbers all over them, transforming them entirely.)

The gallery's opening on January 24, 1938, was the climax to a frenetic couple of months. Peggy spent December through February in Paris, making brief trips to London to see to the hanging of the Cocteau show, which Duchamp was doing himself. She also attended the Paris opening of the Exposition Internationale du Surréalisme on January 17, a show supervised by Duchamp and implemented by Breton and Eluard. While she had ignored England's surrealist show in 1936, this time around she showed keen interest. At the opening, guests arrived at the Galerie des Beaux-Arts on the rue du Faubourg-Saint-Honoré and were met in the courtyard by an ancient taxi, in the driver's seat of which was a stuffed crocodile with a wide grin. The artists had arranged for rain to fall inside the taxi, though the weather outside was fine. In the back seat was a blond mannequin with dead leaves at her feet and snails on her body. More mannequins were inside the gallery, one with a bird-cage on her head, another with a lobster telephone receiver fashioned by Salvador Dali. More dead leaves covered the floor, dusty coal sacks hung from the ceiling, and the air was filled with the smell of roasting coffee. Among the array of odd, wonderful objects – a soup tureen covered with feathers, a chair supported by replicas of four human legs – was a shifting exhibit, illuminated intermittently by flashlights, of such important works as Dali's *Great Masturbator* (1925) and Max Ernst's *Garden Airplane Trap* (1935–36), as well as sculptures by Arp, Giacometti, and Moore and paintings by Magritte, Tanguy, and de Chirico. The event aroused great controversy in the press and among the general public, though it can hardly have been much of a surprise to the Parisian art world, which had already been exposed to what one critic has called the prewar surrealists' 'fourteen-year occupation of the avant-garde territory.'

To Peggy the show was a revelation, and she visited it several times. She found the trappings and the setting greatly interesting, and the paintings and sculpture intriguing. That the vision of some artists was bleak or even threatening she seems to have accepted. Following Duchamp, she cared less for what was visually appealing, appreciating instead the artists' motives and their vision. Moreover, and perhaps most important, she was coming to know the artists: Duchamp brought her to meet the artist couple Jean Arp and Sophie Taueber-Arp in Meudon, outside Paris. This encounter led to what she called 'the first thing I bought for my collection,' an Arp bronze from

1933 called *Shell and Head*. Arp had taken her to his foundry, where she first saw the highly polished sculpture; as she writes in her memoirs 'I fell so in love with it that I asked to have it in my hands.' She was won: 'The instant I felt it I wanted to own it.' In short order Duchamp would also introduce her to Kandinsky and to Tanguy.

Peggy told Emily in the midst of this excitement that she loved being alone and independent, but also admitted again to 'hoaring,' saying, it 'is nothing to be proud of so I won't go into details.' On New Year's Day she wrote, 'I am in Paris working hard for my gallery and fucking.' Peggy was discovering that sexual freedom did not have to mean attachment to any one man. She loved the seemingly instant intimacy that resulted from a sexual encounter. Because she apparently entered into these arrangements expecting nothing, she could walk away unfazed and unhurt, often going on to enjoy platonic friendships with her partners (as would be the case with Brancusi and Mesens, both of whom she would bed). Her amours engaged her emotionally, but she was able to compartmentalize them in a way that most male would-be Don Juans only aspire to, partly because her gallery and professional activity made her feel more grounded and less likely to live in the wake of great men, as she had with Laurence Vail and John Holms. For example, Djuna was then giving her friends a lot of worry by her excessive drinking. Emily gave Peggy to know that her love affairs were equally harmful. Not so, said Peggy:

> When you compare my fucking with Djuna's drinking I think you are wrong again. Djuna's whole life has collapsed because of her drinking. But my fucking is only a sideshow. My work comes first every time & my children are still there. Both the center of my life. Everyone needs sex & a man. It keeps one alive & loving & feminine. If you can't manage to make a life permanently with inferior people, & thank God I can't, you must still now & then indulge in a physical life & its consequences. I went without sex for 5 months . . . last summer. I hope I will never do so again. I find men & man really stimulating but now, thank God I have my own strengths & my inner self to fall back on. John sowed the seeds for this & Garman made them grow by watering. The necessity of falling back on myself.

As this remarkable passage implies, Peggy had learned some important things about herself on her journey to sexual independence: she liked sex, and it made her feel womanly. She realized that she no longer wanted to lead an obscure life in the British countryside with 'inferior people' (presumably partners like Garman, whom she saw as engaged in nothing creative), but rather with people who did things that somehow *mattered*, and that if she wanted her life to be well rounded, she would take her sexual pleasure from such people. But she kept her eyes on the prize: an 'inner self to fall back on,' which protected her from the kind of emotional (and physical) harm Laurence, John, and Garman had inflicted on her. She had her work first, as she makes clear. Perhaps she was deluding herself in believing that her children were of primary import, given the somewhat scattered attention she gave them, but she *believed* they held a central place in her life. Certainly she loved them deeply. Moreover, she had come to an understanding of her 'own strengths,' a striking development in a woman whom no one, with the possible exception of Peggy Waldman, encouraged. And she insisted that her sexuality was part of who she was. It hurt no one, including herself.

Of course, life being what it is, a remarkable man entered her life at just this point, and Peggy fell in love again.

The man was Samuel Beckett, the Irish-born writer who had just settled in Paris for good in a state of permanent exile from his beloved – and hated – native land. Born in a Dublin suburb in 1906 – he was thirty-two to Peggy's forty – Beckett grew up in a comfortable middle-class family, attending boarding school and graduating from Trinity College in 1927. He had made a living as a translator and teacher, but his vocation was writing. In 1931 Chatto and Windus published his long essay on Proust as a volume in its Dolphin series; the firm also brought out a story collection, *More Pricks than Kicks*, in 1934. But Beckett in the late thirties was probably best known for an essay he wrote, at James Joyce's request, about Joyce's 'Work in Progress' (eventually, the 1939 *Finnegans Wake*); Sylvia Beach's Shakespeare and Company published it in *transition* 16/17 in 1929. Known to be an intimate of Joyce, Beckett had recently been subject to the unwanted romantic attentions of the novelist's increasingly unstable daughter, Lucia.

Peggy knew Joyce from her old friend Helen, the former wife of Leon Fleischman but now married to Giorgio Joyce. In fact, it was Helen who invited Peggy along to a family party that included Helen's father-in-law, James Joyce, the day after Christmas 1937. The group convened at Helen and Giorgio's apartment. Peggy realized immediately that she had met Beckett about six or seven years earlier; he had come to a party that she and John Holms gave at their avenue Reille house. From Helen and Giorgio's apartment, the Joyces and Peggy and Beckett went on to dinner at Fouquets. Peggy took Beckett's measure, keenly:

Beckett was a tall, lanky Irishman of about thirty with enormous green eyes that never looked at you. He wore spectacles, and always seemed to be far away solving some intellectual problem; he spoke very seldom and never said anything stupid. He was excessively polite, but rather awkward. He dressed badly in tight-fitting French clothes and had no vanity about his appearance. Beckett accepted life fatalistically, as he never seemed to think he could alter anything. He was a frustrated writer, a pure intellectual.

After dinner Beckett asked to walk her home, and Peggy was somewhat surprised when he took her arm and brought her all the way back to her borrowed apartment. Once there, he asked her to lie down on the sofa with him. They went to bed and stayed there until dinnertime the next day, except for a brief period when Peggy mentioned champagne and Beckett ran out to get some. The idyll was cut short, as Peggy was to meet Arp for dinner, and she was unable to cancel because he had no telephone. She was quite discomfited when Beckett left, saying, 'Thank you. It was nice while it lasted.' Beckett had been gone long enough that Joyce had become worried, but Helen told her father-in-law that Beckett was obviously with Peggy.

Several days passed before Peggy ran into Beckett again on a traffic island in Montparnasse. They went directly to bed (at Mary Reynolds's house, which Peggy had borrowed in the interim) and stayed there for over a week. She remembered this time 'with great emotion'; it was the only happy time they had in the thirteen months during which they were involved. Peggy explains, 'To begin with he was in love with me as well, and we were both excited intellectually.'

There is no reason to doubt this statement, though Beckett's three biographers do, refusing to believe that Beckett's emotions were ever engaged by a woman like Peggy, whom they write off as ugly and almost comical. First, Peggy wrote her memoirs in 1945 and 1946. Beckett was not well known then, with his great trilogy of novels and all of his plays still in the future, so Peggy was not simply name-dropping. Second, when a couple spends over a week in bed, one assumes not only considerable sexual attraction but a lot of time to talk. Beckett, the author of *Whoroscope* (1930) and the future master of the Theatre of the Absurd, clearly found much to talk about with a woman who went 'hoaring' and was at the time immersed in surrealism. Beckett had great enthusiasm for art, and he told Peggy, who still maintained a place in her heart for old masters, that 'one had to accept the art of our day as it was a living thing.' He admired Kandinsky, for instance, whom Peggy would show after Cocteau. But Beckett's personal loyalties skewed his taste; he pushed the work of Jack B. Yeats and a Dutch painter he was very close to, Geer van Velde. Obviously he was aware of the material support Peggy could give to artists he liked; over time she would also get him translating jobs for her catalogues and writing assignments for E.L.T. Mesens's *London Bulletin*. He also loved cars, and Peggy, of course, always had the latest and fastest model.

For her part, Peggy found she could talk to Beckett the way she had talked to John Holms. He brought his published work to show her; she admired his study of Proust and liked Murphy when it appeared later that year, though she dismissed his poetry. What she liked best was Beckett's unpredictable behavior. She never knew when he would show up, which she frankly found 'exciting.' He was always drunk, but he was charming when he drank. She found her professional life obtruding on the time she spent with him, however. She had much to do to prepare for the Cocteau show; Beckett, Peggy writes dryly, 'objected to this; he wanted me to remain in bed.'

'It seemed ironic,' she continues, 'that I should create a new existence for myself because I had no personal life, and now that I had a personal life, it had to be sacrificed.' She had to leave Beckett for a time to tend to her work, and in one of her absences Beckett took an Irish woman, probably a married woman called Adrienne Bethell, into his bed. Nothing came of it, but Peggy was furious and wouldn't speak to him when he telephoned. (He later told her that 'making love without being in love was like taking coffee without brandy.')

Then Beckett went out with a couple to the movies. Returning home, the three were accosted by a pimp begging for money. Beckett pushed him aside, and the man took out a knife and stabbed Beckett in his left side; only his heavy overcoat prevented the knife from reaching his heart. He was rushed to the hospital. Nobody knew his whereabouts until Joyce phoned his hotel and got the news. Meanwhile, Peggy had changed her mind and was trying to reach him to say goodbye before leaving for London for the Cocteau show; she didn't learn of the stabbing until she phoned Nora Joyce. She rushed to the hospital to assure Beckett of her concern.

Beckett was nursed by a French friend, Suzanne Deschevaux-Dumesnil, a talented musician who took charge of all the bureaucratic details relating to his stay in the hospital. It was uncharacteristic of Beckett to be seeing three women at once; generally, he eschewed love affairs. (One exception was Beckett's cousin, also named Peggy, with whom he'd had a long relationship.) Evidently, he was going through some kind of personal crisis having to do with marrying. Eventually, Suzanne, herself six years older than Beckett, would settle down with Beckett, much later marrying him. By that time, Peggy had been made so miserable by the thirteen-month, drawn-out affair that she dismissed her rival: 'She sounded to me more like a mother than a mistress. She had found him a flat and made him curtains and looked after him generally. He was not in love with her and she did not make scenes, as I did . . . I could not be jealous of her; she was not attractive enough.'

All that was far in the future, and for the moment Beckett was confused, and he no doubt made life as miserable for Suzanne as he did for Peggy. Peggy called him Oblomov, after the hero of the Goncharov novel who is so frozen by indecision he cannot get out of bed. Peggy circulated the book, and it made the circuit among Beckett's friends, who found the nickname apt. For the opening of the Cocteau show, Beckett sent a telegram signed 'Oblomov,' which pleased Peggy inordinately. In reality, however, it was no joke: Beckett was as frozen with indecision as John Holms had been. Over the next year he would dither back and forth, while Peggy started taking other lovers, and the affair wound down. But Beckett would always hold a special place in her heart. Only with distance could she see the irony: at the launch of a great career, with newly found self-confidence and excitement about the future – and along comes another man who can't make up his mind. Many women would give up on men after such an experience, and it could be argued that Peggy did, in her own way. Certainly it gave a new edge to her sexuality: she was wary, and for the time being did not intend to let her guard down. If that meant living without love, so be it. She still wanted to have a good time.

9

Out of the Gate

Guggenheim Jeune was a success with the art world and the public from the start. The London papers were full of praise. Many noted what a coup it was to open the gallery with a show of Cocteau, 'who has been for many years the leader and impresario of the moderns in Paris.' Another paper described Cocteau's drawings as 'remarkable feats of imaginative draughtsmanship.' *The Times*, on the other hand, was more interested in the show as a spectacle: 'It is all very lively and entertaining, the artistic interest being in the direct expression of an agile and rather perverse mind than in design or technical qualities.'

The opening itself was a subject for the press. The reporter from *The Sketch* had mixed feelings about the content of the show, but observed, 'though there may be two opinions about the exhibits, there could be only one about the party. It was crowded, gay and successful.' Many reporters commented on Peggy's earrings: six brass curtain rings linked together for each ear. The newspapers were generally complimentary about her; one reporter noted that she was 'very slim,' and commented on her 'attractively jerky way of talking,' meaning, it would seem, that she gestured a lot. Still, many others commented on her 'graying' hair, which prompted Peggy to begin dyeing it an unbecoming black.

'Peggy's influence in London was considerable,' observed the British surrealist Roland Penrose. 'Cork Street was where the important things were happening. Everybody came there, and Peggy brought an international flavor to it all.' Peggy would be back and forth between Paris and London over the next few years, arranging for shows or bringing artists over to meet their public. Marcel Duchamp himself, after all, had hung her first show: only the best for Guggenheim Jeune. From the start, the gallery had great press and a buzz of success.

Peggy's second show confirmed the public impression that Guggenheim Jeune showcased the best European talent. It was devoted to Wassily Kandinsky, who had never been shown in England before. Duchamp had sent Peggy to see the artist in Paris to ask permission to mount a show of his work, a retrospective of his art from 1910 to 1937. Kandinsky was delighted because he was not well known except on the Continent. The painter, of course, had been one of her uncle Solomon's finds. Kandinsky told Peggy that he had an earlier painting Sol had wanted to buy, but he also told Peggy that Rudolph Bauer, his much inferior rival, had urged Sol not to buy any more Kandinskys. At Kandinsky's request, Peggy wrote to her uncle about the painting. She received the following letter from his mistress, Baroness Rebay, extraordinary enough to include most of it here:

Dear Mrs. Guggenheim 'jeune'

Your request to sell us a Kandinsky picture was given to me, to answer.

First of all we do not ever buy from any dealer, as long as great artists offer their work for sale themselves & secondly your gallery will be the last one for our foundation to use, if ever the need to get a historically important picture, should force us to use a sales gallery.

It is extremely distasteful at this moment, when the name of Guggenheim stands for an ideal in art, to see it used for commerce so as to give the wrong impression, as if this great philanthropic work was intended to be a useful boost to some small shop. Non-objective art, you will soon find out, does not come by the dozen, to make a shop of this art profitable. Commerce with art cannot exist for that reason. You will soon find you are propagating mediocrity; if not trash . . . Due to the foresight of an important man since many years collecting and protecting real art, through my work and experience, the name of Guggenheim became known for great art and it is very poor taste indeed to make use of it, of our work and fame, to cheapen it to a profit.

Yours very truly,

H.R.

P.S. Now, our newest publication will not be sent for England for some time to come.

Peggy promptly wrote back to the baroness that she was amused by her letter and that the art critic Herbert Read urged her to frame it and hang it on the gallery wall. She couldn't resist adding that her 'good and growing' collection – she was exaggerating, of course – 'does not & will never include second-rate painters like Bauer.' Evidently assuming that her uncle had not read the baroness's letter, she sent Solomon a copy, adding, 'I do not seek to make money but to help artists.' She stated, '[F]or sixteen years I have lived amongst and befriended artists,' an interesting claim, indicating that she believed all her 'husbands' had been artists (though how she would have included Garman is hard to say, as is whether she came to see that Laurence and John were perhaps not among the top tier of 'artists'). But it is more significant that she now could see her life as having a kind of shape that led to her current position. She wrote to Solomon as an equal, though her interest in art was far more democratic than her uncle's idealistic approach. She wanted to live among artists and promote their work to the public, not to build a secular temple like her uncle's museum. If her project was then 'commercial,' so be it.

The Kandinsky show went up on February 18, closing on March 12, and received excellent reviews. Hugh Gordon Proteus, writing in the *New English Weekly*, observed, 'It is impossible to discuss modern movements in art without referring to Kandinsky. In this country his name is better known than his work. So many-sided is his genius, however, that it is essential to see his work in bulk. And so,' concluded the reviewer, 'the Guggenheim Jeune Galleries . . . perform a public service in organising an exhibition on so handsome a scale, of characteristic Kandinsky paintings, watercolours and gouaches.' This was high praise indeed. But there is no question that in bringing the works of so virtuosic an artist before the British public Guggenheim Jeune set the highest of standards.

All the while, Peggy's personal life was in great tumult. Beckett would come into her life at several junctures over the course of 1938 and into 1939, never especially convenient ones. In February, Peggy was back in Paris, supposedly arranging for future shows but possibly just to see Sam. She joined him on February 2 for a party to celebrate Joyce's fifty-sixth birthday. Beckett had searched the town to find a blackthorn walking stick for Peggy to give Joyce. He himself wanted to give Joyce some bottles of his favorite Swiss wine, Fendant de Sion. Peggy found it at a Swiss restaurant on the rue Sainte-Anne, where she had once been with Joyce and John Holms. When told the wine was for the Irish writer, the restaurant's proprietors agreed to sell her some. At the party, held at Giorgio and Helen Joyce's apartment, a model of Dublin, with a green ribbon running through it, dominated the room. Much revelry followed, and the evening ended with Joyce dancing a little jig.

For this trip Peggy had taken a room in the Hotel Liberia, where Beckett was staying, expecting him to be glad she was nearby. Evidently he was not, for Peggy soon moved to an apartment that Hazel owned on the Ile

Saint-Louis; it had only rudimentary furniture and no curtains, but the light was lovely and a terrace overlooked the Seine. Regardless of Beckett's feelings, Peggy felt that she had achieved a kind of happiness that was new to her experience. She told Emily Coleman that she lived in a 'mad' world now and that she thought she might be able to 'produce something' – though she did not indicate what. She added that Beckett was proving to be a lot like Emily's recalcitrant lover Peter Hoare: 'so terrified that something might happen to him, and that though it has happened, he is damn careful not to let it get any further.' But, she added, the art gallery 'makes a real basis for my life & gives me a purpose & so far I have done it all very well.' She had to admit that she found her success 'surprising.'

What was it that bound Samuel Beckett and Peggy Guggenheim together, in such a way that it was impossible for them to separate even when they had established that there could be no relationship between them? They shared a predisposition for the absurd and a distrust of authority and conventions. Both valued the spontaneous, and both had impressive intellectual energy. They were both funny, in unexpected and understated ways. They liked and disliked the same things. It is not entirely remarkable, then, that they could not seem to give each other up, even when it was clear theirs was not going to be a long-term relationship. Yet, on balance, Beckett needed someone who would make no demands on him whatsoever, someone relatively uncomplicated – and his other new friend, Suzanne Deschevaux-Dumesnil, filled the bill. A lasting romance between Peggy and Beckett was not meant to be, which neither would understand before inflicting further hurt on the other.

With her relationship to Beckett unsettled, Peggy looked elsewhere. She had 'a short affair' with Giorgio Joyce at about this time, causing her some embarrassment when one night Beckett and Giorgio arrived at her Ile Saint-Louis apartment and were both recognized by her maid. Peggy was so mortified that she fell on the stairs and hurt her leg, confining her to bed for several days. It seems likely that she and Giorgio had been thrown together because Helen, Giorgio's wife and Peggy's old friend, was currently undergoing a series of breakdowns that would eventually end in her being relegated to an asylum outside Paris. Naturally there was great distress in the Joyce circle, compounded by Lucia Joyce's own steadily increasing mental instability. Peggy believed 'Helen went mad with change of life,' a condition she also blamed for Djuna's drinking, which was then posing a growing problem to her friends. It's true that Helen's illness had affected her marriage, and it seems that Giorgio and Peggy evidently acted on a mutual attraction in the heat of the moment, without thought of any consequences. But, however unlikely it was that Helen would learn of the fling, it is hard to account for Peggy's sleeping with the husband of one of her oldest friends, especially when that friend was in trouble. (Perhaps Peggy took special precautions not to reveal it; more likely, she and Giorgio were shortsighted in their hurry to go to bed.)

Meanwhile, Guggenheim Jeune was thriving, even in Peggy's absence. After Kandinsky, she showed Cedric Morris – an odd choice for a gallery specializing in surrealism and abstract art, but Peggy and Wyn had a soft spot for Morris and liked his landscapes. The show puzzled the critics, as Morris showed nearly fifty portraits of well-known Londoners, most verging on caricature. One London architect became so enraged that he began to burn a pile of catalogues in the showroom, and Morris flew at him; when the row ended the gallery walls were splattered with blood. The exhibit may not have been particularly impressive, but still the gallery was talked about.

Peggy ran into trouble with customs again with her next show, an exhibition of sculpture by Arp, Brancusi, Pevsner, Moore, Calder, and others. Under a 1932 law designed to discourage the import of gravestones made on the Continent, raw materials entering Britain were treated as stone and wood carvings and were subject to stiff import duty unless they were held to be works of art. (Brancusi had gone to trial in 1928 over a similar condition in the United States, when his Bird in Space was subjected to a heavy duty unless it was determined to be a work of art – which it subsequently was in court.) In questionable cases, customs officials consulted the director of the Tate Gallery. J. B. Manson, clearly no fan of modern art, ruled that the Guggenheim Jeune sculptures were 'not art,' announcing that the pieces 'were all the sort of stuff I should like to keep out.'

The subsequent hullabaloo in the press brought Guggenheim Jeune even more publicity. Peggy commented to a reporter that the whole business was 'monstrous,' adding, 'I think it is a disgraceful thing that we should be under the dictatorship of Mr. Manson, as though he were the only person to decide what is art.' Manson elaborated in another interview, further signaling his contempt for art of the sort represented in the show: 'In my opinion, the works submitted were not works of art . . . They were of the sort of stuff which has played havoc with our young art students in recent years . . . When I am told that an ostrich egg in marble [a Brancusi work] represents the birth of the world, something must be wrong.'

Peggy delegated the battle to Wyn Henderson, who circulated a petition signed by London's foremost art critics, including Herbert Read and Clive Bell. Discussion reached the House of Commons, which ruled that the works could be imported as art and the show could go on – which it did, viewed by hordes of the curious public. Poor Manson gave up his post and subsequently fell to pieces: he announced (unaccountably) to *Time* magazine that he had a 'black-out' at an official luncheon in Paris shortly after, at which he startled the other guests, he said, by 'suddenly crowing like a cock.'

Wyn Henderson could see that Peggy, while pleased with the gallery's success, continued to be preoccupied with Beckett, and, around Christmas 1938, urged her to go to Paris for a while. Beckett was happy to see her, but he continued to waver. Peggy claimed that they had replaced sex with 'wild' drinking and walking all over the city in the middle of the night. Peggy was sure she would be good for him, but he responded that he was 'dead' inside. One night at his apartment she insisted that she stay the night; in the early morning Beckett left, apparently terrified. Peggy got out of bed and wrote a poem, which began, 'A woman storming at my gate / Is this inevitable fate?' The poem described what she thought were Beckett's doubts, closing, 'Shall I kill her holy passion? / Destroying life, not taking action?' She left the poem on his desk and fled for England.

She had since succumbed to Beckett's arguments that she give a show to his Dutch friend, the painter Geer van Velde, and turned her attentions to hanging the show. She did so without much enthusiasm because she thought that van Velde's work was derivative of Picasso's – and the critics would agree. Nevertheless she bought several paintings, either under made-up names or as gifts for friends, for she wanted to make van Velde happy for Beckett's sake. She opened the May 5 show with the usual raucous party.

Van Velde and his wife, Lisle, in London for the show, spent a weekend at Yew Tree Cottage in Petersfield in May with Peggy and another couple; Beckett joined them there. The first night Beckett confided to Peggy that Suzanne was his mistress and that she had found him a flat and made curtains for him. When he asked if she minded, Peggy said no. According to his biographers, Beckett acted strangely during this visit: Peggy took the party down to the coast in her Delage, and while walking along the beach Beckett suddenly shed his clothes and jumped into the icy water, swimming far out from shore, so far that his head was just a black spot bobbing in the waves, as his alarmed friends watched. Finally he turned, swam steadily back, dried himself with his clothes, and then put them on – without saying a word – acting, in fact, like one of his own characters.

Shortly after, Peggy clumsily tried to provoke Beckett to jealousy by having a very public (and short – a few days at most) dalliance with her neighboring gallery friend E.L.T. Mesens; she also had designs on the *London Bulletin*, the newspaper Mesens circulated that covered the gallery scene, hoping to take it over and enliven its rather staid pages. Neither scheme came to much. It was not particularly wise, choosing as a bed partner someone who was technically a competitor. Mesens, who had popularized and now promoted the work of his countryman and friend Magritte, had a surrealist collection of his own and was very much a mover and shaker in London's art world. But Peggy simply liked him, later describing her potential rival as 'a gay little Flamand, quite vulgar, but really very nice and warm.' She seems to have bedded him almost on impulse – certainly with no expectations or, conversely, any worry about the consequences.

After the Mesens interlude, Peggy returned to Paris, where she witnessed a scene in Beckett's apartment that posited one explanation for Beckett's inaction. He and van Velde were trying on items of each other's clothing and talking of exchanging them. Peggy later wrote, 'It was a rather homosexual performance, disguised, of course, with the most normal gestures.' She told Emily summarily that Beckett couldn't give her what she wanted '[b]ecause he is a pederast at heart.'

There is no question that Beckett's sexuality was restricted and complicated and that he preferred the company of men, forming friendships that, it could be argued, were homoerotic in nature. Though he lived with and much later married Suzanne, it seems that their sex life ended shortly after they threw in their lot together. But there is no indication that Beckett ever had homosexual relations or that he consciously wanted to. Still, Peggy's awareness of the sexual proclivities of others was fairly keen. She sensed a tension in the flat that day and, for the sake of her pride perhaps, formed a conclusion about Beckett's sexuality that explained his reticence. By this time, both of them knew they would be better off apart. But neither of them could make the final break.

Peggy sent Beckett a letter saying she wanted to say goodbye before she went back to London. Ignoring it, Beckett proposed that they drive the van Veldes to their new place in the south of France. They drove in Peggy's Delage to Marseilles – Beckett, who Peggy said drove as recklessly as John Holms, did the driving – and took Geer and Lisle on a day trip to Cassis; the married couple did not know what to make of Beckett's relationship with Peggy. Leaving the van Veldes at their new home, Peggy and Beckett drove back to Paris together. Stopping in Dijon for the night, Beckett took a double room with two beds for them. And in the middle of the night when Peggy tried to climb into Beckett's bed, he jumped out and said she had cheated. When Peggy asked why he had booked a double in the first place, he said that it was 30 francs cheaper than two singles. Despite this contretemps, they spent the next day together in comfortable companionship. Each was nicer to the other, and when they parted, they did so 'with sorrow,' according to

Peggy, 'Beckett as usual regretting he relinquished me.' In a familiar pattern, even this bittersweet parting did not end their relationship, which would sputter on for four more months.

Peggy had to hurry back to Paris to meet the painter Yves Tanguy, the subject of her next exhibit at Guggenheim Jeune; she drove him and his wife, Jeannette, to Boulogne, where they took the ferry to England. She had met Tanguy the previous fall and liked him, finding him honest, unpretentious, and sweet. At thirty-nine, Tanguy was two years younger than Peggy; he had been born in Paris to an administrative official and had spent most of his boyhood in Brittany. Following in the footsteps of his father, who had previously been a sea captain, Tanguy joined the merchant marine as an adolescent and soon found himself in the French army, where he met the playwright, poet, and future filmmaker Jacques Prévert, who brought him up to date on the Paris art scene. After his release from the service, Tanguy joined Prévert in Paris, where he gave more thought to painting and began to draw. While riding a bus in 1923, he caught a glimpse of a painting by Giorgio de Chirico (presumably in a gallery window) and ran off the bus to investigate. Admiring the Italian painter's fantastical and geometrical composition, Tanguy on the spot declared himself an artist and set out to teach himself how to paint. In 1925 he presented himself to André Breton, who took him into the surrealist fold. In 1927 he had his first one-man show at the Galerie Surréaliste in Paris.

While Tanguy's bizarre desert landscapes would seem to suggest considerable emotional complexity, he was in fact a very simple man. 'He had a lovely personality,' observed Peggy, 'modest and shy and as adorable as a child.' His hair often stuck straight up, particularly when he was drunk, which was often. 'Tanguy is completely *un*intellectual, unworldly & disinterested in money and worldly things,' Peggy told Emily. 'He is like a simple tailor.' He and his wife had never been to England and were most eager to see it, and their enthusiasm was infectious; Peggy later wrote that they 'were so unspoiled and different from all the blasé people I knew that it was a pleasure to be with them.'

The Tanguy exhibit ran from July 6 to 16, 1938, and was a great success. Like Kandinsky, the French painter was not very familiar to English audiences, and they responded to the newcomer with warmth. *The Times* reviewer wrote, 'Mr. Tanguy is a most exquisite craftsman, not to be bettered in any Academy, and the significance of his works should promote endless discussion.' Peggy sold a number of paintings, and bought two herself, *Toilette de l'air* (1937) and *Le Soleil dans son écrin* (1937). The latter was a desert scene visually darker than was usual for the artist, with an elongated yellow phallic object joined in the far distance by two similarly shaped objects, all of them casting shadows that bear little relation to their actual shapes. It oddly frightened her, she later said, but she recognized it as one of Tanguy's best.

By this time Peggy and the artist had developed a sexual attraction, perhaps fueled by all the alcohol at the steady stream of parties in Tanguy's honor. At a party hosted by Mesens in the Hampstead home of his boss, Roland Penrose, Peggy and Tanguy began their heated affair, leaving the gathering together for her flat. Further assignations were difficult to arrange because of Tanguy's wife, who grew suspicious, but sometimes Wyn Henderson kept Madame Tanguy busy so Peggy and Tanguy could sneak off for the afternoon. The Tanguys soon grew bored with their host, Peter Dawson, an English surrealist who had hung the show with Tanguy, and came down to Petersfield with Peggy. Childless themselves, the Tanguys adored Pegeen and Debbie Garman (who was spending her holiday with Pegeen), and Tanguy and Pegeen solemnly exchanged paintings. Yet Jeannette Tanguy became increasingly suspicious and jealous in Petersfield, and one day the local pub called and asked Peggy if the drunk and weepy Frenchwoman on their hands perhaps belonged with her establishment.

But at the gallery sales were brisk, and Tanguy found himself rich for the first time in his life. His success seemed to fuel his amorous risk-taking. When Peggy put the Tanguys on the boat to France in late June, she quickly began plotting how to get Tanguy to 'elope' with her. She followed him to Paris and lured him back to England, where they had a lovely idyll. Tanguy gave her a drawing of a woman with a feather on it which she thought looked like her; he signed it 'pour Peggy, Yew Tree Cottage, 20 juillet 1938.' He also made her earrings for her collection, painting landscapes on oval disks, one in blue and one in pink, and hanging them by little chains. And he devised an erotic drawing that he had engraved on her Dunhill lighter, which she would leave in a London taxicab years later. At a party someone asked her if she was Madame Tanguy; she and her lover joked that she was Madame Tanguy *de Londres*.

Just then, Beckett appeared in her life yet again, on his way to Ireland. He noticed a photograph of Peggy and Tanguy on the mantel in her flat, both of them evidently in high spirits. He could not hide his curiosity, and Peggy confessed that she had other lovers, blaming Beckett for her double life. Peggy was leaving for Paris with Tanguy later that evening and offered to lend Beckett her flat. He agreed, but then tried to get her to stay overnight with him. When Peggy refused, Beckett entered into the farcical scheme of things by offering her and her lover his rue des Favorites flat while he was in Ireland.

Peggy agreed immediately, and she and Beckett happily went off for a merry dinner with Djuna Barnes and William Gerhardie (her novelist friend from John Holms days) before Peggy left for France.

It was a strange time, and Peggy really did not like causing so much grief in Jeannette Tanguy's life. She was not trying to break up the marriage, and in any case Tanguy had had affairs before. When Tanguy told her Jeannette just sat at home and cried, however, Peggy became quite upset. Inevitably, Jeannette discovered that Peggy was in Paris, and there were scenes, Jeannette once throwing a piece of fish at Peggy in a café, which further upset Peggy, who had grown tired of scenes in cafés during her marriage to Laurence.

Tanguy was beset on all sides. André Breton, recently returned from Mexico with a collection of primitive art, had issued one of the excommunications that characterized his group of surrealists, singling out the poet Paul Eluard. Max Ernst and Joan Miró had been found wanting and packed off in 1926; de Chirico too had been drummed out; Dali was told he had sold out (which left him utterly unfazed). Now, Breton and Eluard had a battle royal over Communism, and Eluard, disillusioned by Breton's doctrinaire Trotskyism, took a good swath of like-minded surrealists with him. Tanguy, who worshipped Breton, had to make sure he did not run into any of the banished surrealists when he and Peggy went out to cafés, while she of course kept her eye out for Madame Tanguy.

Not surprisingly, the relationship could not bear the strain. In the late fall, back in London, Peggy had a fling with her other Cork Street neighbor, Roland Penrose, himself a noted surrealist painter as well as a collector. Extremely attractive to women, Penrose, Peggy discovered, had one eccentric habit; he liked to tie up his sexual partner. Once he used Peggy's belt, but another time he brought out a pair of ivory handcuffs that he locked with a little key.

Peggy would relate all of these details in her autobiography in the most matter-of-fact fashion imaginable. (It is impossible to tell what she made of it at the time, given the deadpan, laconic way she describes the incident; by the time she wrote about it, she was well on her way to envisioning her past as the adventures of a very modern, unflappable woman – though it is likely that Penrose's predilections took her aback at the time.) Certainly she had no illusions that Penrose was more than a fling. Once again, she was choosing her lovers a little too close to home. Though Peggy and Penrose remained friends, he would later make derogatory comments about her behind her back. And he, like Mesens, was a power to be reckoned with on the art scene – in fact, Penrose far more so than Mesens, though Penrose was nicer about it. He was also attached to the stunningly beautiful and talented photographer Lee Miller, who was in Egypt at the time. Peggy had not known about this liaison when she took Penrose to bed, but as soon as she learned of it, she told him to go to Egypt and get Miller if he cared anything about his own future. Penrose subsequently did.

Tanguy picked this moment to reappear on the London scene, and he immediately saw what was going on. Although Peggy broke off with Penrose and stayed with Tanguy while he was in London, the Frenchman was distinctly unhappy. Having money had confused him, he told Peggy; he wished he had not got so much of it all at once. He often sat in cafés, rolling currency up in a ball to throw it at the other patrons. He returned to France in September, leaving the relationship in suspended animation.

In November, Peggy made a remark in a letter to Emily that sounds mystifying at first but also makes a good deal of sense: 'I'm not getting married,' she said, 'as I can't concentrate.' The year had been turbulent. War was approaching. 'The war scares us all the time,' Peggy told Emily in September. 'I wish I could decide on something to do.' That month the Munich crisis rocked the world: Hitler demanded that Czechoslovakia surrender the Sudetenland, its German-speaking district, and a full-scale European war seemed imminent.

Peggy brought all the artwork in the gallery down to Yew Tree Cottage; it did not belong to her and she feared for its safety in London. She thought that she and the children should get away and made plans for them to leave for Ireland, taking Djuna along. She frantically wired Paris telling Tanguy to leave, as she had a not unreasonable fear that both London and Paris would be bombed.

Then, almost overnight, the crisis passed. Neville Chamberlain arranged the infamous international conference in Munich at which the Czechs surrendered the Sudetenland in exchange for a guarantee of security from France, and the British prime minister left for home, declaring, 'Peace in our time.' As Europeans and the Americans among them breathed a sigh of relief, Peggy returned to her own frantic pace.

She had kicked off her second season with a show of children's art (an idea borrowed from the French surrealists), including works by Pegeen and her classmates Anna Campbell (the daughter of the South African poet Roy Campbell who married another Garman sister, Mary) and Lucian Freud (grandson of Sigmund and son of Hazel's friend Lucie; though he would of course become the famous painter, Peggy rightly claimed no credit in foreseeing his future). Then, after one of her usual scouting trips to the Continent, she followed with a collage show, including works by her old friend Mina Loy, some suggestive pieces by Laurence, and contributions from Ernst, Braque, Arp, Picasso, Picabia, and others.

Around this time, a British reporter, Theodore Goodman, stood back and took a look at Guggenheim Jeune and its achievement:

> Miss Guggenheim has given us the first London Gallery in which com-
> merce has no part at all. Her aim is to introduce to the art student, those
> painters whose art is not facile or easy enough to attract the commercial
> galleries and which only gets a showing after the artists have achieved
> fame in the ordinary way. Miss Guggenheim is willing to experiment. She
> would probably be the first to admit that one or two of her experiments
> may have not quite come off, but nothing she has shown has been with-
> out interest.

Peggy would, of course, have been extremely pleased to read that she was not afraid to experiment; it was a quality that made her gallery stand out. And she was proud of taking chances on artists who were not yet known (something she did in her personal life as well). But it was not quite clear what distinction the reviewer was making when he said that Guggenheim Jeune was not a commercial gallery. Perhaps he had in the back of his mind that the proprietor did not need to make money, having a considerable fortune behind her. And it is true that Peggy did not run the gallery expressly to make money; indeed, she may just possibly have shown 'safer' artists if that had been her primary object. But the gallery was not meant as a vanity operation, however little money it was making. Over the years at Guggenheim Jeune and in her subsequent New York gallery, she liked to show at Christmastime affordable paintings and objects suitable to be given as presents. Christmas 1938 was no exception. Guggenheim Jeune showed ceramics by Jill Salaman and caricature dolls and small paintings by Marie Vassiliev; Peggy even took out an advertisement in *Queen* magazine for the show, boasting: 'Original Christmas Presents at Really Moderate Prices.' Of course, she cannot have expected large amounts to roll in for such shows. But the point is that the distinction between an operation that made money and one that did not was one she made, and she intended hers to be a commercial venture – even hoping, against the odds, that it might turn a profit. Not until the second season did she come to understand how unprofitable it was, despite her intentions.

For Peggy, however celebrated the gallery was, the scene was getting a little stale. In November she wrote Emily that the gallery went on 'more and more dully.' She was frustrated by the London public, which she felt was indifferent to modern art. She thought about closing Guggenheim Jeune in June for good and going to live in Paris. In any event, she intended to go to Paris at Christmas for a month, she told friends. Her chaotic love life had made her mistrust her own judgment in the day-to-day work of the gallery and to turn over most matters to Wyn. 'I have reached the stage where I ask her advice about everything now,' she complained.

At this time, Peggy's friends were nothing but trouble, Djuna especially. She was having a great crisis, aggravated by heroic drinking. Djuna's favorite brother was in a sanitarium after a nervous breakdown. Her own nerves were in terrible shape and she made huge scenes; Silas Glossop, the lover she had briefly taken up with in the summer of 1937, could sometimes quiet her, though their sexual relationship was over. Peggy volunteered to pay for sessions with Dr. Carrell, Antonia White's psychiatrist, or for a stay in a nursing home. But Djuna had little patience with Peggy; she remembered an incident at Yew Tree Cottage – or said she did – when Peggy had sat up in bed and said, 'I am so rich, what shall I do with it? I can't think.' That summer Florette's maid had delivered to her in Paris a pearl necklace of Florette's worth at the time about $6,000. Djuna muttered darkly about Peggy's 'swanning' around town wearing the necklace.

Djuna and Peggy had a big falling-out over Tanguy's show, which would reverberate for a long time to come. Peggy asked Djuna to call her friend the collector Edward James – an extremely big fish in the surrealist world who had recently commissioned Dali's lobster telephone, and someone Peggy would have wanted very much to win over – and bring him around to the gallery so that Peggy could sell him a Tanguy. Djuna balked, saying, 'What have you ever done for me that I should do this for you?' Peggy retorted that all Djuna's friends had done a lot for her, and again asked that Djuna do her this one favor. Eventually, Djuna did phone James, but she would always hold this request against Peggy, despite the fact that Peggy would send her a monthly allowance for as long as Peggy lived. Djuna's friends were at their wits' ends about her drinking. Finally, Laurence, in London in November to drop off Sindbad, intervened and took Djuna off to Megève. But the problem was a long way from being solved.

Meanwhile, Emily Coleman, the dark angel of the trio, was behaving most mysteriously. She had left for America at the beginning of 1938 and took a lover named Henry in Montreal. Then word reached her London friends that she had taken up with a cowboy, Jake Scarborough, whom she married in 1939. Letters between Emily and her friends grew more infrequent as Emily's became more and more mystical and she began to write of 'channeling' dead people like John Holms, at which point her diary becomes virtually unreadable. She inserted herself once too often in quarrels between Djuna and Peggy, only making matters worse for all concerned. Peggy found it difficult to navigate between her old friends' complaints and her current ambitions, and each of the three was perpetually aggrieved with the others.

Peggy went to Paris for a month at Christmas both to celebrate the holiday and to see various artists she hoped to show, and she wound up spending seven weeks there. Over the course of her stay she saw Beckett several times and decided that she was finally over him. She was still consulting fortunetellers, and the latest one told her that she should either marry the man of the moment or give him up, commenting that the man Peggy was describing sounded like an 'awful autocrat.' When Peggy repeated this assessment to Beckett, he replied, 'Have you decided not to marry me?' To which Peggy was able to say yes. She made a witticism about having forgotten that she no longer loved him.

Djuna, in a letter to Emily in early 1939, summed up this tangled and frenzied time:

> Peggy is over Sam, and sad about it. 'Where did it go?' she said, like a child when a bubble bursts. Penrose has gone off to get his passion, Lee Miller (in Egypt), Tanguy is still hanging about, but she is no longer in love with him, tho she likes him, he is very sweet and simple, and throws his money about like a drunken sailor . . . So Peggy is high and dry and tired with running about looking at paintings and painters and drinking too much and taking too many sleeping drugs.

This is the first mention of Peggy drinking too much or taking sleeping pills; neither habit ever developed into a significant problem, though without question many of her affairs were fueled by drinking on both sides. (Djuna may also have hoped to deflect attention from her own problem.)

While Peggy was undoubtedly tired after the first season of Guggenheim Jeune, it is wrong to assume, as Djuna did, that Peggy found herself diminished and disheartened. Running the gallery was, at least in part, work she loved. It involved meeting and getting to know artists, choosing works to be shown, overseeing installations, socializing to generate publicity for the gallery as well as sales, and negotiating with buyers – all of which she thrived on, and which demanded that she develop new sets of skills at every turn. Though the gallery was not making money, she was coming to a shrewd understanding of the art world's commercial end. (For one thing, she was beginning to buy artworks for her own collection at very reasonable prices.)

And she was in the milieu where she felt she belonged: among artists, getting to know them (sometimes falling in love with them), supporting and promoting them, and helping them come to understand the commercial art scene together with her. Her autobiographical writing about this time often sounds comical, as Peggy appears to be going from one famous artist to another without making any distinctions among them. But a later colleague of Peggy's, Fred Licht, has wisely pointed out that accusations that Peggy simply slept with one great artist after another, with no sense of perspective, or that she then name-dropped in her memoirs, miss their mark totally. 'Such an assessment presupposes it was her duty to affix personalities to those names for future generations,' writes Licht. Peggy knew, he says, that great artists 'are frequently great bores' in areas other than their talents. We look for examples of how the genius of a Pollock or a Joyce shows itself in social and personal dealings. 'The whole point of her memoirs, however, is that these men and women were not legends to her or to her time,' Licht asserts. 'They were people to be dealt with in the ordinary way, people who had a direct relationship with whatever it was Peggy Guggenheim happened to be doing at the time. Contracts had to be negotiated with many of them; prices had to be discussed; one had to think about when and with whom to invite them and how to avoid the nuisance of their husbands or wives.' It is just this casual approach, says Licht, that enabled Peggy to recreate the 'tenor of her time and her position,' which is the great achievement of her autobiography.

For Peggy found the 'business' of running an art gallery absolutely delightful. It is true that she would become positively gleeful when some of her artists became household names, which accounts for the strangely boastful tone her memoirs can take. But what matters here is that for the time being she was really 'in it' with her artists, the buyers and collectors, the public, and the assorted *machers* of the art world. She was even, in her own way, beginning to see that she might be a *macher* herself. It was a heady time indeed.

If her personal life did not always proceed smoothly, her involvement with men was always passionate and eventful. She had put behind her the years of her twenties and thirties when she was a 'wife' and when she had concentrated on that to the exclusion of everything else. That kind of thing was for women without ambition, she concluded with finality if not bitterness, and Peggy knew, finally, that she had ambition.

10

The Beginnings of War:
The Best-Laid Plans

The course Peggy was now setting for her life was as innovative emotionally as it was professionally. Though she never depended on a man for financial security, emotional security was another matter entirely. In some measure, she had both enjoyed the role of helpmeet with all three of her 'husbands' and yet chafed at it; she had come to feel that suburban living in Petersfield with Garman might as well be jail. In this, her new life, her impulse was still to seek emotional security, but she was learning differently fast. With Beckett, she learned the hard way that sexual and intellectual compatibility did not mean that a couple was destined for a long-term relationship when other obstacles (in this case, Beckett's passive temperament) stood in the way. With Tanguy, Peggy never held out any hope for a major relationship: Jeannette Tanguy made her presence too apparent, and in any event Tanguy was not a forceful enough personality to suit her. As cleverly as she developed her eye for good art, Peggy was learning to discern genius in potential partners. She made mistakes, to be sure, choosing men who were not at all her equals. But her behavior conformed to her new conception of herself as an independent woman.

Guggenheim Jeune's first show of 1939 brought the gallery a good deal of attention. Beginning in 1935, the physician Grace Pailthorpe, a specialist in juvenile delinquency, had been meeting with a young surrealist poet, Reuben Mednikoff, a friend of the poet David Gascoyne, to work on automatic painting and drawing, or creating art directly from the unconscious. The couple – Mednikoff became Pailthorpe's partner – produced surrealist artworks that were of great interest to other artists and the public in the 1930s. The surrealist program was dedicated to accessing the unconscious and finding ways to tap into it for art. André Breton had singled out Pailthorpe and Mednikoff's work at the 1936 surrealist exhibition as perhaps the most exciting development in British surrealism. Pailthorpe published a paper, 'Scientific Aspects of Surrealism,' in the art world's most cutting-edge publication, the London Bulletin, in late 1938, evoking a flood of letters to the editor. The Pailthorpe-Mednikoff show at Guggenheim Jeune in January 1939 drew a lot of press and a sizable public; audiences, then as now, were fascinated by the question of the origins of art, and automatic art seemed to provide some sort of key, however clumsy. No one claimed great aesthetic stature for these artists (though interest in their productions, particularly Mednikoff's, has revived in recent years), but Peggy's exhibit placed her squarely in the cultural vanguard.

Peggy followed the Pailthorpe-Mednikoff exhibition with a less exciting but very strong show of the Austrian surrealist Wolfgang Paalen, who was to found the influential art magazine Dyn (1942). In Paalen's work – Peggy bought Totemic Memory of My Childhood (1937) – fantastical creatures populate desertlike stretches of unreal landscapes. After Paalen, Peggy showed the English artist John Tunnard, whose colorful gouaches were more realistic and far less forbidding; he did not really become an important surrealist until the 1940s. But Tunnard, who wore round spectacles and loud coats and ties, was a colorful character who reminded Peggy of Groucho Marx and who enlivened his own show with his frequent presence. A visitor, looking at his work, asked the room at large, 'Who is this John Tunnard?' The artist, overhearing, turned three somersaults and landed in front of the visitor, announcing, 'I am John Tunnard.' Peggy bought his PSI (1938).

Peggy spent three weeks with Djuna Barnes at the Hotel Madison in Paris in January, and wrote to Emily Coleman that her friend was doing much better emotionally than she had been for more than a year. But back in London on February 10, Djuna tried to kill herself, taking an overdose of Veronal; Peggy sent Dr. McKeand, John Holms's doctor, to take care of her, and asked him to be careful not to reveal his identity to Djuna, who would be upset by the connection. Peggy was entertaining the idea of sending Djuna to stay at the ranch Emily shared with her new husband in Arizona, a bizarre plan she would promote for over a year. She wrote Emily that while Djuna would love to live with her, 'I prefer to live alone. I am very quiet again and have no love affairs but I don't want to have Djuna on my hands.' Djuna should leave London, where, Peggy felt, she was getting no writing done. Djuna had written nothing of consequence since Nightwood, which had been published in October 1936 with an introduction by T. S. Eliot, to some acclaim.

Another old friend surfaced in February, Emma Goldman, who after the publication of her autobiography had conducted a series of whirlwind lecture tours, increasingly on anti-Soviet topics. Peggy and the aged anarchist had had no contact for almost six years. Emma, still in exile from the United States and now living in London, sought Peggy out. 'It cost me a lot of effort to do so,' Emma wrote Emily. 'You will laugh when I tell you that when I arrived [at Peggy's gallery] my heart thumped violently.' Peggy was not there, but on her way out Emma ran into her old friend on the stairs. 'We recognized each other of course, but I felt a certain chill in the reception she gave me . . . [T]he fact that we kept standing in the hall the few minutes we talked and that she did not ask me up to the studio, makes me think that she really was not very eager to renew the old relationship.' She followed up with a letter to Peggy, telling her that going to see her 'required more courage than in the olden days when I had to face the police.' She hoped to see Peggy soon again, she wrote.

Emma was keen in picking up on Peggy's coldness. She received no reply to her letter. Emma had longed for a chance to explain to Peggy what was, after all, true: that 'to do her justice [in my autobiography] I should have had to write about her life with Lawrence [sic], her divorce and all the other things that followed.' Peggy, at this juncture, would not have relished rehashing the days when she had been a meek, abused, and degraded wife. Emma knew nothing about her life with Holms or with Garman, not to mention her current life, in which she was developing a new professional self-assurance and enjoying sexual freedom. Any interest Peggy may have had in Emma's anarchism had vanished after her experience with Garman's Marxism, though she still held many left-wing views. In almost every way, Peggy was a very different person from the one Emma knew in 1928. She had said good-bye emotionally in the aftermath of the publication of Living My Life in 1931, when Emma accused her of general cheapness and meanness. Emma's reappearance at Guggenheim Jeune was a reminder of a life of which she wanted no part and no reminder.

Emotionally speaking, Peggy was cleaning house. 'Once I got Mr. Beckett out of my life I felt like a new woman,' Peggy announced to Emily. '[N]ow I don't take anything seriously & I can have little affairs without hysterics. Very pleasant.' She described in the same letter a weekend spent with the writer and critic John Davenport and her new lover, Julian Trevelyan. Trevelyan was an important surrealist painter who had been at Cambridge with a group of promising young men, including Davenport (who would later cowrite a satirical novel with Dylan Thomas); Humphrey Jennings; Malcolm Lowry, who would go on to write Under the Volcano (1947); and Anthony Blunt, who would become an eminent art historian but is better known today as a Soviet spy. Trevelyan wrote poetry in college, but Jennings saw talent in some drawings he had done and convinced him to switch to painting, which Trevelyan did with alacrity, studying in Paris. When Peggy met him, he was married, and he and his wife, Ursula, lived on Durham Wharf in Chiswick, where they threw large parties at which some guests took mescaline.

When Peggy met Trevelyan, twelve years her junior, his wife was sick and he was at loose ends. She took him home with her one night. Afterward, he was remorseful, thinking of his wife, and the affair might have ended there, but work-related matters threw Peggy and him together. Trevelyan had organized a Spanish Relief Committee, and he and Peggy were planning a three-night auction of artworks to benefit Spanish refugees, originally to be held at Guggenheim Jeune but ultimately hosted in a house in Regent's Park, raising several hundred pounds. Then in March, Davenport, unaware of the connection between them, invited Peggy and Trevelyan to spend a long weekend with him and his wife, Clement, in Dieppe (evidently Trevelyan's wife was unavailable). Peggy spent her days talking to Davenport while Julian and Clement were off sketching together. The evenings, according to a letter Peggy wrote Emily at the time, were deliciously fun. One night Peggy said was as wonderful as something 'that John [Holms] might have organized' when Peggy originally met him in Saint-Tropez, in fact, except that 'it was all terribly happy and gay.' The party ended up in a 'charming' bordello. 'Since life with Garman was so depressing,' she wrote Emily, 'I am desperately trying to regain those last years. I feel 20 again.' When the weekend was over, Trevelyan put Peggy on the boat for England, giving her a little bottle of brandy for the trip. The Davenports had not learned that Peggy and Trevelyan's friendship was a romantic one.

'The affair was very vague,' Peggy later wrote in her memoirs, 'but the consequences were disastrous.' She became convinced she was pregnant. The Davenports invited her for another weekend to their stone house in the Cotswolds, without Trevelyan, and Peggy passed the time gardening and pushing a heavy wheelbarrow, halfway hoping to bring on a miscarriage. One afternoon Trevelyan invited her to his house to see Ursula's paintings, and Peggy somehow knew as soon as she came into the room that both she and Ursula were pregnant. Shortly after, in a great irony, Ursula Trevelyan had a miscarriage. Though Peggy would say in her memoirs that she offered her child to the couple, it seems that she was putting a good face on it, as there is no other indication at the time that she told Trevelyan about her pregnancy or its outcome.

Peggy finally consulted her local doctor in Petersfield, who confirmed that she was pregnant but refused to have anything to do with an abortion. Peggy went up to London and saw a German refugee doctor who said she was too old, at forty-one, to have a child. He performed the abortion in a nursing home. When she left the home she was an invalid for the summer, with Antonia White's friend Phyllis Jones staying with her to nurse her and take care of the children. Peggy passed the time rereading Proust, which she enjoyed just as much as she had the first time, parts of it reminding her strongly of *Nightwood*, especially, she thought, in both writers' use of memory and the past.

Perhaps because the abortion had been so hard physically, or perhaps because of the psychological consequences of learning that her childbearing days were over, Peggy treated this event as a kind of turning point in her life. When she wrote about the affair with Trevelyan in her memoirs, she called him Llewellyn, and when she republished *Out of This Century* in 1979, supplying real names for those she had disguised in the 1946 edition, Trevelyan was the only person whose true identity she did not reveal. While she never offered any facts that might explain why she was so reticent about this particular relationship, it seems likely that she formed some connection with Trevelyan's wife, who lost her baby in quite a different way, and so she kept silent. But it is also possible that she did not reveal Trevelyan's identity because this affair was somewhat obscurely traumatic for her. It remains a mystery. What we do know is that henceforth she would try to be on her guard not to enter relationships in which she would risk being the vulnerable party; of course, she was not always able to do so.

Aside from this consequential episode, Peggy was busy with the gallery – where, in June, Trevelyan had a show. Peggy, at the same time, was very excited by the prospect of a show that would run concurrently with Trevelyan's, an exhibition of the wonderful primitive artwork that Breton had brought back from his trip to meet Trotsky in Mexico in 1938. The show was modest – Peggy did not even save the exhibition catalogue – but it cemented her friendship with the surrealists.

In the spring Peggy decided to close the gallery. For the last show at Guggenheim Jeune, Peggy gave a big party on June 22, inviting the German photographer Gisele Freund to show her new color slides of luminaries like James Joyce, H. G. Wells, George Bernard Shaw, Marcel Duchamp, and Leonard and Virginia Woolf. As this gala was right before her abortion, Peggy was feeling so worried and unwell that she found the event difficult to enjoy.

Peggy had, in fact, been looking beyond Guggenheim Jeune for some time. She was not making any money out of it; actually, the gallery had lost $6,000 in its first season, she had recently discovered. 'I felt that if I was losing that money I might as well lose a lot more and do something worthwhile.' She had an eye, no doubt, on the scene in America, where modern art was putting down institutional roots faster than in Europe. The Museum of Modern Art in New York City had opened in 1929, directed by the talented and perspicacious Alfred Barr. Peggy's uncle Solomon and Hilla Rebay opened the doors of the Museum of Non-Objective Painting in a former automobile showroom on West 53rd Street in Manhattan in 1939. Though Peggy did not know it, Baroness Rebay also had plans to open a branch of the museum in Paris to be called the Centre Guggenheim; this would have been, of course, a disaster for Peggy. Europe had a clear need for such a museum, and Peggy thought the venture would be better planned for England than for the politically unsettled Continent.

A modern art museum in England was not an entirely new idea. Helena Rubinstein, the cosmetics entrepreneur who, with her husband, the journalist Edward Titus, established Black Mannequin Press in Paris between the wars, publishing D. H. Lawrence and other moderns, and who was herself a formidable art collector, was interested in backing such an enterprise. From her salon in Berkeley Square, frequented by such artists as Modigliani and Dufy, Rubinstein had preliminary talks with Roland Penrose and E.L.T. Mesens. Both of them floated the idea in various circles, but nothing came of it. (It is interesting to ponder just what the similarly placed Rubinstein thought of Peggy, and vice versa, but no records remain of the two ever meeting.) The project would take a lot of solid capital and an entrepreneurial personality unafraid to take risks, possessing the skill, background, and professional reputation in the field that would lend the project complete authority.

Enter Herbert Read, the son of a Yorkshire farmer whose father died when Herbert was nine and who managed to put himself through night school at the University of Leeds. After a stint in the army (he was awarded the Military Cross), Read somehow got himself established as a cultural critic, teaching occasionally and writing well-received poetry and books of literary criticism. He also became the regular art critic for *The Listener* and was known especially in art circles for his writing on the sculptor Henry Moore. He was also, though this was not the basis for his reputation, an avowed anarchist, publishing *Poetry and Anarchism* in 1938; he would publish *The Philosophy of Anarchism* in 1940. By the late 1930s, he had established himself as 'the best known proponent of modernism in the English-speaking world,' according to his biographer James King. Married and the father of five children, he was at the height of his eminence at this time as editor of the prestigious (but somewhat stuffy, many thought) *Burlington Review*.

When Peggy first approached Read, then forty-eight, about establishing a modern art museum, he 'sensibly withdrew,' according to his biographer. But

Peggy negotiated: if he would give up the editorship of the *Review*, he could take up an outstanding offer to become a partner of Routledge, the successful London publisher, and she would advance him five years' salary to act as director of the museum. Read agreed to work for six months without pay in exchange for the five-year loan. He asked Peggy for references, and to her and Djuna's amusement got one from a friend he respected very much indeed, T. S. Eliot – whom Peggy had never met. (Eliot had of course arranged for the publication of Barnes's *Nightwood*, after the interventions of Emily Coleman – to whom, somewhat strangely, he took a special liking – so he was familiar with Peggy through mutual friends.) In May 1939 Read wrote to his friend, the eccentric art collector and dealer Douglas Cooper, of the 'momentous decision' he was about to make. 'The thing bristles with snags,' he wrote, 'but it will at least be lively.' A sticking point was finances. '[S]he can't endow [the museum],' Read continued in his letter to Cooper. 'The amount she can afford is just enough, but will not leave sufficient income for important purchases.' Read also seems to have contacted someone, who would in many respects be called a rather unlikely person, about the venture: Emma Goldman. Yet the choice was understandable, given their mutual anarchist principles. Emma said she understood his 'struggle and apprehension' at the idea of working with Peggy. 'Yes, indeed, I know Peggy to be kind hearted and very generous with people she cares about,' adding, however, 'But as you say she is *all-zu-menschlich* [all-too-human].' Read was hoping the museum, once established, would draw funds from a wider range of investors and supporters.

In letters to friends, Peggy was breezy about the whole subject, writing to Emily Coleman that Read 'was a little nervous about chucking all his jobs for me when I might change my mind,' but about the finances she was very serious. After her mother's estate was settled, her income was averaging $40,000 a year (in today's terms, roughly $500,000) – just the amount that would be needed to run the museum annually. Peggy, now recovered from her abortion but with Phyllis Jones still living with her, closeted herself and ran 'monstrous mathematical calculations.' She immediately stopped buying clothes, she told Emily, and expected to buy no more new outfits for a year. She traded in the Delage for a more economical Talbot. And, she firmly told friends, she would have to cut back on all stipends, loans, and gifts – a resolution that would cause shock waves of resentment among her circle and that, for this and other reasons, she would not be able to follow through on.

Still, she and Read forged optimistically ahead with their plans. The art collector Kenneth Clark agreed to lease his house on Portland Place to the museum, with Peggy to live on one floor and the Reads on another. (Peggy was nervous about sharing a residence with Mrs. Read after they quarreled about who was to have which floor.) It goes without saying that living in a museum constituted a commitment few in Peggy's circumstances would have made; it is not clear why she or Read felt they had to be in residence, except perhaps to economize.

Peggy planned to set off for Paris with a list Read made up for her and that, unfortunately, no longer survives. He made statements to the newspapers announcing a major show in the fall to begin with Matisse and to trace the development of modern art since 1910, with special emphasis on abstract art and cubism. Significantly, Peggy crossed Matisse off Read's list, believing him not 'modern' in her understanding of the word; for similar reasons, she struck Cézanne and Rousseau, among others. 'I ask his advice & don't always take it,' she told Emily matter-of-factly early on in her collaboration with Read. Significantly, she had gained enough confidence in her opinions – probably confirmed for her in Guggenheim Jeune's success – to trust her own tastes. (This attitude would no doubt have been galling to Read, had he known.)

Over the summer, the venture nearly fell apart. As the plan became a political football on the British art scene, Mesens, who assumed he would be in on the ground floor of such an enterprise, began to find his position eroding, partly because he tried to force others in the art world to take sides either for or against Peggy's venture and therefore weakened his own base. Penrose was a key figure here, as he had offered to lend his significant collection of Picassos for the fall show of the museum – a crucial element – and yet was someone whom Mesens believed to be an ally, more sympathetic to his own plans than Peggy's. Mesens, who after all had had a fling with Peggy and may have nurtured some personal resentments, tried to sow dissent about her participation, referring to her in letters to Penrose over the summer as 'la Guggenheim.' Apparently trying to oust her from the project, he called all surrealists to meet at Barcelona, a restaurant on Soho's Beak Street, and delivered a speech, asking why certain artists were to be included in the new museum and not others. Referring indirectly to Peggy, he said, 'I assert that all flirting with the art world is the most crucial outrage against all the perspectives the Surrealist movement has had in view since its advent.' Though the audience included such surrealists as Eileen Agar, Stanley William Hayter, Pailthorpe and Mednikoff, and Gordon Onslow Ford, Mesens's tirade fell on deaf ears, the others not sharing his ambition or his bizarre personal vendetta against Peggy. The museum idea was not vitally threatened by Mesens's machinations, but they made clear the uphill battle Peggy had to fight: if she wanted to back a museum, someone – for whatever reason at all – could easily accuse anyone cooperating with her of being in it for the money. That

Peggy may have indirectly encouraged such an impression by sleeping with the accuser was also painfully typical; not for the last time, she found herself negotiating a rather difficult minefield of combined personal and professional lives.

Meanwhile, Peggy and Herbert Read – 'Papa,' as she called him – were getting acquainted. Evidently finding him not seducible (though he was only five years older), she worried about the form her relationship with him would take, eventually settling, as her nickname makes clear, on a daughterly role. 'He treated me the way Disraeli treated Queen Victoria,' Peggy wrote later, adding, 'I suppose I was rather in love with him, spiritually.' She bragged to Emily and Djuna that she withheld from him details of her personal life – which, given her involvement with certain artists key to the contemporary scene, perhaps was not always wise. While Peggy was able to see the situation humorously, the relationship was an uneasy one and would remain so.

With plans for the museum in place, Peggy set off for France in August in her new Talbot, with Sindbad in tow; Pegeen was already with Laurence and Kay. In Paris, Peggy sent Sindbad off on the train to Megève to join the Vails and then looked up her recent friend Petra (Nellie) van Doesburg, who had a house in the Parisian suburb of Meudon. Nellie was the widow of Theo van Doesburg, the versatile Dutch abstractionist and the editor, with Piet Mondrian, of the art magazine *De Stijl*; Peggy extravagantly but not entirely inaccurately called him 'a sort of twentieth-century da Vinci.' Nellie's passion was the continued championing of her husband's work, an impulse Peggy could understand. Nellie, Peggy's age, was an attractive, compact redhead who impressed Peggy with her dedication to abstract and surrealist art and her vitality. Stressing, apparently, the fact that Nellie was still interested in liaisons with men, Peggy wrote Emily that her new friend was 'very gay & alive & her life goes on, very full & *active* in every sense of the word.' Nellie and Peggy planned a trip to Peggy's old stamping ground, the Midi, hoping to visit the artist Gordon Onslow Ford in Chemillieu in the Ain near the Swiss border, where he was entertaining a group of surrealists including Roberto Matta Echaurren (known as Matta), Breton, and, coincidentally, Tanguy.

Peggy and Nellie never got to Onslow Ford's, proceeding instead straight to Laurence and Kay's at Megève, where they spent a week. They were later staying with a friend of Nellie's in Grasse when they heard news of the outbreak of war. Peggy came completely undone, though their host kept declaring that the war would be over in a few weeks. She wired England repeatedly to have her collection sent down to Petersfield in case of bombings, and she got in touch with Laurence immediately. He told Peggy that he would decide what the family should do, but in the interim that she was not to leave France and definitely not to return to England, a move that tempted her.

Of course, the plan for a museum was shelved. Read wrote to the sculptor Ben Nicholson, with a distinct note of relief, that plans were off, somewhat unfairly blaming Peggy: 'Never in business matters rely on a single patron particularly if that patron is a woman and an American.' In the face of such outright sexism, Peggy felt powerless, and in the end she paid him 2,500 pounds, half of his five-year salary, making it somewhat unclear why he felt so badly used. Their relationship was suspended, though she would renew contact after the war.

Yet Peggy was geared to move ahead with some form of art-related plan, and at first the war seems not to have fazed her; she began planning an artists' colony to be located somewhere in the French countryside, writing to Emily, somewhat dramatically, that she hoped 'to try to save a vestige of art & humanity,' and adding, 'There is little enough left.' Her object was still to enjoy some prominent role in the art world, however she could. Her ambition, now discovered, would not be thwarted, and she was frustrated by the interruption of her trajectory. She cast about for other ideas. Her British friend Phyllis Jones had retired to the countryside to care for her senile mother and was supporting herself by farming; Peggy began to form plans to 'go in for agriculture,' as she confided to Emily. She and Nellie visited the painter Albert Gleizes and his wife on their farm at Saint-Rémy in Provence, where Gleizes had a plan to grow enough crops to help provide food for the French during wartime; Peggy knew it was impractical, but the idea of an artists' colony dedicated to agriculture appealed to her. For one thing, she liked communal living. Ever since the Hayford Hall days, she had enjoyed living among other adults, particularly friends who were artists or writers. Functioning as a nuclear family (a way of living that Garman had imposed on her) was thoroughly distasteful to her. Living with artists and seeing to their livelihoods was an ideal situation for her, she thought. Throughout the fall of 1939 she and a real estate agent crisscrossed France looking at chateaux, but Peggy could find nothing suitable. Meanwhile Nellie, reporting from Paris, said she had found that the only artists who were interested in the idea of a colony were not very good – certainly none of the artists on Herbert Read's list.

Djuna, in London, was watching these doings with grim amusement. She had reached a crisis: unable to write, she was dangerously alcoholic, and she seemed to have no place among her friends. She did not seem to have the resources to make a life for herself alone. Peggy continued to make plans to send her to Emily in Arizona – absurd on the face of it, for what would Djuna do on a ranch? – and in the meantime tried to get Djuna to stop drinking.

Peggy was still supporting Djuna, but she was also taking a hard line with her, saying she would not give her friend money unless she dried out. Djuna, meanwhile, reached new heights of sarcasm and bitterness over Peggy's plans. She recounted to Emily how she sent Phyllis into hysterics by saying of Peggy, 'Can't you see Ma Guggenheim on a board like a weatherbeaten moose?' She especially made fun of the plans for musical evenings at the museum, saying pithily, 'Can't you see me standing backed up by a zither reciting pages of *Nightwood*?' About the artists' colony she was completely dismissive, pointing out, with some accuracy, that it was doubtful that artistic people would get along well enough to live communally; Peggy had asked her if she wanted to join, which sent Djuna into howls of derision.

These encounters presaged more serious fault lines in their friendship. At one point Djuna told Emily that she had been furious for a week about Peggy and the art museum, but then wondered why she expended so much energy being angry at her friend. She showed some insight, writing that she now understood why 'the thought of P. *living* in a museum' was so intolerable: 'makes a "pensioner" (me) feel in the way.' Being in Peggy's debt was never easy for Djuna, and it was especially difficult when she was in such desperate straits and saw Peggy hatching grand schemes while the rest of the world was gearing up for war.

But Djuna was really quite unhinged at the time, and her jeering at Peggy gave way to paranoia. Peggy had sent Giorgio Joyce's wife, Helen (surely a poor choice, given Helen's instability at the time), to see Djuna in Paris and take her in hand, and Djuna got the idea that both Helen and Peggy shared a 'little Hitler' complex and took pleasure in ordering her about. Peggy was quite crazy, Djuna concluded. '[S]he is mad,' she wrote feverishly to Emily in November. '[S]he has gone the way of her forebears, who would be in asylums if they had not so much money.'

All this bullying, of course, was quite a lot for Peggy to bear. Emily, too, was writing her angry letters. She had asked for money herself and felt Peggy had not given it in the right spirit. Meanwhile, Peggy was still rereading Proust, and every time she wrote Djuna she commented on how much his work reminded her of *Nightwood*. It was all she could do to get Djuna on a steamer to America in November, arranging her fare on the Washington and seeing her off at the station on a train to the coast; even then, a horrible scene took place. Peggy told Emily that Djuna had been in a state of 'drunken neurotic collapse' and that she was willing to pay all fares and expenses if Djuna could get to Emily in Arizona. In the meantime, she wrote, perhaps it was best if Djuna's family took up the slack and put Djuna in a home for a 'drunkard's cure.'

It must have seemed to Peggy that her friendship with Djuna – one of her constant props – was one of the first casualties of the war and that her emotional landscape had changed seemingly overnight. Belief in Djuna's talent and her long-term commitment to supporting it had been no less than a defining aspect of Peggy's life, and now Djuna's very existence appeared to be in doubt. Emily – though they were still writing letters, albeit much less frequently – seemed to have fallen off the face of the earth. Peggy had a new friend, to be sure, but Nellie van Doesburg was self-possessed and independent, hardly a soulmate. Peggy's future seemed cloudy as well, especially as the colony idea fell through. She was dependent on Laurence for guidance under the shadow of war; though his own marriage was in trouble because of Kay's recent infidelity, he took up the role of paterfamilias with ease. Peggy may have seemed indifferent to the rumbles of a real, not phony, war, but she had been frightened, for one thing, by Sindbad's coming vulnerability to a draft, and surely she had some inkling of her own vulnerability as a Jew. Events had caught up with her, and she saw the inevitability of conflict. Indeed, she saw a future that she had never envisioned – her eventual return to the States. She hoped to put it off as long as she could.

11

On the Run

After a fruitless autumn looking at chateaux, Peggy came to realize that the artists' colony was not going to come to pass. She spent Christmas 1939 in Megève with the children and Laurence and Kay, then settled for the summer in an apartment on the Ile Saint-Louis borrowed from the American artist Kay Sage. (Peggy claimed credit for introducing Sage to the recently divorced Tanguy, saying she had brought them together so that the wealthy Sage could help Tanguy out by buying some paintings: Tanguy had subsequently followed Sage to America – coincidentally, traveling on the same boat as Djuna in November – where Tanguy and Sage would eventually marry.) The apartment, a penthouse on the seventh floor, was entered by way of a terrace; it was a studio with three exposures, a silver-papered bedroom, a dressing room, and an elegant bathroom, and Peggy loved to watch the Seine glinting in reflection on the ceiling of her bedroom.

The so-called phony war was on. France and England had declared war on Germany in September, and the invasion of France by Germany seemed imminent. Nonetheless, Peggy, at loose ends in the United Kingdom without plans for a museum or artists' colony, gravitated to France, where perhaps she had closer friends. She was not alone in feeling a distinct air of unreality among the French – as if they expected Germany to stay at bay, even if events indicated otherwise. And she very much had something to occupy her: she passed her time buying pictures. She had started to collect in what seemed to be a somewhat haphazard fashion, usually buying pieces done by artists she had shown at Guggenheim Jeune whose exhibits had not sold well, but along the way she had picked up some significant artwork. Her first purchase was, of course, the risqué drawing by Cocteau on bed sheets that she had bought simply to hurry the exhibit through customs. Perhaps her most serious acquisition to date, according to the foremost scholar regarding

Peggy's early career, was Jean Arp's bronze sculpture *Shell and Head* (1933), which she bought for $3,000.

Peggy's next acquisition was a Kandinsky; she wanted an early one, but all she could afford was the 1938 *Dominant Curve*; she would later manage to acquire some earlier works, paying, in fact, an impressive $2,000 for *Landscape with a Red Spot* (1913). In the summer 1938 painting and sculpture show at Guggenheim Jeune that was nearly shut down by customs, Peggy was drawn to a large sculpture by Henry Moore, but she thought that it was far too large to be practicable for her to own. Months afterward, Moore brought in two small pieces for her to look at, a leaden figure and a bronze; she took the bronze *Reclining Figure* (1938), according to her accounts, for $150. She bought Tanguys freely, perhaps because her Tanguy exhibit was so successful that she had no doubt that his works were good investments; she paid $250 each for *Le Soleil dans son écrin* (1937) and *Palais promontoire* (1930 or 1931), and an unknown sum for *Toilette de l'air* (1937). Tanguy of course also gave her the earrings he had made for her; the July 18, 1938, *Portrait of P.G.*; and the Dunhill lighter he had engraved with a phallus.

These prewar acquisitions of Peggy's constitute the beginnings of one of the twentieth century's great art collections. Although Marcel Duchamp had been a keen adviser to Peggy when she began her gallery, there is no evidence that she consulted him on any of these purchases. In the early days of her collecting, in fact, Peggy was guided not by a well-known artist (Duchamp) or an illustrious critic (Read), but by Howard Putzel, a strange, shadowy figure who first entered her life just as Guggenheim Jeune opened, when he sent her a note from California wishing her luck with her new enterprise. They became colleagues when he lent her some surrealist canvases for her July Tanguy show, and they probably first met in the summer of 1938 at Mary Reynolds's Paris home, just after Putzel closed his own Los Angeles gallery and headed for Paris. By 1939 they had formed a serious connection.

Howard Putzel, in fact, was so elusive that no known photograph of him exists. Born in Spring Lake, New Jersey, in 1898, he was just Peggy's age. His father, an importer, died when Putzel was sixteen, after uprooting the family and taking them to San Francisco. There Putzel tried to carry on his father's work but found himself increasingly drawn to the world of art, soon serving as the art and music critic for a local newspaper. He opened a small gallery and, in 1935, met Duchamp, who steered him to his first purchase, a Kandinsky watercolor. By 1936 Putzel had moved his gallery to Los Angeles, where he was showing Max Ernst and other important surrealists. Besides Duchamp, he cultivated friendships with Walter Arensberg and his wife, and with film figures such as Edward G. Robinson, who also collected. Putzel had an especially sharp eye, it seemed, and a knack for seeking out the right people, both collectors and artists. Physically, he was not prepossessing – he was fair and fat. He suffered from epileptic seizures and heart problems. He drank too much, and seems to have been homosexual, though not openly so. He was also a self-taught genius who was said to be able to recite *Finnegans Wake* from memory.

On a trip to France in the winter of 1938 and 1939, Putzel took Peggy to the studio of Max Ernst, the German painter who had been involved with surrealism since its postwar origins in dada on the Zurich scene. Peggy had heard of the success of a recent Ernst show in England, and her colleague Roland Penrose had quite a collection of Ernsts, which piqued her interest. Ernst's romantic reputation preceded him; he had married first a German and then a French wife, and was much in demand among the ladies, who were drawn by his shock of whitish blond hair, penetrating blue eyes, a profile that can only be described as aquiline, and his intense manner. Peggy was no exception, but present also at the meeting was the English surrealist painter (and famed beauty) Leonora Carrington, who had been living with Ernst for some time.

Peggy very much wanted to buy an Ernst and was about to purchase one if not several when Putzel drew her aside and said to wait. Mysteriously and unaccountably, he told her that the Ernsts were 'too cheap.' Instead, she bought Carrington's *The Horses of Lord Candlestick* for $80.

Peggy did not know what to make of Putzel at first but came to trust him as she understood him better. As she writes in her autobiography, 'At first [Putzel] was nearly incoherent, but little by little I realized that great passion for modern art that lurked behind his incomprehensible conversation and behavior. He immediately took me in hand and escorted me, or rather forced me to accompany him, to all the artists' studios in Paris. He also made me buy innumerable things that I didn't want; but he found me many paintings I did need, and that balanced our account.'

As an adviser, Putzel clashed often with Nellie van Doesburg, Peggy's other guide at this time. Nellie introduced her to Robert and Sonia Delaunay, as well as the sculptor Antoine Pevsner, who conceived quite a crush on Peggy – he was too meek for her tastes – and Jean Hélion, whose huge canvas *The Chimney Sweep* (1936) Peggy bought for $225. Nellie was partial to art influenced by her husband's work, including the work of Pevsner, but she did not confine her suggestions to these.

Peggy's Ile Saint-Louis apartment had room only for her smaller pieces, and she sent the rest of her purchases to storage. Her art was, of course, a concern as the Germans threatened. Peggy was worried about her collection, but otherwise she did not much notice the encroaching war. Her seeming apathy occasioned one big fight with Mary Reynolds, who was, after Peggy Waldman, her oldest friend. Mary, who would be active in the Resistance (her code name was 'Gentle Mary'), was already involved with the nascent French underground. One night she accused Peggy of keeping her head in the sand about the imminent war and its human toll. Worse, she said, Peggy was so indifferent that she would probably mow down fleeing refugees with a van containing her collection if that was what it took for her to get the artworks to safety. Bested in the argument, Peggy left Mary's house crying on the shoulder of a friend. She resolved to concentrate her energies instead of being so scattered and to look actively for ways to help French and European artists.

It seemed that everyone in the art world learned about Peggy's stated ambition – to buy a picture a day – almost overnight. 'Everyone knew I was in the market for anything I could lay my hands on,' Peggy later wrote. 'They chased after me, and came to my house with pictures. They even brought them to me in bed, in the morning before I was up.' No doubt she relished the attention.

But she remained a scrupulous buyer and tightfisted negotiator. She seduced Brancusi over several months, visiting him in his cul-de-sac studio – she was with him when the Germans first bombarded Paris – until all her work went up in smoke when he offered her his bronze *Bird in Space* (1940) for $4,000, a sum she thought outrageous. She forsook him temporarily, in the meantime buying an earlier work, *Maiastra* (1912), his first bird figure, from the sister of the dress designer Paul Poiret. Peggy, whom Brancusi nicknamed 'Pegitza,' had grown quite fond of the sculptor, but set forth with grim determination to renegotiate the terms of the sale of *Bird in Space*. Setting the price in francs rather than dollars, Peggy bought the francs in New York and saved about $1,000, fixing the purchase at $3,000. 'Of everything I own,' Peggy wrote to a friend about the Brancusi bronze, 'I love it the most.'

Sometimes her escapades bordered on the comical. She had found a Dali painting that she got very cheaply, and it was one she liked. She purchased a second, small Dali on favorable terms. But neither was a 'classic' Dali, and so she resolved to buy one of his better-known works. As it turned out, Gala, the artist's redoubtable wife and promoter, was a friend of Mary Reynolds, who arranged a meeting between the two women. Not unexpectedly, sparks flew; Gala told Peggy that she thought Peggy was 'mad' to approach the art world as she did: better to concentrate your attention on one artist, as Gala did, and make him your profession. It was an interesting argument, but Peggy understandably took it as an attack on her way of life. The two women put aside their differences and eventually turned up an acceptable Dali (*The Birth of Liquid Desires*, 1932) from storage in the Dalis' vacant Paris apartment. It was 'sexual enough,' said Peggy, and 'horribly Dali.'

One remark Peggy made in her autobiography would later shock almost everyone who came across it with its incredible, macabre egotism: 'The day Hitler walked into Norway I walked into Léger's studio and bought a wonderful 1919 painting from him for one thousand dollars.' Even the artist, his eye on the sale, was taken aback: 'He never got over the fact that I should be buying paintings on such a day.' Peggy must have been dreaming up this sentence almost since the day she visited Léger's studio. To her it was the essence of surrealism: to buy a picture at the moment a dictator was occupying a nation was an absurd, bizarre happening. It warranted such a sentence. She never considered whether her action might be thought tactless or worse at such a time. In any case, practically speaking, Peggy found no reason for her to adjust her buying habits to accommodate war news. If anything, she wanted to reach as many artists and buy as many artworks as she could as long as prices were so low. As the spring wore on, of course, she could find fewer and fewer artists who had not already fled in advance of Hitler's approach.

That same April day, in a similarly self-absorbed decision, Peggy looked at and chose to rent an apartment on the place Vendôme – in fact, the quarters in which the composer Chopin had died. She hired the Belgian painter and sculptor Georges Vantongerloo to redo the interior, first ordering his workers to strip away the rococo wall decorations. By the time the stripping was completed, however, Peggy realized that finding a safe space for her growing collection was imperative. The cellars of her new building were all reserved as air-raid shelters. She gave up the place Vendôme apartment with regret after only a week or two, sending her landlord 20,000 francs as an indemnity because they had never signed a lease. Léger recommended that she ask for space to store her artworks at the Louvre, and the response to her preliminary request was encouraging. The museum said she could have a small amount of space for storage of her paintings and drawings at an off-site location in the countryside, with no space given over to her sculpture. But at the last minute, according to Peggy, the Louvre deemed her works 'too modern' and 'not worth saving.' Eventually she thought of her old friend Maria Jolas, who had rented a chateau near Vichy to which she could evacuate her bilingual children's school at Neuilly, which Pegeen was attending. Through the intervention of Alex Ponisovsky, Mary Reynolds's brother and an old suitor of Hazel's, Peggy got a message to Maria, who agreed that she could store the collection in the barn at the back of the school, where the teachers were housed.

Meanwhile, Hitler's forces were making their way through the Low Countries and in June would reach Paris. But Peggy could not make up her mind to leave, as if she had fallen prey to the same indecision that plagued John Holms and Samuel Beckett. She had a new friend, a married man named Bill Whidney, and she spent days on end in the spring of 1940 drinking champagne with him on café *terrasses*. She was ashamed of her seeming torpor, especially as friends like Mary Reynolds swung into action to resist the Germans.

Though she seemed indifferent to her own future (or its particular dangers for a Jew), she did hoard gasoline, storing it in tin canisters on her apartment's terrace. On June 11 Peggy and Nellie von Doesburg were sitting outside at the Café de Flore with friends, Breton among them, plotting their route to Megève, where Peggy could be reunited with her children. An adviser told her not to go south under any circumstances; she would meet the Italian army, a potential danger as Megève was very close to the Italian border. She and Nellie – along with two Persian cats that Peggy had inherited from Helen Joyce, whose American family had finally interceded for her and taken her to America – left Paris for Megève on June 12, just two days ahead of the Germans, in Peggy's blue open Talbot, the tins of petrol in the back. By then, she did not even need a permit to travel, as more than a million people were fleeing Paris, and she and Nellie made a nightmarish journey out of the city. The German army, close behind them, were burning some kind of oil that made the air black with soot; when Peggy and Nellie stopped at Fountainebleau for lunch, Nellie's white coat was perfectly black. In Megève, Laurence counseled a wait-and-see approach, and Peggy and Nellie decided to rent a house for the summer on Lake Annecy at Le Veyrier, near Laurence and Kay but far enough to allow for breathing room so that Peggy need not clash with Kay. They would share the house with Jean Arp and his wife, who had fled the Parisian suburb of Meudon.

Sindbad was seventeen and Pegeen fifteen in 1940; the summer would be marked by their developing sexuality. The Kuhns, neighbors on the lake who were in the American movie business, had a son Sindbad's age, Edgar, whom Sindbad knew from his Swiss boarding school, and a daughter a little older, Yvonne. Before long Sindbad was head-over-heels in love with Yvonne, while Edgar Kuhn, as the summer-long drama played itself out, deflowered Pegeen.

A year earlier Djuna had intervened with Peggy on the children's part, telling her that Sindbad needed a more rigorous education than Bedales, his permissive boarding school in Sussex, provided: 'Bedales is a joke, also according to Laurence, as Sindbad thinks of nothing and does nothing but play games.' He did seem completely obsessed by cricket, which is perhaps not unusual in a boy of sixteen. Pegeen, at a school for expatriates outside Paris, showed artistic talent, Djuna thought, even though she painted in a simple, naive style. 'Pegeen if she does want to become an artist, and she says she does, and certainly has the talent, then she should at least study the human body, not in a silly school where they teach balls, but to at least look at what she sees and draw from that.' It seems obvious in retrospect that Pegeen decided to become an artist to catch her mother's attention and perhaps even to gain her love, and that Peggy erred in not providing her with adequate instruction. For his part, Sindbad seems to have taken as naturally to loafing as Laurence, his father, did.

'The children are nearly grown up,' Peggy had written Emily in the spring of 1939. 'Pegeen is getting gaga listening to the radio and going to cinemas. We fight about it perpetually.' At the lake, Sindbad and Pegeen disappeared for hours with the Kuhn children, returning only for meals; Peggy reasoned that this absence was because she did not have a tennis court or a lakefront swimming area as the Kuhns did. It seemed to Jacqueline Ventadour, a Franco-American friend of Pegeen's from school and a visitor for the summer, that the atmosphere was very 'loose.' Peggy was openly taking lovers – a relative of the Kuhns, briefly, and the local hairdresser. At Megève the social situation was equally chaotic. Kay Boyle had chosen her next mate, Baron Joseph Franckenstein (an educated and cosmopolitan Austrian who aspired to be a political reporter) and was living openly with him, which drove Laurence increasingly to drink. (Peggy, unable to resist taking a potshot at Kay, briefly bedded the baron herself.) Sindbad was in an especially tough bind, as Jacqueline saw it, because Laurence made a habit of disparaging anyone else who actually tried to achieve anything – including his son – and Peggy was indifferent to anyone, again including Sindbad, who did not have some kind of inner drive. 'I admired Peggy tremendously,' says Jacqueline, to whom the Vails and Peggy were a kind of surrogate family (Jacqueline got herself expelled from school with dismaying regularity), 'but she was a very destructive person, especially as a mother.'

The next two years would continue to be difficult for both Sindbad and Pegeen. Sometimes it seemed as if Peggy and Laurence simply lost track of them, though they tried hard at being good parents at other times. At Megève, Kay and Laurence encouraged the children in putting out several issues of 'Vail's Modern Almanac,' clever, colorful, handmade creations that showcased art and poetry by Peggy's and Kay's children and their friends. For the November 1940 edition Peggy contributed an abstract cover; Pegeen contributed a watercolor of her mother for another issue, emphasizing her large nose, bright blue eyes, and dark hair. Peggy was experimenting with hair color, in part to keep her connection with the hairdresser alive, but also to settle on a look. 'I am very young in character still,' she wrote Emily Coleman in March, 'and have dyed my hair chestnut.' Finally, in part at the insistence of Pegeen, who did not like all the changes, she settled on a raven black, which made her features very sharp and was not generally as flattering as her previous naturally brown, though graying, hair.

Still, her concerns centered around her collection. Drawing up endless lists of the works she owned, Peggy could measure just what her months of frantic buying had netted her: 'a Kandinsky, several Klees and Picabias, a Cubist Braque, a Gris, a Léger, a Gleizes, a Marcoussis, a Delaunay, two Futurists, a Severini, a Balla, a Van Doesburg, and a "De Stijl" Mondrian.' Of the surrealists, she owned works by Miró, Ernst, de Chirico, Tanguy, Dali, Magritte, and Brauner, plus sculptures by Brancusi, Lipchitz, Laurens, Pevsner, Giacometti, Moore, and Arp. She reckoned that she had spent about $40,000 overall buying artworks.

In the coming months, what unfolded was one of the great odysseys in the history of art – a story of narrow escapes and marvelous ingenuity that often sounds stranger than fiction. Peggy was a Jewish woman living under an anti-Semitic regime, owning a cache of art the Nazis considered 'degenerate,' with a passport from the United States, a country increasingly expected to become an enemy. She had acquired her collection quickly, and many people would have been strongly motivated to abandon it over the next few months. But Peggy held on, feeling that even when it seemed to be mainly a liability that it perhaps represented an essential part of herself.

For the time, it looked to Peggy as if she would be in France indefinitely. Somewhat perversely, however, she was still eager to exhibit her pictures. Part of her thinking was that if the collection had one prestigious showing, her plans to go ahead with a museum after the war would be enhanced, as the collection's reputation would precede her. To set out to show a collection of abstract and surrealist art in war-torn France – just the sort of art Hitler and his regime were condemning – seems almost delusional. Nevertheless, Peggy, not wanting to bother her Paris friend Mary Reynolds, who after all did not approve of her devotion to her collection at such a time, asked her other friend in Paris, Giorgio Joyce, to arrange for the paintings to be sent down from Maria Jolas's school in Neuilly. From there, she arranged for the collection to go to the Musée de Grenoble. The collection languished for several days at the Gare d'Annecy before Peggy learned it was there. But when she did, she and Nellie hastened there to make sure it was well covered with tarpaulins. The director of the nearby Musée de Grenoble, André Farcy, was known to be a supporter of modern art, and Peggy delegated Nellie, who was acquainted with him, to see if he could help. Farcy offered no promises about an exhibit, but allowed Peggy to transport the collection to his museum. He was already suspect to the Vichy regime because of his artistic proclivities, and no less than Marshal Pétain, the Vichy chief of state, was due to pass through Grenoble. So Farcy put Peggy off repeatedly about showing her hold-ings. He hated to see the collection leave the museum, however, so he gave Peggy a room where she could catalogue and photograph the artworks and bring friends and collectors to see them.

Because their summer lease for the house at Lake Annecy was up, Nellie and Peggy moved to Grenoble for the next few months. When the snows came that winter, they were unable to travel. In the meantime, Laurence had decided that they all should leave for America in the spring. The Germans were threatening to occupy the entire country, and the prospect of concen-tration camps could be glimpsed ahead. Peggy was determined to get her collection to America and was even thinking of appealing to the Vichy gov-ernment for help. To add to the turmoil, Peggy and Nellie were fighting like cats and dogs – over nothing in particular. Into this unsatisfactory state of affairs walked an unlikely savior – René Lefèvre Foinet, a specialist in moving art who had handled the shipping of paintings from France to Peggy's exhibits at Guggenheim Jeune in London. Foinet advised Peggy that she could wrap up the paintings and send them off with some linens and furniture as household goods. By this time, Peggy and he were sleeping together and enjoying them-selves immensely, so they took a leisurely two months to inventory everything before packing it with assemblages of linens, cookware, lamps, books, and other odds and ends. Though she would not rest easy until her collection reached the States unscathed, Peggy was able to breathe a sigh of relief.

With her art on its way, Peggy turned her attention to friends in trouble. By this time she had become deeply involved in helping refugees leave Europe for the States. Kay Sage, now married to Tanguy, wired her in Grenoble from America asking her to 'help rescue and finance' the passage of five Europeans out of France: Breton and his wife and daughter, Max Ernst, and a certain Dr. Mabille, the surrealists' house doctor. Peggy agreed to finance the Bretons and Ernst, though (strangely) she refused to help the doctor; perhaps she knew that her resources – not her financial resources, exactly, but her influence with the right people – would have to be hus-banded closely. At the same time, she was working to rescue the artist Victor Brauner, a Jew, who was hiding in the mountains disguised as a shepherd, and she went down to Marseilles to meet with the Emergency Rescue Committee to ensure that her charges could be taken care of.

Marseilles was then the de facto capital of refugee work, a hub for refugees and those who sought to help them; it was home to the Emergency Rescue Committee, which certain concerned U.S. cultural officials had set up when Americans found that France's June 1940 armistice with Germany provided for the 'surrender on demand' of German refugees. The committee was run by the extraordinary Varian Fry, trained as a classicist at Harvard, who through many complicated circumstances had acquired a mysterious list of two hundred European refugees needing to be rescued from Europe. The U.S. government, or whoever financed him, gave him limited funds to accomplish this mission, and issued him virtual carte blanche to use whatever means he saw fit to effect it. The Emergency Rescue Committee was a renegade and romantic outfit – one participant called it 'that amazing Scarlet Pimpernel operation.' Fry, joined by an assistant, Daniel Benedite, and an American woman who would later write a book about her experience, Mary Jayne Gold, was for a time headquartered in a mansion outside of Marseilles known as Air-Bel. Here André Breton held court over the staff of the committee and visiting refugees on their way, with the committee's help, to North Africa, Spain, or Portugal, from whence they could gain passage to the United States. Guests included René Char, Marcel Duchamp, André Masson, and Tristan Tzara, among others. Surrealist games abounded, guests painted on the extensive grounds, and at one dinner Breton decorated the table with a bottle of praying mantises in lieu of flowers. Peggy visited twice, taking Mary Jayne Gold's room during Gold's temporary absence. Gold, an heiress, is known to have provided funds to secure false passports and otherwise assure the refugees' passage; it seems probable that Peggy did the same, as she said of her first visit there, 'I went back to Grenoble after giving Breton and Fry some money.' She gave the committee 500,000 francs in December 1940, and no doubt provided more funds secretly.

On her second visit to Marseilles, Victor Brauner, who came down from the mountains in order to leave the country by way of Fry's committee, met Peggy at the station and took her back to Air-Bel, where Max Ernst was currently in residence. Ernst had spent time in two internment camps, and his companion, Leonora Carrington, evidently mentally ill, had made over their house to a Frenchman to save it from the Germans and decamped for Portugal. Peggy had bought three Ernsts while Max was in the camps, and she was eager to buy more. Moreover, she found Ernst 'very romantic wrapped in a black cape.'

Born in 1891, Max Ernst had grown up in the small German town of Brühl, the son of a teacher of the deaf and dumb who was also an amateur painter. Discouraged from pursuing a career in art, he had attended the

University of Bonn. He continued to paint, however, and became immersed in the dada movement around 1921, turning to collages and the written word to express dadaist sentiments. The French surrealist Paul Eluard was so impressed by his work that he and his then wife, Gala (later Dali's wife), traveled to Cologne to meet him. Shortly after, Ernst left his wife and son to live with the Eluards in a ménage à trois. He became tremendously excited about the idea of psychic automatism and the visual arts, a counterpart to automatic writing, in which the artist used methods like Freudian free association and dreams to access the unconscious without the restraints of the conscious mind. Ernst developed a technique called *frottage*, a kind of automatic drawing that involved rubbing paper over raised or textured surfaces and then using the rubbings to evoke unconscious associations, which was to dominate his artwork for several years. During the 1930s Ernst became quite well known; the dealer Julien Levy held an Ernst show at his New York gallery, and the painter exhibited widely in the surrealist expositions of the decade. Living with Carrington in the French countryside, Ernst had also tried his hand at sculpture, decorating their house with bas-reliefs and concrete constructions.

Much of Ernst's works had a dreamy – or nightmarish – quality. Birds became his totems, in the Jungian sense, and he christened himself 'Loplop, King of the Birds.' In the catalogue for the 1938 Paris surrealist exhibition, Ernst was described thus: 'loplop, bird superior, painter, poet, theoretician of Surrealism from the movement's beginning until today.'

Now, however, Ernst was distinctly at loose ends and feared being caught and again interned as an enemy alien. Married twice, Ernst was very attractive to women. When Peggy met him at Air-Bel, his fiftieth birthday was a day away. He brought out all his paintings, and Peggy agreed to buy a good number of them, mostly his older work. Max threw in some collages as well, and she clearly promised him that she would be a steady market for his work. On his birthday, he asked Peggy when, where, and why he would next meet her; she replied, 'Tomorrow at four at the Café de la Paix and you know why.' An intense physical affair followed. He accompanied Peggy to Megève to spend Easter with the children, whom he impressed with his cape and romantic air.

In the meantime, the Guggenheim-Vail ménage were making their own plans to flee Vichy France, ever more pressured and under surveillance by the Germans. Kay Boyle had reserved ten seats on a Pan Am Clipper flight from Lisbon, the only European point from which transatlantic flights were still being made. There were seats for all the children and for Pegeen's friend Jacqueline Ventadour, whose mother agitated for her to be included and paid her way. Kay's new love, Franckenstein, also had a seat, but Laurence drew the line at traveling with him, and Kay eventually found passage for him on a ship. That left one seat, for which Max Ernst was the obvious candidate. First, however, all kinds of arrangements had to be made in Marseilles. Max's visa to America had expired and he needed an emergency exit visa because of his alien status, Laurence needed a traveling permit, and Peggy, in order to prolong her visa, had filled in a false date in her documents, which had to be corrected.

It was a dangerous time; the Vichy police were rounding up Jews from all the hotels in Marseilles, and Max warned Peggy to admit only to being an American, not a Jew. One morning, with the breakfast dishes still on the table, she received a visit from a plainclothes policeman, who did indeed ask her whether she was Jewish. She replied that she was an American. When he asked whether her name was not a Jewish one, she replied that her grand-father was Swiss. He rifled through her rooms looking for concealed Jews and finally ordered Peggy to come to the police station with him. Fearing that she would simply disappear and that neither Laurence nor Max would be able to find her, Peggy followed the policeman out of the room, where he met in the hall with his supervisor, who unaccountably told the officer to leave her alone. (Peggy believed his mercy was based on the current popularity of Americans with the French, the Americans having recently delivered a shipload of food.) When Peggy complained to the hotel manager about this intrusion, the woman answered, 'Oh, that is nothing, madam. They were just rounding up the Jews.'

Max managed to get out of Marseilles and flee to Lisbon, his canvases rolled up and tucked into his suitcase. It took Peggy three weeks to free up the money for the fares of those traveling on the Clipper. In the meantime she ran across her old friend Jacques Schiffrin, who long ago had given her Russian lessons, and managed to convince Fry's Emergency Rescue Committee to secure him passage on a boat. She tried up until the last minute to get Victor Brauner safely out of the country as well. She had to leave Brauner behind, however, and also Nellie van Doesburg, whom she had tried in vain to help. She simply hoped they would be able to follow her. Laurence and the children had all got off to Lisbon by train, and Peggy stayed behind waiting for Jacqueline Ventadour, and the two of them then traveled down to Lisbon by train together.

The whole party were reunited in the Portuguese capital, but inevitable tensions arose among them. Furthermore, Max told Peggy on her arrival that he had just found Leonora Carrington – in Lisbon – and that she was about to marry a Mexican to ensure passage out of Europe. Max was obsessed with her, and Leonora wavered between going back to him or marrying her Mexican suitor, the whole matter leaving Peggy horribly depressed. All of them were either physically or emotionally drained: Kay was in a hospital, purportedly with a sinus infection, but had Laurence at her beck and call delivering telegrams to her lover on shipboard, which the other adults found ridiculous. None of them had any idea how long they would have to wait in Portugal for passage out; after a couple of weeks they left for Monte Estoril, on the seashore, where the children were happier.

Finally their departure date was fixed, and they all piled onto the Pan Am Clipper. When they inspected their very novel arrangements, Peggy found the Clipper was short one bed, and it looked as if Max was out of luck. But then Peggy took Pegeen into her bed so that Max could have one of his own, which provoked a quarrel between Pegeen and Max. Kay and Peggy, of course, barely spoke to each other. All the children were sick into air bags.

The Clipper experience was a novel one; the plane had made its first transatlantic flight in 1939. It provided the utmost in luxury, with dressing rooms and a dining salon. Four-star hotels provided the food, which was served on real china with real silver, served by white-coated stewards. The adults sat in comfortable chairs, drinking whiskey and looking out at the sea. The trip was broken up by a stop in the Azores to refuel and a stop in Bermuda, where British officials examined the passengers and their papers. The entry into the United States was not propitious; Peggy and her little band had been homeless and living in a state of emergency for almost three months, and most of them were emotionally depleted. With the possible exception of Max Ernst (and perhaps Kay Boyle, whose lover awaited her), nobody wanted very much to be in the States.

12

The States

Peggy had bought a huge sombrero during the brief stop in the Azores, nearly four times the size of a dinner plate, and wore it when she and her party got off the Clipper at the LaGuardia Marine Air Terminal on July 14, 1941: the press thronged to meet her and Max, alerted to the news of the arrival of the well-known German painter and a Guggenheim. There too was Max's twenty-one-year-old son from his first marriage, Jimmy, and the British painter Gordon Onslow Ford and his wife, Jacqueline. Jimmy Ernst described his first look at Peggy:

> One of the women, I guessed her to be about forty, came toward me, her body and walk suggesting considerable hesitation. Her legs seemed absurdly thin even for her fragile, angular figure. Her face was strangely childlike, but it expressed something I imagined the ugly duckling must have felt the first time it saw its reflection in the water. All of the features of that face seemed to be intent on wanting to draw attention away from a naturally bulbous nose. The anxiety-ridden eyes were warm and almost pleading, and the bony hands, at a loss where to go, moved like ends of broken windmills around an undisciplined coiffure of dark hair. There was something about her that wanted me to reach out to her, even before she spoke.

Working in the new Museum of Modern Art's film department, Jimmy had heard rumblings about Peggy supporting his father's flight to the United States, but he had half expected Max to show up with Leonora Carrington. There was trouble over Max's German passport, and, after a night at the Belmont Plaza chaperoned by a detective, Max was sent to Ellis Island for a few days until the matter was straightened out (with letters that Jimmy Ernst brought from Alfred Barr and MoMA supporters, backed up by Peggy's appearance with a representative from ASARCO, the Guggenheim metal-refining business). The next night Peggy and the rest of her clan from the Clipper moved into the Great Northern, an apartment-hotel on West 57th Street, where a party awaited them. According to Jimmy, the guests included Tanguy and his wife, the American artist Kay Sage; Howard Putzel; the Chilean-born artist Matta; the critic Nicolas Calas; and Bernard Reis, an accountant and lawyer well known to many artists, with his wife, Becky.

Howard Putzel told Peggy that her art collection had arrived safely but would take time to clear customs. She was, of course, relieved, but also concerned that she might have to pay duty on some works – the abstract sculpture, most likely – that the authorities deemed not to be art, in a rehash of the controversy that had attended Guggenheim Jeune's importation of sculpture to England in 1938. She anticipated a lot of paperwork and immediately hired Jimmy to be her secretary, at a salary of $25 a week.

Peggy also began looking for what she still called her museum. Finding nothing in New York that met her standards, she decided to go to the West Coast to visit her sister Hazel in Santa Monica and scout a location. Hazel, herself an amateur painter, had, after the tragic deaths of her and Milton Waldman's children, married again to Denys King-Farlow, an Eton friend of George Orwell and later an oil executive. She had borne him two children, John (in 1932) and Barbara (in 1934), later awarded in custody to their father on the couple's divorce. She had recently remarried, to Charles 'Chick' McKinley, an Army Air Corps pilot some years her junior.

Pegeen, Max, Jimmy, and Peggy flew west in late July, while Sindbad stayed behind to visit Laurence, then living in a beach community in Rhode Island. The flight itself, over mosaics of midwestern farmland and the dramatic mountain ranges of the West, made a tremendous visual impression on Peggy: 'The beauties of America are unparalleled in the world and best seen from above,' she wrote Djuna, who was back in New York. 'The colors and patterns of the earth are better than any picture abstract or surrealist.'

When the party arrived in California, Hazel sent word that she had just had a nose job and asked them to delay their visit for several days. Peggy immediately set out to see the competition. At the San Francisco Museum of Art (later the Museum of Modern Art), she and Max were turned away when they asked to see the director, Grace McCann Morley. The museum was exhibiting primitive and pre-Columbian art from the gallery of the New York dealer Sidney Janis, who was there attending to the show; he greeted Peggy and when he heard of the contretemps, called Morley and told her that Peggy was there with Max Ernst. Morley took them out for a big fish dinner;

Peggy warmed to her and asked if the museum would want to borrow from her own collection once it was set up.

Throughout the trip, Peggy clashed continually with Pegeen, then fifteen, mostly in rather typical parent-adolescent fashion. But Jimmy Ernst was mystified by how constant and bitter the fights were, later recalling that the new family preoccupied him with 'a staccato of twists, eccentricities, and combat in the bewildering relationships between Max and Peggy, Peggy and her daughter Pegeen, Pegeen and Max, and finally all three of them with me as a kind of sounding board, battering ram, and totally inept arbitrator.' These conflicts had an edge: Max Ernst had an eye for female beauty, and Pegeen was indeed very beautiful. Pegeen fought with Max, but it is likely that there was an undercurrent of sexual interest between them. Max was soon to buy a thronelike chair for the family's eventual home and allowed no one else to sit in it but Pegeen. In fact, the West Coast trip marked a turn from Pegeen's initial fierce resistance to Max to a kind of flirtation – which seemed to please Peggy, who remarked delightedly in letters to friends about Pegeen kissing her putative stepfather good night without being prodded.

Another source of conflict was Kay Boyle, who had relocated to Nyack, a New York suburb, with her lover Joseph Franckenstein. Max detested Kay because he believed she had urged Leonora Carrington to marry her Mexican suitor, and Peggy, of course, had always objected to Laurence's second wife, but Pegeen had spent two years in Kay's household just before the war and she felt bereft without her stepmother. Kay Boyle was a kind of ur-mother, with her thriving tribe of blond children, and Pegeen, who often felt motherless, inevitably responded to her. Pegeen's letters to Kay were wistful, always addressed to 'Darling Kay,' often adding a postscript: 'I love you always very much.' Kay's decision to leave Laurence for her new lover of course made Pegeen feel even more desolate. 'Oh Kay, do come back, do,' her letters begged.

Pegeen's mood improved somewhat after they flew to Los Angeles and settled into Hazel's house in Santa Monica; she was starstruck, and the proximity of film-world celebrities preoccupied her. On Pegeen's sixteenth birthday, Max and Peggy took her to Ciro's, a restaurant said to be frequented by stars and their entourages, but the girl was disappointed not to see any. On another occasion Hazel gave her an invitation to a charity ball at which a fair number of actors were likely to be present. Pegeen outfitted herself in a simple white gown and a white rabbit stole she bought in Beverly Hills expressly for the occasion and attended the ball alone. What a beautiful sight she was, thought Peggy, as her daughter bravely set forth. Peggy would briefly entertain Pegeen's desire to go to acting school, but their hopes never panned out. For Pegeen, an acting future remained elusive.

In southern California, Peggy and Max also visited the collector Walter Arensberg's Hollywood home, a Victorian house filled with both modernist and pre-Columbian art. Peggy enumerated Arensberg's holdings in her memoirs, concluding, 'His Cubist collection made me very jealous' – Peggy had few cubist works – 'but his later things are not nearly up to mine,' adding, 'In fact where he left off, I began.' Peggy was delighted to be able to report to Djuna Barnes that she spotted *Nightwood* on Arensberg's bedside table.

While her sister was there, Hazel threw a big party for Peggy's birthday, inviting, among others, the American artist George Biddle – known for his antipathy to modern art – and the director of the Wadsworth Atheneum, Chick Austin, who was visiting friends on the West Coast. One couple brought their houseguest, the Japanese-American sculptor Isamu Noguchi; Hazel objected to his presence, arguing that the Japanese were our wartime enemies, and denied them entrance, later telling the collector Judith Malina, 'We were shooting Japs at the time.' At the party, Max and Man Ray had a 'happy reunion,' according to Man Ray's biographer; they had not seen each other since war broke out.

Peggy and Max borrowed her brother-in-law's car to explore the area and look at possible museum sites. Peggy's goal was still to find a place where she could live that could also house a museum; this particular arrangement, odd and unprecedented though it was, seems to have become something of an *idée fixe* with her. While they saw several mansions in various stages of ruin, and even made a halfhearted bid on one, an unfinished sixty-room palace in a Malibu canyon, their bid of half the $40,000 asking price was rejected. They enjoyed their stay with Hazel – Max even gave her lessons on how to paint a leaf – but McKinley began to complain about their repeatedly borrowing his car. So Peggy went out and bought her own, a flashy gray Buick sedan with an automatic shift, then quite a luxury; Jimmy gave his father driving lessons so he could get his license, and the travelers cut short their three-week stay and set out for New York. At the time the trip was a considerable undertaking. Though much of Route 66, the new road between San Diego and Chicago, was in place by this time, the rest of the country was for the most part crisscrossed by small roads, many unpaved, and the party followed Route 66 only through the southwestern states, then turned due south to go to New Orleans.

Peggy had not seen Emily Coleman for some time, and she wrote Emily at her Arizona ranch offering to pay Emily's fare to meet her at the Grand Canyon; Emily asked that they come to the ranch instead. A journal entry of Emily's, however, indicates that she received Peggy's invitation with some trepidation. Jake Scarborough, her cowboy husband, 'kept saying Peggy was "mad" and I was not to invite them. "But I'll offend Peggy," I said to him. "I'm longing to see her."' The meeting was not a happy one. To reach the ranch, visitors had to make a perilous descent into a valley. Leaving Max and Jimmy at the hotel, Peggy drove to the ranch, with Pegeen beside her, and the steep drive terrified Peggy. She was ready to cry by the time she reached the ranch – which was a sorry affair, even more isolated than Peggy had imagined and decidedly ramshackle – and roundly scolded Emily for sending them on such a difficult trip. Evidently Emily's conviction that Peggy had let Djuna Barnes down continued to fester, and Peggy, for her part, was dismayed to think of her brilliant friend living such a sordid, remote existence. In a letter thanking Emily, Peggy apologized for being 'disappointed' and said she was sorry she 'could not have enjoyed the ranch in a peaceful calm.' Peggy remarked on how they seemed to have traded places: 'I entered the world when you left it,' she said, referring to Emily's isolation. 'What a pity,' she added.

Max enjoyed the southwestern states very much, finding to his great surprise that, in a kind of reverse déjà vu, he had previously painted many landscapes whose features resembled the red-brick buttes and mesas that characterized the region's dramatic scenery. He developed a lasting interest in all things Native American, from kachina dolls to Hopi dances. Peggy shared his enthusiasm, though both agreed the lack of society would be deadly, and they pressed on. The Buick continued east, the passengers holing up for several days while Pegeen recuperated from tonsillitis in Wichita Falls, Texas – a God-awful town, to Peggy's thinking – before turning south for New Orleans, where they visited Jacqueline Ventadour and her mother, as well as the Gonzaleses, friends of Hazel's. (After Chick McKinley died in the war, Hazel would relocate to that city.) There, Peggy later wrote, they enjoyed some fantastic meals in the French Quarter and 'felt more at home there than anywhere in America.'

Back in New York in September, Peggy continued her search for a museum site in the city, eventually discovering a wonderful house at 440 East 51st Street, off Beekman Place, known as Hale House, a brownstone set on the East River (incorrectly said to mark the spot where Nathan Hale had been hanged). It had a dramatic two-story living room, where Max placed his throne and where Jimmy Ernst had his desk, and a lovely terrace looking out over the river. That fall Peggy brought her collection there and unpacked it, but soon learned that it was against local zoning regulations to open a museum in the neighborhood. Nevertheless, she installed herself in a bedroom facing the river on the third floor, giving Max a studio with another terrace facing the front. Pegeen had enrolled at the Lenox School, a preparatory school attached to Finch Junior College and the alma mater of many of New York's German-Jewish daughters, but she hated it, finding it a 'snob debutante' outfit; she moved out of the dorm and onto the second floor of Hale House, which she had all to herself. Sindbad enrolled at Columbia College and moved into a dorm there, but often hung around the house. 'Our house on the river is heavenly,' Peggy wrote Emily in December.

When she and Max moved in, Peggy threw a housewarming party for fifty, starting a tradition of memorable evenings at Hale House. Charles Henri Ford, her old friend from the Paris days, now the editor of the surrealist organ *View*, got into a fistfight with the art critic Nicolas Calas at that first party (Breton had recently made a move to merge *View* with his idea for an art magazine, *VVV*, and Calas was very much in Breton's camp), and the battle was so bloody – Calas 'bleeding like a raspberry pie,' observed Ford – that Jimmy Ernst dashed in and got paintings by Kandinsky and by his father out of the way.

Peggy's parties were legendary. A friend observed,

[Hale House] seemed like partyland. I suppose because whenever I went there a big rambling party was going on with people draped everywhere, drinking and talking while someone sat in a sort of booth telephoning. The walls around the telephone were all bescribbled with numbers and messages, and this seemed bohemian, as the rest of the place was on the grand side and the living room was dominated by that outsized Alice-in-Wonderland throne of Max Ernst's.

Some guests criticized the limited board their hostess offered, usually consisting of Golden Wedding whiskey and potato chips. But Leonora Carrington, for one, commented, 'Everyone gathered at Peggy's; she was very generous, always having parties.'

Peggy's parties could be counted on to introduce the unexpected: the appearance of the burlesque artist Gypsy Rose Lee, for instance, or the stray baseball player. Peggy was fast becoming friends with Gypsy, who would soon be a near neighbor. The burlesque artist (who for a time called herself 'the Literary Stripper,' and whom the writer Damon Runyon introduced to an intellectual set, where she more than held her own) was at the peak of her career, having just published a mystery called *The G-String Murders* (1941), and was soon to open in the Broadway show *Star and Garter* (1942). Peggy was immediately drawn to Gypsy's defiance of convention, her wit, and her love of a good party. Max, with whom Gypsy enjoyed a harmless flirtation that Peggy seems to have minded not a bit, painted her portrait, which Peggy offered to buy for her own collection if Gypsy did not want it. Thrust into this artistic milieu, Gypsy turned to painting and sculpture herself, and Peggy would include several of the stripper's works in her shows, which handily brought in lots of publicity. Gypsy became a fixture at Peggy's parties, and Peggy at hers, evidently often in high spirits (Peggy wrote Gypsy on April 3, 1943, 'I hope you have forgiven me for the other night').

Daily living at Hale House, however, was another thing entirely. Max was often mysteriously absent. He had been extremely impressed by Sidney Janis's show of primitive art at the San Francisco Museum of Art and had taken to collecting Hopi and Zuni kachina dolls and masks as well as totem poles. A Third Avenue dealer named Carlebach let him buy pieces on credit, and Max would pay him back whenever he sold a painting. This arrangement was a cause of conflict at home, for Max refused to contribute to household expenses, and Peggy, the buyer of most of his paintings, blamed his new avocation for his absences and his financial laxness. (Max even refused to set aside money for his income tax.) Jimmy Ernst, working at Hale House every day, found he had little in common with his father but took to Peggy instinctively, forming a razor-sharp impression of her; he spoke of her 'lack of affectation, whose shyness suggested a painful past. At the same time there were kinetic flashes of brilliance, charm and a warmth that seemed to be in constant doubt of being reciprocated.' He later remarked on her 'need to love someone.' Jimmy very much appealed to Peggy – she called him 'a cute little boy of 21' in a letter to Emily – and she inclined toward mothering him, once writing him a blank check to buy an overcoat.

While Peggy in July had referred to herself as 'a happily unmarried married woman again,' by the winter she was terribly impatient with Max for his refusal to marry her. She had tried several times on their cross-country trip to get him to do so, but Max always talked his way out of it. After Pearl Harbor, she insisted that she had no desire to 'live in sin with an enemy alien,' however reluctant Max was. In order to escape publicity (and, according to Peggy, to avoid blood tests – why is not clear), they went to Washington, D.C., and collected Peggy's cousin Harold Loeb and his wife and married in a civil ceremony in a Virginia suburb just after Christmas 1941. The marriage gave Peggy 'a feeling of safety,' but it did nothing to stop their quarreling. Peggy was especially wounded by Max's remoteness. As with Yves Tanguy, Peggy used her fluent French to talk with her husband, and she noticed that he never addressed her as '*tu*,' for instance. She was insulted that he never painted her; she could see echoes of herself in some of his paintings, but usually in the form of monsters. Always, she feared that he was still in love with Leonora Carrington, now living in the same city.

Max could be, observers said, a cold fish. 'Max Ernst is the easiest and most delightful of companions,' said one, 'but there is no mistaking the inheritance of taciturnity and stern withdrawal on which he can draw when the occasion demands it.' Peggy bore the brunt of his aloofness. Djuna Barnes, increasingly sober and reconciled with Peggy, told her that the only time Max showed any emotion was when he was with Leonora. Peggy agreed. 'Normally he was as cold as a snake.' Their quarrels were fantastic, at times lasting a period of days and filled with deadly silences.

Their most frightening aspect was that Peggy seems once again to have been behaving masochistically, reverting in some ways to her behavior with Laurence, John Holms, and Garman. It was evident that Max had no respect for her or for what she did. She felt that he would have preferred her to be another kind of woman: 'He admitted that he likes vulgar, stupid girls.' The wonder is that Peggy actually expected him to change, to wake up and notice her, take her seriously. It was terribly difficult for her to accept that her new lover was not very attracted to or even interested in her. Max, it seems obvious in retrospect, may have been interested in Peggy at the outset, but her principal attractions for him were a way to make it safely out of Europe, a steady outlet for his work, a means for making some excellent connections, and financial security. Furthermore, he may have feared deportation without a family tie to an American. When their fights began, he had little motivation to try to make the marriage work, and less so as he realized that he had no more trouble attracting female admirers in the United States than in Europe.

Peggy's motivation in behaving as she did to Max was extremely complex. No doubt, now in her forties, she was beginning to feel her age and may have been more anxious about her looks. She had not minded being alone before Max, she had thought, but thinking back on earlier periods without a male relationship gave her pause. 'It's very strange being married again after $4^1/2$ years living alone,' she wrote Emily. 'I can hardly believe it. In spite of my 30 misadventures [the number of men she estimated she had slept with] I was alone.' Perhaps the most important element in Peggy's psychological makeup was fear of abandonment. The three people she loved best had died, and worst of all had died suddenly and unexpectedly – her father on the Titanic, disappearing without a trace; Benita, taken suddenly in childbirth; and John Holms, dying accidentally during a minor operation. She knew she was going to lose Max. Her only hope may have been that she could control the event in some way, make it happen on her own terms, time it in a way that would soften the blow. Thus she would goad Max, for instance, into admitting that he loved vulgar and stupid women. Though to almost anyone else it would seem that Max had rejected her, in one sense it was Peggy who engineered and authored the demise of the relationship. Not long after, she would go so far as virtually to handpick her successor and put her squarely in Max's way. 'It was a horrible marriage,' Jimmy Ernst said; Peggy 'was the victim right from the beginning.'

Much of this was still to come, however. In the winter of 1941 and 1942, Peggy mercifully had something to distract her, some indication that in other areas her life was moving forward. In January she began assembling a cata- logue of her collection, a huge undertaking that would result not only in a complete record of her holdings but a kind of encyclopedia of modern art as well. At the same time she was rounding out her collection, which brought her great pleasure. Marcel Duchamp was still in France, so Max and André Breton were her advisers in this endeavor; she worked also from the list that Herbert Read had drawn up for her in 1940. She bought two Calders, *Mobile* (1941) and 'Silver Bedhead' (1945–1946), spending $475 and $800, respec- tively. ('Silver Bedhead' was a descriptive title, and her payment represented the sculptor's commission on a remarkable silver headboard with movable parts.) Her new friend Alfred Barr convinced her to trade an Ernst for a Malevich, his *Suprematist Composition* (1915). She also bought works by Amédée Ozenfant (who became a good friend), Duchamp, Breton, Henry Moore, Wolfgang Paalen, Matta, and Leonora Carrington, among others, buying from the artists themselves in some cases, in others through such dealers as Karl Nierendorf, Curt Valentin of the Buchholz Gallery, Sidney Janis, or Pierre Matisse. Her biggest investment was in Picassos: she bought his 1911 oil *The Poet* for $4,250 and his 1937 *Young Girls with the Toy Boat* for a dizzying $10,000, the most she had paid for a single piece. Max was going through an extremely fertile period, and Peggy bought many paintings from him, including, most notably, *The Attirement of the Bride* (1940), for $1,500.

She put in long days working on this catalogue. Eventually a hardcover book, it contained a great deal of text, most importantly an essay by Breton covering the whole course of surrealism (Peggy indulged him by having it printed in green ink, his trademark). Breton, indebted to Peggy because she had promised him $200 a month until he figured out what he wanted to do in America, gladly contributed the piece gratis.

She also asked Mondrian for a preface, and she used another piece that Arp had written for her in Europe. She assembled and added manifestoes from other artistic movements of the last thirty years, such as the Futurists' Manifesto and a 'Realistic Manifesto' signed by Naum Gabo and Antoine Pevsner. She assembled brief biographies of the artists along with statements from each about art or about their artistic vision. Enormous quantities of paperwork made their way through Hale House; the project demanded all of the energies of Peggy and Jimmy – and Max, who often put his two cents in. At the last minute Peggy decided the catalogue was too dull. Breton came up with the idea to include photographs of all the artists' eyes with their biographies, requiring, of course, more work (especially because some of the artists were still in Europe) – as did arranging for and assembling photographs of the artworks, much of which they accomplished with the help of Alfred Barr, to whom Peggy gave pride of place in her brief acknowledgments. The resulting 156-page volume she called *Art of This Century* – the title was the contribution of Laurence, then waiting out the war in rural Connecticut but journeying in frequently to the city – and it had a Max Ernst drawing on the cover. Thanks in part to Jimmy's publicity efforts, the book, though it had no commercial publisher and received no reviews, was quite a success, at least in the limited milieu of the New York City art world. One bookstore arranged window displays around it, and Peggy was much gratified by the attention. She must have taken special satisfaction in imagining Hilla Rebay's response to the volume, and what the baroness might have said to Uncle Sol about it.

Around the time the catalogue came out, Peggy struck up a friendship with two people who were to become mainstays of her life for the next thirty years: the lawyer and accountant Bernard Reis and his wife, Becky. Bernard was a native New Yorker. Born in 1895, three years before Peggy, he had earned his law degree from New York University; Becky was from Pennsylvania and had attended the University of Michigan. (They had a daughter, Barbara, close to Sindbad's age.) Since 1925, when the Reises had become fast friends of the sculptor Jacques Lipchitz, Bernard's clients had been almost exclusively artists. Pink-faced and almost always smiling, Bernard was seldom seen without a cigarette smoldering at the end of a long holder. Becky, a small woman, displayed her collection of heavy, oversized ivory, plastic, and wooden bracelets up to her elbows; she used a lorgnette, noted one observer, through which she peered 'with the amused eyes of a tiny owl.' Peggy acquainted her new friends with her museum plans, and Bernard warned her of the particular problems in administering a nonprofit institution; it might be wiser, he told her, to think of adding a for-profit element – like a gallery – that would allow her to deduct expenses associated with maintaining her collection. Slowly, Peggy was coming around to that idea. Her collection was by now quite large, however, and it would be difficult to show it all in a gallery space, especially after reserving room for exhibits of art for sale.

The Reises were known for the parties they gave at their East 68th Street townhouse, which were attended by a cross section of New York's artistic community. They also opened up their summer house in Amagansett to artists. The American David Hare, soon to turn to sculpture from photography, commented, '[A]t that time the Surrealists were looking for somewhere in America to meet and for somebody who would give them free drinks and dinner. It was that simple.' The Reises welcomed such European modernists as Léger, Mondrian, Chagall, and Pavel Tchelitchew (Charles Henri Ford's friend) – wartime émigrés. But the surrealists were much more in evidence: Matta, Kurt Seligmann, Ernst, Masson, Gorky, of course Breton, and the honorary surrealist Duchamp, who had arrived in the United States in February 1942. 'It's as if one transplanted a whole culture from one continent to another,' commented a *Fortune* writer.

At such gatherings, it was Breton's habit to decree rounds of Truth, in which he required participants to answer the frankest of questions – almost always about sex – with the utmost seriousness (casual remarks were not permitted and violators fined). In his usual fashion, Breton approached this game as if it were a laboratory exercise rather than a piece of fun, but the players usually enjoyed themselves nonetheless, partly no doubt because of the salacious secrets revealed. During one game of Truth, Peggy pointedly asked Max whether he preferred sex at the age of twenty, thirty, forty, or fifty; Ernst's answer is not recorded.

By the summer of 1942 Peggy thought a vacation was in order, and she and Max decided to summer on Cape Cod. While Peggy made a trip to Washington in a further effort to get Nellie van Doesburg out of Europe (she could not), Pegeen and Max went to Massachusetts without her, renting a house in Wellfleet. When Peggy arrived, she found the house completely unsuitable and moved the ménage to Provincetown, where they shared a house with Matta, who was there for the season. But Max had neglected to inform authorities of his change of residence – something he was required to do as an enemy alien. This, added to his cryptic answers to questions asked by the arresting officers – the result of his imperfect command of English – and the presence in the Matta household of a shortwave radio, brought Max under suspicion for espionage. It was only with great difficulty – along with the help of a sympathetic Boston district attorney who had had some dealings with the Guggenheims and the intercession of Bernard Reis with the Board of Enemy Aliens – that Max was allowed to go on his way. He was left with a fetishistic horror of unfamiliar radios, fearing they might be shortwaves.

This incident effectively ended their summer plans, much to the dismay of the temporary residents of Hale House, which in Max and Peggy's absence had been transformed into the equivalent of a bachelor pad for the summer. Peggy had told Marcel Duchamp he was free to stay there, and both Jimmy

Ernst and Sindbad were using it for assignations with their girlfriends. Duchamp had recently created a *Boîte-en-valise*, a deluxe box-in-a-suitcase that contained reproductions of all his previous artwork, and he had arranged to have materials to make fifty more of the same shipped to Hale House, where he was already busy assembling them. (Peggy remarked on how amusing it would be to go off on a country weekend and to discover on arrival that one had mistaken the valise for one's suitcase.)

A number of interesting developments in Peggy's life and in the New York City art world occurred that summer. Duchamp was instrumental in bringing a new American artist to Peggy's attention. One afternoon at Hale House, while a thunderstorm raged outside, Duchamp answered the ringing telephone. On the other end was the reclusive artist Joseph Cornell, then known only to a few devotees as the creator of imaginative and thoughtful shadow boxes. Cornell, an outsider whom Julien Levy had discovered, was becoming canny about New York's art scene, and he had summoned the courage to call Peggy to interest her in his work. Reaching Duchamp himself, whom he had met several years earlier at Julien Levy's gallery, was, he wrote in his diary, 'one of the most delightful and strangest experiences I ever had.' Cornell invited Duchamp out to his home on Utopia Parkway in Queens to see his work, and Duchamp wound up buying two of his boxes. Peggy acquired two boxes herself, *Ball and Book* (1934) and *Thimble Box* (1938), and later acquired several more. By some accounts, she did not really appreciate Cornell's work as fine art, giving away many of his boxes as presents (she would give *Thimble Box* to Charles Seliger, one of the gallery's artists, when she closed the gallery) and, years later, handing one to a visiting child as a plaything.

John Cage, the avant-garde composer, who had met Max at an Ernst show in Chicago that spring, was another visitor that summer, and, after an inauspicious beginning, was to become an important friend of Peggy's: in July, he and his wife, Xenia, accepted Max's invitation to visit in New York City. Arriving from Chicago with only 25 cents, Cage used a nickel to dial Hale House; Max did not recognize his voice and hemmed and hawed before asking the caller to come around for drinks. Cage reported the dispiriting exchange to Xenia, who said they had nothing to lose and a lot to gain and made him call back. When he again reached Max and this time identified himself, he was told that his room had been ready for weeks and to come right over.

Cage was dazzled by the atmosphere at Hale House, where he and Xenia encountered 'people whose names were written in gold in my head – Piet Mondrian, André Breton, Virgil Thompson, Marcel Duchamp, even Gypsy

Rose Lee . . . Somebody famous was dropping in every two minutes, it seemed.' But his experience with his hostess was not as pleasant. Peggy, who hoped to inaugurate her art center (she had stopped calling it a museum) in the fall, asked Cage if he would present a performance of percussion music at the as yet undetermined opening. Cage agreed, and had his percussion instruments shipped from Chicago. In the meantime, he arranged a concert at the Museum of Modern Art for a celebration it was mounting to commemorate the twentieth anniversary of the League of Composers. When Peggy learned of this commitment, she flew into a rage, canceled his performance at her opening, and refused to pay, as she had agreed, for the shipment of Cage's equipment, informing him that he and Xenia had better make plans to move on. Cage burst into tears and left the room; in the next room he found a man in a rocking chair smoking a cigar. 'It was Duchamp,' Cage later said, who asked Cage why he was crying. Cage never remembered exactly what Duchamp said to him, but recalled, 'He was by himself, and somehow his presence made me feel calmer.' Miraculously, Cage's friendship with Peggy would survive (though neither picked it up again for years). But the incident also signaled Peggy's competitiveness and her desire to make the opening of her collection an auspicious event. Showcasing a new discovery like Cage – he was at the very start of a promising career – would have been a coup. But if a competing institution beat her to the punch, her plans were spoiled.

Later in the summer, Peggy again turned her attention to finding a space for her art center, which she now thought of as definitely including a gallery. The plan was to put her 'permanent' collection on exhibit, emphatically *not* for sale, and to attach to it a gallery that would show changing exhibitions of artworks *for* sale. Peggy's attempt to land new talent for the opening suggests the direction her thoughts on the matter were taking. When she settled down to concrete planning, she initially had in mind that the space would include an auditorium seating 150 (where, presumably, Cage was to debut). What she was envisioning, in fact, was much more along the lines of an art center than it was of a gallery or museum, though she and everyone else would come to refer to it simply as a gallery.

Peggy's gallery would not be the first venue for modern art, of course. The Museum of Modern Art (MoMA), Chick Austin's Wadsworth Atheneum, and her uncle's Museum of Non-Objective Painting, among a few others, were already established (though the cavernous rooms of the last were usually empty of visitors), as were galleries such as Julien Levy's, which had opened in 1931 and showed surrealists like Dali, Giacometti, Magritte, and Ernst. Levy also mounted several photography shows and was drawn to those he called the 'neo-Romantics,' like Tchelitchew. A *Vogue* survey of New York

galleries in 1938 observed that Levy's gallery was 'principally for the sophisticated and the young,' and that his eye was 'focussed on the Parisian scene,'
which would no longer be terribly important in Peggy's vision.

Other leading New York galleries included the Durand-Ruel, run since
the turn of the century by Edwin Holston, the American representative for
the 125-year-old French firm. A venerable institution, with walls 'covered
with dull brown velvet,' it was dimly lit and was said to be 'soothing and
refreshing.' Its specialty was French impressionism, and it catered to many
eminent collectors. Marie (Mrs. Averell) Harriman's 57th Street Gallery,
'small, well lighted,' also specialized in French art, as did the Valentine
Gallery, run by the 'suave, energetic, and genial' Valentine Dudensing, who
loved to gossip about his acquaintance with Picasso. Farther north, the
Wildenstein gallery on East 64th Street was housed in a building with 'a
Louis XVI façade brought, stone by stone, from France.' Visitors were shown
in by way of a long marble hall to a Louis Quinze room hung with eighteenth-
century portraits and a room given over to Fragonards and Watteaus. The
French-born Georges Wildenstein, who wore his Légion d'Honneur pin on
his lapel, '[w]ith exquisite taste' served up eighteenth-century French art
'with the same astuteness and faith as his distinguished confrères in London
and in Paris.' Carroll Carstairs, late of Knoedler, had a small gallery on the top
floor of a 57th Street building showing old masters with a smattering of moderns. In the back was a kitchenette run by 'a French factotum,' which
provided food for openings and intimate lunches with collectors: he turned
out 'pheasant with bread sauce for luncheon, or other dishes a little on the
rare and elegant side.' The venerable Knoedler Galleries, founded in 1846,
occupied 'a solid, handsome building' on 57th Street specializing in old masters, 'occasionally dabbling, rather like a non-swimmer in the surf, with the
Moderns.' Knoedler had been instrumental in building collections such as
those of Henry Clay Frick, Isabella Stewart Gardner, and Andrew Mellon.

This was not a field in which Peggy could compete, even had she the
inclination to do so. Her father had bought paintings from Durand-Ruel and
Knoedler, but Peggy, who as a young woman came to appreciate old masters,
could never afford them, and by this stage they were hardly her major artistic interest. Firmly entrenched in surrealism and abstraction, the backbone of
her collection, she intended to mount shows of artists like de Chirico and
Giacometti, but she did not focus, as did the other gallerists who showed
some modern works, on France. She also hoped, as she had with Guggenheim
Jeune, to discover new artists who might not come from Europe at all; in fact,
it was in this regard that her gallery would change the course of art history in
the twentieth century. She had no interest, moreover, in running a stuffy

place where great collectors would be wined and dined and where an atmosphere of reverence held sway. She envisioned a vibrant and innovative gallery
that would be a real experience to visit, that would draw guests in and
encourage them to interact with the art and with any artists or critics they
might meet there. She had begun to think that the gallery space itself could
be an innovation. She knew she wanted something out of the ordinary.

By Christmas 1941 Peggy had found a suitable space, a north-facing
double loft on the top floor of 30 West 57th Street. The older, more established galleries like Rosenberg, Durand-Ruel, and Knoedler were on East
57th Street; Peggy's gallery, on the West Side, was next to one of Manhattan's
finest fashion stores, Jay-Thorpe; on one side of the gallery entrance was a
jeweler and milliner, on the other side a corsetiere. Because the loft was on
the seventh floor and had no street frontage to advertise it, Peggy knew that
her gallery would need to be a place that was talked about, a must-see for the
cognoscenti; more than that, she hoped to attract the general public. Her
plans demanded that the space be distinctly modern and striking, and she
solicited opinions about how best to arrange for its design. Breton and
Howard Putzel urged her to hire the architect Frederick Kiesler, thought to be
a visionary in such matters. Marcel Duchamp may also have directed her
attention Kiesler's way, as the Austrian had recently photographed his *Large
Glass* (1915–1923); Duchamp would stay in the apartment shared by Kiesler
and his wife, Steffi, for almost a year, beginning in October 1942. 'Peggy
attracted a good many people who helped her,' said the critic James Johnson
Sweeney, citing Duchamp, Herbert Read, Nellie van Doesburg, and Matta.
'[B]ut she also had her own views and she acted on them.'

Kiesler, a sculptor as well as an architect, was a Viennese immigrant, less
than five feet tall, whom Jimmy Ernst described as '[a]cting alternately like an
elfish puck or a stern philosopher.' He was known as a designer of stage sets
as well as the interior of the Eighth Street Playhouse; in the late twenties, he
had directed the construction of display windows for Saks Fifth Avenue. He
was known equally well as the writer of several poetic, imaginative works on
architectural and design theory. In fact, with Duchamp, Kiesler was one of the
most visionary minds of the twentieth century. Few of his designs were built –
perhaps the reason he does not have the recognition he deserves today – but
in the last century he lived among America's greatest writers and artists,
influencing their innovations and coming up with striking new concepts of
his own.

'Dear Mr. Kiesler,' Peggy wrote in February 1942, 'I want your help. Will
you give me some advise [sic] about turning two tailor shops into an Art
Gallery?' Thus began a rather remarkable partnership. At the time the

director of the laboratory of the School of Architecture at Columbia University and scenic director at the Juilliard School of Music, Kiesler had articulated his theories about art and space several times since his arrival in the United States in 1926. In 'On Correalism and Biotechnique' (1939), he had written, 'The exchange of inter-acting forces I call co-reality and the science of the laws of interrelationships, *correalism*. The term *correalism* expresses the dynamics of continual interaction between man and his natural and technological environments.' Kiesler believed in showing art in relation to the totality of experience – and the gallery he designed for Peggy could be described as a *Gesamtkunstwerk*, or total work of art, like a Wagner opera. He demanded a free rein, and Peggy gave it to him. His insistence that there be no barriers between the public and the art was perfectly in keeping with what was to be a hallmark of the gallery and the dominant aspect of Peggy's collecting life: a democratic impulse that broke down the barriers between high art and popular culture and insisted that art be viewed in a human framework, not aestheticized as in a museum.

One of Kiesler's theories was that paintings should never be displayed in frames. He explained: 'Today the framed painting on the wall has become a decorative cipher without form or meaning, or else, to the more susceptible observer, an object of interest existing in a world distinct from his. Its frame is . . . a plastic barrier across which man looks from the world he inhabits to the alien world in which the work of art has its being. That barrier must be dissolved.'

Moreover, in keeping with the concept of the gallery as *Gesamtkunstwerk*, Kiesler designed extensive lighting schemes, arranging to have one series of lights switched on and off automatically every three seconds, spotlighting artworks; he also arranged to have recordings of noises sounding like an approaching train played in time with the lights. (The switching lights and noises were eliminated soon after the gallery opened because so many visitors complained about them.)

Kiesler also designed innovative devices to display artworks, addressing the large size of Peggy's collection by showing as many as possible in a small space as well as affording new ways to explore the viewer's stance in looking at art. Visitors viewed her several Paul Klees, for instance, by means of a paternoster, a device that showed the paintings every ten seconds; the viewer could look for a longer period by pulling a lever. The visitor looked at the contents of Duchamp's *Boîte-en-valise* (1941) by looking into an eyepiece and turning an enormous spiral, like a ship's wheel, which revealed successive pieces of the work. These devices, shown in what Kiesler called the Kinetic Gallery, were meant to allow the viewer to interact with the art.

Kiesler also gave a great deal of thought to seating, combining it in sev-eral ways with the viewing of the artworks. Though she had to give up the idea of an auditorium, Peggy wanted the gallery to seat ninety, and Kiesler accordingly devised folding chairs of blue canvas as well as rockers designed from plywood and linoleum. Similar to the rockers were what he called his correalist furniture, biomorphic shapes made out of the same materials as the rockers, which could be used as stands for artworks, for seating, or, when lined up horizontally, as long table-like structures; into these were fitted cut-off baseball bats that would display paintings.

Setting to work in June after months of planning, Kiesler spared no expense, using oak for the floors instead of pine and, in the so-called Abstract Gallery, linen on the walls instead of cotton; poor Jimmy Ernst got caught in the crossfire over the bills, which temporarily cost him his friendship with the architect. Peggy would also clash with Kiesler about costs, though their friendship withstood the quarrel, and in 1943 she would offer him a show (which did not take place).

The space Peggy chose for her gallery was in a double loft, so Kiesler had in effect four different spaces to work with; it was in the shape of a square circle. Visitors entered the gallery from a door leading to elevators in the center of the floor, roughly in the north part of the Abstract Gallery. In this space, Kiesler positioned blue fabric in undulating fashion so that the walls appeared to curve, giving a sail-like appearance, and he reinforced it by lacing the material to the ceiling and floor. The unframed paintings – works of geometric abstraction by artists such as Kandinsky and Picabia – were individually spotlighted and hung from triangular structures of rope inter-spersed with sculptures positioned on the correalist furniture.

Passing by a desk occupied first by Jimmy Ernst, then Howard Putzel, and later by a literary critic named Marius Bewley, visitors turned right and encountered the first of the viewing devices, the Klee box, and, behind it, a window to the next space in which a Kurt Schwitters painting hung with a Jean Arp on the other side. Then they entered the Daylight Gallery, a space that looked north onto 57th Street. The windows were covered with a new kind of sheer fabric called ninon. Here Peggy had a desk (she also had a seldom-used office in a room beyond the Abstract Gallery) and showed her ongoing exhibitions, making this the only part of the floor that was a true commercial gallery. Kiesler had devised what he called painting libraries, actually racks on rolling wheels that held and displayed paintings, drawings, and prints; Peggy wanted as many of the artworks in her collection to be seen as possible, and these 'libraries,' like the viewing devices, made it possible to display most of her collection. Robert Motherwell, one of the artists who would show at the gallery, singled out this feature as remarkable: '[The gallery] could be treated as a place to browse . . . You were invited to take the pictures in your hands – like a print or a book – and move them back and forth so that you could see a line or a surface more clearly in different kinds of light.' No other gallery allowed visitors to hold artworks in this way.

Turning right, before entering the Surrealist Gallery, visitors came across the Duchamp viewing device; beyond that, the Surrealist Gallery had concave walls made of eucalyptus. On these, paintings were mounted on wooden 'arms.' Other paintings and sculptures were displayed on the correalist furniture and in still more painting libraries; in this gallery were hung Peggy's Dalis, Delvauxs, and Magrittes. In the south part of the gallery were two storerooms, housing art not on display. The floors of the gallery were painted turquoise, Peggy's favorite color.

Peggy's conception of an art center that challenged received ways of viewing and experiencing art set her apart from other collectors and gallery owners of her time; indeed, it took sophistication and daring to return to the United States and decide to open a gallery that would be not just a showcase for her collection but an innovative and radical experience, designed by someone with vision. Kiesler proved himself just such a visionary, whose aim was to get visitors to view art in innovative ways, responding to it interactively and appreciating it in its totality. The name of the gallery, like Peggy's catalogue title, was to be Art of This Century. It would put Peggy Guggenheim centrally on the map of twentieth-century culture, and it would change the course of modern art.

13

'When Art Wore a Rose':
Highs and Lows

In 1963, about twenty years after Art of This Century opened, Ethel Baziotes, the wife of William Baziotes, the New York artist who rose to prominence after Peggy displayed his work at her gallery, wrote in a letter to the leading U.S. art critic of the century, Clement Greenberg, to say how glad she was that 'Bill, myself, Bob Motherwell and you, Clem, came out of the same golden period. Peggy Guggenheim – Mondrian – the Surrealists – Art of This Century. The champagne years – when Art wore a rose. Besides important things happening life had a wonderful quality. It had a sort of F. Scott Fitzgerald and Hemingway quality. I think this had to do with Peggy being a twenties person. To my mind nothing that ever followed, has ever had the same zing.'

The 'champagne years' began with a spectacular opening on Tuesday, October 20, 1942, from 8:00 P.M. to midnight; $1 admission was charged, with the proceeds going to the Red Cross. The hostess appeared in a white gown – which contrasted spectacularly with her black hair and crimson lipstick – with a different earring in each ear: one, by Alexander Calder, represented abstract art, while the other, by Yves Tanguy, designated surrealism. She was trying to say she embraced both.

Peggy, ever mindful of the need for publicity, issued a press release that explained how the collection began and included a listing of the individual rooms in the gallery. The release commented, 'Miss Guggenheim hopes that "Art of This Century" will become a center where artists will be welcome and where they can feel that they are cooperating in establishing a research laboratory for new ideas.' The release went on to quote her directly: '"Opening this Gallery and its collection during a time when people are fighting for their lives and freedom is a responsibility of which I am fully conscious. This undertaking will serve its purpose only if it serves its future instead of recording the past."'

The press, perhaps intrigued by this forward-looking statement, had a wonderful time with the opening; coverage ranged from a long review in a Butte, Montana, daily to a photograph in the pages of *Town and Country* magazine of Frances Scott Fitzgerald (the daughter of Scott and Zelda) looking at Duchamp's *Boîte-en-valise* through its viewing contraption. The *New York Times* reviewer, Edward Alden Jewell (whom Peggy would call 'Mon Bijou de l'Epoque'), said that as a venue for showing modern art, '[I]t is the last word.' Henry McBride, the reviewer from the *Sun*, wrote, inelegantly, 'Frankly, my eyes have never bulged further from their sockets than at this show.' *Time* and *The New Yorker* both compared the show to Coney Island, not unfavorably. Emily Genauer, in the *New York World-Telegram*, wrote enthusiastically, 'Going through the rooms is a mystifying and delightful experience. You feel like a child with a new toy that does all sorts of unpredictable things.' Perhaps the review that pleased Peggy the most was an underhanded rebuke to the baroness and Uncle Sol: 'If the Museum of Non-Objective Art is built, one of the sanest and most ingenious efforts to find a better way to show pictures will be at hand for comparison.'

The comparison to her uncle Solomon's venture is an interesting one. As opposed to the temple of high art that Solomon Guggenheim and the baroness Hilla Rebay intended – complete with ubiquitous piped-in Bach – Peggy's interactive gallery, which made looking at art *fun*, was accessible to a general audience and not just wealthy buyers. Peggy's was a highly democratic enterprise. As her press release indicates, she envisioned not just a gallery but an art center, where ideas would be freely exchanged, where art was not static and removed but rather immediate and engaged – thus her decision to show new, unproven artists, which would finally be Art of This Century's greatest contribution. Its mission, truly, was not to 'record the past' but to 'serve the future,' a mission completely foreign to museums and galleries of the day.

Jimmy Ernst has said of the gallery's early days that 'daily attendance was consistently large,' despite Peggy's early adoption of an admissions policy, requiring the visitor to deposit 25 cents in a Spanish tambourine near the door – a practice Putzel would soon convince her to drop.

Putzel overheard the whispered names of 'various members of New York's fabled Jewish aristocracy . . . Loeb, Straus, Gimbel, Seligman,' and in fact Solomon Guggenheim's wife, Peggy's aunt Irene, bravely visited the gallery, though she risked a disagreement with her husband and, perhaps, the wrath of the baroness, who would have seen it as a betrayal of Solomon's efforts. According to Jimmy, Aunt Irene thanked Peggy lavishly for handing her a catalogue, whereupon Peggy informed her that the asking price was $2.75. Aunt Irene had only a $20 bill, and Peggy sent Jimmy out for change.

It was quite clear that Peggy's gallery was that rare phenomenon in the art world – a popular success. Galleries like Alfred Stieglitz's An American Place and museums like MoMA drew crowds, to be sure, but by and large they attracted the cognoscenti. Though other galleries' shows were reviewed by art critics of papers like the *Sun*, the *World-Telegram*, and the *Herald Tribune*, exhibits at Art of This Century were more often the subject for news stories in these papers, and no other galleries received the national coverage Peggy's did – not only in far-flung newspapers but in middlebrow publications like *Time* and *Newsweek*. (Art of This Century was featured in *Vogue* fashion spreads three times.) The gallery's impact was indelible; it is not too much of a stretch to compare it to the American artistic event of the century, the Armory Show of 1913, with its then scandalous modernist content, which had rocked the popular imagination and drawn enormous crowds. Peggy's gallery became a must-see even for tourists; it is not surprising that the popular First Lady, Eleanor Roosevelt, would pay a visit on a trip to New York in 1944.

The very atmosphere of Art of This Century set itself apart. The musician John Cage called the gallery 'a kind of funhouse . . . You couldn't just walk through it, you had to become part of it.' Though a fair share of visitors did progress through the rooms quietly, as they did in museums, perhaps murmuring to their companions, the gallery quickly evolved into just what Peggy had envisioned: an art center. The 'erratic setting,' said a critic, 'provided a recklessly liberal point of encounter and discussion. One never knew which artist would be arguing loudly with what other artist or critic.' For the émigré artists, it became a place where they could gather as they once did in cafés; Breton, for instance, could be found there on most days. But in the early days, observed Jimmy Ernst, its great weakness was the absence of American artists from the mix: 'Admission of Onslow Ford, Gorky, Esteban Frances, Jerome [sic] Kamrowski and Baziotes to the circle seemed possible but was held in abeyance . . . [S]uch names as Jackson Pollock, Mark Rothko, Willem de Kooning . . . were met with incomprehension when they were mentioned by Matta, Howard Putzel or me.'

Although a surrealist, Matta was open-minded about his American colleagues. Along with Putzel and Jimmy, he convinced Peggy to present a show of new art once a year. And Putzel felt even more strongly than Jimmy that the center of the art world was shifting, even then, from Paris to New York, telling a friend in 1940 that with the exception of Picasso, 'nothing really new was painted in Europe . . . This continent will very likely be the new home of art.' Peggy liked the idea of showing new art, telling Jimmy that it would be nice to have 'a sort of *salon du printemps*, where I don't have to buy if it doesn't fit.' The first of the gallery's changing exhibits seems to indicate that Peggy was swayed by such arguments: she showed, along with Duchamp's *Boîte-en-valise*, the American Joseph Cornell's shadow boxes, which she designated 'Objects,' and bottles with collages on them made by Laurence Vail. (For Peggy's catalogue, Laurence quipped, 'I used to throw bottles and now I decorate them.' He still emptied them first, of course.) Peggy bought for her permanent collection a screen Laurence had decorated with collage images of cityscapes thronged with people, and she would buy several of his bottles over the years.

From the beginning, then, Peggy worked to correct her collection's European bias, increasingly showcasing new American talent. For this new talent, the exposure was incredible, many times career-making. 'None of the other galleries had anything like the character of Peggy's place. It was quite different; everyone went there; it was a gathering place, and it gave young people an opportunity they might never have had,' said the critic James Johnson Sweeney. Robert Motherwell noted that artists who showed in the Daylight Gallery, where artwork was for sale, enjoyed the juxtaposition of their work with Peggy's collection. 'The works in the permanent collection – especially the Surrealist collection – were masterpieces. If you were having a one-man show as a youngster, and you were having it here flanked by this collection, it was an amazing experience.'

At the time, Peggy was, except for the aristocratic and entrenched Marie Harriman, the only female gallery owner in New York; indeed, Peggy's decision to let Kiesler build his vision in the gallery set her apart from many women of the time. Duchamp, recognizing this, suggested that for her second show she mount an exhibit of all-women's art. This exhibit trumpeted her interest in American artists, juxtaposing them with such internationally known figures as Leonora Carrington, Frida Kahlo, and Leonor Fini. Called 'Exhibition by 31 Women,' it opened on January 5, 1943, and included works by Djuna Barnes (who contributed *Portrait of Alice*), Carrington, Buffie Johnson, Kahlo, Gypsy Rose Lee (a self-portrait), Louise Nevelson, Meret Oppenheim (who had shocked viewers at a recent MoMA show with her fur-lined tea set), I. Rice Pereira, Kay Sage, Hedda Sterne, Dorothea Tanning, and Sophie Taeuber-Arp, among others. As she often did, Peggy included family members and friends who were sometimes talented, sometimes not – in this case, her sister, Hazel; her daughter, Pegeen; and Barbara Reis, Bernard and Becky Reis's daughter. Peggy set up a jury to choose which artists to include, consisting of Breton, Max, Putzel,

Jimmy, the influential James Johnson Sweeney (once a secretary of James Joyce's), and herself.

Peggy must have been dismayed when the American painter Georgia O'Keeffe, who was presumably invited to show in the exhibit, turned up at the gallery and announced that she was most emphatically not a 'woman painter.' Jimmy recorded this fact in his memoirs, describing O'Keeffe as 'formidable,' and noting that she showed up at the gallery 'with a small entourage' to face an 'awed' Peggy. Peggy chose to overlook this moment in her memoirs, though she records that the first piece of modern art she held (upside down) was an O'Keeffe painting, back in the days when she worked at the radical bookstore Sunwise Turn. O'Keeffe's was an imperious and rather august presence, and Peggy's shyness made it unlikely that they would have talked freely when O'Keeffe appeared at her gallery, despite many points of connection.

Peggy lamented often that she should have left the number of women artists at thirty. For, in an interesting development, Art of This Century sent Max to each of the selected women's studios to choose the piece to be included in the show. Quite possibly this idea was Peggy's. She wrote in her autobiography, 'I made Max work hard for this show.' Inevitably, he fell in love with one of the women, Dorothea Tanning, whom he and Peggy had met the previous year, once at an exhibit at Julien Levy's gallery and again at one of Levy's parties. Peggy, while conceding that Dorothea was 'pretty' and 'quite talented,' dismissed her as a *fille de rien*, 'pretentious, boring, stupid, vulgar, and dressed in the worst possible taste.' Max chose two of Tanning's paintings, one of them the celebrated *Birthday* (1942), the other the truly scary *Jeu d'Enfant* (1942), which showed a child tearing and burning wallpaper behind which lurked horrifying creatures. She was a surrealist already heavily influenced by Ernst's work.

Peggy felt herself partly to blame for pushing Max into the arms of another woman. She regretted that she had recently told him that he made love badly. More importantly, however, she and Duchamp had activated a long-simmering, mutual sexual attraction. In her memoirs, she wrote dismissively, 'While Max was away [for a show in New Orleans] I was untrue to him for the first time, with Marcel, at last after twenty years.'

Then on February 17 Peggy wrote Emily that Max had spent a night alone with Tanning and that he was 'infatuated' with her. It was her own fault, Peggy said, 'because I spent nights out and gave him the same freedom,' adding, 'I told Max I would give up Marcel if he would give up Tanning but Max said if he did he would have a grudge against me and it would do no good.'

Twenty years before, she and Marcel had circled through the Paris streets pawing at each other but were stymied as to where to find a bed; now she had bedded 'the king of the bachelors.' Detractors of Peggy like David Hare and Pierre Matisse dispute this claim, as Duchamp's biographer, Calvin Tompkins, has pointed out. But Duchamp had a penchant for women with plain faces and beautiful bodies, confiding his predilection to his friend Henri-Pierre Roché. That he and Peggy should choose each other seemed eminently natural to no less than Breton, to whom Peggy turned, in her unhappiness about Max, seeking psychoanalysis, remembering that Breton had been a psychiatrist during World War I. Breton declined but heard her out, observing that because of the affair with Duchamp, Max, out of pride, would never come back to her. Peggy later wrote, 'He wanted to know why I did not live with Marcel instead of fussing with Max.' She told him that sharing a few nights was one thing, but she and Marcel could never have a 'serious affair' because of his long attachment to her friend Mary Reynolds.

The affair died down. Peggy referred to it later as a 'vague affair,' adding, 'We were almost like brother and sister, we had known each other so long.' Duchamp was her 'father-confessor,' she said, to whom she confided her problems with Max and, later, her interest in other men.

In early March, Peggy endured the humiliation of seeing Dorothea Tanning at an opening at Julien Levy's gallery, 'all dolled up surrealistically,' wearing a dress with holes in it that revealed photos of Max. Just like that, Peggy was cured, writing to Emily in late March, 'I now wonder how I endured him for so long,' adding, with hindsight, 'I should have left him [earlier] and spared myself the humiliation of Tanning.' Her only regret, she wrote, was that everyone thought Max had left her. 'I pushed him into the affair . . . Tant pis,' she wrote dismissively.

While Peggy's personal life was in turmoil, her gallery was thriving. 'Exhibition by 31 Women' had caught the critics' attention. The Times's Edward Jewell led the way, proclaiming that the show 'yields one captivating surprise after another.' The news, one critic wrote, was that it was a surrealist show. Bob Coates, writing for The New Yorker, singled out Still Life by Meraud Guevara (a painting of a bowl of eggs), the work of Leonor Fini and I. Rice Pereira, and the newcomers Kay Sage (for her At the Appointed Time) and Tanning.

Peggy's next show featured Jean Hélion, the French painter who had recently attracted attention in the newspapers for his account of escaping from a prisoner-of-war camp in eastern Germany, making his way across Europe with a fake passport and from there to the United States; he was in the midst of turning it into a book, They Shall Not Have Me (1943). Peggy charged an admission fee to the Hélion show, sending the proceeds to Free French Relief. On February 8, 1943, the opening day, Hélion gave what many found a moving lecture on his escape from the Nazis. Peggy threw a party at Hale House after the opening, and it was there that Hélion first caught sight of the seventeen-year-old Pegeen. At thirty-nine, the painter was old enough to have been her father, but he could not forget the beautiful girl with long blond hair and luminous, large eyes.

Hélion's painting was abstract; in France he was a noted theorist of abstraction, regarded as an artist who approached the genre with intellectual rigor. The paintings on display at Art of This Century were crisply rendered, colorful abstracts that the New York Sun's critic called 'cool, elegant, and detached.' Edward Jewell announced in the New York Times, 'Here is non-objective art of real substance and originality.' Hélion himself was very handsome and winning, and cut something of a swashbuckling figure because of his wartime experience; the show made an impact because of the paintings' obvious force and the creator's widely talked-about charm, but Hélion would soon disappoint many collectors and critics by turning back to representational art.

The next exhibition was intended to showcase the original covers of Breton's art and literary magazine VVV, a rival to Charles Henri Ford's and Parker Tyler's magazine, View. But a series of arguments between Peggy and the editor, David Hare, as well as her falling-out with Max, led to its cancellation. Max, an adviser to VVV, had promised her a certain amount of ad space without charge, but Breton rescinded this offer. So Peggy cast about for other ideas, and Jimmy came up with a good one, suggesting that she mount 'Early and Late,' a show devoted to the earliest and most recent paintings by a series of artists. In the show, which ran from March 13 to April 10, 1943, Peggy included three works of Salvador Dali – perhaps to spite Breton, who in disgust had anagrammatically dubbed the surrealist-turned-celebrity Avida Dollars.

Next came 'Collages,' from April 4 to May 15, Peggy's first show to include a significant number of American artists, one of whom was soon to become famous. Among the group were Joseph Cornell, Ad Reinhardt, David Hare, Jimmy Ernst, Alexander Calder, Gypsy Rose Lee, and Laurence Vail. That these artists were all American signaled the approach that would distinguish Art of This Century from competing galleries. The difference between Peggy and Julien Levy, for instance, was 'the quick, succinct transformation of her program in just five seasons, from Surrealism into Abstract Expressionism,' while Levy was 'adamantly a Surrealist to the end,' according to an art historian writing about Levy. This transformation, in turn, was what defined Art of This Century's success.

Also included in this show was Jackson Pollock, whose contribution has unfortunately been lost. Pollock, whom Peggy would later count as her single greatest discovery, had only recently come to her notice. Max had left Hale House in March, and Peggy no longer turned to Breton for guidance in the art world; even Duchamp had come to play less of a role. In their place, she was turning very often to her old bulwark, Howard Putzel, and increasingly to James Johnson Sweeney, soon to be placed in charge of the sculpture and painting divisions at MoMA. Sweeney had first encountered the works of the Wyoming-born Pollock in the spring of 1942, when the graphic designer, photographer, and arts supporter Herbert Matter came to him after seeing Pollock's paintings at his studio. Sweeney told Peggy that 'this man was doing interesting work.' With that, he left the next move to her.

Putzel, meanwhile, had met Pollock that summer, introduced by the artist's friend, the painter Reuben Kadish, who had known Putzel since the late thirties. Kadish remembered that Putzel immediately used the word genius to describe Pollock. At first, however, Peggy was slow to act. Even a recommendation by Matta, who had been holding an informal workshop in automatism with Pollock, Motherwell, Baziotes, Peter Busa, and Gerome Kamrowski, left her cold. But when Putzel urged that she show a piece by Pollock in her 'Collages' show, Peggy finally agreed. The show received only mild praise, with the *New York Herald Tribune* noting flatly that it was 'both historical and contemporary.' No review mentioned Pollock's work.

Again urged on by Putzel, Peggy announced a Spring Salon to be held from May 18 to June 26. On the first of May, the *New York Times* announced the jury: besides Peggy, it would include Piet Mondrian, Duchamp, Sweeney, and James Thrall Soby (Sweeney's predecessor at MoMA). The artists considered had to be less than thirty-five years old. A steady stream of hopefuls appeared at the gallery's door with their portfolios. Putzel, however, made a selection of Pollock's work at the painter's 8th Street studio and brought it to the gallery himself.

On the day the jury was to meet, Peggy and Jimmy Ernst were lining up the various candidates' contributions against the wall when Mondrian arrived and looked around, coming to a stop in front of Pollock's *Stenographic Figure* (1942), a powerful abstract covered over with what seem to be mathematical signs. Peggy had had a soft spot for Mondrian ever since she had visited the painfully shy artist in his studio the year before to see his latest pictures. On that occasion he had danced with her to some boogie-woogie music and then kissed her chastely. Seeing him focused on the Pollock, she went up to him and said, 'Pretty awful, isn't it? That's not painting, is it?' But Mondrian did not move away, and several minutes later Peggy approached him and said,

'There is absolutely no discipline at all,' adding that she was sure Pollock's work would not be chosen for the spring show – a potential problem as Putzel and Matta had recommended him so highly. Mondrian answered, 'Peggy, I don't know. I have the feeling that this may be the most exciting painting that I have seen in a long, long time, here or in Europe.' Peggy protested that it was not the sort of thing she had expected Mondrian to admire. He replied that just because it was not like his own work did not mean he did not respect it, adding, 'I don't know enough about this painter to think of him as "great." But I do know that I was forced to stop and look. Where you see "lack of discipline," I get an impression of tremendous energy. It will have to go somewhere, to be sure.' But right now, he said, he was 'very excited.'

When the show went up, Stenographic Figure was included. And the critics, like Mondrian, were excited. The New Yorker commented about the Spring Salon, 'Despite a faint air of the haphazard about the hanging and a certain amount of deadwood in the painting, the new show . . . deserves your attention.' The New York Herald Tribune critic found it 'a lively, if not a distinctly impressive show' with fewer new names than one might have hoped. But Peggy's friend Jean Connolly singled out Pollock's contribution in the May 29 Nation, writing, '[F]or once the future reveals a gleam of hope.' She commented on works by Matta, Motherwell, and a few others as 'paintings it would be a pleasure to own,' then added, 'there is a large Jackson Pollack [sic], which, I am told, made the jury starry-eyed.'

It would be a bumpy road ahead, to say the least, but with Art of This Century's Spring Salon of Younger Artists, Pollock's career was effectively launched.

Max Ernst had moved out of Hale House in March 1943, taking Kachina, his pet Lhasa apso, with him: Peggy so loved the dog that she debated trying to get joint custody of Kachina in the upcoming divorce. Eventually, she let Max have her, but on the condition Peggy could adopt two of Kachina's puppies, which she soon received and came to adore much as she had their mother. She was not alone in the house for long. Laurence Vail had recently broken his leg in a skiing accident, and because he could not negotiate the stairs of his fourth-floor walkup, he moved into Hale House for a month, where he let Peggy take care of him. Before very long he was involved with Jean Connolly. Jean, née Jean Bakewell, was born in Pittsburgh in 1910 and grew up in Baltimore. She was still married to Cyril Connolly, editor of the British magazine Horizon, and had recently recovered from an affair with Clement Greenberg; she had taken over the writing of Greenberg's Nation columns when he was in the service. An independently wealthy and striking woman, she had been part of Christopher Isherwood's campy circle in Hollywood in the late 1930s; the artist Michael Wishart remembered her with a 'permanent retinue of Ganymedes.' She was to become an important friend to Peggy and moved in with her before the end of the year.

By the end of March, however, Peggy, at forty-four, was able to write to Emily that she had fallen in love again, with a Scottish cultural gad-about named Kenneth Macpherson. 'It won't get me very far,' she added, 'but at least it is an affair and occupies my mind.' This equanimity belies the tone Peggy would take in her memoirs, which she would start in 1944 and in which the chapter about her relationship with Macpherson is titled 'Peace.' Sadly, this was not to be the case.

Kenneth Macpherson had met the imagist poet H.D., in 1926, when he was twenty-four to H.D.'s forty. The son of a Scottish painter, he was descended from six generations of artists. Macpherson was the second husband, after Robert McAlmon, of the poet H.D.'s lover Bryher (Winifred Ellerman, herself a talented writer and the daughter of a British shipping magnate); theirs was a *mariage blanc*; for much of it, Macpherson was having an affair with H.D. He had written two not very good novels (published by Bryher), had directed several films (including the 1930 silent film *Borderline*, which starred H.D. and Paul Robeson), and had produced a film magazine called *Close-Up* from 1927 to 1933. Around 1930 he ended his affair with H.D. and began a series of affairs with men, often African-American. The artist Buffie Johnson introduced him to Howard Putzel and through Putzel, Macpherson came to Hale House to buy art; over time, he bought (presumably with Bryher's money) from Peggy's collection several Ernsts, Tanguy's *Toilette de l'air*, a Klee, a Miró, a Picasso, and a Braque.

Dr. Hanns Sachs, a psychiatrist whom Macpherson consulted, had diagnosed him as having a 'mother fixation,' a result of his mother's proclivity for younger men. Perhaps that was part of his appeal to Peggy. It did not hurt that Macpherson, forty, had a British accent, was over six feet tall, and recalled visiting Bryher's parents at their London house on South Audley Street at the intersection of South Audley and Curzon; Peggy was very familiar with Curzon Street, having visited someone there the day before Sindbad was born, and this slight connection pleased her. Macpherson was also, because of a generous income from Bryher, financially comfortable, which worked in his favor, because Peggy did not have to worry about financial motives on his part. At a meeting in early 1943 she sat next to him for a performance of Mozart's *Don Giovanni* and thought she detected an attraction between them.

When they met, Kenneth had just recently arrived in New York from Europe, where he said he had worked for British intelligence. It may have been in this capacity that he had offered an affidavit at the request of Alfred Barr's wife that had helped enable Max Ernst to get into the United States in 1941. Kenneth Macpherson was a handsome man with reddish gold hair, who did no work of any sort, as far as Peggy could tell, but spent his days listening to music and preparing for parties and evenings out. He also drank more than anyone she had known since John Holms. The range of his sexual tastes and when she knew of them is not precisely clear, but very early on he instructed her never to use the word *fairy* but to say *Athenian* instead. In early April she wrote to Emily, 'He . . . paints his face with Max Factor like Pegeen,' which ought to have given her pause.

Peggy persisted in thinking of Kenneth as a lover, though they do not seem to have had sex more than a few times. By June, Max and Dorothea Tanning had left from New York for Sedona, Arizona, where they would later move permanently in 1946. Because Sindbad had been drafted into the U.S. Army in February, and Pegeen was leaving soon for an extended trip to Mexico, Peggy gave up Hale House, which the owners had sold out from under her, and was living in a succession of hotels. Evidently she and Kenneth were getting along well enough because they decided to rent a place together. Soon they found a very unlikely apartment, a duplex on the top two floors of two adjacent five-story brownstones that had been converted to apartment buildings at 155 East 61st Street (now number 153). Accessible by elevator from the street floor to the fourth floor, the top two floors were connected by a sweeping Regency staircase as well as a set of back stairs. There was a kitchen but only one bathroom on the top floor, while the floor below had four bathrooms. They took a lease, which Peggy insisted be in Macpherson's name, presumably to avoid publicity, but also, perhaps, for fear of seeming too controlling, and to cement what she hoped would seem to be the heterosexual nature of the arrangement.

Over the Fourth of July, Peggy went to Florida to see Sindbad, whose army unit was stationed there, a visit that stretched to two weeks. Kenneth had told her and Putzel that he would rent a house on Long Island for the summer and invite the two of them out, but that evidently fell through. Peggy began to talk about their renting a camp in the Adirondacks or the Maine camp of her British friends the Reeveses. The Maine camp won out because it was cheaper, but at the last minute she and Kenneth decided it would be too far away. Laurence Vail and Jean Connolly had taken two houses on Candlewood Lake in Connecticut; another house stood between theirs. When Peggy heard this news, she looked into renting it. On learning that the property association refused to rent or sell lakeside land to Jews, she turned to a new friend, the writer and composer Paul Bowles, and asked him to sign the lease for her. (If she made any connection to her grandfather's experience of being turned away at a hotel, she didn't say so.) Bowles, himself in a marriage in which both partners were bisexual, agreed to the scheme.

Peggy had met Bowles that spring, when a new company she formed called Art of This Century Recordings produced Bowles's Flute Sonata, performed by the French flautist René Leroy, and his Piano Sonatina, played by George Reeves, on five sides, with Two Mexican Dances, a piano duet performed by Arthur Gold and Robert Fizdale, on the sixth. (The recording would be issued the following year, and seems to have been the only venture of Art of This Century Recordings.) Peggy met and liked Bowles's (Jewish) wife, Jane, whose novel *Two Serious Ladies* had just been published. At Candlewood Lake, Peggy was known as 'Mrs. Bowles,' a situation that wrought much hilarity when the Bowleses came out for the weekend, bringing Kenneth with them. It was a perfect month, except that Kenneth spent the night in her bed only once – when she was frightened by a prowler – and even then he did not have sex with her.

Peggy moved into the duplex on her return, and Kenneth remained at his old apartment to await delivery of some furniture. Jean Connolly, too, soon moved in with her again. When Kenneth eventually appeared, he spent all his time on Peggy's floor of the duplex because his floor was being extravagantly decorated. Though Max had taken the Lhasa apso, Kachina, he had left behind the couple's two Persian cats, Romeo and Gypsy; Kenneth's boxer, Imperator, rounded out the household. When the gallery reopened for the fall season, Peggy brought Imperator to work every day.

Other changes in Peggy's quotidian life became apparent that fall; for one thing, Kenneth was very particular about her wardrobe. Previously, except when she wanted to go all out, her daily attire usually consisted of a 'light, summery dress' like a shirtwaist, according to a high-school-age artist who visited her gallery almost weekly. She often donned ankle-length bobby socks, reasoning that they were comfortable and gave her weak ankles some protection; one observer notes that Walter Winchell often poked fun at this habit in his gossip column. She favored bright red, a color that Kenneth insisted she give up entirely. He preferred her in blue, and especially liked her in a dark blue suit with a row of brass buttons, telling her that her *gamin* quality was most attractive. (Though he had once helped her outfit and make herself up as a boy for a party, when they arrived at the gathering he ignored her, perhaps fearful of talk.) She also added to her wardrobe of coats – mostly secondhand furs from the Ritz Thrift Shop – but Kenneth prevailed on her to buy a new sable coat, which he insisted she hike up before sitting down, in order to preserve the nap. Despite his skill with Max Factor – and a whole dressing table full of cosmetics – Kenneth does not seem to have helped Peggy with her makeup: she still limited her toilette to hastily applied eyebrow pencil and a bold, often smeary line of red lipstick. (Observations about Peggy's wardrobe and appearance in New York in the forties are often juxtaposed with remarks on the impression she made in her middle and later years, when it was said that she was far more elegant than she had ever been in New York.)

As the decade progressed, she would add pounds to her previously very slender frame – though Anne Dunn, the wife of her unofficial nephew Michael Wishart, remembers that, 'Though her waistline grew, she maintained an appealing angular quality – the same birdlike wrists and ankles' that could still make this unconventional-looking woman appear attractive. There was no question, however, that her habit of dyeing her hair jet-black harshened her complexion and features, and the mop-top style in which she wore her hair did not help matters. And, of course, there was the nose, 'her unfortunate nose, a putty-shaped blob,' according to the *View* editor John Myers. But 'she had style,' as one observer said. 'There was something about the way she held herself, the way she gestured.' Yoko Ono, who later became a friend, comments that Peggy was 'not at all ugly,' adding, 'When a woman is powerful others will go to any lengths to criticize her – and denigrating her looks is one of the easiest means around.'

The new ménage worked surprisingly well, though Kenneth could get angry at some of Jean's habits: she helped herself to anything in the duplex, once, unforgivably, taking the last bottle of Scotch in the house. And Kenneth's own behavior could sometimes be annoying. He took to closing the doors behind the kitchen and pantry on his floor from the other rooms; Peggy and Jean could use the cooking area by way of the back stairs but were denied access to the rest of his apartment. At other times, though, Kenneth seemed to want to make it known to the world that Peggy was his mistress. He cooked and served her lunch every Sunday on his floor, for example – he was a fine cook, far easier in the kitchen than Peggy, who was only mediocre – and if her phone downstairs rang, he would rush to answer it. As it was, many of Peggy's friends – and Kenneth's as well – were mystified as to what their arrangement was. He took multiple sex partners, but so did Peggy, and neither of them told the entire truth about their activities – but these were not considered grave sins in their milieu. In this context, the relevant question is, Did he make her happy? He does seem to have had sex with her in the beginning, and to have reassured her often by holding her in his arms and otherwise showing physical affection. He seemed to want to live with her. Was he hiding his sexual preferences, or were his motives more complicated?

Many women relish the attention offered them by gay men, especially in helping them with their appearance, but what exactly are the terms of that exchange? What happens, finally, between a homosexual man and a hetero-sexual woman – especially between two people living in relative intimacy? It is impossible to miss the sense that a very delicate balance of power reigned in the duplex.

It would be too easy to see Peggy as mired in yet another masochistic relationship. True, even her supporters were aware of her lack of self-esteem. Her friend Eileen Finletter's comment that there was something 'off' about Peggy, a central absence of confidence, and Anne Dunn's speculation that Peggy had no self-regard, which was picked up by others, are both relevant here. Peggy had always had a touch of the masochistic in her relationships, but, in the case of Kenneth Macpherson and her life in the duplex, this flaw explains the situation incompletely. For the most part, Peggy was happy there: most of the time, she felt loved, she lived in beautiful surroundings, she enjoyed her new involvement in fashion – and her gallery was a huge success, almost entirely due to her efforts. 'I love my independent life,' she told Emily. 'I have Marcel and my lesbian friend McPherson [sic] and my hard working girl's life.' Still, something about the situation did not sit easily – and over the next few months the various agendas floating through the duplex would begin to make themselves clear in disturbing ways indeed.

Peggy's professional life, at least, was to become considerably simplified by a new goal: she was to devote the next four years to furthering the career of Jackson Pollock.

14

Two Stories: Pollock and Pegeen

The 1943 fall season at Art of This Century opened with another crowd pleaser: 'Masterworks of Early de Chirico,' a one-man show featuring the art of the Greek-born Italian artist. Three paintings were from Peggy's collection: *The Rose Tower* (1913), which she had bought for $2,525; *The Dream of the Poet* (1915), $750; and *The Gentle Afternoon* (1916), $1,725. The other thirteen paintings were borrowed from museums and private collections. One well-known work, *The Melancholy and Mystery of the Street* (1914), which showed a girl rolling a hoop in an empty plaza, caught both Peggy's and Kenneth's fancy, and Peggy tried desperately to buy it, to no avail; the owner wouldn't part with it.

The show was received warmly. The *New York Times* stated unequivocally, 'You cannot afford to miss seeing [the paintings] if you are interested at all in probing the modern genesis of Surrealism.' Though the critic probably intended to stress the importance of the show, he or she was also stating an essential fact about de Chirico's work: 'Masterworks of Early de Chirico' *were* his masterworks, painted from 1910 to 1920; after 1920 his style changed almost completely, and he disavowed his early works. The features of 'early' de Chirico – the vast urban squares, empty but for a figure or two or perhaps a statue, lit by the bright sun with marked shadows and characterized by odd, sometimes competing perspectives – impressed the European surrealists enormously, though the Italian artist never considered himself part of their movement.

In fact, however, the reception of de Chirico and those surrealists like Magritte, Ernst, Delvaux, and, especially, Dali, whose work was marked by a photographic precision, was something that divided the European surrealists from the younger American artists. Called by the art historian Werner Haftmann 'veristic' surrealism, these European works accessed the unconscious and produced bizarre juxtapositions of realistically rendered images, like Dali's drooping watch. On the other hand, American artists looked to surrealism for its ideas, its foundation in dreams, its embrace of at times repugnant figures and images, but rejected its emphasis on realistic, or veristic, renderings. Haftmann has described this strain of surrealism, which the Americans picked up on, as 'absolute' surrealism, best illustrated in the work of Masson, Picasso, and Miró – and to a lesser extent, Tanguy. The nature of this development can be understood by looking at the role of Matta in the forties art scene and the development of abstract expressionism.

Educated in Chile as an architect, Matta had studied for three years with Le Corbusier in Paris. But he was dissuaded from an architectural career in 1937, when he saw in *Cahiers d'art* a reproduction of Duchamp's *Passage from the Virgin to the Bride* (1912). At the magazine's offices, he looked up Duchamp's home address and presented himself there, a meeting that convinced him to follow the way of Duchamp rather than that of Le Corbusier. Shortly afterward, he met Breton, who welcomed him 'as a loved son, an heir apparent.' Like Tanguy, Matta reached American shores in 1939, earlier than the other Europeans and, like Duchamp and unlike the other European artists, he was relatively fluent in English. He immediately sought out such American artists as Gorky, de Kooning, and, especially, Robert Motherwell. Motherwell's response to Matta was extreme: 'He was the most energetic, poetic, charming, brilliant young artist that I've ever met.' Matta's work suggested a way for modern painters to break free from the strictures of cubism; his paintings of these years show morphological abstractions, 'drawn' in black or white paint, the inspirations for which Matta believed he had received by accessing the unconscious, which offered a surer image than the eye could provide.

For reasons that some have construed as self-serving or ambitious and others as purely intellectual, Matta wanted to take the idea of surrealism in new directions, correctly sensing that the movement had qualities to offer that young American artists, fed up with Depression realism and eager to seek out a new aesthetic, would find especially well suited to their concerns. To this end he held small gatherings in his 12th Street studio (designed by Kiesler, the apartment had curved walls), including, in the beginning, surrealist parlor games. In the Breton-derived 'Exquisite Corpse,' each participant would write one word on a corner of a piece of paper and then fold it over; after the last person took a turn, the paper was opened and the absurdist sentence read aloud. (The game took its name from the result of an early experiment of Breton's, 'The exquisite corpse shall drink the young wine.') The idea was to introduce the young participants – Motherwell,

Baziotes, Peter Busa, and Pollock – to the concept of automatism and the beauty or impact of random juxtaposition. Through tapping into the unconscious without the censorship of the conscious mind, the artist could summon up images that seemed to have little relation to physical reality. Matta's meetings evolved into more meaningful sessions in the fall and winter of 1942. He asked his guests to create art in automatic or unconscious response to themes he provided for them, like fire, or the hours of the day. Though the artists grew somewhat impatient with the intellectual content Matta insisted on finding in this activity and his polemical and dogmatic approach, they did like the process otherwise and the art that came out of it. Also, the organicism of the activity made sense to them. Although the informal group dispersed, Matta had wrought a kind of alchemy. It was, to some American artists, as if Matta had validated abstraction, paving the way toward the large canvases of abstract expressionism.

Pollock seemed perhaps most resistant to the structured nature of Matta's gatherings. Once Matta told the artist to roll a pair of dice every hour and record the numbers. 'That was more than Jackson could take,' said Peter Busa. 'He just got up and walked out.' Matta's insistence on the occult – he talked about interplanetary communication and extrasensory perception – was not helpful to most of the other artists, nor were his teaching methods. As the art historian Martica Sawin has pointed out, 'For none of the painters involved was [Matta's circle] a definitive commitment, but it opened the possibility that a few young Americans might indeed develop a new style that advanced beyond Europe's last avant-garde and that they might form a group, and be known, if not as automatists, then as something else not yet named.' As Busa later told his erstwhile mentor, 'It was your presence, Matta, that personalized Surrealism for us . . . Surrealism was a fuse that lit up the American scene.'

Jackson Pollock was in those days raw, uncouth, barely socialized, a child of the hardscrabble American West, yet possessed of an explosive talent – he could not be less like the two artists whom Peggy found most congenial to her, Duchamp and Breton. He was born in 1912 in Cody, Wyoming, to a father who moved restlessly from place to place, trying to find a farm he could work for a profit, and a mother who, according to Jackson's sister-in-law, 'saw all her sons as potential geniuses, [and] wanted them to be artists of some kind.' Pollock, the youngest of five sons, grew up in Arizona and California, first studying art at Manual Arts High School in Los Angeles. His school years were marked by generally rebellious behavior, and he is said to have started drinking in his early teens.

Pollock came to New York in 1930 and enrolled at the Art Students League. The regionalist Thomas Hart Benton became an important mentor, and, with the work of Albert Pinkham Ryder, an important early influence. Pollock became acquainted with the murals of the Mexican artists José Clemente Orosco, David Alfaro Siqueiros, and Diego Rivera. After traveling extensively in the United States, he settled in New York City and worked on the WPA Federal Art Project from 1935 to 1942. In 1936 he was part of an experimental workshop in New York run by Siqueiros, another formative experience. Along the way he came under the influence of a remarkable man, the painter and critic John Graham, who would direct him to the unconscious and to Jung, and, perhaps most importantly, to Picasso, whose *Guernica* (1937) Pollock first saw in 1939. At about this point he fell in with Matta and the surrealists.

In 1936 he met the woman he would marry nine years later, Lee Krasner, a daughter of Orthodox Jewish parents from Brooklyn and a striving and dedicated painter who studied from 1937 to 1940 with the artist Hans Hoffman, a legendary teacher. 'Lee was an intense, serious person who didn't go for small talk or nonsense . . . Mature and strong but by no means affectionate, she could be a good friend if you went along with her ideas,' said an artist friend. She could be blunt and was not afraid to be critical of Pollock's work, but essentially she took a maternal role in his life, even suspending her own painting for some years.

Pollock was by 1943 a troubled, even tortured man who was already a severe alcoholic. Contrary to established myths about him, concerned family members and Lee did see to it that he got help; in 1938 he had been hospitalized for four months and treated for alcoholism, and thereafter he saw a succession of Jungian analysts in an attempt to curb his drinking and his rages and to tame and also free up his unconscious, or recognize the usefulness of psychic automatism to release unconscious imagery. (Pollock's constant attempts to find a cure for his inner turmoil belie the legendary view of the man, which insists he was completely self-absorbed and hell-bent on self-destruction.) By the early forties he was producing dense abstractions with bold, disturbing images that were highly indebted to Picasso and rich in symbolism. *Stenographic Figure*, the painting that so impressed Mondrian at Art of This Century's Spring Salon of 1943, shows a rather horrifying female creature reaching out a paw to a withered male figure, but the depressing image is rendered in luminous, sure colors, with mysterious symbols and numbers in the background, perhaps showing the influence of Matta's teachings.

It was almost impossible then, and is still very hard for many people today, to 'like' Pollock's early work. Those paintings, with their heavy symbolic content, strike many viewers seeing them for the first time as profoundly disturbing. 'You had to work to like them,' said fellow artist and friend Peter Busa. 'They were not easy paintings. But the closer you looked and the more you thought about them, the more you saw and the better they looked.'

Peggy came only gradually to an appreciation of Pollock's work. In the summer of 1943, she decided to visit Pollock's studio and see his work en masse, with an eye to offering him a one-man show. Unfortunately, the day appointed for her visit, June 23, was Peter Busa's wedding day, and Pollock inevitably stumbled home drunk to find that Peggy had arrived before him. Peggy was already furious at having to wait, and complained bitterly about having to climb four flights of stairs. When she finally saw his work, she expressed admiration but told Lee and Jackson that she would be sending Duchamp over to take a look. Duchamp, when he came, merely murmured his approval.

Peggy took the gamble of producing a Pollock show, perhaps because Putzel, who had complete faith in Pollock's talents and his future stature, immediately stepped in and began negotiating with him. Art of This Century gave Pollock a one-man show in November. To allow Pollock time to prepare for the show, and to continue to work afterward, Peggy agreed to pay him $150 every month for a year. At the end of the year, she deducted the $1,800 advance from the total proceeds of sales from his painting, minus a one-third commission. Pollock would make money only if the gallery sold $2,700 worth of work; if it sold less than that, he was to make up the shortfall in paintings. Peggy also stipulated that he would paint a mural to hang in the lobby of her apartment building, the mural to be delivered on time for the show's opening day. Pollock's elation was, as might be guessed, considerable; to celebrate, he went with Howard Putzel and fellow artists Mark Rothko and Charles Seliger out to dinner at the Minetta Tavern and then to a double bill of *Dracula* and *Frankenstein* (both 1931) at a Times Square movie theater.

It was an unprecedented contract. It was rare indeed at the time for a patron to show such faith in any one artist, to provide such free and generous rein. It was astonishing to Pollock's artist friends, who were not in the scene for the money. 'We were delighted, overjoyed by an occasional $100 sale,' says Charles Seliger, one of Peggy's young artists. To his fellow artist Gerome Kamrowski, Pollock's contract was the equivalent of a World Series-winning home run by a local hero: 'One day – I think it was a September day – there were two big success stories: Frank Sinatra was swinging big at the Paramount Theater, he'd made like thousands of dollars, and Jackson Pollock had gotten this contract from Peggy Guggenheim. He was the first American painter that I know of to receive a contract in my time as a painter.'

*

Peggy's eye was sharp enough that she regarded her total support of Pollock as a worthwhile gamble. As Jimmy Ernst observed, 'She was very proud of having helped Pollock, and she did. I don't know what would have happened to him at that time; nobody was going to take a chance on *that*.'

Because Peggy had very emphatically decided to take a chance on *that*, she issued a statement to the press a week before Pollock's one-person show opened: 'I consider this exhibition to be something of an event in the contemporary history of American art . . . I consider [Pollock] to be one of the strongest and most interesting American painters.' Not an outrageous comment today, it might seem – but Peggy was speaking long before the dramatic poured paintings that became Pollock's more familiar legacy. Even in Pollock's most difficult and tortured early works, Peggy saw genius – and was willing to stake her reputation on it.

The November 1943 show did not disappoint, though in retrospect responses such as Bob Coates's in *The New Yorker* – 'At Art of This Century there is what seems to be an authentic discovery' – seem awfully tepid, especially given Peggy's commitment and Putzel's enthusiasm. James Johnson Sweeney had also decided to stick his neck out over Pollock, contributing an introduction to the show's catalogue. 'Pollock's talent is volcanic,' he wrote. 'It has fire. It is unpredictable. It is undisciplined. It spills itself out in a mineral prodigality not yet crystallized. It is lavish, explosive, untidy.' Thus defending himself and Pollock against too ready judgments – though Pollock would, in fact, take great offense at Sweeney's words about his lack of discipline – the critic nonetheless concluded, 'Among young painters, Jackson Pollock offers unusual promise in his exuberance, independence, and native sensibility. If he continues to exploit these qualities with the courage and conscience he has shown so far, he will fulfill that promise.' Peggy, in her memoirs, wrote, 'In a way, Sweeney replaced Mr. Read in my life,' recalling the role that the British critic had played when she set out to amass her collection. She often referred to Pollock as her and Sweeney's 'spiritual offspring.'

Some critics took a tone of honest yet tentative surprise: Maude Riley, the reviewer for *Art Digest*, wrote, 'We like all this. Pollock is out a-questing and he goes hell-bent at each canvas.' But the opinion that mattered most – and not because the reviewer was famous, for his reputation had not yet been made, but because it was so confidently expressed – was that of the *Nation* reviewer, Clement Greenberg, newly returned from the armed services. Although not unequivocal, Greenberg seemed to sense that something portentous was happening: '[Pollock] is the first painter I know of to have got something positive from the muddiness of color that so profoundly characterizes a great deal of American painting.' He concluded with a similar double-edged comment, yet he made it clear that Jackson Pollock had captured his interest. Rightly, he saw Pollock as still too hampered by the influence of the great modernists: 'Pollock has gone through the influences of Miró, Picasso, Mexican painting, and what not, and has come out on the other side at the age of thirty-one, painting mostly with his own brush, [but] in his search for style he is liable to lapse into an influence.'

Neither Pollock nor Peggy felt exactly vindicated by the opening – and perhaps especially Peggy, who would sell just one Pollock, a drawing, during the show, to Kenneth Macpherson. But there was an unmistakable sense that positions were being taken and sides drawn – in short, that art history was being made.

Even beyond the day-to-day ambiguities of life with a bisexual man possessed of an outsized ego, life was not going smoothly in the duplex on East 61st Street. Peggy had looked the other way for a long time as far as her daughter was concerned. Pegeen had matured into a willowy blonde with sad eyes, large breasts, and a distinctly beseeching expression: she had the Nordic good looks of the Vails, but her face bore a marked resemblance to her mother (though she lacked the infamous nose): both mother and daughter, according to Anne Dunn, had a distinctive habit of drawing air in through the mouth and tucking their chins back into their necks. Somewhat like her mother, Pegeen could be very outspoken and very shy at the same time. Sometimes alcohol, to which she was very susceptible, was the culprit. 'But she could be fun and funny – full of laughs,' maintains Eileen Finletter: she had her mother's dry wit. Yet Finletter also had the distinct sense that Pegeen 'let things happen to her,' that she was a passive agent in her own self-destruction. According to Michael Wishart, Peggy's honorary nephew from her Garman days, Pegeen's was 'an exquisite and delicate temperament.' He could never remember her long golden hair without thinking of Ophelia.

Pegeen had been painting since she was a child, but her style remained primitivistic, naive. Wishart found her painting 'mysterious' and commented that she represented daily life in her artwork as if 'made from barley sugar.' Pegeen's paintings, brightly hued, usually showed girls with long blond hair, like herself, their breasts exposed and their pink nipples painted in – not unlike the child-woman she seems to have been herself. Herbert Read wrote a preface to a much later exhibit of hers with extreme hyperbole, but what he said has some resonance: 'This gaiety . . . Pegeen by some miracle or subterfuge has retained. I have known her since she was a child, and have seen her grow in bodily stature and worldly wisdom; but a brilliant and seemingly ephemeral fire-bird, which she released in those early years, has survived and brightly takes the air when her brushes make their wand-like motions.'

Pegeen had been loudly unhappy since early adolescence and had battled with her mother incessantly throughout Peggy's courtship of and marriage to Max Ernst. She was deeply hurt when her stepmother, Kay Boyle, to whom she was very close, left her father, Laurence, for Joseph Franckenstein. (In 1941, she wrote a letter to Emily Coleman, saying, 'I hardly ever see Kay, much to my disappointment. Well I guess there's no use crying over spilt milk. I just can't bear thinking of Megève, and all the happy times we had there.') Max had been something of a champion of hers, and she must have felt dev-astated when he, too, went out of her life, following the departures of other father figures like John Holms and Douglas Garman. One can only guess at her reaction to Laurence's upcoming marriage to Jean Connolly. And Pegeen resoundingly hated the Lenox School, where she was finishing her second year, and had no intention of going on to Finch Junior College, the institu-tion affiliated with Lenox. Her mother, presumably otherwise engaged, did not come to her graduation from Lenox in June, though she gave Pegeen money for a dress. The Mexican artist Rufino Tamayo, whom Pegeen had met through Peggy, picked out a beautiful white dress for her for the occasion, but for Pegeen the day was spoiled because of her mother's absence. The girl would never forget this lapse.

After graduation, Pegeen set out for Mexico, where she had spent the pre-vious summer, taking with her Barbara Reis, the daughter of Peggy's accountant, and another friend. Peggy seldom heard from her but received occasional word through Laurence because Pegeen wrote frequently to Bobby Vail, the Vail-Boyle stepsister closest to her in age. Time passed, and Barbara Reis came home safely. But in October, Peggy received a phone call from Becky Reis, Barbara's mother, telling her that she had heard from Leonora Carrington – then living in Mexico – that Pegeen 'was in the most dangerous company,' as Peggy put it in her memoirs. Becky said Peggy should go after her daughter at once or find someone to go for her. Peggy tried to get a plane reser-vation, but no seat was available for a week. Meanwhile, she and Laurence tried to telephone Pegeen, only to get through to Acapulco finally and be told that their daughter would not come to the phone. Peggy phoned Leonora in Mexico City and asked her to rescue Pegeen, but Leonora said this would involve too much 'responsibility, authority, and money.' Then a wire came from Pegeen and, after that, several letters, saying she had a plane reservation and would be home soon. Peggy canceled her own plane reservation.

Though Peggy does not say so in her memoirs, it appears that Laurence finally went to Mexico to rescue his daughter. The whole wretched story then fell into place: Pegeen had spent time aboard the *Sirocco*, the yacht belonging to Errol Flynn, the actor and Nazi sympathizer, who had been accused several times of statutory rape. On board she acquired a venereal disease. From there she had gone to live with the dirt-poor family of an Acapulco diver named Chango, with whom she had fallen in love. After retrieving Pegeen, Laurence dropped her off at the door of Peggy's building at around midnight.

Peggy was delighted and relieved to see her daughter, and Pegeen was happy to see her mother in the apartment she had urged Peggy to take in the spring. Quite naturally, however, Pegeen was confused by the presence of Kenneth Macpherson, whom she perversely called 'Daddy.' Kenneth seems to have realized the incongruity of the situation. Soon he was complaining about the noise Pegeen's high heels made on the wooden floors and the way her voice carried throughout the duplex. About five weeks after her return, Pegeen wrote several plaintive letters to Emily Coleman, telling her of her sulfa cure (for the venereal disease), which left her feeling weak, and how much she missed Chango.

Pegeen had come back to New York City only conditionally, holding out the threat that she might return to her diver boyfriend in Acapulco at any time. There was not much to hold her to New York; the idea of college had been shelved. With most of the boys her age either away at war or in college themselves, she had little male companionship. Peggy might have seen that Pegeen was badly in need of a father figure, perhaps remembering her own loss of her father at a young age. Peggy also knew how much she had regretted never attending college, but she seems to have given up on Pegeen's education. Perhaps now she simply wanted to keep her daughter near her.

Pegeen picked up on the hopelessness of her situation. 'Life seems so shallow and absurd,' she wrote Emily. Even things that had once pleased her seemed ridiculous now: 'I go to parties a lot, where I see all the "Surrealists" and suddenly burst out in a hysterical laugh. It's all lost its former charm.' Not long after she wrote Emily a series of letters talking about suicide: 'I despise myself,' she wrote, 'I went rotten. I'm mouldy,' signing off, 'Sorry to have bothered you.' She particularly hated relying on her mother for money. According to Pegeen, Peggy would give her some cash, then take it back, saying, 'You can't have your own way in everything,' and flounce out of the room. In ten minutes, though, she would be back, thrusting the cash at Pegeen. 'Being bribed by her money drives me crazy,' Pegeen wrote. It was a terrible drama illustrating Peggy's mothering talents, or lack of them, as she pantomimed giving, removing, and capriciously restoring her love for her daughter.

Peggy found her daughter 'pathetic,' as she later wrote. (She was impatient with all of Pegeen's talk about Chango, complaining to Emily that she was being 'so stupid and romantic.') When she found out that Emily and Pegeen had been corresponding, she was furious. What Pegeen really needed, Peggy thought, was a man.

At the time of his first one-man show at Art of This Century, Pollock had agreed to paint a mural to hang in the entrance hall of Peggy's apartment building, but it was some time before he got around to the task. The previous spring he had taken a job, ironically enough, with Solomon Guggenheim's Museum of Non-Objective Painting. After failing to impress the baroness with his portfolio, he was performing custodial duties and stretching canvases. Because he worked the noon-to-6:00 shift and seldom rose before 10:00 in the morning, he had little enough time to paint. In any event, the job did not last long. Soon after he signed the contract with Peggy, he either quit or was fired.

To make a large enough space on the wall of his studio to hang the canvas for Peggy's mural, Pollock had to take out a wall that separated his studio from one that had been his wife Lee's. (She was now spending all her time nursing Jackson or doing promotional work for him. Peggy, for instance, had asked her to stuff and address twelve hundred invitations to Pollock's show – and then scolded her in front of everyone in the gallery for making mistakes on three of them.) About the approximately twenty-by-eight-foot canvas, Pollock told his brother, 'It looks pretty good, but exciting as all hell.'

The stories around the timing of the painting of the mural and its hanging are numerous, and most are wrong. Legend has it that Pollock painted the mural in one fell swoop the day before the opening, from dusk one day to dusk the next, and that he rolled up the canvas and carried it, with the stretcher, to Peggy's apartment building on the day of the show. But the paint would not have been sufficiently dry for him to do so. Also, a twenty-by-eight-foot canvas saturated with paint would have been too heavy for one man to carry – not to mention the over-sized stretcher, even broken down. The definitive history of the painting that Lee Krasner called, simply, *Mural*, remained a mystery for some time.

Legends abound about the hanging of *Mural* as well. It has been said several times that when Pollock brought the painting to Peggy's building, he found the canvas was too high for the wall, and that Duchamp, when called in to help, lopped eight inches off the bottom of it. But none of the edges of *Mural* are cut, as is clear in photographs of the completed work. What really happened, according to Francis V. O'Connor, the leading Pollock authority, is that the painting was wide enough but not tall enough to fit the space. O'Connor says that Pollock probably measured the space correctly – he wrote his brother on July 29, 1943, that the piece was to be eight feet eleven and a half inches tall and nineteen feet nine inches wide – but bought a stretcher that was eight feet tall, almost a foot shorter. It is true that Peggy called Duchamp in to help when Pollock repeatedly phoned her about the difficulty in hanging it, but it is unlikely that the rather inventive device that the 'workman' she mentioned – surely a technically skilled framer – devised to make up the difference, in the form of a frame that would fit the space, can have been made in a matter of hours.

However, the discovery of a letter from Peggy to Emily Coleman postmarked November 12, 1943, announcing that the painting was finished and had been hung (presumably by the time of the opening on November 9), together with a previously unexplained postcard from Pollock to his brother saying he had painted the mural that summer, puts the lie to most of these legends. 'I painted quite a large mural for Miss Guggenheim's house during the summer. 8 feet by 20 feet; it was grand fun,' Pollock wrote to his brother Frank on January 15, 1944. He would have had plenty of time to touch it up after the initial session, which photographs and conservators have confirmed he did. And he would not have needed to trundle the wet canvas to Peggy's, as it would have long been dry. The new date also allows time for the framing and hanging of the painting, which was so complicated that it could not have been done over the course of one day. Peggy's November 12 letter to Emily states, 'We had a party for the new genius Jackson Pollock, who is having a show here now. He painted a 20 foot mural in my house in the entrance. Everyone likes it except Kenneth. Rather bad luck on him as he has to see it every time he goes in and out.'

Just as the history of Mural was murky, so too is the nature of Peggy's relationship with Pollock. It is very unlikely that they went to bed together, whether successfully or not. In her memoirs, Peggy said flatly, 'My relationship with Pollock was purely that of artist and patron, and Lee was the intermediary.' Peggy was nothing if not a good storyteller, and she surely would not have hesitated to produce a good sexual tale had there been any basis for it. But Pollock was not her type at all. Tall and balding, he had smoldering good looks, but his physical presence was somewhat overwhelming, and bearish men did not appeal to Peggy. She preferred verbal partners, as her own talents were in that line, and Pollock was not always articulate, especially with someone who stood in any kind of a power relation to him, as Peggy did. And while she could hold her own with almost every drinker – and though Laurence, John Holms, and even Kenneth Macpherson were probably alcoholics – Peggy, perhaps as a result of her marriage to Laurence, did not like violent men, and with every year was less tolerant of unpredictability. Pollock, it is equally clear, would not have found her attractive; he had problems with women, particularly powerful ones. Nor would he have been likely to jeopardize his financial future, however drunk he might have been on any given occasion. Lee Krasner, herself somewhat formidable, would have made it very clear to Pollock that Peggy was his last and best hope.

The painting of *Mural*, as it turned out, constituted something of a breakthrough in Pollock's work. The largest piece he had yet completed, it seems to have freed up his imagination and led him to put his whole body into applying paint to the canvas, an engagement with the material that would mark his later, poured paintings. *Mural* was more abstract than his earlier painting; the arabesques of color over black shapes, the calligraphic nature of the design (which contained very little pouring), and the raw energy that characterize *Mural* mark it as a transitional work in his development.

Legend also has it that Pollock oversaw the hanging of the painting and then went upstairs to the duplex, where Jean Connolly was giving a party, and peed in the fireplace; Peggy's more conservative memory is that he walked naked into the room. If this indeed happened, it would have been only one time among many that the painter tried her patience. However open-minded and bohemian-leaning Peggy might have been, Pollock's antics were often beyond the pale, to her mind. 'Pollock was drunk so much of the time,' Peggy wrote to one of the editors of the painter's *catalogue raisonné*, 'that one did not see him too often. He could not be invited to come and meet the people who bought his paintings, which was a great handicap . . . It was difficult to invite [him and Lee Krasner] to parties, as he drank so much, and did unpleasant things on such occasions. He was very sweet when not drunk. I think he was a very frightened person, and felt trapped in the city life. He probably would have been happier in the western prairies.'

Sales often depended on how collector and artist got along. Some artists were comparative delights to a gallery owner like Peggy. Motherwell, for instance, was urbane, good-looking, articulate, and hailed from the same social class as his well-off collectors. Pollock was another story entirely. And Peggy had to sell his work to justify his stipend. It was a grim, upward progress, but both painter and patron were thrilled with Pollock's critical success and the reflected glory in which Peggy could bask.

15

Making a Mark

In the spring of 1944 one of the people whose advice Peggy relied on most heavily announced his decision to move on: Howard Putzel had plans to open his own establishment, the 67 Gallery at 67 East 57th Street, in part supported by funds advanced him by Kenneth Macpherson. Peggy, who said of Putzel, 'He was in a way my master: surely not my pupil,' had much in common with him. They were born just six days apart, and they both lost their fathers at almost the same age. Putzel was content to work behind the scenes for a time, pleased to see artists whom he had supported and directed to Peggy thrive, but no doubt he had ambitions of his own. He seems to have had few material resources – certainly he owned little art. In New York, his mother lived at the Plaza Hotel, but evidently she shared none of her wealth with her son. At the 67 Gallery, Putzel slept on the bathroom floor.

Putzel's new establishment got off to a strong start: he showed recent ballet designs by Eugene Berman and then mounted an impressive exhibit called 'A Problem for Critics,' which featured Krasner, Rothko, Masson, Pollock, Richard Pousette-Dart, Charles Seliger, Rufino Tamayo, Gorky, and Adolph Gottlieb next to Miró, Arp, and Picasso; the critics dutifully tried to sort out the rather open-ended problem the show set before them. Never in good physical condition – he was plagued by alcohol-related problems, heart irregularities, a thyroid condition, and epilepsy – Putzel died a year later, and his body was found in his gallery. Most attributed the death to his heart, though some, including Peggy, considered it a suicide.

It was Emily Coleman who found a new adviser for Peggy. The gulf between her and Peggy had widened as a result of Emily's recent conversion to Catholicism through the writings of the French theologian and philosopher Jacques Maritain. Emily became so devout that she left her cowboy second husband because the Church did not recognize her divorce from her first. ('To me the whole thing is childish irrational and extremely unintelligent,' Peggy wrote Emily in April.) But Emily was passing through New York in July and brought with her Marius Bewley, a literary critic who had had bad luck so far in securing an academic position. More openly homosexual than Putzel, Bewley was a native of St. Louis but had acquired an English accent at Cambridge, where he was educated; he reminded one visitor of 'an English vicar.' He would come to work for Peggy in the fall. Though he possessed few developed aesthetic preferences in art and would never advise Peggy as directly as Putzel had done, he was a frequent contributor to *View* and quickly picked up the subtleties of the art world's social scene.

Bewley also added a new sexual undercurrent to the scene at the gallery. As did Kenneth Macpherson, the homosexuals in Peggy's circle deployed the term *Athenian* as a code word for homosexuality, and Athenian matters preoccupied Peggy and Bewley in 1945. Julian Beck, a talented twenty-year-old painter, first exhibited at Art of This Century in a group show in 1945. Something more than a flirtation went on between Bewley and Beck, though they may not have consummated their relationship. Beck at the time was 'flashily beautiful,' according to a companion: very thin, very tall, with a long mane of blond hair, a hairstyle quite rare for men in those years. He was a ubiquitous figure at the gallery, always underfoot, it seemed. Peggy welcomed his presence until he began bringing with him an eighteen-year-old girl, Judith Malina. Malina characterizes herself then as a bobbysoxer with schoolbooks under her arm, far too 'square' to interest Peggy, whom she found intimidating. In fact, Peggy seemed to resent her presence, particularly as she began to treat the gallery as 'a local soda fountain,' says Malina. Bewley, who had convinced Peggy to show Beck's work, became jealous of Beck's attention to Malina and grew resentful; one day, in a rage, he tore up a portfolio of drawings that the artist had brought to the gallery for consideration.

By this point Peggy was deeply concerned with her assistant's flirtation with the dashing painter; perhaps she was interested in Beck herself, or perhaps she was championing Bewley as a romantic partner for Beck, but at any rate she wrote Beck a decidedly strange letter, worth quoting in its entirety: 'After careful consideration of your new problem in changing your sex I have decided that it would be better for you not to be connected with this very Athenian gallery. It can do you no good, and possibly great harm, and with all my maternal and friendly interest for you I feel obliged to ask you to take away your drawings. I deeply regret this as I like your work exceedingly well, but one cannot allow art to come first in life in such delicate matters.' Bewley no doubt had a hand in composing this letter, but Peggy clearly backed him.

Malina and Beck would marry in 1948. Beck gave up painting, and the couple went on to found the experimental and politically engaged Living Theatre. Malina stresses that, while Peggy surrounded herself with a number of 'pretty boys,' no discrete gay group was associated with the gallery, despite Bewley's interests. Peggy, still living platonically with Kenneth Macpherson (who had taken up with a new boyfriend whom Peggy bedded first, mistaking his interest in Kenneth for an interest in her), felt comfortable in a gay milieu.

Indeed, Peggy's sex life was becoming frenetic in this New York interval. There was a compulsive aspect to it that even friendly observers noted. Sara Havelock-Allen, a British friend of Peggy's, has advanced an interesting theory about Peggy's behavior. 'Going to bed with so many men made her feel less ugly. Each new conquest made her feel attractive.' It is indeed likely that Peggy saw her liaisons as confirmation that she was still desirable, and that they bolstered her often shaky feelings of self-worth. Certainly, very forthright in such matters, she showed no reticence in pursuing others.

The experience of the artist Jock Stockwell, a veteran of the Lincoln Brigade in the Spanish civil war and a passing fancy who came into Peggy's life in 1946, bears out this impression. He brought a portfolio of drawings for her consideration, but she showed interest instead in the twenty-nine-year-old Stockwell himself. She took him for a drink at the Russian Tea Room, commenting, after he returned to the table following a trip to the restroom, 'Nice tush.' They repaired to the gallery, where Peggy took him into the little, seldom-used office she maintained behind the Abstract Gallery. They had sex five times over the next three days, according to Stockwell, who characterized Peggy as 'very demanding sexually.' He admired her as a woman with that much money and that much freedom, but she showed no further interest in him after the three-day fling. He thought she did this kind of thing 'on a regular basis,' and believes she had another, more pressing love interest at the time.

More than once, Peggy and the bisexual Charles Henri Ford, the artist, writer, and editor of *View*, went out and picked up men on the street. 'They were the same,' one observer notes, 'both sexual predators.' One evening Peggy and Charles brought a young man they met at a party back to Peggy's apartment; while the man and Peggy were engaged, Charles was getting undressed; Peggy looked over her partner's shoulder and eyed Charles. 'Nice body,' she said. Both took their turn and Peggy slipped the young man a $20 bill, which led Charles to remember the pickup later as their 'bandit-boy.'

Fabulous parties were the order of the day while she was living with Macpherson. The previous October the socialite Alice De Lamar had thrown a big party for the fifth anniversary of *View* at her estate in Weston,

Connecticut, renovating an old barn by installing hardwood floors for dancing and putting in bathrooms and a kitchen just for the occasion. A big
bonfire in the field next to the barn made the party site easy to find. Peggy
called it a 'wonderful pre-war party, a Bal Masqué.' She described the event
for Herbert Read: 'I was old fashioned and wore an eighteenth century
slightly Pietro Longhi dress in which I jitterbugged until five in the morning,
carrying my train over my arm, then drove back to New York at dawn, watching the sun rise.' Boys arrived on roller skates dressed as nuns, and Charles
Henri Ford and Parker Tyler were dressed as leaf children. The art-world fixture John Myers, impersonating the eighteenth-century French poet Alfred
de Musset with a laurel wreath on his head, recorded in his diary, 'When
Peggy Guggenheim whirled by, wearing a Venetian gown with a tricorn on
her head, the skirt billowed out revealing not only her bare legs but also the
fact that she had absolutely nothing on beneath her dress.'

Peggy had a new distraction as well. Having spent the summer visiting
friends on Long Island and Fire Island (for a while she stayed at a cottage
rented by David Hare and Jacqueline Lamba, who had left Breton, her husband), Peggy had begun writing her autobiography. Clement Greenberg first
suggested the idea to her, and he interested the Dial Press in the volume.
Peggy took up the project with alacrity, telling Emily in October 1944 that
she had written about 360 pages. 'I only live and breathe for my book,' she
said. She had always loved writing, producing voluminous letters marked by
an earthy wit and a quick intelligence. The various diaries she had tried to
keep were always abandoned eventually, but she suspected that she had a
talent for writing. After she finished the first draft of her autobiography in
early 1945, she started in on a novel – evidently unfinished – writing a friend,
'Last night I started a new book & was surprised to discover how easy it was
to write a romantic novel.'

The gallery, of course, took up most of her time. Peggy gave three one-
man shows to American newcomers in the fall of 1944, perhaps emboldened
by Pollock's success. The first, William Baziotes, had shown his work in the
gallery's Spring Salons of 1943 and 1944; this was his first one-man show.
Greek-American, Baziotes was born in Reading, Pennsylvania, and had what
his wife, Ethel, says was a 'Saroyanesque childhood,' poor but happy. Moving
to New York in 1933, he eventually got work with the WPA Federal Art
Project, which began in 1935. Especially close to Matta, he was a believer in
accessing the unconscious through psychic automatism. He was inspired also
by Miró and Picasso, but his greatest influences, insists his widow, were
Baudelaire and the French symbolist poets. Baziotes's painting featured richly
colored biomorphic shapes. Interestingly, like a number of artists – Miró,

Derain, Braque, Vlaminck – he was an amateur boxer, and said to be quite good. When Peggy first visited Ethel and Bill Baziotes to see his work in their apartment-studio on Broadway and 103rd Street, they had only an unpainted chair for her to sit in, which promptly gave way, sending Peggy to the floor with her skirts flying up. 'But she wasn't embarrassed,' says Ethel. 'She was a good sport.' A friendship developed with the couple: Ethel especially found Peggy 'piquant' and noted 'her wonderful sense of humor.' A week or so after she first visited them, Peggy sent a wool bathrobe of Sindbad's and 'a wonderful Palm Beach suit' over to Bill. 'She was very maternal,' says Ethel.

Baziotes hung his own show in the company of Robert Motherwell, a good friend. Before the opening, he was so nervous that he fainted. The reviews of his show were mixed; Maude Riley, writing for *Art Digest*, commented, 'If many of the canvases seem repetitive, and if some of them seem somewhat unsure, these faults are less impressive than the many virtues.' Critics would be slow to warm to Baziotes's work, but when they did, they were very enthusiastic. Peggy bought two large gouaches and a small oil, paying $450, then quite a substantial sum. Ethel Baziotes thinks Peggy actually preferred Baziotes's art to Pollock's; she talked about him even more enthusiastically, in Ethel's view.

Peggy followed the Baziotes show with a one-man show for Robert Motherwell, featuring his paintings, drawings, and *papiers collés*. Motherwell was an intellectual young man who came from the state of Washington and initially studied philosophy at Harvard. He was much impressed by surrealism, and, like Baziotes, was an enthusiastic admirer of Matta and automatism. The reviews of his show were almost all admiring: the reviewer for *Art Digest*, typically, noted Motherwell's 'intense enjoyment of the materials of his medium.' In contrast to Baziotes, Motherwell was an easy artist to write about. Clement Greenberg noted this distinction in an important review that appeared in *The Nation*, calling Motherwell 'less upsetting because more traditional and easier to take.' Baziotes was Dionysian, he observed, and Motherwell Apollonian. Motherwell had only to find his own personal 'subject matter' and stop intellectualizing. Greenberg complimented Peggy for her 'enterprise' and 'acumen' in showing Baziotes, Motherwell, and Pollock. It is 'no exaggeration,' he concluded, 'to say that the future of American painting depends on what [Motherwell], Baziotes, Pollock, and only a comparatively few others do from now on.'

Following these two important shows was an exhibit of sculpture by another promising young artist, David Hare, until recently an editor of *VVV*. Because Hare was now having an affair with Breton's wife, this show no doubt marked Peggy's independence from the French surrealist; giving Hare a show sent a clear signal to Breton. But it should be noted that all three of these shows were assembled hastily; an exhibit of Giacometti's sculpture, originally announced for the fall of 1944, had been moved to January. This confusion underscores Putzel's importance in keeping the gallery on course and his successor Marius Bewley's relative inexperience. (Peggy had begun to complain that Bewley could not be trusted to run the gallery in her absence. 'Marius can't be left alone. He doesn't even notice when lights go out,' she said.)

Aside from writing her autobiography, much of Peggy's time that winter was given over to personal matters. Pegeen, who had recently announced her intention to model for a female artist friend for $1 an hour, had been living in a Greenwich Village studio for some months. Though her mother had noticed his attraction to Pegeen at the time of his Art of This Century show in the spring of 1943, she was unaware that Jean Hélion was seeing a good deal of her daughter. She probably would have approved, believing Pegeen needed a father figure in her life, but few details are known beyond the fact that on December 3, Pegeen, then nineteen, secretly married the forty-year-old painter. At the time, Hélion was gearing up for a show at the G Place Gallery in Washington, D.C. This modern art gallery, known to insiders as the G-String Gallery, was opened in 1943 by Peggy's old friend Caresse Crosby with David Porter, Caresse's lover. Peggy renewed her friendship with Caresse at Hélion's opening in January 1945. But Caresse's relationship with Porter was now over, and while in Washington, Peggy took up with Porter herself.

David Porter was a young Chicagoan with an avid interest in art; turning to painting and collage in the 1950s, he would become an artist of some note as well as a collector. Fourteen years younger than both Caresse and Peggy, he had an intense manner that endeared him to women. One of Peggy's earliest letters to him, in January 1945, simply stated her desires: 'I had a wonderful time in Washington with you and was very happy with you. I miss you. I want to be with you again soon.' They helped each other put together shows, frequently swapping various works of art. Porter, for instance, gave a show of women artists in early June 1945; Peggy mounted one almost simultaneously. (Porter evidently pressured Peggy to get the show up, for she replied, 'Can't the women wait a little? Women are always waiting for men anyhow.') They exchanged Valentine's Day cards in February; Peggy once told Porter he was number two among her lovers; he gathered that Samuel Beckett was number one.

At the same time, however, Peggy became involved with another man, this one married. Her new interest was Bill Davis, who with his wife, Emily,

A portrait of Peggy, circa 1938, the year she opened her London gallery, Guggenheim Jeune

Yves Tanguy and Peggy, at the height of their affair, July 1938

Sindbad and Pegeen
with their mother,
mid-1930s

Peggy (center) with
Jacqueline, Aube, and
André Breton, Château
Air-Bel, outside
Marseilles, 1941

The Vail family in 1941, left to right: Apple, Laurence, Pegeen,
Kay Boyle, Clover, Bobby, Kathe, and Sindbad

Max Ernst, 1946, with a detail from
The Temptation of St. Anthony

Group portrait, New York City, 1941.

Top row, left to right: Jimmy Ernst, Peggy, John Ferren, Marcel Duchamp, Piet Mondrian. Middle row, left to right: Max Ernst, Amédée Ozenfant, André Breton, Fernand Léger, Berenice Abbott. Front row, left to right: Stanley William Hayter, Leonora Carrington, Frederick Kiesler, Kurt Seligmann

Peggy's autobiography: front jacket art by Max Ernst, back
by Jackson Pollock. The Dial Press, New York, 1946

Peggy on a piece of
Frederick Kiesler's
correalist furniture
in her Art of This
Century gallery, 1942

Pegeen, around the time of her marriage to
the artist Jean Hélion, circa 1943

Jacqueline Ventadour with her husband,
Sindbad, and Jean Hélion with his
wife, Pegeen, circa 1946

Peggy's friend, the writer
Mary McCarthy, Venice,
early 1950s

Raoul Gregorich,
Peggy's last love,
early 1950s

Peggy sunbathing on the roof of her palazzo on
the Grand Canal, Venice, 1953

Peggy with her much-married sister Hazel, at a
London party in January 1965

Peggy with her Calder sculpture at an exhibition of her collection in the Tate Gallery, December 31, 1965

A lifetime in passport photos

was a Pollock collector. As macho and crude as they come, Davis was also a fearful snob and relentless in his pursuit of women. Born in New York City in 1907, he was nine years younger than Peggy; henceforth, almost all her lovers would be younger men. While she told Porter he was her number two lover, she later reported to Cyril Connolly that Davis was 'the best lover she ever had'; perhaps Porter had been wrong in guessing Beckett number one.

Meanwhile, in the early months of 1945, shows of Mark Rothko, Laurence Vail, and Giacometti opened at Art of This Century. The Russian-born Rothko had first come to Peggy's attention through Putzel, and his 1943 *The Entombment* had been part of the 'First Exhibition Show in America of Twenty Paintings' in April 1944. Rothko was a big enthusiasm of David Porter's, and Porter in fact penned a foreword, never used, for the Art of This Century show. It was not Rothko's first one-man show, but was the first devoted to his new, more abstract style. As the art historian Melvin Lader has pointed out, the ensuing rush to classify Rothko highlighted the growing critical consensus that an entirely new movement was afoot among the young American artists. Was Rothko's work surrealist, as Sidney Janis had claimed in December 1944, or neither surrealist nor abstract, as Maude Riley said in a review of the January show, or, as Porter decided in his discarded foreword, a blending of romantic and abstract styles?

The Giacometti show, which Peggy had postponed from the fall of 1944, followed on the heels of the Rothko exhibit, as did a show of collages, mostly on bottles, by Laurence Vail. But the spring event that rounded out the 1944–1945 season, making it, according to Lader, 'the most important [season] in the history of Art of This Century and . . . a milestone in the history of contemporary art,' was Pollock's second one-man show, held from March 19 to April 14, 1945. The season went on to include an important show of work by the surrealist Wolfgang Paalen, one of his wife, Alice's, work, and the show devoted to women's art in June. But the season's importance lay mostly in the shows Peggy gave to rising young artists – Motherwell, Baziotes, Rothko, and Pollock.

The Pollock show included the large paintings *Totem Lesson 1*, *Totem Lesson 2*, *There Were Seven in Eight*, and *Two*; other canvases included were *Horizontal on Black*, *Night Mist*, *Night Magic*, and *The Night Dancer*. Because *Mural* had never been officially shown, Peggy invited guests to stop at her 61st Street apartment house to see the painting in the lobby. Some reviewers did not know what to make of the show. 'I really don't get what it's all about,' confessed Maude Riley in *Art News*. Parker Tyler, writing in *View*, complained that Pollock's 'nervous, if rough, calligraphy has an air of baked-macaroni,' and said that Pollock did not seem very talented.

But Clement Greenberg complained that he could not 'find strong enough words of praise' about the show. He anticipated the public response, admitting that Pollock 'is not afraid to look ugly – all original art looks ugly at first.' According to Greenberg, the show established Pollock 'as the strongest painter of his generation and perhaps the greatest one to appear since Miró.' He later conceded that his outspoken praise was perhaps a delayed reaction to Pollock's first show.

Greenberg's anticipation of a new kind of abstraction was starting to take and his championing of Pollock established him in the forefront of American cultural criticism. Born in 1909 to Russian-American parents in the Bronx, Greenberg had studied at Syracuse University but had no formal art training. His 1939 essay 'Avant-Garde and Kitsch' vaulted him into the ranks of the New York intellectuals who clustered around the *Partisan Review*, the journal where the essay was published; he had a vision of what the post-war American art world would look like. Thenceforth he was nothing less than a kingmaker in the art world; his nod could make or break an artist's career.

For Pollock, Greenberg's words had an immediate effect. When Pollock's contract with Peggy came up for renewal in April, Peggy doubled his monthly allowance and claimed all the pictures he painted in the next year, excepting only one that the painter could keep for himself. But Pollock was on a down-ward vector in his personal life, his days given to bingeing and fighting. Lee Krasner, hoping to fend off disaster, insisted that they get married. She also insisted that they leave New York City that summer, renting a house on Gardiners Bay on Long Island. The summer did indeed put Pollock back on a more stable course, and, encouraged, Lee suggested they think about taking a winter rental in the same area.

That fall, with some difficulty, Pollock and Krasner found a church will-ing to allow a religiously mixed wedding. Lee Krasner wanted Peggy and the critic Harold Rosenberg to serve as witnesses, while Jackson wanted Rosenberg's wife, May, to be a witness. When Krasner approached Peggy about it, Peggy said, 'Why are you getting married? Aren't you married enough already?' Peggy declined to appear, leaving the distinct impression that she did not approve of Lee. The wedding took place on October 25, 1945, with May Rosenberg and the church's janitor serving as witnesses.

At about the same time, Krasner found a house for them to live in for the winter, a simple farmhouse on Fireplace Road in Springs, near Easthampton on Long Island. They rented it at $40 a month for six months, with an option to buy the property for $5,000. Krasner soon approached Peggy about buying the house for them, telling her that Pollock was indeed more relaxed and creative in the country. The local bank was prepared to give them a mortgage of $3,000, but that still left the $2,000 needed for a down payment. According to Pollock's biographers, Peggy told Krasner to go ask the rival gallery owner Sam Kootz for the money. Taking Peggy at her word and probably anticipating the outcome, Krasner approached him and he agreed – on condition that Pollock leave Art of This Century for his gallery. When Krasner reported this deal, Peggy was livid; it confirmed her suspicion that Kootz was a poacher, especially since Baziotes and Motherwell had recently defected to him, lured by promises of more money.

In the interim between Pollock's first show and a second show in March 1945, Peggy managed to persuade a reluctant Alfred Barr to approve the purchase of She-Wolf (1943) for the Museum of Modern Art for $600. She arranged a visit to Springs in early February, taking Bill Davis with her to look at the property and assess Krasner's claims that Pollock was much steadier in the country. 'Things couldn't have turned out better!' Pollock wrote to his friend Reuben Kadish. 'Peggy and Bill were here over the weekend & she liked the place and got the spirit of the idea.' David Porter also advised Peggy to lend the couple the down payment, and eventually she agreed. But her terms were strict; she deducted $50 from her otherwise interest-free loan, and demanded that Pollock put up as collateral three paintings, including Pasiphaë (1943–1944). The loan documents were signed later that month, and Pollock and Krasner now owned the house in Springs.

The fall 1945 season opened with an Autumn Salon, including works that Art of This Century had previously displayed by Baziotes, Hare, Motherwell, Pollock, and Rothko. Other up-and-coming artists included in the exhibition were Willem de Kooning, Clyfford Still, Adolph Gottlieb, Charles Seliger, Jimmy Ernst, Peter Busa, and Richard Pousette-Dart. Seliger was a very young artist who had been a keen observer of Art of This Century since its opening. He had read about Kiesler's fantastic designs and the opening party at Peggy's gallery in Time magazine when he was living in Jersey City, where he had recently moved with his mother. One of the first things Seliger did after the move was to visit the gallery. On entering, he recognized Jimmy Ernst, who had appeared in a small photograph accompanying the Time piece. Seliger did not meet Peggy then, although he glimpsed her sitting at her desk; when he did meet her, he was struck by her 'intense black hair, red lipstick, and casual dress and sandals,' as well as her Calder earrings.

Seliger had left high school after the tenth grade and had no formal art training, but he had read and enjoyed Amédée Ozenfant's Foundations of Modern Painting (1931) and Herbert Read's Surrealism (1936), and he was turning out biomorphic paintings and surrealist fantasies. Jimmy Ernst, flattered when Seliger recognized him, asked the young artist if he would join him in painting the walls of the Norlyst Gallery, which Ernst's girlfriend, Eleanor Lust, had opened in fall 1943. This collaboration led to Seliger's inclusion in group shows at that gallery. Ernst also convinced Seliger to submit a painting for consideration in Art of This Century's 1944 Spring Salon; it was rejected, but Howard Putzel gave him a great deal of encouragement. Shortly before Putzel died in the summer of 1945, he told Seliger that Peggy had bought his *Cerebral Landscape* (1945). Peggy wrote to Seliger in August, offering him a one-man show in the fall. Sam Kootz's gallery was storing Seliger's paintings at the time, and Peggy was determined to get them to hers. She packed Seliger into her open touring car and took him on a hair-raising drive across the city to get them: Seliger remembers 'nearly [having] killed half the people in New York.' Just nineteen when his painting was first shown at Art of This Century, Seliger remembers Peggy's loyalty and fierce championship of her artists. He was her 'war baby,' she often said. And Seliger recalls, 'There was no question about Peggy – if you were one of her artists she was really there for you. She was great. Very, very informal. Poorly organized but she got it done . . . And everyone – artists, critics, art historians, celebrities – came through her gallery. If you were showing there you knew anyone worth knowing, any important person in the art world, saw your work.'

And others did as well. Seliger was waiting at an uptown stop for the Fifth Avenue bus when he realized that Jean-Paul Sartre was among those waiting with him, looking astonishingly like a 'cloak-and-suit' man. Seliger introduced himself, and the two of them rode uptown on the top of the bus, smoking their pipes. Sartre wrote down Seliger's name and said he would look up his work. The next day Peggy called to say that Sartre had visited the gallery.

Seliger stresses how idealistic artists were in the 1940s. 'There wasn't much money to be made,' he says. 'There was a generosity and camaraderie among artists. There was always the economic struggle for the artist, yet there was less competitiveness because artists helped each other.' He even tells a story about Pollock – whom he never once, he emphasizes, saw drunk – that reveals a certain graceful humor otherwise missing from accounts of the painter: Seliger got into an elevator with Pollock. A friend outside the elevator said, 'Careful, Charles – don't stand too close to Jackson – he may influence you.' 'No,' Pollock answered as the doors closed, 'he may influence me.'

Seliger also stresses the centrality of Art of This Century: 'There had never been a gallery at which you could find everybody of any significance [in the art world].' Peggy did not play the *grande dame*, Seliger stresses. Her speech was, indeed, 'clipped and precise.' But the 'air of distraction' she projected was really a sign of her 'shyness.' Actually, despite this air, 'She was bright and alert, nothing got past her.' But Seliger sensed something sad about Peggy: 'She was really a much lonelier and sadder person than anyone really realized.' Still, she and her gallery were a moving force in 1940s New York: 'Peggy had great spirit. There was no real dealing going on. She was just her natural self. She was the whole thing all by herself, erratic, peculiar, yet somehow organized, somehow totally aware of everything going on.' And Seliger adds, 'It was a wonderful, exciting time . . . it really was an "avant-garde," the real thing.'

Seliger's one-man show at Art of This Century ran from October 30 to November 17. Duchamp, Pollock, Rothko, Baziotes, Tamayo, and James Johnson Sweeney showed up at the opening, Seliger recalls (Sweeney bought his 1944 *The Kiss* from the show). Other guests included Laurence Vail ('often mistaken for Max Ernst, who he clearly resembled'), Djuna Barnes ('always with a cigarette in her mouth and dressed in mannish suits'), and Frederick Kiesler, the gallery's architect ('a small lively man with large concepts and dreams'), who became Seliger's lifelong friend. Breton, 'who with his Olympian manner gave the impression of gentle calmness,' took out a pen and wrote down for Seliger, in his usual green ink, names of galleries in Europe to which he could send photographs of his work. Seliger had invited his high school art teacher to the opening and was proud to introduce the surprised woman to Mondrian.

Though reviews were mixed – Edward Alden Jewell found the shapes 'bizarre' and the colors 'bilious' – Peggy was dead set on furthering Seliger's career. She scheduled a group show for December 1946 and asked him to contribute; by that time the Museum of Modern Art had bought his *Natural History: Form within Rock* (1946).

That season, the gallery's fourth, included shows given to several relative unknowns who never really thrived in the art world, but Peggy also gave shows to Janet Sobel (January 2 to 19, 1946) and David Hare (January 22 to February 9), along with first one-man shows to Clyfford Still (February 12 to March 2) and Robert De Niro (April 23 to May 11). From March 9 to 30, she showed her daughter's work with that of Peter Busa.

Peggy also gave another show to Pollock (April 2 to 20), which included *Totem Lesson 1* and *2*, from his 1944 exhibition, *The Night Dancer*, *There Were Seven in Eight*, and *Two*. Works that he had completed since he and Krasner moved to the country included *Circumcision* and *The Little King*. Clement Greenberg was prescient when he described the show as 'transitional.' Pollock was working toward the large, visionary poured paintings that would make him famous, filling the entire canvas as a field of action that had not yet become completely abstract. The show received an unofficial stamp of approval from the art world. The critic for *Art News* wrote, 'Jackson Pollock is one of the most influential young abstractionists, and he has reinforced his position in a recent exhibition.' Greenberg voiced disappointment that his latest work contained no strong large canvases like the *Totem* paintings of the previous year, but concluded that the show confirmed him as 'the most important easel-painter under forty.'

All this activity and keen critical attention portended a turning point in cultural history as the so-called New York School became ascendant. The infusion of ideas and energy that the wartime émigrés brought to the American art scene was a potent tool in the mix. But a sense that modern American art was something sui generis permeated the art world, as critics like Greenberg and Rosenberg, with their strong interest in young American artists, moved to the forefront and as magazines and newspapers began to cover art in ways they had not before the war. But the fame that came along for artists, like seafoam on this new wave, was a mixed blessing. 'The support of . . . well-placed cultural pundits,' writes Dore Ashton in *The New York School: A Cultural Reckoning*, 'with the inevitable dependence of the artist on their initiatives, was at once a blow to the pride of the bohemian artist and a source of both secret joy and secret despair.' The trajectory of Jackson Pollock's career, here gaining momentum, and its amazing arc, as well as its rapid end, is well known. But in New York City in the mid-1940s he was just glimpsing the heights ahead. In no small part it was happening at, and because of, Peggy Guggenheim's Art of This Century.

In 1945 and 1946 Peggy was much preoccupied with the editing and publishing of her memoirs, which she tentatively entitled 'Five Husbands and Some Other Men.' On the face of it, this title suggests that Peggy felt she had structured her life around the men who passed through it, especially her five 'husbands,' presumably Laurence Vail, John Holms, Douglas Garman, Samuel Beckett, and Max Ernst. Despite having established herself on her own terms as a force in the art world, she still seemed to define herself in terms of men. But the working title, as a way of ordering the narrative of her life, also typified her wry humour. She may well have felt that the public 'reads' women's lives often by the men with whom they kept company rather than their real achievements. In this respect, the working title conveys a sense of irony of the type to which Peggy was drawn.

The editing was a painful and drawn-out process. Djuna Barnes read most of the book, according to Peggy, 'not with the idea of editing it to improve its style, which Laurence does.' According to Hank O'Neal, Djuna's friend, editor, and secretary in her old age, 'Djuna Barnes was proud to point out that she once forced Guggenheim to eliminate from one of her early memoirs a particularly lurid section dealing with Marcel Duchamp. Barnes convinced her that if the text remained as originally written, Mary Reynolds, who was then supporting Duchamp, would probably throw him out and he'd starve.' Djuna was annoyed that the manuscript contained 'so much screwing, as if that mattered at all.'

Of course, Djuna herself would be part of the narrative, and Peggy, ambivalent as always about the woman she continued to bankroll, toyed with inserting some nasty passages involving her friend. On January 24, 1945, she had written Emily Coleman that her memoirs would include the story of how, in the summer of 1938, Djuna refused to bring the collector Edward James, a friend of hers, to Peggy's London gallery to buy a work of Tanguy's. Peggy eventually struck the story, but included the old one about Djuna and Peggy's cast-off underwear.

Early on, the Dial Press lawyers warned Peggy that if she used the names of real people she would be in danger of libel suits. Peggy, outraged, contacted the civil-liberties lawyer Morris Ernst (no relation to Max), who had been instrumental in getting *Ulysses* published in America; not surprisingly, he declined to represent her. Instead, Peggy made up names that often concealed the players transparently. She called Laurence 'Florenz Dale,' Clotilde Vail 'Odile Dale,' Kay Boyle 'Ray Soil,' Garman 'Sherman,' Ronald Penrose 'Donald Wrenclose,' and so on. She also referred to many people by their true names. Inexplicably, Pegeen became 'Deirdre' while Sindbad's name appeared unchanged. Beckett became 'Oblomov,' while John Holms, Tanguy, and Max Ernst kept their names.

Peggy's treatment of Max Ernst became a sticking point between her and Jimmy Ernst, to whom she showed an early draft of the chapter that chronicled her second marriage. He objected strenuously to her portrait of Max and the story of Max's leaving her for Dorothea Tanning ('Anacia Tinning'). 'Well, I don't care if you think it is terrible,' Peggy replied. 'I am not going to change one comma in it. Your father can consider himself fortunate that I am not more explicit.' Jimmy, who had long since given up his job at the gallery, thought the manuscript 'barely avoid[ed] vulgarity' and that it was 'tailor-made for the scandal press and would hurt her almost as much as the intended subject of destruction, my father.' He added tersely, 'Peggy and I did not see each other for a long time after that.' Actually, the finished book does not seem 'spiteful' about Ernst in the least. In fact, Peggy treats him fairly gently, highlighting her own shortcomings in their relationship. It remains unclear as to why Peggy would show her memoirs to Jimmy and then ignore his advice.

Others who looked over the manuscript were Lee Krasner and Mary McCarthy, the latter a relatively new friend; McCarthy didn't like it and told Peggy her dog had eaten it. Dwight Ripley also read the manuscript. An Anglo-American collector who lived with the botanist Rupert Barneby in Dutchess County, New York, Ripley was supposed at one time to have proposed marriage to Peggy. (Evidently this was a huge joke in 'Athenian' and art-world circles.) Peggy added new parts and cut others, sending the manuscript back several times to her typist. 'I like the book, in fact, I am in love with it, though I see its faults,' Peggy told Emily.

As March 1946, the publication date for the book, finally titled *Out of This Century*, drew nearer, Peggy began to have second thoughts. She expected her old friend Herbert Read to come for a visit and was delighted that his trip would coincide with the Pollock show in April, but she worried about his reaction to the book, hoping that it 'won't make you hate America unduly.' She doubted, though, that she would 'have the courage to allow [him] to read it.'

Peggy had nothing to be ashamed of. The book opens with three chapters about her ancestry ('I didn't say anything awful about the Guggenheims,' Peggy said when told her family was displeased, 'only about the Seligmans') and her childhood, which she described as almost unrelievedly bleak. These chapters, as well as the following ones about her marriage to Laurence and her relationship with John Holms and Douglas Garman, establish how thoroughly she was grounded in the bourgeois tradition of her wealthy German-Jewish ancestors, and how hard-won her struggle to get free of that world had been. It details the founding of Guggenheim Jeune and the shows she put on there, conveying a vivid sense of what the art world was like in those heady modernist days. The same holds true for her descriptions of the establishment of Art of This Century and the emergence of young American artists there.

Though she does detail her many loves, the pictures she gives of them are often tremendously valuable. We get a side of Beckett, for instance, that is missing from traditional accounts of him, and that is far more insightful in explaining his complicated sexuality than are his several biographies. Peggy does mention her affair with Duchamp, but only in passing (perhaps at Djuna's suggestion), and conveys much more thoroughly than do art history annals his subtle shaping of her tastes and his influential presence in the international art world (while he professed to be aloof from it). Breton emerges fully rounded as the figure he no doubt was: a stern and purist, if well-meaning, overseer of his surrealist court. Indeed, in the very immediacy Peggy's position afforded her as patron, friend, and sometime lover of artists on the brink of fame, her book is a valuable modernist document, an artifact of the emergence of modern American art in the twentieth century.

Overnight, the book – which appeared in a yellow and black dust jacket by Pollock with an Ernst design on the front cover – became a sensation. *Art Digest* commented that everyone on 57th Street had a copy. Guessing games as to the identity of Peggy's thinly disguised characters enlivened its reception. But the critical word was, overwhelmingly, derogatory. *Time* wrote breezily, 'Stylistically her book is as flat and witless as a harmonica rendition of the *Liebestod*.' B. V. Winebaum, reviewing the book for the Sunday *New York Times*, complained, 'To hide a singular lack of grace and wit, she loads her sentences with italics and parentheses.' Elizabeth Hardwick in *The Nation* commented on the 'limited vocabulary, and the primitive style,' calling the book 'an unconsciously comic imitation of a first-grade reader.' The art critic Katherine Kuh said she had no problem with tell-all books if they were written well, but that Peggy was not 'a gifted literata.'

The critics' real quarrel, in fact, seems to have been with her morals. Peggy was charged with vulgarity (in writing about her affairs) and decadence (in having them in the first place). Katherine Kuh went on to say that Peggy 'has done the cause of modern art no kindness by mixing it irrevocably with a compulsive recital of her own decadent life.' Harry Hansen, writing in the *World-Telegram*, blamed her not only for her morality (or lack of it) but for the bad taste she showed in admitting it freely: he condemned '[t]he complete absence of moral responsibility,' adding, 'The more I read this type of writing, the more I begin to understand the social and artistic usefulness of restraint.' Some private remarks by Aline Saarinen, wife of the architect Eero Saarinen, sum up the argument of those on the side of convention and good taste: 'I have read her unspeakable book. And it shocks me deeply. I am not shocked that she went to bed with everybody (before I married Eero I led a promiscuous life) but I *am* shocked that she would talk about it – write about it,' Saarinen wrote to Bernard Berenson. In other words, the book was insufficiently hypocritical.

Criticism, then, surfaced on three fronts: Peggy's prose style; her behavior, which observers found promiscuous and immoral; and her candor, for writing about her affairs in the first place. Putting aside the criticism of her style for the moment, the two other areas bear consideration. On moral grounds, the attacks were puzzling: Peggy's behavior was well known, especially to members of the art set – and certainly was not out of the ordinary for many readers of her book. Middle America was not her audience. Presumably her readers were reasonably sophisticated and aware that adults may have sex outside marriage. The age-old double standard, of course, reared its head here; women, even mature, unmarried women, were expected in the 1940s to be sexually chaste, and if they were not, they must hide the fact or be silent about it – certainly not trumpet it as Peggy did in *Out of This Century*.

Peggy's 'vulgarity' lay also in admitting that she enjoyed her sexuality, enjoyed the freedom to bed whomever she wanted at will, which, to many readers, was not only immodest but unforgivable. This aspect of the criticism gave rise to another, subtler implication: that the author must be a sad, bitter, hurt, and lonely woman. Katherine Kuh concluded her review by saying, 'She leaves us with a picture of a lonely woman, too hard, too hurt, to have retained normal sensitivities.' So sad and so embittered, that is, that Peggy's life itself was abnormal.

These days, of course, such condemnation would not be so automatic. Peggy regarded herself as an independent, self-sufficient woman, and she believed that her unfettered sexuality came with this territory. *Out of This Century* was about Peggy's pride in transcending her bourgeois upbringing. The long sections on her marriage to Laurence and their crazy antics, her love affair with John Holms and her creation of an alternative 'family' made up of like-minded friends, and her relationship with Douglas Garman and her decisive rejection of 'wifehood' attest to her pride in being able to make over her own life with a new, bohemian existence in which nothing was taboo. Similarly, her narrative about the string of lovers she took before, during, and after her marriage to Max Ernst celebrates her freedom from traditional morality. Her book makes clear that her quest had been to live among, support, and act as muse for artists, and naming her artist-lovers was her way of proclaiming her success in this quest.

Possibly complaints about Peggy's prose style derived from instinctive responses to her behavior and her candor – thus, for instance, Saarinen's outrage and Kuh's disparagement of Peggy as not 'a gifted literata.' In fact, those critics who responded most warmly to her candor were those least bound by convention: Janet Flanner, the lesbian writer, for example, praised Peggy's 'detachment in looking back on life. I felt she was telling the truth, a rare event in a listener's life.'

There is indeed a distinct literary style in *Out of This Century*. Far from being 'primitive,' it is off-the-cuff and often funny. Peggy knew that she said witty things, and she had a distinct fondness for the surreal in everyday life. Just as the surrealists sought to shock, so did she. Admitting that she married Max Ernst because she 'did not like the idea of living in sin with an enemy alien' lets the reader know just what she thinks of the notion of living in sin and the lunacy that Max be adjudged an enemy alien. Gore Vidal, a consummate stylist, once said, 'What I really liked about Peggy was her writing. She was almost as good as Gertrude Stein. High praise. And a lot funnier.' (Vidal, in what we might here call a Guggenheimesque turn of phrase, later insightfully observed that Peggy 'was like Daisy Miller – with rather more balls.')

But Peggy's was not a classic wit. Her writing was hit-or-miss, and sometimes unintentionally funny; often her sense of timing was off, something that is fatal in a comic. She did not mind being herself a figure of fun: she was often not in control of her wit, and when she was flummoxed was capable of making odd utterances that she hoped would be construed as funny or smart. When a *Time* writer cornered her and asked questions about *Out of This Century*, Peggy tried to deflect him. 'It's more fun being a writer than being a woman,' she said; the reporter evidently found the idea absurd and nonsensical enough to conclude his column with it, declining further comment.

Peggy Guggenheim was emphatically not a stupid woman, however, and one should always look for sense in what seems to be her nonsense. What if she did feel that writing – getting up and messing with one's manuscript, without dress code or demanding human interaction unless one deliberately sought it out – was preferable to the performance of being a woman, putting on high heels, stockings, and makeup, and sallying forth to meet and greet customers and trying to sell pictures or cultivate relationships with possible buyers? To please oneself or to please men? To enjoy freedom from convention as opposed to living the life of a wife or a mistress? And, if so, what were the consequences?

16

Becoming a Legend

Peggy Guggenheim after *Out of This Century* was an entirely different person from the one she was before her memoirs appeared, at least in the mind of the public and even in the minds of some who thought they knew her well. Before the book, the public saw her, when they saw her at all, as an heiress with an interest in modern art. Some knew her as the wife of the German surrealist Max Ernst. New Yorkers and art cognoscenti were aware of her encouragement of Jackson Pollock and other emerging American artists. Rumor had it that she was an eccentric.

But the book's publication created a legend: a sinfully promiscuous woman who lived a bohemian life among artists despite her considerable wealth. (The distinction explained in the book between poor and rich Guggenheims meant little to readers to whom the Guggenheim name signified only great riches – she was still richer than most people.) For the book to have appeared while her gallery's doors were open may have been an error in judgment, making it possible for the uninformed simply to write her off as crazy and to downplay her contribution to art history. Clement Greenberg's championing of Peggy and her role may have saved her within the art world, but those not in the know (who read the book or heard about its contents) may have seen her as a fool. Today, of course, in the age of tell-all memoirs, a genre especially popular among younger women, Peggy's autobiography would seem almost tame. But in her lifetime the die had been cast, and it became easy to see her, especially as she aged, as faintly ridiculous.

Peggy's memoirs attracted notice, also, because of her forthrightness in admitting personal failures. She admits that she had deceived herself about Max; she admits that she deceived herself about Kenneth Macpherson (whom she had left behind in the duplex). She revealed her own vulnerabilities, and in those days such a thing was just not done. She gave a full picture of her treatment at the hands of Laurence, relentlessly underlining her own masochism. Also, although any attention to the facts of her life show her as a fairly purposeful businesswoman, *Out of This Century* presents a self-indulgent society woman who stumbled into collecting and running an art gallery with no idea what she was doing – which was hardly the case. In short, she had shot herself in the foot.

Peggy had never really liked being back in the United States, with the exception of 'the magnificent scenery of the far West,' as she wrote Herbert Read in a 1946 letter. 'It is difficult to tell you what to avoid,' she told Read, who was planning a visit at the end of March. '[A]fter five years here I should say avoid everything.' Nothing in America was pleasant, she said, and 'the only way to endure it is to work hard all day, and to drink hard from 6 on.' She was afraid to go back to Europe right away, she said, as she had become 'spoilt by the materialistic side of American life' – which was all that life in America had to offer. Pegeen and Hélion would be leaving for France in April, and Laurence, now married to Jean Connolly, was going back in June; Sindbad, who had been discharged from the U.S. Army in May after serving in France as a translator, was still there. Peggy decided to test the waters, going to Europe for a couple of months in the summer. Before leaving, she lined up an apartment for her return to New York, agreeing to rent the upper two floors of Louise Nevelson's brownstone on East 30th Street. (Peggy had met the artist through the gallery's selection of a Nevelson sculpture for the 'Exhibition by 31 Women' in January 1943.)

She flew to Paris in the second week of June. Staying in the Lutétia, she spent time with Pegeen, pregnant with her first child, and with Sindbad, who had married his and Pegeen's childhood friend Jacqueline Ventadour (who had returned to France to serve with the Free French during the war). Jacqueline was pregnant as well. Peggy barely commented on any anticipation of being a grandmother – indeed, it was around this time that she began to refer to the litters of her two Lhasa apsos, Emily and the White Angel, as her grandchildren.

In the summer of 1942, during her brief stay in Wellfleet with Max Ernst, Peggy had made the acquaintance of the *Partisan Review* writer and theater critic Mary McCarthy, then married to Edmund Wilson. They had become friends in wartime New York, sharing such friends as the lesbian couple Sybille Bedford and Esther Murphy, who would, after the war, spend most of their time in Europe, often crossing Peggy's path. McCarthy published her first book, *The Company She Keeps*, in 1942, to excellent notices. A series of six related episodes about a young New York woman and her life and loves,

it was devastatingly witty and unerringly accurate about the social mores of
the 1930s. McCarthy herself, born in 1912 and thus fourteen years younger
than Peggy, was a dark beauty, smart and unconventional, taking lovers freely
and marrying often; she would soon leave Wilson for Bowden Broadwater, a
foppish young man of indeterminate sexuality who worked intermittently as
an editor and had a wit that kept pace with her own – at least for a time.

John Myers, a gallerist in the 1940s, began in 1946 a series of Friday
evenings at which intellectuals like the anarchist and writer Paul Goodman
and the art critic Harold Rosenberg read work in progress; at one memorable
meeting in the spring of 1947 McCarthy read a story that would later become
one of the most scandalous chapters in her bestseller about Vassar graduates
in the city, The Group. A member of the group goes to bed for the first time
with a man she hardly knows and afterward he sends her to be fitted for a
diaphragm. It is a delicious story with a particularly wonderful discourse by
the heroine's husband about the etiquette of diaphragm use in an adulterous
affair, just the sort of thing that would appeal to Peggy, who was in the audience that evening with Niccola Chiamonte, Dwight and Nancy Macdonald,
and Harold and May Rosenberg.

Peggy was drawn by McCarthy's sharp and cosmopolitan outlook;
McCarthy, in turn, found Peggy, with her eye for art and penchant for artists
and Athenian lovers, fascinating. McCarthy's stories and Peggy's memoirs
broadcast all kinds of sociological messages about class, money, and sexual
mores in prewar and wartime Europe and America. Although at first
McCarthy was one of Peggy's harshest critics, enjoying the mean gossip about
her, she later became one of her ardent supporters, and had perhaps the
keenest instincts about Peggy of all who observed her.

Whether by design or by chance, Peggy ran into McCarthy and
Broadwater on her summer trip to Europe in 1946. Peggy was wavering about
going to London, which she loved but feared to see in its bombed-out state,
and Bowden and Mary easily convinced her to go to Venice with them
instead. They were traveling with a friend of Bowden's, Carmen Angleton,
whose brother, James Jesus Angleton, was about to become CIA director of
counterintelligence. Mary, on her first visit to Europe, admired Peggy's ease
with travel and love of life abroad. In the story she wrote about Peggy, 'The
Cicerone,' the narrator writes that while she is only a tourist, the character
based on Peggy, Polly Grabbe, is 'an explorer.' In comparison, the young lady
and her companion who encounter Polly 'would always appear to skim the
surface of travel.' Miss Grabbe, McCarthy writes, 'did not lack courage.' In
fact, 'She had learned how to say goodbye and to look ahead for the next
thing. Paris, she quickly decided, was beautiful but done for . . . a shell now

inhabited by an alien existentialist gossip, and an alien troupe of young men who cadged drinks from her in languid boredom and made love only to each other.'

It was on the train to Italy, McCarthy would later say, that Peggy made the decision to move to Venice for good, with London and Paris out of the question. She had always loved the watery city, and it had been relatively unaffected by the war, unlike other places in Europe. Her son-in-law, Jean Hélion, showed perception about her motives, telling an earlier biographer, 'Peggy could be a queen in Venice. It suited her and her pictures very well. In New York or Paris, she could not be the first person, as she was in Venice, to show modern art.'

The four travelers endured a horrific and much-interrupted train ride south, ending up in Lausanne, where Mary came down with mononucleosis. Peggy stayed for a while to find a doctor – with whom she flirted shame-lessly – and to nurse her friend, but soon left for Venice. When Mary and Bowden resumed their trip, they met an Italian man called Scialanga, whom they dubbed Scampi. He was a most perverse tour guide who showed Mary and Bowden the second-best (and therefore, to his mind, the nontourist and thus the best) sights and restaurants. Suspecting he was a bounder, they went on with him seemingly against their better judgment; he fascinated them, partly because they knew little about him, for all his talk. When he announced that he had to cut short his wanderings and head directly to Venice, they gave him a letter of introduction to Peggy, even though they were also tempted to drop a warning note into the envelope.

When Mary and Bowden arrived in Venice, Peggy professed indiffer-ence to Scampi – he was a type she knew well, she said, out only for money – and used him as a kind of guidebook when she wanted the name of a restau-rant or an Italian phrase. Mary and Bowden were stupefied to hear that Peggy slept with Scialanga one night. Peggy later provided them with rather explicit details. They were frustrated because Peggy could deliver no real news of their elusive fellow traveler; Peggy took him into her bed without strings of any kind and knew no more about him than Mary and Bowden did.

The story McCarthy fashioned from this series of incidents, 'The Cicerone,' is a brilliant meditation on what can most blandly be called tourism – the adventures of Americans in Europe and their interchange with 'native Europeans.' McCarthy saw that Peggy's experiences abroad were worlds apart from her and Bowden's: 'Sexual intercourse, someone had taught her, was a quick transaction with the beautiful, and she proceeded to make love, whenever she traveled, as ingenuously as she trotted into a cathedral: men were a continental commodity of which one naturally took advantage, along with the wine and the olives, the bitter coffee and the crusty bread.'

According to Miss Grabbe, it was easier to learn languages in bed, and when abroad she infinitely preferred Europeans to their American counterparts, who were all businessmen. 'The rapid turnover of her lovers did not particularly disconcert her; she took a quantitative view and sought for a *wealth* of sensations. She liked to startle and to shock, yet positively did not understand why people saw her as immoral. A prehensile approach, she inferred, was laudable where values were in question – what was the beautiful *for*, if not to be seized and savored?'

'The Cicerone' was more than a meditation on travel. It was Mary McCarthy's attempt to come to an understanding of the woman who so fascinated her. Her portrait of Peggy is dead on, but at this stage McCarthy too was inclined to view her friend as somewhat ridiculous. ('An indefatigable Narcissa, she adapted herself spryly to comedy when she perceived that the world was smiling; she was always the second to laugh at a prat-fall of her spirit.') Over time, after enduring (and engineering) bitchfests and gossipy dissections of Peggy's character, McCarthy resolved never to hear an unpleasant story or remark about Peggy, whose 'huge gay, forgiving heart,' as Mary would later write in one of Peggy's Venice guest books, had finally won her over.

Back in New York in the fall of 1946, Peggy got ready for Art of This Century's fifth season, though her heart was not really in it. Masson and Breton returned to Europe, and many of the other émigré artists decamped for more rural settings. As Peggy saw firsthand in Paris, their ideas were no longer in the ascendancy. Sensing Peggy's waning commitment to the art business, Clyfford Still and Mark Rothko left for the gallery opened by Betty Parsons in October 1946, joining Baziotes and Motherwell among the artists who had showed at Art of This Century and then had gone elsewhere. And despite the attention Peggy and her gallery had received, the hard – and frustrating – truth was that the artists she was in effect subsidizing had been slow to gain recognition. While the new American artists received lavish praise from cognoscenti like Clement Greenberg, and achieved wide notoriety, they simply did not sell; it was not until 1950 that significant collectors appeared and the new artists' success was assured. Peggy was tired of unsuccessfully trawling for buyers.

With her children married and having children of their own, Peggy saw other loose ends in her life tied up. Max Ernst was determined to get a divorce and marry Dorothea Tanning, with whom he had settled in Sedona, Arizona.

In September, Ernst wrote to Bernard Reis, the financial adviser he shared with Peggy and several other artists, saying that he was 'mired' in Reno, awaiting word from Peggy. He had sent registered letters by airmail to Peggy and her lawyer three weeks before. He assumed he would hear from her, but in the meantime he feared the worst: 'The only trouble is her well known mercurial temperament. By caprice, she could refuse to sign.'

Dorothea, perhaps understandably, saw darker motives in Peggy's delay. She already believed that her predecessor had interfered with Max's becoming an American citizen. In the course of his application the authorities, Tanning claimed, took out a copy of Peggy's book and tried to make him answer the charge of stealing an American's wife (Tanning had been married when she and Max first met). But the divorce became final on October 21, and Ernst married Tanning three days later, in a double wedding with Man Ray and Juliet Brower.

Meanwhile, Peggy – who was living in an apartment rented from a man who wrote bridge columns because the Nevelson apartment had fallen through – had opened her gallery's doors with a retrospective of the German surrealist Hans Richter (October 22 to November 9). Richter was one of her 'projects.' In 1944 he had asked her for a loan to make a film called *Dreams That Money Can Buy* (1948), a surrealist picture that Man Ray would eventually codirect and that he was still working on at the time of his show. An Art of This Century Production, the film featured a sequence of nudes descending a staircase, for which Peggy had lent her spiral staircase in Hale House. In the exhibition, stills of the film joined Richter's paintings from 1919 to the present.

After Richter, Art of This Century gave a joint show of the work of the art critic and painter Rudi Blesh and the painter Virginia Admiral (November 12 to 30), and then a group show that included the works of John Goodwin, David Hill, Dwight Ripley, Charles Seliger, and Kenneth Scott (December 3 to 21). Four of the men were already or would become important friends: Seliger was Peggy's 'war baby'; Dwight Ripley she spoke of as her suitor; John Goodwin (half brother of the sculptor David Hare) would visit her frequently in Venice; and Kenneth Scott became an important clothing designer in Milan whose creations Peggy loved. Over Christmas the gallery showed two women artists, Marjorie McKee and Helen Schwinger.

But the next big event was another one-man show by Jackson Pollock. According to his biographers, Pollock 'begged' Peggy for this last show before the gallery closed, desperate to make inroads on the number of paintings he had to sell before he would realize any profit (he was hoping for this show to open in 1946, not, as it turned out, 1947). The best slot she could give him, however, was January 14 to February 1, not a great time for sales – too soon after Christmas and too early to be considered a spring show. She included *Mural* in the show, though the painting had to be viewed in the lobby of her old building on East 61st Street; she was unable to sell it and would donate it to the University of Iowa in 1948, taking a tax deduction of $3,000.

Pollock completed all of the paintings for the show by the end of November, and divided them into two groups, 'Accabonac Creek' (for the paintings he had done in the upstairs bedroom studio of the Springs house) and 'Sounds in the Grass' (for those he had completed on the floor of the new studio space in the barn). Most of the former were small abstractions, including *The Tea Cup* (1946); the eight colorful, all-over canvases of the latter group included *The Blue Unconscious* (1946), *Eyes in the Heat* (1946), and *Something from the Past* (1946). Two of the paintings, *The Tea Cup* and *Shimmering Substance* (1946), sold even before the show opened, to Peggy's sometime lover, the collector Bill Davis.

Greenberg praised the show as Pollock's best since his first one-man show in 1943, and thought that the paintings represented a next step in the artist's career. 'Pollock has gone beyond the stage where he needs to make his poetry explicit in ideographs' like *The Tea Cup* and *The Key* (1946). 'What he invents instead has perhaps, in its very abstractness and absence of assignable definition, a more reverberating meaning.' What attracted viewers most was Pollock's new palette: teal blues, honest reds, pinks, and lime greens. Also, rolling out the canvas on the floor had given him a new freedom to treat it as a large all-over piece rather than a classic composition. Pollock was experimenting with pouring and dripping his paints, though his breakthroughs with this technique did not really come until later that year. The reviewer for *Art Digest* liked the 'thoughtfully related pastel colors' of *Shimmering Substance* and the 'controlled yellows' of *Something from the Past*. In general, the show sold well, but Peggy still had many Pollocks from 1946 and earlier on her hands. She gave away as many as twenty gouaches and small paintings, usually as wedding presents (she gave Mary McCarthy a Pollock gouache when she married Bowden Broadwater in late 1946, for example). 'I never sold a Pollock for more than $1,000 in my life,' she told a reporter much later.

After the Pollock fortnight, Peggy mounted a show (February 1 to March 1) of the primitive painter Morris Hirshfield, who had died shortly before; a one-man show of the new American painter Richard Pousette-Dart (March 4 to 22); and another show of David Hare's sculpture (March 25 to April 19).

The last show at Art of This Century was one of which Peggy was very proud. As a nod to her friend Nellie van Doesburg, who had helped her considerably in assembling the collection before the war, she mounted a retrospective exhibition of Nellie's late husband, Theo van Doesburg. Peggy had not been able to get her friend out of France before the war, though she had gone to Washington for that purpose in the summer of 1942, and now she had to sell two works, Henri Laurens's cubist sculpture *Man with a Clarinet* (1919) and a Klee watercolor, to raise the cash to bring Nellie over from France. Nellie brought her husband's works with her on the plane.

The gallery closed its doors on May 31. Peggy had finally found a gallery owner willing to represent Pollock: Betty Parsons, though Parsons would do so only until Pollock's contract with Peggy ran out and would not then offer him a new one. 'I suppose it was the best thing I have done,' Peggy said about her support of Pollock. Her other artists, if they had not earlier decamped for other dealers, did so now, not without regret. The gallery was shuttered, the curved walls sold through Charles Seliger to his then employer, the Franklin Simon department store, for $750; Peggy then gave Seliger two of Kiesler's correalist chairs, which were later lost by a furniture repairman. Other fixtures she sold for a few dollars or gave away. She put her art collection in storage, though she also gave artworks to a variety of institutions around the country. A number of artworks, sadly, she destroyed – some Jimmy Ernsts, and some damaged paintings by Baziotes. 'She did some very strange things when she left,' says Seliger.

The quick and somewhat careless dismantling of Art of This Century indicated, among other things, Peggy's decisiveness in putting the gallery behind her. She was, quite simply, tired:

> I was exhausted by all my work in the gallery, where I had become a sort of slave. I had even given up going out to lunch. If I ever left for an hour to go to a dentist, some very important museum director would be sure to come in and say, 'Miss Guggenheim is never here.' It was not only necessary for me to sell Pollocks and other pictures from the current show, but I also had to get the paintings circulated in traveling exhibitions . . . I had become a sort of prisoner and could no longer stand the strain.

She had not made any money from the gallery; in fact, it had lost money every year, ranging from $2,600 in 1942 to $8,700 in 1946. Peggy's books were meticulously kept, with everything from $7,000 for Kiesler's fees to 75 cents for postage penciled in. Bernard Reis's books indicate that the collection – an inventory of which was, unnecessarily, attached to her yearly statements – increased in value from $76,500 to $90,000 over the five-year life of the gallery, mostly because she kept buying new pieces.

Peggy had been relentlessly and avidly pursuing, collecting, and selling art for almost ten years. Her avocation had been a great deal of work, and it did not make her appreciably richer than she had been. Perhaps because of its financially lackluster performance, she was for some while unable to see the considerable impact of Art of This Century. It was not until much later, when she realized how eager visitors to Venice were to see her collection, that she opened it to the public. With time, she understood the impact the gallery had had on the course of modern art – but by that time the incredibly high prices set for the abstract expressionists' works were unreachable even for someone of her means, and soon she would grow disgusted with the entire art scene. The surfacing of several Pollocks that the artist had clearly painted during the term of his exclusive contract but had never turned over to her did not help matters. She came to feel, in Pollock's case at least, that she had been taken advantage of. But she also came to feel immeasurably proud of her collection, and the foresight it indicated on her part, so that the question of what would happen to it after she died assumed paramount proportions as she aged.

Critics would soon assign an important place to Art of This Century. 'With all the museums and all the doings, [Peggy's gallery was] almost beyond a doubt the most important of all in that brief historic half-decade from 1942 to 1947 when events reached a crisis and a new American modern art was struggling to get born,' wrote Rudi Blesh just ten years after the gallery closed in one of the first popular books on modern art. '[N]o one has ever forgotten that marvelous place where sculptures hung in mid-air and paintings leaped out at you on invisible arms from the walls, where miniature pictures revolved in peepshow cabinets, where Marcel Duchamp displayed his life's work in a suitcase, tables became chairs, and chairs became pedestals.'

The special nature of Peggy's achievement deserves comment. In stark contrast to the secular temple to high aesthetics that Sol Guggenheim and the baroness were creating with the Museum of Non-Objective Painting (with its piped-in Bach), Art of This Century mixed 'high' art with popular culture. It is indicative, for instance, that the erstwhile stripper and popular novelist Gypsy Rose Lee was a neighbor and close friend of Peggy's and showed frequently in her gallery; Gypsy made one of the 'lowest' forms of entertainment mainstream fun. The very layout and design of the gallery was intended to make the art accessible and viewing it an entertaining and friendly experience for anyone, not just the wealthy collector. This innovation was unprecedented in the history of American art exhibiting.

And it was quite deliberate. Peggy not only brought émigré artists and a new generation of American artists together, she brought to the New York art scene the cultural freedom and egalitarian spirit that she had breathed in

Montparnasse in the twenties, where world-renowned artists and writers mixed with barflies, entertainers, prostitutes, and street people. Art of This Century, with its interactive exhibits and its atmosphere of play, was a natural draw for newspapers and magazines, and it is not surprising that Peggy's shows invited news stories almost as often as reviews. Other galleries presented distinguished shows of important artists, but the media sensed a phenomenon in Peggy's gallery that could change popular tastes and popular culture, not just the buying habits of the wealthy. Moreover, the gallery thrived in a day when the very rich – including the Guggenheims – were themselves among the most avidly followed celebrities. Thus the press was naturally drawn to this venture.

With the daring mix of high and popular culture at Art of This Century, Peggy had at last made good on the gauntlet she had thrown down over twenty years before when she refused to live the life her family and her class expected of her. She had created a place for art completely antithetical to the grand edifices in which her family and their fellow patrons enshrined their possessions. The artists of Art of This Century, after they became successful, entered popular culture in a way that earlier artists had not or could not. With Art of This Century, Peggy's democratizing vision became a reality.

Clement Greenberg, in an eloquent tribute in *The Nation* in 1947, just after the gallery's last show closed, predicted that the importance of Art of This Century, and Peggy's role directing it, would only increase as the artists she discovered and promoted came into their own. Her departure, he said, 'is in my opinion a serious loss to living American art.' Peggy's way of life and her memoirs – what Greenberg called her 'erratic gaiety' – may have misled the public, who perhaps did not fully appreciate her importance: '[B]ut the fact remains that in the three or four years of her career as a New York gallery director, she gave first shows to more serious artists than anyone else in the country (Pollock, Hare, Baziotes, Motherwell, Rothko, Ray, De Niro, Admiral, McKee, and others). I am convinced that Peggy Guggenheim's place in the history of modern art will grow larger as time passes and as the artists she encouraged mature.'

Asked about this statement in 1980, the critic said, 'I stand by what I wrote. Her place in history has grown in the last thirty-odd years; no question about it.' Serious art historians and cultural critics indeed credited Peggy with playing a pivotal role in the history of modernism and the rise of abstract expressionism. Without her, the artists Greenberg named either would not have thrived or perhaps would have gained recognition much later in their careers – and some might have given up on their work because of a lack of critical response or sales.

In the decades since, Art of This Century has received serious consideration from art historians as the recent book, *Peggy and Kiesler: The Story of Art of This Century* (2004), makes clear. The shift of attention in the art world from Paris to New York and Peggy's part in that shift is itself the subject of more than one book – most notably, Martica Sawin's 1995 *Surrealism in Exile and the Beginning of the New York School*. Sawin admits that '[m]uch has been claimed and disclaimed' about the influence of the surrealists on the new generation of American artists, but argues, '[I]t is incontrovertible that not only was there a new breed of painting developing in New York by the mid-1940s, sometimes referred to as abstract surrealism, but also that it was emerging among those artists who had the greatest amount of contact with the Surrealist émigrés, painters such as Arshile Gorky, William Baziotes, Robert Motherwell, Gerome Kamrowski, and Jackson Pollock.' The art historian John Richardson, reviewing a 1979 reprint of *Out of This Century*, called Peggy 'a canny impresario of the most important art movement to emerge in this country.'

But in more anecdotal books aimed at the general public, Peggy's role in art history has been curiously downplayed, she has often been denigrated personally, and her taste in art has been questioned. While Charles Seliger was a lifelong friend who would correspond with her and make a point of seeing her on her rare visits to the United States, some of the artists she discovered and promoted tried to minimize her role in their careers or even told nasty stories about her. David Hare was perhaps the worst culprit. He complained that Peggy flirted with him constantly, and explained his failure to respond to her advances by saying, 'She was fun. She was lively. But I mean she was as ugly as sin.' Hare told an earlier biographer that Duchamp would never have slept with someone as ugly as Peggy. He told and retold a story of going out with Peggy to dinner and returning to his studio with her 'absolutely stoned.' He claimed that he showed Peggy his work and that she agreed to give him a show but telephoned the next morning to ask whether she had actually agreed to do so. She thought she had, she said, but she was not sure. Clearly meant to disparage, such a story was nevertheless not very shocking in the context of the time. Peggy was indeed drinking a lot in the forties, as her remark to Herbert Read about drinking from 6:00 on every night makes clear, but she ran with a hard-drinking crowd and her behavior was not particularly out of the ordinary; in fact this is the only account of her being drunk to come out of the entire five years she was in New York City – perhaps surprising, given that entertainment was practically part of her job description. Hare was also a font of misinformation, making things up out of whole cloth. He claimed to have witnessed Duchamp's chopping off eight inches of

Pollock's *Mural* to make it fit in Peggy's foyer, which never happened, nor was Hare present when Duchamp saw that a frame was needed to make the picture appear large enough to fill the space.

But Hare was not the only one. 'Too many male artists were reluctant to credit her role in their successful careers,' comments Yoko Ono, later a friend. Besides artists, other observers of Peggy's New York years invented nasty stories and aired them years later for the biographer Jacqueline Bograd Weld: Rupert Barneby (Dwight Ripley's friend) said that Peggy 'looked like a hag' in clothes that were 'absolutely awful' and seemingly noted every gray hair that her dye job had missed. And even her admirers tripped over themselves to deliver the cruelest possible descriptions of her nose.

What started in the 1940s would continue. Many nasty stories sprang up around Peggy over the decades: some still surface occasionally today. Evidence of her cheapness was so widespread that it is nearly impossible to count the anecdotes; her generosity is well documented too, but hardly ever given the credit it deserves. The general assessment was not only that she was unimportant but that she was a fright, a predator, and finally a joke. As Greenberg himself said, her 'erratic gaiety' – it's a good term – and her memoirs contributed to this impression. But there is more to it. Peggy was a powerful person during her five years in New York: as one of America's leading art impresarios, she could make careers. Some observers are uncomfortable with a woman wielding so much power: such a woman must not only be retrospectively erased, she must be eviscerated. American culture has seldom been receptive to the spectacle of a woman with frank sexual desires – especially one whose activity does not flag in middle age or even beyond. Some people are particularly threatened by erotic energy in a woman of power and influence.

In short, American culture has apparently needed to see Peggy Guggenheim in a less than flattering light. The ideal world Clement Greenberg assumed when he said that Peggy's importance would only be heightened over time, as the artists she helped along matured, has by and large eluded us.

17

A Last Stand

I do not in the least regret having left New York,' Peggy confided from Italy to Clement Greenberg in 1947. 'Am happy I took the plunge & I am where I belong if anyone belongs anywhere these days.' Mary McCarthy spotted her in Paris seated outdoors at a Left Bank café with a glass of vermouth and a pile of saucers on her table. 'Isn't it divine?' she called out to Mary and Bowden Broadwater, 'Don't you love it, don't you hate New York?' She set her sights on nothing less than a palazzo in Venice, where she could look at all her lovely art and enjoy a constant stream of visitors bearing the freshest news and gossip about old friends and the art world. She envisioned little herds of Lhasa apsos sweeping across the marble floors. 'Don't you think they would be divine trooping about in large quantities?' she wrote Becky Reis. She longed to buy a gondola and float through the canals of the magical city.

Reestablishing herself in Europe, Peggy first stopped in England in the spring of 1948 to collect the old furniture from Yew Tree Cottage, in storage for the last ten years. She was delighted when a local jeweler, who had been holding Florette's silver tea service on consignment, returned it with no questions asked – no receipts, no proof of ownership. She remembered how much she loved England (and English men, for whom she had a distinct weakness). Of course, she found London much changed – buildings destroyed in the Blitz, food scarcities, the city itself 'bedraggled and in need of paint.' Moving on to Paris, she found that city depressing as well, though she was pleased to get some good black market food and other luxuries.

While staying in a Venice hotel and looking for a palazzo, Peggy received the great good news from Bernard Reis that he and her American lawyers had finally succeeded in something they had been trying to do ever since she had closed the gallery: they had broken one of her trusts. Peggy now had enough cash to indulge in palazzo-hunting.

Her gratitude to Reis was considerable. With this move, he cemented her allegiance to him, as well as her personal friendship with him and his wife, Becky. From this time on, she wrote to Reis – or sometimes to Becky, when she had not heard from him – several times a week, sometimes several times a day. The children's allowances, charitable donations, the exchange rate, payments to her father's mistresses, trusts for her grandchildren, not to mention the overarching subject of Peggy's later years, the disposition of her palazzo and her collection – all were matters on which she consulted Reis. Becky kept her in couture wear, giving her, among other garments, a stunning pleated Fortuny gown that had to be sent to London for cleaning and repleating, and shipping her a steady supply of American cleaning aids that Peggy found vastly superior to those available in Italy. When she needed a male dog to mate with her female dogs, the White Angel and Emily, Peggy asked Becky to choose and bring to her in Venice a male Lhasa apso, black if possible. (Becky managed to do so, the dog was named Pecora, and the breeding commenced.) The Reises visited almost every summer, especially in the years when Venice hosted a biannual international art show, and showered Peggy with expensive art books at Christmastime. No two people were closer to Peggy over the next thirty-odd years – though several fallings-out punctuated the friendship.

Reis was greatly in demand by newly rich artists, some of them overwhelmed by the responsibilities and complications that came with the windfalls they were beginning to realize from selling their work in the changing New York art world. Reis had been born to a New York working-class family and attended New York University law school at night. By day he was a legal secretary and served as the sole support of his parents. He began his career in a field that with hindsight seems curious indeed: he was one of the founders of the consumers' movement, in 1937 publishing a book called *False Security*, about how the middle class was regularly duped in the stock market. He founded, directed, and acted as treasurer for Consumers' Research beginning in 1932.

Becky insisted that Bernard's background qualified him to guide and protect members of the art world. 'My husband, Bernard, growing up a poor boy himself, realized that the artist is the most unprotected creature in the world' and that artists need 'a guiding spirit and a loveable one.' As her statement indicates, her husband involved himself intimately in his clients' lives: 'As a friend and confidant,' writes one observer, 'he relished his clients' personal problems, interesting himself in their love lives (including marital and extramarital affairs and discords), their clothes, diets, and especially any medical or psychiatric difficulties . . . No detail of an artist's life was too picayune for

Reis's attentions.' Inevitably, some clients found his involvement too intrusive, or questioned the soundness of his advice. '[W]hen clients left his aegis, they often went away angry, having found his financial advice faulty or his interest in their personal lives meddlesome.' Among such disgruntled clients were the writer Lillian Hellman, the director Joshua Logan, and, among the artists, de Kooning, Naum Gabo, Esteban Vicente, and Motherwell. Reis's career would implode in 1970 over his unethical management of the estate of Mark Rothko, an artist who trusted and depended on him completely. Peggy, too, would have her own disagreements with Reis, and, given her closeness to him and Becky, would find these disagreements devastating.

But Reis was well placed for success when the art world's geographic center and cast of characters shifted in the 1940s and, especially, the 1950s. Around 1950, the tide began to turn financially for many artists, with young Americans like Baziotes, Motherwell, Pollock, Rothko, and Hare commanding ever higher prices. Reis could advise them on setting prices, investing their money, establishing trusts, and he could help them with tax matters. To many, like Rothko, Reis became a very important friend, a confidant in whose ear artists could pour all of their doubts and concerns about the future. As such, and because he was an important collector who often accepted works of art in exchange for financial or legal advice, and also because the Reises' East Side townhouse was a mecca where artists met with one another as well as with dealers and collectors, Reis was a man of tremendous power in the art world. Intimacy such as the Reises shared with Peggy was not unusual for them, although it is somewhat bizarre to imagine a busy Bernard Reis reading a letter about Peggy's latest tax worry as well as a plea for Becky to send her some silver polish.

Peggy had her heart set on a palazzo, and thanks to Reis she had the means to acquire one, but in the process the deals she made had a way of falling through. One such property, with more than fifty rooms and a huge garden, was occupied on the *piano nobile* and mezzanine by a tax bureau that she would have to evict before moving in; moreover, the owner was in South America and responded to queries late if at all. While the deal was hanging fire, and knowing how cold, lonely, and enshrouded by fog Venice could be in the winter months, Peggy took a four-month lease on a house called the Villa Esmerelda on Capri. She made the trip with Laurence and his new wife, Jean, in November.

Kenneth Macpherson, with whom Peggy had parted amicably when she moved out of the duplex the year before, also had a villa on Capri, given to him by Bryher, which he shared with the writer Norman Douglas. In fact, he had been due to pick Peggy up in Venice and drive her to the Capri ferry, but, as irresponsible as ever, he never showed up. Still, she was glad to be reunited with him on the island, though commented that he seemed 'a little vaguer than ever if possible.'

Peggy's four months in Capri had the quality of a last hurrah. Her house was on the side of a cliff, a fifteen-minute walk from the town, and was reached by 150 steps. On Christmas Eve, Peggy threw a party for thirty-five at which her guests consumed the same number of bottles of champagne. At one point Peggy was putting up several vacationers, including one, she wrote, who, though homosexual, 'seemed sufficiently normal as to prefer me' to another man. His swain, in dismay, took an overdose of sleeping pills, fell asleep, and nearly burned down the villa. 'However, people in Capri do mad things,' Peggy said by way of explanation, 'and no one can be responsible for their actions.' She was no exception, telling Djuna that she had 'a lot of friends social and sexual,' but closed another letter by saying that she would spare her friend such details, 'as I know what you think of the sordid side of my otherwise so spiritual existence.'

While she was in Capri, word reached Peggy of a great honor. The Twenty-fourth Venice Biennale, the Venice institution that had mounted an international art exhibition every other year since 1895 and that was held on parade grounds on the lagoon separating Venice from the Lido, invited Peggy to display her collection in that year's show, beginning in June, the first exhibition since the war. Her inclusion had come about because of a new friend – an Italian painter, Giuseppe Santomaso, whom Peggy had met at her favorite restaurant, the All'Angelo, which was owned by Vittorio Corrain, soon to be a close friend as well and her part-time secretary. Artists frequented the trattoria, often exchanging works of art for a meal; on its premises she also met the Italian painter Emilio Vedova, another artist whose work she would collect. Santomaso evidently said a word to a higher-up in the Biennale bureaucracy, and of course Peggy's collection and her presence in Venice were well known. Most countries had entire pavilions given over to their art, but in 1948 the Greek pavilion was vacant, as the country was beset by civil war. Count Elio Zorzi, the ambassador of the Biennale and already one of Peggy's admirers, formally extended the invitation to show her collection there; the commission agreed to pay any expenses and duties involved in bringing it from storage in America.

Peggy was delighted by this turn of events. The only modern artists widely known in Italy at that time were, besides the Italian futurists, Picasso and Klee; Italians knew nothing of the surrealists or the new generation of Americans, and Peggy hoped her collection would both shock the crowds and expose them to something new and wonderful. She was frustrated when she found that she would not be allowed to hang her show until three days before the Biennale opened. The art looked strange to her on white walls, familiar as she was with Kiesler's trappings in Art of This Century, but beautiful, she thought. A skylight provided excellent natural light. But she particularly enjoyed the earliest days of the festival when she was alone representing the United States because the art for the U.S. pavilion was late in arriving.

On June 6, the morning the Biennale opened, Peggy, wearing Venetian earrings in the shape of large daisies, welcomed Luigi Einaudi, the president of Italy. The same morning, Peggy was paid a visit by the American ambassador James Dunn and his consular staff. Though she may or may not have been aware of it, her collection's appearance at the Biennale was very much in the interest of the U.S. government, which in the early days of the Cold War was seeking cultural capital of every sort. The newly formed CIA was expressly committed to waging what amounted to a cultural battle for the hearts and minds of Europeans beginning its postwar funding of American artists and writers with an eye to winning such a battle.

Peggy's pavilion received enormous publicity, most of it praise, which did not escape the attention of American officials. She held court in her pavilion almost daily. In other words, Peggy's presence was part of the show, as it had been at Art of This Century. Every day she brought her two dogs, who were given little dishes of ice cream at the Paradiso, a restaurant just outside the exhibition gates. She of course loved the idea that a Guggenheim pavilion was included in an exhibition of national pavilions; it made her feel, she wrote, 'as though I were a new European country.' The whole experience delighted her.

The Biennale regularly brought, as it would every time it was held, a steady stream of visitors to Venice; in 1948 Peggy was forced to put up her guests at a nearby hotel. Matta came to visit, as did the Reises; Chagall and his wife; Peggy's old friend Alfred Barr and his wife; and Roland Penrose, now married to the photographer Lee Miller, who photographed the Biennale and Peggy for Vogue. In August she gave a party for her fiftieth birthday. She wore a seventeenth-century-style Venetian dress with crinolines beneath it, and 'crowds' of guests consumed 'rivers' of French champagne.

Earlier that year, the palazzo inhabited by the tax bureau had eluded her and she had looked at others. Leaving her hotel, she had moved into an apartment owned by the Curtis family of Boston, which occupied three floors of the Palazzo Barbara on the Grand Canal. The Curtises had lived there since 1875; before that, Robert Browning had been a resident; John Singer Sargent, a Curtis relative, had painted a portrait there; and Henry James had written The Wings of the Dove (1902) while a guest. Peggy rented the top floor, reached by a steep, winding stone staircase.

Finally, Peggy spotted a new prospect. This one would not slip from her grasp. In her autobiography she says the secretary of Count Zorzi, the Biennale's ambassador, found it for her, and Pegeen convinced her to take it. Construction of the Palazzo Venier dei Leoni had started in 1748 by an old Venetian family (two members were doges), who were said to have kept lions in the garden. Construction had been halted (because of Napoleon's 1797 invasion) after just one floor was complete. In the twentieth century, the poet and patriot Gabriele d'Annunzio, in whose hands it had somewhat mysteriously fallen, made a present of it to his lover, Marchesa Luisa Casati, who gave huge parties at which naked youths painted gold posed aloft columns in her garden. One boy, it is said, suffocated from the paint, which caused the marchesa to leave Venice in a hurry.

In turn, the palazzo was bought in 1938 by Viscount Castlerosse, an Irish aristocrat whose many occupations included writing gossip columns. His wife, Doris, inspired the Cole Porter lyrics 'Where is Venetia, who loved to chat so, / Could she still be drinking in her sinking pink palazzo?' The Castlerosses built six modern marble bathrooms and installed central heating, but the Palazzo non Finito, as it had come to be known, remained one story high. Since the thirties, it had mostly stood empty, though the actor Douglas Fairbanks, Jr., rented it from the viscountess's brother for a year.

When Peggy saw it, the Palazzo Venier dei Leoni was a low, white marble structure almost entirely engulfed by vines on the Grand Canal in the Dorsoduro district, roughly across the canal from the Piazza San Marco and near the Salute cathedral. The poles to which gondolas were traditionally tied up on the canal were painted turquoise and white, which pleased Peggy, who considered turquoise 'her' color. In time, she commissioned a gondola, said to be the last one made by the revered Casada. She also had a motorboat, christened *Cleopatra*, that would take her and her guests far beyond the somewhat dirty and shallow Lido to a lighthouse on a rock that was excellent for swimming. The garden – a necessity because of the dogs – was one of the largest in Venice; Peggy would install in it a stone Byzantine throne on which she was often photographed. On the side facing the Grand Canal, she installed a Mario Marini sculpture, *The Angel of the Citadel* (1948), of a horse and its ebullient rider, who sports a huge erection. Marini made the phallus detachable, and Peggy would remove it on feast days when the nuns passed by. But its repeated theft led her to ask Marini to solder on a permanent replacement.

Peggy bought the palazzo for approximately $60,000, or about $500,000 today, but not without much calculation of exchange rates and cables to and from Bernard Reis. She had the roof mended and most of the walls painted white; in the dining room she installed the Venetian table, chest, and chairs that she and Laurence had bought so long ago and that she had retrieved from Yew Tree Cottage. For the living room, painted dark blue, she bought two Elsie De Wolfe sofas, upholstered in a beige leatherette that withstood the dogs well; the sofas had wide backs that one observer notes were excellent at parties, providing 'double-decker' seating. In her bedroom were her fanciful and airy Calder headboard and the two von Lenbach paintings from her childhood – one of her alone and one of her and Benita. Her collection of more than one hundred pairs of earrings hung, as usual, on one wall. The interior of the palazzo remained very much a work in progress; one visitor recalls that the radiators were covered in orange primer and left that way for years.

It was some time before Peggy's collection caught up with her after her permanent move to Venice. It was scheduled for a show in Turin in the fall of 1948, just after the Biennale, but at the last minute the Communist city officials rescinded the offer, calling her art 'degenerate.' In the spring it went to Florence and from there to Milan. By the fall of 1949, however, enough of it was back in her hands that she was able to hold a show of sculpture in the garden. But she had not as yet discovered a way to avoid paying the 15 percent duty for bringing the collection permanently into Italy, despite having agreed to leave it to the city of Venice after her death. Eventually she would arrange for it to be shown in Amsterdam, Brussels, and Zurich in 1951 and to be brought in at a lower valuation. She fancifully described its being transported over a pass in the Swiss Alps at 4:00 in the morning, with a niggling amount of money paid to 'some very ignorant and sleepy douaniers, whose demands were very modest.' She then paid the duty on it – which had been reduced from 15 to 10 percent in the interim.

Over time, Peggy made a number of changes to the palazzo. She cut back the greenery severely so that the building presented to passersby on the Grand Canal an expanse of gleaming white marble quite modern-looking in its simplicity. She hired architects to draw up plans to add a second story to the building. Because it was unfinished, and had few architectural adornments, the palazzo was not protected by historic designation, but the red tape required to get approval for the second story proved too great a frustration. Instead, in 1958 she would add what was technically known as a *barchesa* (as structures like this were called in the countryside, where they were built for storage of grains and hay), a one-story annex on the southeast side of the palazzo and at right angles to it, which she would later connect to the main house; for this, she needed the permission of the U.S. State Department because of a common wall shared by her and the American consulate. She moved most of her surrealist art out to this wing and for one season she did not let visitors into the palazzo proper. At the same time she converted some basement space she had used for storage as well as two maids' rooms into underground studios where Pegeen and various Italian protégés painted; one subterranean room was devoted exclusively to Pollocks – which would prove rather unhealthy for the canvases. In 1961 she would commission the American sculptor Clare Falkenstein to design and build a pair of gates to the San Gregorio entrance to the palazzo and garden. Falkenstein made these of welded iron studded with bits of Venetian glass, and Peggy professed herself entirely pleased with them.

The palazzo evolved into a museum, which she opened officially after her collection was installed in 1951. It was not the museum of modern art she had dreamed of opening in London eleven or twelve years before, but it was impressive nonetheless. At the opening for her sculpture show in 1949, Peggy had a glimpse of the difficulties of life in such a place: 'It is very strange living in a museum,' she wrote, 'and I don't like it at all. If I want to get across the hall in my dressing gown or a sun bathing costume I find myself rather out of luck.' She had to order velvet ropes to keep visitors out of the bedrooms, 'as is done in chateaux on the Loire.' She opened from three to five on Mondays, Wednesdays, and Fridays in the summer only. She did not charge admission, but she did sell a mimeographed catalogue for 75 cents, necessary because the pictures were unlabeled. Perhaps she wanted to create a need for catalogues, but equally likely she did not care to be reminded that she was living in a museum.

In opening her palazzo and her collection to the public, Peggy was making an audacious statement, culturally speaking. And by setting up her museum in such a prominent spot in Venice, she was boldly placing not only her collection but herself on display. Word rapidly began to spread that the Palazzo Venier dei Leoni and its American owner were among Venice's not-to-be-missed attractions. Given its location and the quality of the collection, the palazzo became over time a tourist attraction – not something Peggy had foreseen when she bought it. Eventually, she closed off her bedroom and the guest rooms from the rest of the palazzo and absented herself during the hours it was open, sometimes retreating to the roof to sunbathe.

Peggy used the word *lonely* to describe her early years in Venice. With one significant exception, she did not have a man in her life. Her relationships with her children were highly problematic and becoming ever more so, she busied herself with visitors and parties to the extent that she could. The winters were cold and unpleasant, and, whenever she could, she spent them elsewhere – usually in Paris or London. The most enduring objects of her affection were the dogs, and she preoccupied herself with their health and breeding. The number of dogs fluctuated; in the end the little corpses of fourteen dogs were buried in the garden with her. She gave them strange names, after people who were important in her life: Sir Herbert (so named before Read, its namesake, was knighted), Pegeen, Emily. A friend of her daughter relates that Jean Hélion and Pegeen were infuriated that Peggy would name a dog Pegeen and that Hélion, backing out of a driveway near the Lido, by an accidental turn of the wheel ran over and killed the animal, 'much to Peggy's dismay and Pegeen's secret joy at Jean's unconscious inner support of her feelings.' Naming a dog after a daughter is a peculiar gesture, to say the least, and calling her dogs her daughters, and their broods her grand-children, speaks to Peggy's spectacular maternal confusion.

As they had before, rumors persisted about Peggy's frugality. The sculptor Joan Fitzgerald, an American friend, remembers filling in for Peggy on an open day at the palazzo. Fitzgerald received strict instructions: on the back of each painting were two numbers, one representing the price to hold out for, the other the lowest acceptable price. If a collector bought a painting, Fitzgerald could give him or her a glass of vermouth – but only then. Fitzgerald remembers that few visitors came in, and no buyers. She took the mimeographed catalogue with her on a tour of the collection, writing little notes on each entry, and then took it home with her at the end of the day. That evening Fitzgerald received a phone call from Peggy, wanting to know why a catalogue was missing.

Related tales abound – about meager food at parties, about her giving her servants inferior food or haggling with them over tiny sums. 'The house was always too cold, and there was never anything to eat,' says John Hohnsbeen, who would become Peggy's live-in secretary in the 1970s. She was known to decant cheap Japanese whiskey into empty single malt Scotch bottles. One observer remembers going to an Arthur Rubenstein concert at La Fenice and afterward being one of a restaurant party that included Oona Guinness (a far wealthier heiress). The bill was delivered to Peggy, who, to the observer's horror, started to divide it up – whereupon he paid the entire bill himself, which he could not afford, to save everyone embarrassment. On the other hand, Yoko Ono, a friend of Peggy's through John Cage, believed she got 'an unfair shake' regarding these accusations of quotidian cheapness: 'She was a shrewd woman,' Ono says, 'and wasn't going to be taken advantage of with an inflated restaurant bill. Of course she checked such bills.'

Once again, these petty cheapnesses must be set against Peggy's larger generosity. She increased Djuna Barnes's stipend periodically, almost doubling it when Mary Reynolds, who had also been sending regular sums to Djuna, died in 1950. She continued to give Laurence an allowance, and at one point in the 1950s, after his wife, Jean, died, paid $12,000 to bail him out of a breach-of-promise suit. Also in the 1950s she learned that Robert McAlmon, her old friend from 1920s Paris, was down on his luck, suffering from tuberculosis. As a result she sent monthly checks to him until his death in 1956. One of the most telling examples of this admixture of cheapness and generosity comes from the artist Anne Dunn, once married to Michael Wishart. (His mother, Lorna, was Douglas Garman's sister.) While Dunn and Wishart were guests at the palazzo, Dunn's mother sent her a Swiss franc note worth $100. Peggy shepherded them all over Venice, spending an entire morning trying to get it cashed at the most favorable exchange rate. Not much money was saved that way, to be sure, but Dunn felt that Peggy wanted her and Wishart to have as much money as possible so they could prolong their stay. 'She was generous with her time,' says Dunn.

Then, too, Peggy was aware of her reputation for penny-pinching and was, according to John Loring, a close friend, 'very deft in upsetting people's expectations.' Once, she invited the Reises and a number of visiting grandchildren to dinner and made a point of telling everyone that she was paying and they should order the most expensive dishes on the menu. The Reises – who were, according to Loring, in comparison to Peggy, 'hall-of-fame' cheap – were sure that Peggy would renege on her offer and expect them, at least, to pay their share. They ordered a cup of minestrone and a plate of spaghetti with tomato sauce, telling the waiter they would split the food. When the check arrived, a mischievous Peggy paid it in full.

Mary McCarthy, writing of Peggy's fictional counterpart in 'The Cicerone,' mentions her 'pretty, tanned legs.' Peggy tanned religiously, often naked on the roof of the palazzo; employees in the *prefettura* on the right bank of the canal noted that her first nude appearance signaled to them the beginning of spring. This habit caused some embarrassment when Paul Bowles came to visit in the early 1950s with his young Moroccan friend Ahmed. Peggy sent word through a servant to Ahmed and Bowles after breakfast, asking them to join her on the roof. Ahmed was shocked to find her naked, and Bowles led him back downstairs. Peggy urged them to come back, saying she would put on her bathrobe. But Bowles explained to her that Ahmed found it wrong for a woman to appear nude in front of strange men. Peggy responded, 'How strange. You mean they don't do that where he comes from?'

If Mary McCarthy was kind to notice Peggy's pretty legs, she was more critical of her friend's tanned visage. Peggy's fictional counterpart, Polly Grabbe, has a 'brown face [that] had a weatherbeaten look, as though it had been exposed to the glare of many merciless suns; and her eyes blazed out of the sun-tan powder around them with the bright blue stare of a scout.' Other guests remembered her 'piercing' blue eyes. She was still dyeing her hair a glossy black and carelessly applying a crimson gash to her lips. But she dressed elegantly after she moved to Venice, favoring clothes fashioned by the Milanese dress designer Ken Scott, a friend since he showed his work at Art of This Century. Seeing some unique slippers in a painting by the Venetian Renaissance painter Carpaccio, she commissioned a shoemaker to make her copies of these open sandals that came to a point above the inset of the foot, in a rainbow of different colors. 'She got much more proper' after her move to Venice, said a British neighbor, referring to her dress in public. Marius Bewley reported on Peggy in a 1951 letter to Clement Greenberg: 'She's looking much better than she did in America. She dresses better, with a great deal of style, looks younger, and drinks far less.' (Though one detractor says Peggy 'often' drank too much, she found that her intake reduced as she aged, though she especially enjoyed an 'iced vodka' before lunch and dinner.)

In 1963, at sixty-five, Peggy would give in to time's demands and dye her hair white, later letting it grow in naturally gray. Everyone would agree that it was a distinct improvement. 'I liked her best in her Gray Period,' Charles Henri Ford was moved to quip. Charles Seliger, seeing Peggy on a visit to the United States in 1969, thought she looked much better at age seventy-one than she had in her forties. Rather than primary colors, she wore beiges and browns – and stylish fishnet stockings – that went very well with her blondish gray hair. 'Imagine!' she said to Seliger. 'I was wearing the wrong color hair for forty years!'

In Capri in the winter of 1947 and 1948, Peggy had consulted a fortuneteller, who told her that her move to Venice was not going to be permanent and that she would fall in love and marry a man already known to her. Peggy racked her brain but could not imagine a likely candidate. In 1950 she had an affair with an admiral in the U.S. Navy when his ship docked in Venice. She told Becky Reis about it, saying, 'It was all quite exciting – I had always wanted to know how these people conducted themselves in love and now I know,' confirming Mary McCarthy's sense that she was a kind of sexual explorer. 'It was a lot of fun,' she added in her letter to Becky, 'but you know the Navy moves on.'

Increasingly, however, Peggy surrounded herself with homosexual men, who she felt understood her. Charles Henri Ford remained a good friend, and he and his friend the painter Pavel Tchelitchew (whose art Peggy did not like) were frequent guests in the palazzo. In Rome she stayed with the photographer Roloff Beny, who would take her along on a trip to India in 1955. Another man she traveled with (to Egypt, in 1964) was the Vassar professor and Wyndham Lewis critic Bill Rose. The American painter Robert Brady lived in Venice in the 1950s, and in subsequent years she visited him in Mexico. The pianists Arthur Gold and Bobby Fizdale, who had played on an Art of This Century Recording in the 1940s, eventually settled in Venice and became good friends of Peggy's.

Truman Capote's first visit with Peggy was in 1948 or 1949, and on this occasion he first encountered her in the palazzo's reception room. She rather liked him, and she was delighted when she learned that he had written a short story based on the Hans Richter film she had financed, *Dreams That Money Can Buy*. He turned up periodically, often staying for several weeks and making her share his dieting regime, which meant going to Harry Cipriani's every night for fish. In the fall of 1950, Peggy visited Capote and his then lover, Jack Dunphy, in Sicily; Peggy flirted outrageously with the hired driver and also tried to cheat him out of a tip, for which Dunphy dressed her down in the lobby of a Palermo hotel. They all put this experience behind them, but Capote never tried to travel with Peggy again. He would write maliciously about her, however, in an installment from *Answered Prayers*, his long-promised novel about the social stratosphere, parts of which were published in *Esquire*. Though the hero, P. B. Jones, a bisexual hustler, compares the Peggy character to a 'long-haired Bert Lahr,' he admits that he came close to marrying her:

> It was pleasant to spend a Venetian winter's evening in the compact white Palazzo dei Leoni, where she lived with eleven Tibetan terriers and a Scottish butler who was always bolting off to London to meet his lover, a circumstance his employer did not complain about because she was snobbish and the lover was said to be Prince Philip's valet; pleasant to drink the lady's good red wine and listen while she remembered aloud her marriages and affairs.

Aside from this passage, which Peggy was unlikely to have seen, Capote never let Peggy know if he thought her ridiculous; her company was too good to pass up.

Despite surrounding herself with a bevy of gay men, Peggy found love in Venice for perhaps the last time in her life. From 1951 to 1954 she reeled through a tumultuous relationship with a man who was twenty-three years younger than she. Raoul Gregorich was dark-haired and handsome, 'like Tarzan,' according to John Hohnsbeen. He came from Venice's mainland industrial suburb of Mestre and had a somewhat questionable past that Peggy persisted in seeing as romantic. The details are sketchy; evidently during the war Raoul was involved in what seems to have been a prank, ambushing the wealthy German Prince von Thurm-und-Taxis at a pass outside Venice. But Raoul brandished a gun and, according to some accounts, wounded the prince. Whatever actually happened, he ended up serving a prison sentence. Peggy believed that he had been part of the resistance during the war and that the ambush was a noble if misguided effort of the movement. Some observers found Raoul's background disturbing; John Richardson, who with his friend the art historian and collector Douglas Cooper was a good friend of Peggy's in her Venice years, was quoted as saying, 'Raoul was bad news, really bad news.'

But Raoul's background did not square at all with reports of his demeanor with Peggy. It's not known when or how they met, or what he was doing at the time, but many people had ample opportunity to observe the couple. Raoul was quietly attentive, not at all interested in art or art-world gossip, appreciative of Peggy's attention and, to be sure, her financial largesse. Though he had some serious girlfriends on the side, Peggy never knew about them (or, if she did, she did not care). Raoul seemed genuinely smitten by her. 'As for me I'm terribly in love with Raoul,' Peggy wrote Becky Reis on October 1, 1951. 'We get more and more connected even though we don't live together.' The relationship was, as sometimes happens when both part-ners' emotions are pitched high, tempestuous: Peggy wrote Djuna Barnes in the summer of 1952, 'I'm terribly in love . . . It's been going on about a year with various intermissions and lots of rows.' At the moment, however, all was peaceful between them: 'He's madly beautiful and has nothing to do with my world; most unintellectual.' To Emily Coleman she wrote that it was a won-derful affair especially because Raoul was not intellectual, but reiterated that the relationship was rocky: '[W]e fight like hell half of the time but the other half we are very happy.' Peggy, ever keen to spot inferiority complexes in others, worried that Raoul sometimes felt uncomfortable when the talk was over his head; perhaps that was the origin of some of the rows.

The other bone of contention was Raoul's first love, which was cars. Perhaps under his influence, in 1953 Peggy ordered a 'beautiful new motor boat' with 'a terribly fast motor,' which could make it to the Lido in five min-utes. The year before she had bought 'a lovely little Fiat car with a special Ghia body that got a prize in the auto show in Turin.' She had always enjoyed buying top-of-the-line cars, but only Raoul could have interested her in a Turin auto show prizewinner. Raoul wanted Peggy to buy him a sports car; he also asked her to set him up with his own car rental business and then an auto mechanic's shop, both of them on the mainland outside Venice. The latter she agreed to, but the sports car was a sticking point. During an especially rocky time in their relationship in the summer of 1954, she reported to Emily Coleman that they had broken up: 'R left me because I think he hoped I would give in about the car. This is his usual blackmail stunt; it didn't work however . . . he had the impertinence to tell me he wasn't a gigolo for nothing and then he phoned to apologize, but said there was no use to come here to fight. So has ended three years of Italian insanity. We must all admit love is a disease.'

This remark suggests a new slant on their relationship: Peggy was locked in the same battle that had always characterized her relations with those on the receiving end of her generosity, especially with individuals whose pride forbade them from being obsequious in return (like Emma Goldman, like Djuna Barnes). In such situations she grew suspicious, oversensitive to what she perceived as ingratitude. She had no problem with recipients like Laurence Vail or her father's cast-off mistresses who accepted her generosity without comment, but those who accepted it begrudgingly, afraid that accepting her gifts affected the balance of power between them, understandably peeved her and made her, in turn, think that she was being taken advantage of. It made for almost intolerable situations. In Emma Goldman's case, the relationship could not survive this impasse; in Djuna Barnes's case, arriving at a level of mutual comfort took almost two decades (and even then they hardly ever saw each other).

In Raoul's case, tragedy intervened. Peggy eventually broke down and bought him the baby blue sports car he had agitated for, and they were briefly reconciled, only to part once again. Raoul, while driving the same baby blue sports car, swerved to avoid a motorcyclist on a road outside Venice, crashed into another car, and died instantly. Peggy was devastated, and tried to sort out just what had made the relationship so stormy. 'I'm terribly sad and unhappy. I never thought this would happen to me again,' she said, referring to the death of John Holms, at the age of thirty-seven to Raoul's thirty-three.

It's terrible to love an Italian and besides that he was 23 years younger than I am, and he only cared about cars and did not feel happy at all with most of my friends, and he felt so inferior which made him do awful things and say awful things. I suffered terribly for three years and now I'm miserable. Such is life; isn't it a hell. I was so lonely for years before I met him and then when I met him I fell madly in love with him. It was all very difficult as I found it so difficult to talk to him; he was like a child mentally but he was so completely natural and real.

The 'dreadful thing,' she added, 'is that I helped him to start a business which eventually was to kill him . . . It was absolutely his fate to die this way: like a Greek tragedy.'

18

What Remains

Peggy's main focus, in the aftermath of her affair with Raoul, was Pegeen, and specifically Pegeen's love life. She cared for her daughter passionately and wanted only the best for her, but she had difficulty expressing her love, a shortcoming that had already taken its toll on both her children. Pegeen, married to Jean Hélion, had two boys, Fabrice (named for the Stendhal character), born in 1947, and David, born in 1948. Eileen Finletter, then married to the aspiring writer Stanley Geist, was introduced to the Hélions in 1949 by Charley Marks, an American painter who had met Hélion through Giacometti. Geist and Jean became friends, as did Eileen and Pegeen. 'Pegeen had a sort of "amuse me" quality,' Finletter recalls. 'She was wonderful with babies until they were around three or four. Then she would turn them over to housekeepers.' Pegeen suffered from depression, and her marriage to Hélion was troubled. Yet the couple had a third child, Nicolas, born in 1952. Pegeen slept with other men, her infidelities took their toll on their marriage, and she and Jean finally divorced in 1958.

Soon after Nicolas was born, Pegeen became involved with the Italian artist Tancredi Parmeggiani, known as Tancredi. Peggy had taken an interest in his work in 1952, after the American painter Bill Congdon introduced him to her, and she eventually installed him in one of the palazzo's basement studios next to one used by Pegeen. Tancredi was a spatialist who had signed the manifesto of the Movimento Spazile in 1947, and a handful of critics thought he showed promise. Peggy gave him a show in her palazzo in 1954 and bought many of his paintings. Not long after, Pegeen and Tancredi were in the throes of a passionate affair. Their involvement continued intermittently through the early 1950s, but Tancredi eventually moved to Rome, where he married and had two children. In 1964 he drowned himself in the Tiber.

Pegeen's relationship with her mother always seemed to be her deepest and most frustrating, however. 'Pegeen was in love with her mother,' says the Venetian artist Manina, whose work had captured Peggy's attention, though Peggy never bought any of her paintings. 'I was on a vaporetto with Pegeen. As we passed Peggy's palazzo Pegeen grabbed my arm so tightly she left a bruise. "If that collection ever goes up in flames," Pegeen said, "You'll know who did it."' Pegeen hated the collection, Manina says. 'It was her rival for her mother's love.'

Peggy took her daughter on a trip to England in 1957, hoping, observers said, to solve her problems by marrying her to a British aristocrat (though she had no one specific in mind). They went to some galleries on Cork Street, among them the Hanover, which was showing the British artist Francis Bacon's *détournements* of van Gogh paintings. At the opening, the artist Ralph Rumney met Peggy and her daughter. 'It was a *coup de foudre*,' Rumney, then twenty-four to Pegeen's thirty-three, recalled. 'Love at first sight.' The next day he saw Pegeen again at the opening of a collective show at the Redfern Gallery in which his paintings played a large part, and this time he followed her in a taxi to a Soho party, where they finally connected. A few days later Peggy came back to the Redfern Gallery and tried to make a deal with Rumney for a painting of his, *The Change* (1957). 'It's Pegeen's,' Rumney said. Peggy turned to Pegeen and hissed, 'You're fucking your way to quite a collection.'

Pegeen became ever more deeply involved with Rumney. The couple eventually made their way back to Paris, where Ralph, with the help of a small inheritance, bought an apartment on the rue du Dragon, installing bunk beds for Pegeen's sons. But Pegeen wanted to go to Venice and reconcile with her mother; Ralph agreed, and, hoping mother and daughter could sort things out, rented a large apartment in Castello near the Questura, dividing his time between Venice and Paris. Pegeen refused to see her mother unless Ralph was present. Meanwhile, Peggy was writing letters to Bernard Reis about 'that awful boy,' whom she considered to be after Pegeen's money.

According to Rumney, Pegeen had a full-fledged drinking problem when he first met her. 'She would hide bottles of Scotch behind books, things like that,' he said. She had seen many therapists, and was psychoanalyzed from 1955 to 1956 by a Russian doctor, but her doctors only added prescriptions for tranquilizers and barbiturates to the mix. Eileen Finletter saw Pegeen's analyst at a party during a time when Pegeen seemed to be anorexic. Like her mother, Pegeen had always eaten scantily, but this was something else entirely. She was growing progressively weaker, and it was clear she meant to starve herself. Although he was a Freudian, the analyst said, 'This goes beyond Freud.' According to her friend, Pegeen had a 'lack of will, a fundamental weakness.'

But Peggy could not or would not see this. To her mind, Pegeen's problem was Rumney. If he were removed, she would be fine. Peggy tried to enlist
Sindbad in the cause, but Sindbad, with problems of his own, resisted her
attempts. He had recently divorced his wife, the former Jacqueline
Ventadour, who in a strange turn of events had fallen in love with Pegeen's
husband, Jean Hélion. Her marriage to Sindbad and Pegeen's to Hélion were
effectively over and had been so for some time, but it was a difficult situation
nonetheless, and continued to be so after Jacqueline and Hélion married in
1958. Sindbad was unsure of his vocation; in 1949 he had started a literary
magazine called *Points: The Magazine of Young Writers*, in which, with the
help of his father, he published work by Brendan Behan, James Baldwin, and
other young writers in Europe. Though it was relatively successful – 'it was
one of the first signs of French culture picking up after the war,' says Iris
Owens, a girlfriend of Sindbad's before he remarried – Sindbad lost interest
before long. 'Peggy liked strong people and Sindbad never really had much
drive,' says his former wife, Jacqueline. Peggy helped him with *Points*, but
Sindbad eventually went back to selling insurance for one firm after another,
alternating with forays into real estate. He played cricket obsessively in his
spare time. 'Laurence was not much help. He was deprecating to anyone
who tried to achieve anything,' says Jacqueline Ventadour Hélion.

Sindbad bridled, in fact, when Peggy tried to involve him in his sister's
affairs. He then tried to involve Bernard Reis, sending the accountant letters
that passed between him and Peggy on the topic. It was symptomatic of the
family's troubles that Peggy's financial adviser functioned as a kind of family
counselor. In characteristic Vail-Guggenheim fashion, Sindbad called these
matters 'all the histoires.' He worried that he would lose his allowance from
his mother, and, like his sister, Pegeen, he was forever thrown into confusion
as Peggy toyed with decisions about her legacy. With Iris Owens, he discussed – not entirely in jest – stealing the Picasso that hung in the palazzo's
foyer.

In Ralph Rumney, Peggy met her nemesis – or so she thought. Actually,
he had more in common with her than she ever bothered to learn. Born in
1934 in Newcastle and raised in Halifax, where his father was a vicar,
Rumney was a rebel from his schooldays, when he was roundly denounced as
a pervert by the bishop of Leeds for purchasing the complete works of the
Marquis de Sade; he was also expelled from the Young Communists League
for 'lack of moral rectitude.' After enrolling briefly in an art school, Rumney
left for Paris, where he continued to paint and fell in with the Lettrists, a
group of artistic and intellectual provocateurs who believed that the individual was a spectator of his or her own life and could escape this condition

only by appropriating the materials of consumer culture and using them against it. After his show at the Redfern Gallery in 1957, Rumney and Pegeen went with fellow Lettrists to the tiny Italian village of Cosio d'Arroscia, where Guy Debord, later the author of *La Société du Spectacle* (1967), founded the Situationists International, a new movement based on Lettrist principles that quickly grew to be a major artistic and political force in the decade leading up to the Paris insurrections of 1968. Debord, like André Breton before him, was very strict; Rumney was the first Situationist to be expelled, later the same year, for failing to meet a deadline for an article on the psychogeography of Venice.

'Pegeen wasn't political. We were in love and inseparable, so she came along' to the Cosio d'Arroscia meeting at which the Situationists International was formed. '[Pegeen] thought it was my own private obsession,' Rumney recalled. But Pegeen's attraction to Ralph had a certain logic, as his work and his political and cultural stance represented a kind of continuum with much of the work her mother had patronized over the years. The surrealists, too, had criticized elements of popular culture and, in some cases, regarded their activities – from 'studio' art to films to public happenings – as contributing, potentially, to a revolutionary opening up of society. Several of the Situationists, including Debord, knew Breton and regarded him as an intellectual godfather.

But Peggy was set against Rumney from the start. If in the past she had found something in common with insurgents like Emma Goldman, that time of her life was decidedly over. In fact, she had pushed from her mind any memories of the anarchist movement that had loomed so large in politics and art during her younger years. When Judith Malina, the widow of Julian Beck, whom Peggy had banned from Art of This Century when he turned from Athenian ways, came to Venice with Hanon Reznikov (whom she would later marry) in the late sixties, she decided to visit Peggy, bearing no grudge about what had happened some time ago. Conversation turned to Alexander Berkman, or Sasha, to whom Peggy had been quite close at the time of her friendship with Emma Goldman, Berkman's lover. Peggy reminisced about Emma's Jewish cooking. But Reznikov said something about the fact that Berkman shot Henry Clay Frick, for which Berkman had served some fourteen years in jail before he met Peggy. 'FRICK?!' Peggy shrilly hooted. 'He shot FRICK?' Perhaps, from her current vantage point, she felt she had less in common with the anarchist than she did his victim (including, to be sure, a significant art collection).

Much about Rumney simply scared Peggy, reminding her of her own past and her marriage to Laurence Vail. Like Laurence, Ralph seemed to dabble in the arts; like Laurence, he drank. When Pegeen became pregnant with Ralph's child, Peggy bombarded Bernard Reis with questions about the child's legal status. Hélion, in fact, sent a notary after Pegeen and Ralph denying the paternity of the child, Sandro, born in 1958. Sandro's birth did nothing to bring Pegeen and Peggy any closer, and they remained at daggers drawn for several years. Around this time Peggy took Rumney to lunch and offered him $50,000 to stay away from Pegeen. Ralph demurred, but when he told Pegeen, she said he should have taken the bribe so they could spend the money.

Other matters competed for Peggy's attention. She had continued to add to her collection after she left New York City and she made a point of it. To a museum director interested in showing her collection, she said, 'I do not like your list. It looks as though I had stopped collecting after Pollock.' She had not stopped, though the art world was changing overnight, making it harder for her to find bargains. She watched in amazement as Pollock's' star rose and his prices skyrocketed. An August 1949 article in Life headlined 'Is he the greatest living painter in the United States?' Following this publicity, Pollock had a fall show at Betty Parsons's at which almost all the paintings sold. He was 'Jack the Dripper,' sales rose exponentially, and the public took note. Peggy did what she could to further Pollock's reputation in Europe, showing six of his paintings at the 1948 Biennale. In the summer of 1950 she arranged a show of the twenty-three Pollocks she owned in the Sala Napoleonica at the Museo Correr on the Piazza San Marco. At night, the show was lit up, and Peggy loved looking at the paintings while sitting in a café. But she noticed that her name was being left out in stories about Pollock's success; one description of her as the painter's 'first dealer' especially upset her. She blamed Pollock for this lapse before he died, and after his death her blame shifted to Lee Krasner, whom she felt was personally responsible for trying to expunge her name from the record. General feelings about Pollock and Krasner's ingratitude led her to tell Krasner, on a European trip in 1956, that she could find no room for her in Venice; thus she was spared being Lee's host when a phone call told her the tragic news, that Pollock had died in a car accident.

With an eye to her future reputation, in 1959 Peggy turned to a writing project. 'I've written a book called Confessions of an Art Addict,' she wrote Bernard Reis in 1959. 'It's about ART ONLY.' She condensed Out of This Century, leaving out most of the personal matter, and brought the autobiography up to date, concentrating on the details of opening and maintaining the palazzo, her travels and those of the collection, and her observations on the art world; the result is a fairly bloodless volume. Peggy admitted as much, writing in a later edition containing both autobiographies, 'I seem to have written the first book as an uninhibited woman and the second as a lady who was trying to establish her place in the history of modern art.'

Meanwhile, unable to afford the prices the abstract expressionists now commanded, Peggy looked for talent elsewhere. In 1950 she bought the Scottish painter Alan Davie's *Untitled*, also known as *Peggy's Guessing Box* (1950); later she would acquire two more of his works. In 1954 she reported to Bernard Reis that she had bought *Empire of Light* (1953–1954), 'that wonderful painting of Magritte with the lamp lit house in the daytime.' The same year she added Arp's *Fruit Amphore* (1951). In April 1957 she went on something of a spree in Paris and London, buying a Karl Appel (*The Crying Crocodile Tries to Catch the Sun*, 1956); a sculpture by the British artist Leslie Thornton (*Roundabout*, 1955); *Osage* (1956), a painting by the American artist Paul Jenkins; and *February 1956* (*Menhir*), a relief by the British artist Ben Nicholson (1956). In the same letter she said that she hoped to buy a number of Giacometti sculptures for her garden, but the sale fell through. The same year she bought Francis Bacon's *Study for a Chimpanzee* (1957), which she liked so much she hung it on the wall next to her bed. In 1959, she bought a mural-size painting, *Ireland* (1958), from the artist Grace Hartigan; she wrote Hartigan saying that she had hung it prominently, on her sitting room wall. In 1964 she would buy Jean Dubuffet's *Fleshy Face with Chestnut Hair* (1951); in 1960 she bought two untitled 1958 de Kooning works, an oil and a pastel drawing. In 1971 she would tell Reis that she had bought an Enrico Baj (*Perdu*, 1967) and a César compression (*Compression*, 1969); she already owned César's *Man in a Spider's Web* (1955). In 1968 she would add an oil by Graham Sutherland (*Organic Form*, 1962–1968). To her collection of Italian works by Tancredi, she added Edmondo Bacci's 1958 *Event #247* and *Event #292*, a Giuseppe Santomaso (*Secret Life*, 1958), a 1951 Emilio Vedova called *Image of Time* (*Barricade*), a Piero Dorazio (*Unitas*, 1965), a Pietro Consagra relief (*Mythical Conversation*, 1959?), and an Arnoldo Pomodoro (*Sphere No. 4*, 1963), among others. She invested as well in small glass sculptures executed by the Venetian artist Egidio Constantini from sketches by both Picasso and Pegeen.

Few of these works would be considered controversial. Peggy said many times that postwar art collecting was not for her, buying solely on the basis of investment. Much of what she saw she did not like, especially pop art, telling a reporter she 'loathed' it: 'It's got nowhere, and I can't see where it was trying to go.' In 1968 she would expound at some length to Bernard Reis, who was evidently trying to put together a show of artists who had exhibited with her: 'I can't bear the painting of Barney Newman. I hate all that school of painting including [Mark] Rothko's present work & I would not want my name associated in any way with it. Also a lot of the painters I showed at "Art of This" aren't worth showing again & one could not leave them out if one wanted to show everyone who had been exhibited by me.' Rothko became a particular object of distaste, though she never explained why: a 1970 show of his work at the Biennale would move her to tell Reis, 'It's advertised that Rothko is the greatest American painter. I think that is exaggerated.'

It is interesting to contemplate just what separated the painters like Rothko whom Peggy disliked and those like Pollock whom she extolled. They were more or less of the same generation and from the same scene. One possibility is that some, like Rothko and Newman, were moving further toward unarticulated planes of color; Peggy may have seen a static quality in their images that she did not like. It is possible, as well, that she did not like these artists as people; or, rather, since the age difference between her and them was so great, that she couldn't see herself surrounded by them. Artists were what compelled her in the art scene, and these artists were a continent away from her. By installing Tancredi in her basement, she was again attempting to live among artists, but the Italian art scene never took off in ways she had hoped, and Tancredi disappointed her personally, complaining to all of Venice when she tried to put him on an allowance. Peggy found herself at a distinct remove from the actual making of art, and her energies were simply not engaged from such a distance.

It was evident that to Peggy, Jackson Pollock, and not Mark Rothko, would always be 'the greatest American painter.' But she had no comment about Pollock's tragic death in 1956, and by that time, she was starting to have suspicions about her former protégé. She had her eye on the prices his work was getting, and what she saw began to trouble her. She was convinced that more Pollocks from the years 1946 and 1947 were turning up, and she believed that all work from those years was contractually hers. She began looking into the matter, and warned Bernard Reis that she was thinking of bringing a suit against Lee Krasner.

But many things distracted her from such litigation. Through the American poet Alan Ansen, a good friend, Peggy became acquainted with the Beat writers, for whom Venice was an obligatory stop. The first of these was William S. Burroughs, author of the controversial novel about a heroin addict, *Junkie* (1953), who met Peggy when Ansen brought him to a party at her palazzo for the British consul. Ansen explained that the thing to do was to kiss Peggy's hand when he met her. A drunken Burroughs said, 'I will be glad to kiss her cunt if that is the custom.' Peggy's friend Robert Brady overheard this comment and made Peggy bar Burroughs from the palazzo.

It did not surprise Peggy that Ralph Rumney was acquainted with this crew. Ansen had a very small apartment, and Rumney opened his home to other Beats who came to town. Peggy attended a poetry reading at Ansen's in 1958 when the poet Peter Orlovsky threw a sweaty towel at his boyfriend, Allen Ginsberg. 'Disaster! It landed on Peggy Guggenheim's head,' Rumney later said. 'She made a scene and stormed out.' She withdrew an invitation for a party at her palazzo in honor of the critic Nicolas Calas. A contrite Ginsberg wrote to Peggy, with characteristic frankness: 'I've never been in a great formal historic salon before and naturally have been eager to go there, be accepted, see the pictures at leisure, sip big cocktails, gaze over [the] grand canal, be a poet in Venice surrounded by famous ladies, echoes of *Partisan Review* & the 20s & Surrealists, butlers and gondolas . . . I'd like to come. I don't want to leave Venice without big high class social encounters.'

When the story of the incident reached Burroughs, he wrote to Ansen, 'It was hardly in the cards that Peggy Guggenheim should find Allen and Peter congenial. However, it does seem to me she is being a bit unreasonable to move in admittedly bohemian circles and simultaneously demand conventional behavior.' Burroughs had a point, but Peggy was on her guard in these years. Though she and Ginsberg had more in common than she could see – both had large, forgiving hearts, despite Peggy's occasional vindictiveness – she was put off by his long hair and his drug taking.

Other Beats fared better. The poet Gregory Corso wrote a poem called 'Venice, 1958,' which contains the line, 'I eat! And well!' He and Peggy had what can only be characterized as a courtship in early 1958, chronicled in Gregory Corso's recently published letters to his Beat friends. He described his first meeting with her very tersely: 'It could be called successful,' except that she kept worrying about one of her ailing dogs and 'was even thinking of flying in a specialist from Zurich to consult.' They got drunk together, according to Corso, and he confessed that he had been in jail. Describing his second, much happier meeting to Allen Ginsberg, in a February 13 letter, he said they had a

> very very funny conversation, we were both drunk, but Alan [Ansen] was drunkest, he demanded she try heroin . . . It was all mad, the evening ended with a long long embrace and a kiss on some Piazza . . . Thus my date with Peggy . . . She is a woman who does demand manners, that is certain. I tried telling her that Peter [Orlovsky] realized that she was a great personage therefore decided to impress this great personage, and the best way he thought was the flying towel. She said

that that is no way, because one need not put up with that, that she
would like to be impressed with an enduring thing.

Peggy brought up the topic of sex, but Corso had his eye on the thirty-
four-year-old Pegeen, and hardly thought of Peggy in that regard. In one
telling, he said that Peggy wanted to go to bed with him and, although he
declined, they remained friends. But in a letter to Ginsberg he reveals how
tenderly he felt for her and how important a figure she was at this time of his
life:

Good news. I had wild alone ball dancing thru Picassos and Arps and
Ernst with P.G., she digs me much, I told her all about me prison, etc.
etc. . . . . She is a very sweet person, sad at heart, and old with memories.
But I make her happy, she laughs, and I am good in that way. We spoke
of sex, we spoke of sex, but I don't know what to do about that. She
wanted me to stay over the night, but I couldn't, and didn't, and I am
glad because she walked me late at night to boat to Ansen's, and sat on
barge with me and told me great things about she and Beckett and her
life, and it was pleasantly sad and good, thus Venice is becoming
romantic for me, in this fashion.

He took Peggy's measure with insight and compassion:

Very strange, marvelous lady. Didn't you see that in her? How did you
miss it? Perhaps you didn't have time, but she really is great, and sad,
and does need friends. Not all those creepy painters all the time. I told
her painters were making her into a creep, she laughed, led me to the
boat, there we sat and when boat came fifteen minutes later, I kissed
her good-bye, while I watched her walk away I saw that she put her
hand to her head as though she were in pain. I suddenly realized the
plight of the woman by that gesture. She is a liver of life, and life is
fading away. That's all there is to it.

At a subsequent meeting, when he turned up late, she gave him an expensive
watch, taking it off her wrist and handing it to him 'with wry sarcasm.'
    Corso told the story of his acquaintance with Peggy with cynical detach-
ment. He said his first mistake was refusing to go to bed with her. His second,
he said, was following her out into the garden heading for the grave of her
'favorite pet dachshund.' He said, 'Gee, what a nice backyard you have,' at
which Peggy took offense. Then, at a party at the palazzo, the phallus on the

Mario Marini sculpture was stolen. Peggy confronted Corso, who said, 'It was that German artist, Hundertwasser, that fucker took it.' That was his third mistake, Corso claimed. But what really got him barred from the palazzo was his confession that he was interested in her daughter. The unpleasant tone of this telling of the story is at odds with the very real affection Corso seems to have felt for Peggy.

Alan Ansen had frequent run-ins with the Venetian police. Like another of Peggy's gay friends, the art collector and dealer Arthur Jeffress (who 'left a substantial sum in his will to the welfare of British sailors provided that not one penny should go to officers or Wrens'), Ansen had a weakness for sailors, as did Peggy; she would roll out the red carpet any time the fleet was in town. But one night two sailors Ansen had brought home attacked him, forcing him naked into the street and into a bar on the corner, where he grabbed a chair to defend himself. After that, the city fathers refused to renew his *soggiorno*, and he had to go to Austria and then come back into the city to get a new residency permit.

In 1959, for Peggy's sixty-first birthday, Ansen wrote a masque, 'The Return from Greece,' performed on August 3 in her garden. It was dedicated to the poet James Merrill and his companion, David Jackson. 'Ansen wrote it,' Jackson told a friend, 'and four others plus Alan in a blond string wig and draperies (as Venice) did it, with Peggy, Jimmy, and I on thrones wearing leaves, listening.' The New York City art dealer John Myers was the master of ceremonies, and Peggy's secretary, Paolo Barozzi, played a garbage man. One feature was the account by the character representing the city of Venice of the summer's events there, especially Corso's visit and the stop of the U.S. Naval cruiser *Des Moines*. The performance was successful enough that Ansen would follow it with two more productions at the palazzo, 'The Available Garden' in 1960 and 'The First Men on the Moon' in 1961. A fourth was planned, but in 1962 Ansen was at last expelled from Venice on a morals charge. He moved on to Athens, where Peggy would subsequently visit him 'at least twice,' according to Ansen.

More reliable old friends also turned up in Venice in the late 1950s. John Cage, friendly again with Peggy after their misunderstanding in the 1940s, was a frequent visitor, often with his companion, the dancer Merce Cunningham; for example, when they performed together at La Fenice, in 1960, 1964, and 1970, they stayed each time with Peggy. She describes Cage visiting her 'now and then between times for a minute.' Perhaps his most memorable visit was in the winter of 1959, when he stayed five weeks, appearing on an Italian TV quiz show, *Lascia o Raddoppia* (Leave It or Double It), and being tested on a pet subject of his, mushrooms. He hoped to win

$2,000, and, as Peggy wrote Bernard Reis, 'As he answered all the questions and no one else is a rival he will probably win.' While the show ran, women called from windows to Cage on the streets of Venice below and wished him luck; he had become a small celebrity. Win he did, taking away $6,000, with which he bought a Steinway and a Volkswagen station wagon. After his first appearance on TV, Cage recorded a composition he called 'Sounds of Venice,' in an electronic studio. Peggy went with him to the recording session, and was delighted when a technician came to the palazzo to get some sounds of a house painter singing and the dogs barking. But the dogs refused to bark and made unholy sounds when the house painter tried to provoke them, 'a great disappointment,' Peggy told Bernard Reis.

The performance artist Yoko Ono, who was one of Cage's admirers in the early 1960s, remembers that Cage spoke very highly of Peggy and brought her to one of Ono's performances in 1961. The following summer, Cage and Ono invited her along on their tour of Japan, and Peggy and Ono were occasional roommates. Though Peggy was outspoken about not being a particular fan of either's music, she was, according to Ono, 'open-minded and intelligent – she was in modern terms a very hip girl.' With similar parallels in their lives – both had come from privileged, strait-laced backgrounds and had been determined to break away – they had 'become girlfriends on a human and personal level,' and remained so, Peggy visiting Ono in the Georgian mansion near Ascot that she shared with John Lennon, and Ono visiting Peggy in Venice whenever she came through, often with her daughter, Kyoko.

Though old friends like Emily Coleman and Peter Hoare (separately – they never did get together) came through Venice frequently, reminding Peggy of her past, Peggy maintained few family ties as the 1950s stretched into the 1960s. Grudgingly, she allowed her sister Hazel to stay with her from time to time, but discouraged her sister's visits when she was not part of a couple, for Hazel on her own was a bit of a loose cannon. The photographer Lyle Bongé, Hazel's godson, whose mother, the artist Dusti Bongé, was a good friend of Hazel's, remembers Hazel playing 'ring-around-the-bed' with him in the 1950s. 'Don't feel like you're fucking your mother,' she said to reassure him, 'I'm much older than she is.' He remembers her as 'delightfully wacky. I should have written down everything she said.' But Hazel had her troubles. Once, a broken fingernail led, improbably, to her confinement in a Paris nursing home, which took on her treatment for barbiturate addiction for months on end. The nursing home evidently was after her money and had no plans to release her. Hazel's New Orleans and Paris friends conspired to get her out, which they eventually accomplished. Hazel, for her part, competed with her sister in all kinds of ways. In a less than loyal move, she befriended Kay Boyle and maintained a correspondence with her. Long after Peggy's death, Hazel was complaining about her sister, writing Boyle in 1990 that her sister was 'a strange confused unhappy woman enamored of her . . . self-importance.'

One unpleasant encounter in the late 1950s left Peggy uneasy about the way posterity would view her collection and her role in it. Aline Saarinen, the wife of the architect, was writing a book to be called *The Proud Possessors*, about legendary American collectors. She spent some time in 1957 gathering material for the chapter dedicated to Peggy, 'dissecting' her with people like Mary McCarthy. Alfred Barr would not give her any ammunition, responding to Saarinen's query with the statement, 'I am completely convinced of her kindness and fundamental goodness.' Saarinen engaged in a chummy discussion by mail with the art critic Bernard Berenson, who seems to have felt Italy was too small for both him and Peggy Guggenheim. In a September 23 letter to Saarinen, Berenson – through whose books Peggy had received her earliest art history training – recounted his visit to her pavilion in the 1948 Biennale. He opened by calling Peggy 'a foul horror, an anthropomorphic, creepy, crawly thing.' (Berenson's antipathy to modern art is well known, but it is not clear why he viewed Peggy in such a harsh light.) At the festival, according to Berenson, she had greeted him, saying, 'Mr. Berenson, all I am and all I have ever done is entirely due to your influence over me.' He told Saarinen that his 'spontaneous' answer to Peggy was 'And this is the result?' Mary McCarthy, he said, had been with him that morning and tried to defend Peggy, 'but, I thought, very feebly.' Saarinen paid a visit to Peggy in Venice, a meeting Peggy later said she should have known was a mistake.

When *The Proud Possessors* was published in 1958, Peggy was dismayed at her sensationalistic portrait, though outwardly she took it, according to Herbert Read, 'in her usual good spirit.' She correctly perceived that Saarinen had not liked *Out of This Century*, disapproving of Peggy's morals. 'If your puritanical reactions to my memoires made you so critical and hostile,' Peggy wrote Saarinen on October 29, 'you would have done much better to have left out everything that did not deal with your subject. Surely no one is interested in your reactions to my personal life. I take great offense to your allusions to this.' The two would soon meet at a 1959 party given by the Alfred Barrs in New York; Peggy told Saarinen bluntly that she was a puritan and thus could not understand what it was like to take a lover. Saarinen was proud to report to Berenson that it was a sign of her 'long awaited maturity' that she did not correct Peggy. It was an unfortunate skirmish between two strong-minded women, each convinced she was right.

Peggy, 'a proud possessor' indeed, had her collection to think about: where it would travel, and, more pressing, what she would do with it after she died. It had been over ten years since Peggy had had any contact with her uncle Solomon or her Guggenheim cousins, though sometimes one or two of the latter would pass through Venice. In the meantime, there had been a changing of the guard. The Solomon R. Guggenheim Museum, housed in the noteworthy building designed by Frank Lloyd Wright, was set to open in August 1959. Solomon had died in 1949, shortly after commissioning Wright to design a building to house his Museum of Non-Objective Painting; the baroness was its director until her resignation in 1952. Harry Guggenheim, Peggy's cousin and the former U.S. ambassador to Cuba, served as president of the board of trustees of the Solomon R. Guggenheim Foundation, which oversaw the now renamed museum. With his ascension, the clan's disdain for Benjamin Guggenheim's branch of the family seemed to have lifted, especially as Harry had ambitions for the institution that now had an instant-landmark location on what would be known as Museum Mile on Fifth Avenue. He welcomed Peggy when she traveled to New York City in April 1959 to see the as yet unopened museum.

Wright had designed an extraordinary building: a corkscrew structure that allowed works of art to be placed along one long ramp leading up from the ground floor. When her cousin Harry gave her a tour, Peggy did her best to like the building but found it altogether uncongenial. She had to admit that, with the planned all-white interior, it would make a striking background for the art. She sympathized with 'poor Sweeney,' she said, who inherited this 'millstone' of a building along with the museum's holdings. Referring to it as 'Uncle Solomon's garage,' Peggy felt that it would have been much better located in Central Park rather than on the East Side of Fifth Avenue, where she thought it looked cramped – greatly overestimating the extent of her family's influence.

While in New York, Peggy went to an opening of her old friend Mina Loy's work at the Bodley Gallery. Along with Peggy, Marcel Duchamp, Joseph Cornell, and Kay Boyle were on the guest list; Djuna Barnes came as well. Charles Henri Ford's beautiful sister Ruth and her actor husband, Zachary Scott, gave a party for Peggy at their apartment in the Dakota on West 72nd Street, another reunion of sorts. Peggy wrote that she also went to a cocktail party at the West Side home of Ben Heller and his wife, who had recently bought Pollock's *Blue Poles* (1952). During Pollock's lifetime, the painting had sold for the then considerable price of $6,000; the Hellers had bought it for $30,000 (and would sell it for a record $3 million in 1973). This no doubt irked Peggy, for she had given away countless Pollock gouaches and several oils, and often without realizing any tax advantages; she had given *Cathedral* (1947), for instance, to Bernard and Becky Reis in 1949. She had spied Pollock's 1947 drawing *War* in a Rome gallery in 1957, and since then had been gathering evidence that Lee Krasner had been cheating on Art of This Century's 1946–1948 exclusive deal with Pollock.

After two years Peggy's patience ran out, and she returned to New York City to file suit in federal court against Krasner for a settlement of $122,000 on June 8, 1961. She told a reporter that she had uncovered the existence of fifteen works of art created in the time she had subsidized Pollock. The suit charged that Pollock had defrauded her by not giving her these works and that Lee had further defrauded her by keeping them. She sought, she said, the 'reasonable market value' of the works. Staying with the Reises again, she quarreled with Bernard over his management of the case – he kept stalling, unwilling to alienate Krasner – and moved out, going to the apartment of an English friend.

A year before, Reis had written to Krasner that Peggy believed she owned the 1946 *Composition, Shimmering Image* (1947), *White Horizontal* (1941–1947), and *Eyes in the Heat II* (1947), as well as *War*. The lawsuit would drag on for four years before Peggy settled out of court and dropped the case. In the settlement, Krasner gave her two small Pollocks then said to be worth $500 together.

In 1960, Peggy wrote to her old friend Emily Coleman that for three years she had been having 'perpetual histoires' about Pegeen and Ralph Rumney, 'whom I can't bear and whom I never want to see.' Ralph was becoming a bête noire, beyond anything he might have done. She knew that Emily, who had met Ralph in London in 1958, had taken a liking to him, and continued, 'I think he has used Pegeen to get out of his financial misery and went even to the point of giving her a baby to gain his ends. I don't think they are happy together and I don't believe either of them is in love with the other. I think Pegeen can't bear to be alone so she stays with him not having the courage to look for someone else. Also the child is in his name so she does not know what to do. I daren't interfere as it only makes things worse.'

Peggy thought, she said, that Hélion was too old for Pegeen 'once she grew up.' Ralph was drunk 'all the time,' she wrote; Pegeen stayed with him only for 'security.' There is no question that Rumney drank too much; indeed, his friends called him 'the consul' after the alcoholic hero of Malcolm Lowry's *Under the Volcano*. But Pegeen drank heavily as well, and was developing an addiction to Valium and sleeping pills. None of these habits improved after she married Ralph, though she was always happiest with an infant and would remain so until Sandro was three or four. Then her demons returned. Ralph would later say that he rescued her from suicide threats too many times to count.

In October, Peggy wrote to Bernard Reis that Pegeen had married Ralph in order to legitimize Sandro. She reported as well on their sorry finances. Neither Pegeen nor Ralph sold paintings with any regularity. A story was going around Venice that they were keeping warm by burning some Victor Brauners that Pegeen had somehow got her hands on, lighting their wax surfaces for heat (Brauner had devised a technique for painting on wax). They divided their time between the rue du Dragon apartment and their rented apartment in the Castello. After their marriage, however, Pegeen and Ralph bought a 150-square-meter apartment with terrace on the Ile Saint-Louis in Paris, after Pegeen sold off a Max Ernst to raise the capital. (Peggy insisted that they put the flat in Pegeen's name, which the couple agreed to do.) Among their few treasures were some Cocteau drawings; Cocteau was Sandro's godfather and had tried to intervene with Peggy on behalf of Pegeen and Ralph. Pegeen received about $200 a month from a trust set up for her by her grandmother, Florette, and, until Peggy cut her off, about $150 from her mother. (Peggy often gave her large cash gifts, however, and seemingly endless 'loans.')

Peggy was clearly trying to ensure that Pegeen would not make the same mistakes she had made, but she never seems to have recognized that she herself had done best when she was without a man, when she discovered her independence after her first three 'marriages' – to Laurence, John Holms, and Garman. The only future she could envision for Pegeen was for her to enter a man's orbit, and she was determined to control Pegeen's choice of men. Hélion had been a safe choice for a partner, in her eyes, as he had been part of Peggy's circle and thus familiar, and because, as an older man, secure in his career, he could give Pegeen the security she seemed to need so desperately. When Pegeen began to take lovers, Peggy seems to have approved, perhaps sensing that Pegeen had needs that her husband was not meeting, but Peggy did not seem fully aware of the hash Pegeen was making of her life. Peggy felt that Ralph represented a real danger. She worried that she was losing her daughter to a man altogether too much like the men – creative yet dissolute – whom she herself had so often favored. Perhaps she remembered that her own mother had tended to look away rather than to see Peggy's problems with Laurence, and now she was going too far in correcting this fault.

Fundamentally, Peggy failed to see that her daughter was depressed and unhappy – and had been, probably, since girlhood. It showed in Pegeen's demeanor; it showed in her painting. Ralph Rumney was perceptive about her artwork: 'Her paintings, especially the pastels, are very deceptive if you only look at the surface where, at first glance, there is nothing but life, color, festivity. It's only after a deeper contemplation that you perceive the poignant beauty and anguish that her work breathes. Her work reflected her experience.'

Yet no one ever saw the possibility of intervening in Pegeen's life and getting her some help – though Peggy no doubt approved and even gave financial assistance for her daughter's psychoanalysis in 1955 and 1956. Peggy never seems to have noticed that Pegeen was barely eating, that she went from affair to affair, that she was drinking too much and taking too many pills. It is no surprise that Pegeen should have threatened suicide as often as she did: she seems to have desperately wanted her mother's attention. But when she did have Peggy's attention, neither had the vocabulary to talk about their emotions. The only thing the people who loved Pegeen could do, as they saw it, was to keep her alive. Making her happy did not seem to be a possibility.

As she aged, moreover, Peggy tried to tighten her grip on her daughter. As her body began to betray her, she felt as if she were losing control, and the only way to hang on was through Pegeen. And she thought that her only means of regaining control was money. That Peggy was making plans for her legacy when Pegeen became involved with Ralph did not help matters any. As had been true throughout her life, Peggy had very complicated ideas about gift giving, especially when money was involved. Ingratitude was her great fear, along with any feeling of entitlement on the part of the person receiving her generosity. Above all she feared that she was loved only for what she could give financially.

And the countervailing fear was that Pegeen would no longer need her and would leave her. Mother and daughter seem to have constantly played out this fear, breaking with each other and then reconciling again, as if to prepare themselves for the final separation. Pegeen seems to have genuinely loved Ralph, and that thoroughly frightened Peggy, whose daughter was no longer under her sole control.

By this time, Peggy was in a frenzy of concern about her will and the disposition of her estate. After her visit to America to see the new Guggenheim Museum in 1959, her cousin Harry had written indicating that if she had ever considered leaving her collection to the museum, it was no longer something of great concern or interest to him. As if he underestimated her intelligence, he wrote that he had once thought it might occur to her. 'However, after thinking the matter through, I most sincerely think that your Foundation, and your Palace, which has, thanks to your initiative, become world-renowned, should, after your death, be bequeathed, as you have planned, to Italy.'

Peggy, understandably, was incensed. She had, as Harry's careful wording indicates, instructed Bernard Reis to set up a foundation as early as 1957, though she had been dithering ever since about who should be on the board. She initially wanted Sindbad and Pegeen to have seats, as well as Vittorio Corrain (a friend from her earliest days in Venice), her painter friend Robert Brady, and the Canadian photographer Roloff Beny, also a close friend. But as one child and then the other fell out of her good graces, the makeup of the board changed. And while the foundation existed mostly for tax reasons, the question of whom she would leave her two most prized possessions to – her collection and her palazzo – was beginning to haunt her.

After Harry let her know that the collective Guggenheim nose was turned up, Peggy looked elsewhere. She found no shortage of advice. At the end of 1960 she wrote Bernard Reis that she wanted to make Sindbad and Peggy, his new wife, and Sindbad's three children (two by Jacqueline Ventadour and one by his second wife, Peggy) a gift of $15,000 each – while giving nothing to Pegeen. In the same letter, she told Reis that Herbert Read thought she should leave the museum – presumably the palazzo and the collection – to the Cini Foundation or the Venice Bell'Arte. The director of the Venice Modern Art Museum thought she should leave the palazzo and the collection to the city and let the museum run it. In any case, Peggy wrote, she wanted the children to waive whatever claims they might have. By the end of 1960 she had made up her mind to leave everything she owned, except the palazzo and her collection, to her children and to ask them to renounce any other claims. (She added a new clause about her dogs, for Sir Herbert had gone blind, and she felt she could not leave a blind dog to Becky Reis, the current canine legatee.) The palazzo and the artworks would go to her foundation.

But as soon as she settled on this plan she changed it, as she would continue to do until she was nearly on her deathbed. In early 1961 she announced that she was leaving the collection to Venice – an announcement hastened by Italy's threat to levy a 15 percent tax on it. It would be best taken care of, she told Chauncey Newlin, the American lawyer for the Guggenheim Museum, by the Modern Art Museum there (Galleria Internazionale d'arte Moderna di Ca' Pesaro). But by October she changed her mind again. She had always, she said, thought of England as her 'spiritual home,' and she would go to live there 'like a shot,' but for the dogs. The Tate Gallery had come courting. Negotiations took up almost all of 1961, with Sir John Rothenstein, the Tate's director, making subtle and then not so subtle inquiries. In 1962, the Venetian authorities again made her waver when they awarded her honorary citizenship in Venice, a relatively meaningless tribute that pleased her nonetheless. But there were complicated tax reasons for not leaving the collection either to Venice or to the Tate; on top of the difficulties of settling a complex estate involving more than one country, the rules governing gifts and trusts were byzantine. For art to pass from one country to another, import and export duties and taxes were involved. For these reasons alone, then, she was advised that it was best that the collection stay in the same place. Still, Peggy set plans in motion to show her collection at the Tate in 1965, the museum officials acting in hopes that she might decide in their favor. Peggy shipped off the collection to England in late 1964, clearly favoring the Tate at this point.

But something happened in the interim. On August 6, 1964, Harry Guggenheim wrote Peggy in response to 'your inquiry concerning the possibility of the Solomon R. Guggenheim Foundation ultimately taking over the administration of your gallery in Venice and operating it.' Peggy responded, 'I am so very happy that you have not excluded my idea as an eventual possibility.' Another bold suitor had come on the scene, and this one from the family fold – the very family she had renounced with such vigor.

19

Last Days

Age encroached. Peggy wrote Djuna Barnes from London that she saw Willa Muir, their old friend from the years in England in the 1930s, at a party for Herbert Read's seventieth birthday in late 1963; Willa was in a wheelchair, and she didn't seem to recognize Peggy when she spoke to her. Djuna, for her part, wrote Peggy that she heard that Alice Toklas, still living in the house she had shared with Gertrude Stein and a succession of standard poodles, had fallen and broken both legs and was having a terrible time sorting out 'hospitals, home, property.' It was a fearsome state to contemplate for a woman like Djuna, who lived the life of a hermit in her tiny apartment on Patchin Place in Greenwich Village. Djuna also wrote that her arthritis was bad and her asthma prohibited her from traveling. Physically, Peggy had few complaints, but following a 'heavenly' trip to Tripoli and Egypt with Bill Rose in 1964, she was very 'washed out.' She told Djuna that she had 'hardly enough energy to get through the day.' (Djuna sympathized, responding, 'We are on the autumn road are we not.')

But the mood would pass; generally, Peggy enjoyed a vigorous old age. She walked a precarious line between being a figure of fun and a dignified lady from an earlier time. Called *l'ultima dogaressa*, or the last (female) doge, she was granted a certain status in Venice by virtue of her long tenure there and her general good citizenship. Too often, though, she let herself be photographed wearing outsized sunglasses and surrounded by her brood of little dogs. She sailed around Venice like a presiding spirit from an earlier time – the eighteenth century, perhaps. Fortunately, however, some of the institutions that had spurned her in the past – like the Louvre, and, most notably, the Guggenheim – were at last offering her some well-earned recognition, which she of course accepted with enthusiasm.

One of the high points of her life was the show of her collection at the Tate Gallery in London in 1964 and 1965. The exhibit opened on New Year's Eve in 1964, and a formal dinner in Peggy's honor followed on January 6, 1965. Almost her entire collection had been shipped to London, including Oceanic and primitive art that she had bought in the 1950s, although the Marini horse and rider was left behind. In a neat suit, her silvery hair cut short with a fringe of bangs, Peggy held court with aplomb, cheerfully meeting with journalists and TV newscasters. Museum officials noted that the show attracted about 86,000 visitors and extended it from February 7 to March 7. The show was having 'a terrific success,' Peggy wrote Djuna. She was feted everywhere, and Pegeen and Sindbad both came from France to join in the celebrations.

Sindbad was now happily married and the father of two young girls, as well as his sons by Jacqueline Ventadour. But he was still directionless, interested mainly in eating and drinking well and in following cricket, playing the game every Sunday at the Standard Athletic Club in Meudon. His performance in the insurance business was lackluster, and 'He is working at a stupid job and does not know what else to do,' Peggy told Emily Coleman. 'It's very sad.' (It never seems to have occurred to her that this was more than his father had done.)

Sindbad and his father had still not got beyond the Vail propensity for flinging furniture in public places. The novelist Herbert Gold has recently described a scene between Sindbad and Laurence in Paris in the 1960s:

> My friends in Paris, Lawrence [sic] Vail and his son, Sindbad . . . were fighting and throwing tables at each other at the Old Navy on the boulevard Saint-Germain. It was a voluptuously operatic public quarrel, scraping the inside of the Oedipus complex with an extravagance befitting their expatriated money and self-indulgence, Americans in Paris enjoying café life while trying to beat the shit out of each other. Not quite traditional father-son stuff . . . A couple of *flics* engaged the battlers in conversation. When they asked the Vails what was their occupation, the words 'tourist,' 'painter,' 'writer' or 'editor' – all somewhat applicable – would have appeased them.
>
> Lawrence, who exhibited his old wine bottles with tasteful wax drippings in a Left Bank gallery, drew himself up with cool dignity and said: 'Rentier.'
>
> Man who lives by his income. Remittance individual. Dependently wealthy.
>
> The cop arrested them both . . .

[Sindbad] could have said he worked, but chose not to. It was none of the cop's business – this was principle.

Gold was making a larger point about a certain stratum of the idle rich that by the 1960s was fast disappearing: 'Upper Bohemians tend to be subsidized folks with soul and a need beyond what they have been given.' But it is a poignant and finally sad vignette. Sindbad had never outgrown his adolescent infatuation with cricket; little else interested him. He vaguely wanted to achieve something – thus the magazine, *Points*, which had folded by then – but he did not try very hard. Peggy's collection to him meant little more than a meal ticket, and he was not very good at hiding his views, although he loved his mother in his own, complicated way.

Pegeen was a greater concern. Her reliance on drugs was unquestionably an addiction, still complicated by heavy drinking. The problem became so bad, in 1966, that Ralph Rumney took her to Laurence's apartment by pre-arrangement; once they got her there they locked her in a room to force her to go cold turkey. The ordeal was unbearable for her, and she struggled so hard that the two men could not bear it and released her. Another time Ralph arrived at the Paris apartment one day to find Pegeen missing. After some frantic telephoning, he learned that nineteen-year-old Fabrice, at Peggy's direction, had taken his mother to a Swiss clinic. Ralph had been trying to get her to reduce her drug intake, but at the clinic, to his dismay, she was put back on Valium. He and Peggy each blamed the other for Pegeen's condition, using much the same argument – that each was using Pegeen's addiction as an opportunity to pry her away from the other's influence. Rumney later said, 'I think Peggy did everything she could to destroy our relationship and to have control of her daughter. For Pegeen, the situation was unbearable . . . She was depressive, or rather, I would say, anguished. Pegeen's problem, in my opinion, was that she wanted a real relationship with her mother, but her mother was incapable of having human relationships or giving affection.'

Peggy had her reasons for disapproving of her daughter's husband. Ralph 'could be mean,' says Eileen Finletter. Indeed, in the early 1960s her husband, Stanley Geist, barred Ralph from their home after he ruined a party by getting very drunk and knocking things over. 'He drank all the time and never ate,' says Finletter. 'He was good-looking but cadaverous at the same time.' (Peggy told Bernard Reis in July 1958, '[Ralph] looks more like a corpse than ever.') But 'he had a sweet nature,' says Finletter. 'You could talk to him about things like literature, anything cultural, for hours – he always had interesting opinions.'

After the founding of the Situationists and his expulsion, Ralph said,

'Life got rather boring and dreary. Or normal, shall we say. Bringing up children, desperately trying to get enough money to keep the family alive, working quite hard, trying to keep Pegeen alive.' Pegeen, whom Anne Dunn describes as 'pudique,' or discreet, alternated between confiding in her mother – telling her everything, really – and not speaking to her at all. According to Ralph, she and Peggy were not speaking in February 1967. Peggy would later say, however, that Pegeen had recently – that same month, in fact – told her explicitly that for the sake of her children, she would never kill herself.

Ralph was in Venice in late February, fulfilling a mural commission for a hotel and pursuing another for a nightclub. He found himself, on February 27, by a series of mishaps, in the office of the chief of police. The officer behaved very formally, demanding to see Ralph's papers and various other proofs of identity, to the point that Ralph thought it comical, as he had known the policeman for fifteen years, and said so. The policeman put him in a damp jail cell overnight. At court the next day he was expelled from Italy and taken, handcuffed, to the French border by train. When he returned to the Ile Saint-Louis apartment, he learned that Pegeen already knew everything that had happened; Peggy, who had somehow, Ralph believed, engineered the arrest and the expulsion, had told her. Pegeen was frantic at the news, fearing that Venice was henceforth closed to her as well. The two drank and argued far into the night until Ralph, exhausted, went to bed.

The next morning, Ralph got up and took the boys to school, believing that Pegeen was asleep in the vacant maid's room. Returning home, he went back to bed. When he next woke, around noon, he went to the maid's room to wake up Pegeen. The door was locked, but through the keyhole he could see the key on the other side. Hearing no answer when he banged on the door, he put a piece of paper under the door, and jiggled the key from his side until it fell onto the paper, where he retrieved it. Letting himself in, he found Pegeen on the floor. He picked her up, put her on the bed, and when he saw that she was not breathing, called the police. Pegeen had choked to death on her own vomit. 'It's still a mystery, you know,' Ralph would recall more than thirty years later, 'how you can be very close to someone and be powerless to intervene in their personal tragedy. I saw myself then, and still do, as someone who kept her alive. On this last occasion, I failed, you could say.'

In Mexico, Peggy received the news of Pegeen's death in a telegram. Dry-eyed, she spent the night in disbelief, hanging on to the fact that her daughter had promised never to kill herself. As denial lifted by degrees, she decided that Ralph had killed Pegeen. When it became clear that this was not true, she still held him to blame, demanding that the Paris police and her lawyers find some reason to arrest him. Returning immediately to Venice from Mexico, she focused on her grandson Sandro. She had the police issue a civil warrant for Ralph on the specifically French charge of not coming to the aid of someone in mortal danger.

Ralph, meanwhile, summoned Hélion to tell his sons, Nicolas, David, and Fabrice, about their mother's death when they came home from school. But he did not know what to do about Sandro; he let Laurence Vail, whom Ralph had notified and who turned up immediately at the scene, lead the eight-year-old away. Ralph would not see his son for another ten years. The Guggenheims and Vails moved quickly, sending Sandro off to Laurence's daughter Kathe, then on a skiing vacation with her children in France. Ralph, knowing that he was being sought by the police, took refuge in a clinic run by the maverick psychoanalyst Felix Guattari, where he was put to use teaching painting. After a few weeks, he slipped back into England. He tried to see Sandro, to no avail. Dixie Nommo, an English friend whom he ran into at a café, told him that the Guggenheim lawyers had offered him $10,000 to testify against Ralph. Ralph despaired of the situation. 'I suppose if I'd suspected for a minute what was happening,' he said later, 'I'd have nipped off to England with the boy straightaway.' When Sandro turned eighteen – Kathe Vail, the daughter of Kay Boyle and Laurence, raised him after Pegeen's death – he would look for his father by calling every Rumney in the London and Paris phone books until he found him, as neither Laurence nor Peggy would tell him Ralph's address.

Persecuting Rumney and making sure that Sandro was tucked away took up most of the rest of 1967 for Peggy. 'Peggy loved Pegeen more than anyone,' Emily Coleman told Djuna Barnes. 'This will just about kill her.' And Djuna, in turn, wrote Peggy, 'It truly kills the heart.' She reminded Peggy that no one could know just what happened, that the whole story was 'like a grisly early Italian Opera plot.' Djuna could hardly believe it: 'Strange to think of the down-thrust chin, the floating golden hair, the stubborn and lost wandering walk . . . to know it is not there – but, once the grief is over, then "Thanks be to God!!" . . . she can't be tormented anymore.'

Peggy never really recovered from Pegeen's death. Afterward, her correspondence became dull and she was less given to witticisms, indicating few sources of pleasure. She also lost her sense of purpose. Her life assumed a narrower focus, as she became more obsessive about day-to-day details regarding such things as travel – which she didn't much enjoy anymore – and life in the palazzo. Her perspective narrowed to one thought: what her legacy would be.

Her grandchildren brought Peggy little pleasure, though she gave each one a gift of $15,000 when they married. She had been disappointed when

Pegeen brought her four grandsons in a row and no granddaughters. But Peggy saw more of Pegeen's boys, to whom she grew close as they were growing up, than she did of Sindbad's two boys, Clovis and Marc, or of his two daughters, Karole and Julia, by his second wife, Peggy. Fabrice, Pegeen's eldest, introduced her to the ways of the younger generation. He visited her at Easter in 1961, and Peggy reported to Becky Reis that 'luckily' he was gone all day and returned only at 11:00 at night: 'He is terribly in love and is not quite 14 years of age. Imagine.' But she got used to it; in the fall of 1966 she reported, 'I have had a lovely summer here full of grandchildren and their girlfriends. Imagine already. They come here on PRE HONEYMOONS.' In another letter she commented, 'They come here with their girlfriends. Even the little one of 15 already has a steady. How young they start.' The grandchildren thought she asked inappropriate questions about their sex lives, but no doubt they enjoyed the relaxed atmosphere around the palazzo.

Nicolas Hélion was the grandchild most interested in Peggy's collection. He would name one of his children Benjamin, after Peggy's father, and offered to change his name to Guggenheim; Peggy, when told of this, answered blandly, 'Go ahead.' In 1973, Nicolas wrote to the Guggenheim's director, Tom Messer, asking that he be considered as curator. The first question he had was about the salary; Messer explained to him, in his words, 'the distinction between a trainee and a salaried position.' Nicolas had no formal art history training; Messer made arrangements for enrollment in college, but the boy evidently lost interest.

Too many times Peggy's exchanges with her grandchildren were marred by poor communications; her lack of a vocabulary for discussing emotions was a contributing factor. In the early 1970s Peggy visited Sandro at his Swiss boarding school. Over lunch, she asked him what he would like for his birthday. Sandro's classmates were mostly rich and lacked for nothing, including expensive stereos. Sandro said that was what he wanted, and, to his delight, Peggy took him to Geneva that afternoon and bought him one. She came back to his room, watched him set it up, and then asked him to dinner with her. Sandro, eager to show the stereo to his dorm mates, asked if he could have lunch with her the next day instead. 'She drew herself up in a great huff,' Sandro recalled, 'left, and involved the school's headmaster in the whole affair. She left the next day without seeing me. I behaved badly, but really we were both behaving like thoughtless adolescents. That kind of thing prevented me from getting close to her.' Sandro also found life at the palazzo 'gloomy. The servants were the only normal people around.'

Laurence, called 'Grappa' by his grandchildren, never recovered from Pegeen's death either: 'Ralph finished off Pegeen,' he wrote in a letter to

Djuna Barnes, but he said that Peggy also was responsible: 'She loved Pegeen, but jealously, possessively – for over 20 years she has done all she can to break up Pegeen's relationship with whoever she was living with, husband or lover. So Pegeen had a miserable life – it was a perpetual tug of war between Peggy and the man Pegeen was living with. Pegeen was the rope between the two. And the rope snapped.'

Laurence was suffering from cancer at the time, and an operation for ulcers in 1967 had left him with only part of his stomach. Djuna reported to Peggy that she had seen him in New York, when he made a last trip to see his daughters by Kay Boyle: 'so old, so ill, so shattered, yet holding together with incredible ferocity . . . and I must say courage, that is, to have dared to travel alone . . . tho a wind lays him, like a leaf, in the gutter, crossing streets, staggering up to bed.' He died in April 1969, 'very gallant to the end,' said Peggy. 'Laurence was the greatest – the best of the lot,' says his grandson Sandro.

The Guggenheim Museum had not stopped courting Peggy, broaching the idea of 'a Guggenheim Jeune long summer show at the Guggenheim in New York' as early as late 1965. Before Pegeen's death in 1967, Peggy committed herself to the idea, although negotiations over dates continued for the next two years. Tom Messer made a summer visit to Venice in 1967, and a show was planned to open in January 1969. But Peggy drove a hard bargain, demanding that the museum agree to restore the paintings they borrowed. The artworks arrived safely in New York in November 1968, Peggy approved the catalogue copy, and all was set for the opening on January 15.

Peggy's trip to America just prior to the opening was a nightmare; she missed a connecting flight and her luggage was lost. Finally she received a case of clothes at her hotel, but without her shoes. Peggy went to the dinner in her honor in a white lace dress and knee-high beige boots, telling a reporter, 'They're my security because my ankles are weak.' At a dinner given by her cousin, the publisher Roger Straus, Peggy was seated between Lillian Hellman and Edmund Wilson; Wilson, who had been told by Straus that Peggy had 'mellowed,' evidently did not listen to her very carefully, for he wrote in his journal that she was 'a good deal preoccupied with her children.' Perhaps Peggy had been talking about her dogs.

Peggy was dismayed when she saw the exhibit. The pictures seemed to her to look 'like postage stamps' on the museum's expansive white walls, though she noted with pleasure that, because the walls curved, they were hung by contraptions that owed something to Kiesler's baseball bat-like devices at Art of This Century. The press wrote enthusiastically about the exhibit – and about Peggy. *Time* magazine called the show 'not only a brilliant visual statement but also a monumental historical document that ranges from cubism to abstract expressionism and includes Picasso, Arp, Braque, Léger, Gris, Severini, Miró, Mondrian, Ernst, de Chirico, Brauner, Kandinsky, Still, de Kooning and Pollock.' On display were 175 of the 263 artworks in her collection. 'I never dreamt,' she told a reporter, 'that the collection would be shown at my uncle's museum in New York and that one day I would see it descending the ramp like the nude descending the staircase.' It is hard to underestimate the *frisson* Peggy must have experienced in seeing her surrealist works in Sol's secular temple.

In late January, the board of Peggy's foundation met, and its members – Sindbad, Roloff Beny, Herbert Read, Vittorio Corrain, Bernard Reis, and Peggy – agreed to turn the collection and the palazzo over to the Guggenheim Museum at her death, at which point the foundation would dissolve. The *New York Times* reported the deal on March 25, by which time Peggy was back in Venice. 'We have some very great cubists, futurists, and neo-plasticists,' Messer, smiling, told the *Times* reporter. 'But the phases of Dadaism and surrealism are not represented in our collection at all. She has such artists as Max Ernst, Dali and Yves Tanguy, which will be a tremendous boost to the totality of our collection. Her 11 Pollocks will supplement our one.' Peggy was relieved as well. Just before the announcement, she wrote Djuna Barnes, 'I'm glad I came as I settled the collection's fate after my death. The Guggenheim Museum will look after it here in Venice. That is what I most wanted.'

But Peggy continued to fuss over the transfer. The museum had damaged Picasso's *The Poet* (1911) by varnishing it, she said. After the palazzo was robbed twice in 1971, the museum installed a security system, which Peggy never quite got the hang of. (The New York people dragged their heels at paying for it, however, trying to do so by buying a Cornell box from the collection. Peggy stood firm.) Negotiations over the condition of the works of art and water damage to the palazzo complicated matters; as Messer said, '[F]or some time the decision to accept her gift remained an issue among the [Solomon R. Guggenheim] Foundation's trustees, many of whom doubted the prudence of accepting an unendowed palazzo and collection – no matter how valuable.'

By 1973 Peggy's representative in most of these negotiations was John Hohnsbeen, a young man originally from Oklahoma, educated at Stanford and Columbia universities: he had been a dancer with the Martha Graham troupe before turning to art dealing. Once the lover of the architect Philip Johnson, the blond, blue-eyed Hohnsbeen was known for his all-white New York apartment, designed by Johnson, which set off the single color in the place, the ice blue of his dressing gown. Hohnsbeen became Peggy's companion and assistant; his art training was significant enough for him to aspire to become the collection's curator. He lived in the palazzo from the spring to the fall, wintering in warmer climates for his health. Much of the time he was in Venice he spent by the pool at Cipriani's, joining Peggy for a modest lunch at the palazzo; he had a busy social life and often returned to the palazzo only late at night. Peggy was pleased to have someone staying with her and trusted Hohnsbeen, who enjoyed the social life at the palazzo and his proximity to the art.

Hohnsbeen describes the first two years of his residence in the palazzo as assistant to Peggy as 'magical. She treated me like a prince. Breakfast in bed, everything.' But soon, as Peggy's physical condition began to deteriorate, her world grew smaller. The collection was open as before, for only two hours a day on Monday, Wednesday, and Friday. One after another of her servants left, and she did not replace them; toward the end she was attended by just two servants, Isia and Roberto. There were few visitors and little or no food in the kitchen; Hohnsbeen remembers that every meal began with canned tomato soup. He found Peggy's decline very painful, though he admits that spirited social occasions sometimes dispersed the gloom. The paintings, untended, were getting damper and damper, and some were flaking paint.

Peggy dismissed one of her gondoliers in 1977; the remaining one, Bruno, also held a city job as 'corpse collector,' according to Hohnsbeen (he transferred corpses to funeral homes). Peggy no longer took the gondola out in the morning but only in the early evening, 'the irresistible hour,' as she put it, when the light on the lagoon waters was golden. She would direct the gondolier through the city's canals with a barely discernible flick of her hand. Tourists relished glimpses of her sailing about in the boat, her Lhasa apsos surrounding her. Peggy's was the last private gondola in Venice, and she was proud of the distinction. When she first bought the craft, in 1956, she wrote Djuna Barnes that 'I adore floating to such an extent, I can't think of anything as nice since I gave up sex, or rather since it gave me up.'

In 1975, ten years after the Tate had feted her, the Louvre mounted a show of Peggy's collection at the Orangerie, showing about two thirds of it. Her bequest of the collection and the palazzo to the Guggenheim Museum after her death was now official. The collection had much more space in Paris than it did in Venice, and Peggy told Djuna she thought it looked better in the roomier surroundings. Though she felt triumphant at showing the collection in the place that had refused it custody during the war, she quarreled with the curators about the placement of one of the Brancusis. In Paris, however, she met and befriended the literary sensation Françoise Sagan and renewed her friendship with Mary McCarthy, who fed her oysters at a dinner during which they rehashed their 1946 trip to Venice, including the Scampi episode. McCarthy remembered a time when on another visit to Venice she had to go to Padua, about an hour's drive from Venice. Because of a recent near accident, she asked a friend to drive her, but he backed out at the last minute. According to McCarthy, Peggy 'discerned (yes, discerned, incredibly, for I didn't tell her) that I was afraid to drive to Padua, and volunteered her services. She drove me to the station and hopped on the train to Venice . . . All this was done in a spirit of gayety. "I couldn't let you go alone," she remarked, "especially after I remembered the ending of A *Charmed Life*" in which the heroine is killed in a car crash.'

'I have never, never forgotten this and have loved her ever since,' McCarthy later said. She would no longer brook any gossip about Peggy, although she herself had spread so much of it over the years. Earlier, she had put the question to Bernard Berenson (not the best authority, given his par-ticular dislike for Peggy), 'Why is [Peggy] so ostracized? Her morals are no worse than the next Venetian's. At her best, she is fresh and amusing, like a naughty child.'

In 1976 a problem surfaced about a painting in the collection, *Contraste de Formes*, a 1913 canvas Peggy had bought in 1967, believing it was a Léger. 'Peggy had always bought artworks directly from artists,' her grandson Sandro points out. 'So fakes were not something she worried about.' She had asked someone at the Tate to look at the painting in Paris, but she bought it before she heard the Tate official's report, paying $60,000 for it, more than she had ever paid for an artwork and more than she thought the painting was worth. For this unwise purchase she blamed the Tate, and it possibly contributed to her decision not to leave her collection there. Douglas Cooper (a friend) and Eugene Victor Thaw, art historians and dealers, had spotted the painting as a fake soon after Peggy bought it, but did not tell her. Rumors circulated about it, but in the meantime it held pride of place in her collection, hanging in the entrance room opposite the Picasso bathers, on a wall that has since been opened up with a second door to the dining room. In 1976 Tom Messer raised the question of whether the red, white, blue, and black painting was authentic – and John Loring, an American friend in Venice, pointed out that the Tate officials had raised this concern after Peggy bought it. Peggy objected when Messer said the painting would not be included in catalogues of the col-lection once the museum took it over; it was 'her favorite painting,' Peggy answered. But Messer prevailed and Peggy agreed that he could dispose of the inauthentic Léger. Around this time Peggy had the painting taken down and put in storage. 'She never talked about it,' says Hohnsbeen. But Messer had reminded her several times that he needed her permission in writing to leave it out of the collection, and she finally did so in 1979, two months before her death, saying that she authorized Messer to dispose of the painting by sale or exchange but adding the contradictory statement, 'Also insist that anything I will to the Guggenheim Museum can never be sold.' Tom Messer has not said how they resolved the issue.

In 1974 Peggy had met Philip and Jane Rylands through her friends Lady Rose Lauritzen and Lauritzen's American husband, Peter. Philip Rylands was finishing his doctorate on the Italian painter Palma Vecchio, and Jane was teaching at a U.S. Army base. Philip was British and his wife American, a combination with inherent appeal to Peggy. The Rylands performed a great number of services for Peggy; they bought her dog food and other supplies at the PX, and Philip's status as an art historian, Peggy felt, would lend her collection a certain amount of prestige. Over the next five years they became very close to her, so much so that Hohnsbeen, who might have expected to be the curator of the collection after her death, was gradually displaced. Despite the measure of cheer the Rylands brought her, Peggy's decline was heartbreaking to see, says Hohnsbeen, remembering her eightieth birthday in 1978, when Peggy's eyes were 'wide and unseeing.' An operation in England that winter would remove double cataracts from her eyes, making it possible for her to read Henry James, a favorite occupation in her last years.

Physical ills had come to plague Peggy in the late 1970s, bringing her vigor to an end. She had what she thought was rheumatism but which turned out to be arteriosclerosis, and she traveled to various places in Europe for treatment. In 1976 she fainted because of high blood pressure and broke eight ribs, requiring a three-week hospital stay. The arteriosclerosis made it difficult to walk – a problem in Venice, where there were, as Peggy pointed out to Djuna in 1978, 'no normal taxis and lots of bridges.' In the spring of 1978 she suffered a heart attack, and Hohnsbeen wept at her bedside. She celebrated her eightieth birthday that summer with a cocktail party on the Gritti Palace terrace; the birthday cake was a model of her palazzo, and all the bells in Venice were ringing because it was the day the new pope, John Paul I, who had been the patriarch of Venice, was named. 'I think life goes on too long,' she wrote Djuna.

She and Djuna often felt they were the last two standing. Emily Coleman died in 1973, and both women monitored the declines of Silas Glossop and Peter Hoare, two friends from England in the 1930s. Peggy increased Djuna's stipend in 1970, and in 1971 conspired with Bernard Reis to see that she received a so-called Rothko scholarship, given by Mark Rothko's estate – the artist killed himself in 1970 – which provided aid to aging artists and writers. (Peggy heard only faint rumors of the scandal surrounding Rothko's death and the division of his estate, and Reis's complicity in it.) After some confusion – Djuna was rumored to refuse prizes, which delayed the award – she received a much-needed check for $2,500 with no strings attached.

The two women diligently kept up their correspondence, Djuna always bemoaning her age (she was eight years older than Peggy) and complaining about the many admirers whom Peggy sent to her. Djuna found herself besieged by thesis writers, fans, and would-be biographers, many of whom had received her address from her friend. Peggy, on the other hand, approved of two biographies of her life in the 1970s, the first an official, authorized book by an American journalist, Jacqueline Bograd Weld, and the second a kind of oral history assembled by Virginia Dortch, the wife of the Italian artist Piero Dorazio. Eventually, Peggy learned not to send people on to Djuna, saying she 'no longer received' such people. But even so she did not understand Djuna's reticence. 'I think it is a great pity that you don't want anyone to write about you. Don't you want to be immortal? How can you be so private? It's all too bad.' Djuna scoffed, in return, 'Being immortal? Being biographed? – so? Do you really think immortality is a matter of talking to unknown, unrelished persons?'

It would appear that the two friends simply could not agree on anything. But in the same letter, having learned that Peggy was planning to publish a new version of her autobiography, joining *Out of This Century* (with people's real names) with her 1960 *Confessions of an Art Addict* and adding some new material plus an afterword about life in Venice, Djuna asked that, as long as she was assuring her own immortality, Peggy take out the 1920s detail about Djuna being 'caught' at her typewriter wearing Peggy's secondhand silk underwear in Paris. Being caught had not annoyed her or she wouldn't have worn the underclothes, she wrote. Rather, she was startled when someone came in her room, unannounced and without knocking. 'All of which is long ago, and matters little now,' Djuna admitted. 'But when my name is mentioned, some information appears that is incorrect.' Vanity was the quality the two friends shared to the end.

Universe Books in New York was in the process of reprinting *Out of This Century*. Gore Vidal, who had known Peggy in New York in the 1940s, supplied a brief and fond foreword. He provided a wonderful evocation of New York life in the 1940s, when parties at Hale House were the order of the day: 'In a sense . . . I still think that somewhere, even now, in a side street of New York City, that party is still going on and Anaïs [Nin] is still alive and young and *chéri* is very young indeed, and James Agee is drinking too much and Laurence Vail is showing off some bottles having first emptied them into himself as part of the creative process and André Breton is magisterial . . . and a

world of color and humour is still going on.' The volume presented a far
more balanced view of Peggy than had *Out of This Century* when it had
appeared in 1946 because she provided some context for her contributions to
the art world, and because the events she described had grown more distant
and the world more tolerant.

In the fall of 1979 Peggy cracked a bone in her foot when she fell getting
into her gondola; her feet and ankles, fragile since girlhood, signaled the
beginning of her end. The bone would not heal even after rest, and she
decided to have an operation. She went by boat to the Piazzale Roma and
then by ambulance to the Camposanpiero, a hospital in Padua, after saying
goodbye to her one remaining dog, Cellida, who died shortly after. She
brought along a volume of Henry James stories. She suffered a pulmonary
edema shortly after her arrival and, when she had recovered enough for the
operation, she decided she did not want it, although she still hoped to be back
in her palazzo, with the collection, by Christmas. She had few visitors. To
John Hohnsbeen, she would only say, 'There's no reason on earth for you to
stay here to see me. The next time you see me I'll be dead.' She changed her
mind again about the foot operation, but a fall to the floor one night left her
with several broken ribs. Although she asked that her son not be called,
Sindbad visited nonetheless, and when he saw her in the hospital she asked
him to kiss her. On December 22, Venice was flooded by torrential winter
rains, and Sindbad and the Rylands were busy moving artworks out of the
palazzo's basement for safety. On December 23, when Sindbad was having tea
at the Rylandses', a phone call came from the hospital in Padua; Peggy, who
had suffered a stroke, was dying. Philip Rylands called back after relaying the
news to Sindbad to ask what they could do, and the hospital told them it was
too late; Peggy had died, from complications of the stroke.

Tom Messer arrived from the United States the very next day with a key
that opened the gates to the palazzo and the palazzo itself, which Peggy had
given him the previous May. Sindbad was annoyed to be told he could no
longer stay there; no one seemed to understand that the collection was now
a museum and that, for insurance reasons alone, no one could live there.
(The housekeeper, Isia, who in the confusion had nowhere to go and was desperate to stay put, actually announced to the press that she would be the
director.) Messer made a brief inventory of the palazzo and its contents and
had dinner with Philip Rylands at the Bauer-Grünwald Hotel, offering him
the position of curator *pro tem*. The Rylandses spent the next two months
trying to put the collection in order before the official reopening in April,
which was marked by a confused dinner party that left Peggy's family with
little hope that the new regime would heed their interests. During one of

Messer's interminable speeches, a tipsy Sindbad was heard to growl, 'Big deal.'

Peggy's will, which she had changed several times, left her money and securities to Pegeen's children and to Sindbad, her gondola to the naval museum of Venice, and her modern art books to her grandson Nicolas. Her dining room furniture had already been given to the Guggenheim, and John Hohnsbeen, left to choose one artwork not left to the Guggenheim, chose a Picasso pot. Everything else in the house – furniture, jewelry, other books, and artwork not part of the museum – was to go to Sindbad and the grandchildren; Sindbad's daughters, Karole and Julia, were to have the two von Lenbach paintings of Benita and Peggy and the earring collection.

The amount of money Peggy left was in dispute. Originally, it appeared that Sindbad would receive $400,000 and each of Pegeen's children $100,000. But the estate turned out to be much larger, and in the end Sindbad received about $1 million and Pegeen's children the same, which they divided equally. But the grandchildren would come to resent the fact that Peggy left not one piece from her world-famous collection to any of them.

The transfer was seamless, and the Guggenheim took over with stunnung swiftness. Peggy's decision had been made so long before that the museum had been able to put in place an agenda for the small collection, so that they were poised to reopen it by Easter, just four months after her death. On April 4, her ashes were buried in the garden, next to the graves of her dogs.

Pegeen's heirs brought suit against the Guggenheim Foundation in 1991 for mismanaging their grandmother's legacy, in particular by effacing Pegeen's presence from the collection and the palazzo. As a result Pegeen's paintings and the glass sculptures Constantini made from her designs were reinstalled in what the collection designates as the 'small room' – originally the bathroom off Peggy's bedroom. A family committee now represents the heirs' interest, and Sandro Rumney has hopes of seeing a show of all the family's art there one day: Pegeen's wistful primitives, Laurence's bottles and screens, and Ralph Rumney's oversized canvases. Many onlookers complain that, as it is now set up, the collection preserves little of Peggy's essence, although her name is now prominently displayed on the canal side of the palazzo. The art historian Fred Licht, officially a curator of the collection, remembers that he was severely criticized when he ordered the removal of Peggy's bed, disliking the crude jokes some visitors made about it. What was important about it was the Calder headboard, which the foundation kept. There is a new building opposite the palazzo along the street side, housing offices, a café, and a shop; visiting the collection is more like visiting a small museum than it is like visiting a person's home, but Peggy's presence is undeniable.

This is pretty much what the visitor sees today, although as the Guggenheim expanded into an international chain of museums in the late 1990s, a projected second outpost in Venice, to be located in warehouses past the Salute, threatened to subsume it. More recently, however, the board has curtailed these expansionist gestures and the Peggy Guggenheim Collection appears to have secured a modest place for itself. Since 1997, the *barchesa* has displayed twenty-six artworks on a long-term loan from the collection of Gianni Mattioli, which include major works of the Italian futurists, including Boccioni, Carra, Russolo, Balla, and Severini; paintings by Morandi; and a portrait by Modigliani. The Patsy R. and Raymond D. Nasher Sculpture Garden shows sculptures on loan from the Nasher collection in Dallas, along-side Peggy's sculpture holdings in the building's original garden. The Solomon R. Guggenheim Foundation also owns the U.S. pavilion at the Venice Biennale, supported by the Peggy Guggenheim Collection. Otherwise, how-ever, the collection houses only artworks that Peggy chose, the so-called permanent collection. There are those who think the core collection is not vital enough, that it should be pruned and added to, but Peggy and her heirs felt strongly that it should be static and unchanging, representing her unique and specific vantage point.

As such, the Peggy Guggenheim Collection stands as a rebuke to the art world that has burgeoned in the years since Peggy closed the doors of Art of This Century and moved her collection to Venice. Peggy was the rebel of the philanthropic Guggenheim family, and it is easy to conclude that she lost her battle: aggressive dealers and well-funded Olympic-sized institutions like the Guggenheim have joined forces to forge a modern-art business cum tremen-dous profit machine, building a market accessible only to affluent buyers and at the same time as rankly commercial as Disney World. Peggy's vision of a community of artists and patrons that would embrace the general public and seek to connect with popular culture rather than simply aestheticize it can sometimes be seen as quaint and far-fetched. But Peggy's vision did not die. The egalitarian, popular spirit she brought to New York from Montparnasse, which mixed baseball players and bohemians and was equally open to both ambitious artists and anyone curious enough to wander in, can be traced through such phenomena as Andy Warhol's Factory (the idealized version, at least) and Keith Haring's Pop Shop. Peggy's vision of a truly vital art world may be elusive, but it survives.

All too often, however, the Peggy Guggenheim Collection has had to compete with the legend that has grown up around Peggy herself, a legend not always flattering. The popular myth fixes her as a ridiculous aging woman given to wearing silly oversized sunglasses, a sexually voracious predator with-holding of money and love. An otherwise thorough and reliable 1986 biography by Jacqueline Bograd Weld wholesaled some of the nastiest gossip about her, thereby fixing the image. John Hohnsbeen feels that because Weld knew her subject only in the last years of her life, when her world was con-stricted to the musty palazzo walls, hung with flaking paintings, she could not capture the vibrant, accomplished, and active woman who assembled the fine collection and carved out a creative and fulfilling life for herself.

Carping criticisms of the collection miss the point as well. Peggy never compared the 'greatness' of her art to anyone else's; and she wanted it pre-served as it was – the possessions of an alert and responsive patron who collected not from a distant remove but from the midst of the art world, a world she helped to shape. Peggy lived among artists as she collected their works, and her choices affected the course of twentieth-century art history. The woman who bridled when Emma Goldman left out of the record of her life a summer that was the turning point of Peggy's own (the fall of 1928, when she left Laurence Vail) was very definite about what she wanted her contribution – her collection – to be. It was not definitive and she never tried to make it so; the collection records the history of choices made from a spe-cific point of reference. But its value is not only personal: the collection and the palazzo constitute her best biography, in part because they are so much more than her story alone.

As Mary McCarthy pointed out, Peggy was well aware of the burlesque aspects of her life; she often put them on display. But she also desperately wanted and deserved to be taken seriously. It is hardly surprising that she rel-ished the ministrations of museum directors in her later years. At last, attention was paid her, and for what really mattered: her collection. The Peggy Guggenheim Collection, housed in the beautiful palazzo that was her home, is one of the great personal museums of the art world. Peggy's presence is indelible.

'ART OF THIS CENTURY INVENTORY OF ART WORKS AS OF DECEMBER 31, 1942'

The following was given as schedule 1 in an audited financial report for Art of This Century gallery, drawn up by Bernard J. Reis for the year 1942. The spellings of artists' names and renderings of the titles of artworks are preserved as Reis had them. This report is in the Bernard and Rebecca Reis Papers at the Getty Research Institute.

ARTIST	NAME	DESCRIPTION	YEAR	COST
Abbott, Berenice	'Saints for Sale'	Photograph	1937	$14.00
	'Rooster Facade'	Photograph	1937	$14.00
Archipenko, Alexander	'Boxing'	Terracotta Sculpture	1913	$880.00
Arp, Jean	'Great Composition'	Collage	1915	$200.00
	'Overturned Blue Shoes With Two Heels Under A Black Vault'	Relief in Wood	1925	$200.00
	'Shell & Head'	Bronze Sculpture	1933	$300.00
	'Mutilated & Stateless'	Object	1936	$50.00
	'Paper Torn According To the Laws of Chance'	Collage	1938	$50.00
	Drawing		1940	$51.00
Balla, Giacomo	'Automobile & Noise'	Oil	1912	$100.00
Bellmer, Hans		Drawing	1939	$33.33
		Drawing	1939	$33 33
		Drawing	1939	$33.34
Brancusi, Constantin	'Maistra'	Bronze Sculpture	1912	$1,000.00
	'Bird In Space'	Bronze Sculpture	1940	$3,000.00
	'The Fish'			$1,000.00
Braque, Georges	'The Waltz'	Oil	1912	$1,500.00
Brauner, Victor	'Faux Collage'	Collage	1938	$30.00
	'Fascination'	Oil	1940	$200.00
	'Woman into Cat'		1941	$200.00

ARTIST	NAME	DESCRIPTION	YEAR	COST
Breton, André	'Portrait of the Actor A.B.'	Poem-Object	1941	$300.00
Calder, Alexander	'Mobile'	Wire Sculpture	1941	$475.00
Carrington, Leonore	'Horses of Lord Candlestick'	Oil	1938	$80.00
Chagall, Marc	'Farm Reminiscence'	Oil	1911	$1,200.00
Chirico, Giorgio de	'The Rose Tower'	Oil	1913	$2,525.00
	'The Dream of the Poet'	Oil	1915	$750.00
	'The Gentle Afternoon'	Oil	1916	$1,725.00
Cornell, Joseph	'Ball & Book'	Object	1934	$60.00
	'Thimble Box"	Object	1938	$30.00
Dali, Salvador	'The Spectral Cow'	Oil	1926	$175.00
	'Woman Sleeping in a Landscape'	Oil	1931	$250.00
	'The Birth of Liquid Desires'	Oil	1932	$825.00
Delauney, Robert	'Disks'	Oil	1912	$425.00
	'Windows'	Oil	1913	$250.00
Delvaux, Paul	'The Break of Day'	Oil	1937	$500.00
Doesburg, Theo Van	'Composition'	Oil	1918	$200.00
	'Counter Composition'	Oil	1920	$150.00
Domela-Nieuwenhuis, Cesar	'Composition on a Round Base'	Construction	1936	$200.00
Dominguez, Oscar	'Nostalgia of Space'	Oil	1939	$80.00
Duchamp, Marcel	'Sad Young Man in a Train'	Oil	1912	$4,000.00
	'Valise'	Object	1941	$40.00
Duchamp-Villon, Raymond	'The Horse'	Bronze Sculpture	1914	$300.00
Ernst, Jimmy	'Dying Dragon Fly"	Drawing	1941	$26.00
Ernst, Max	'Dadamax'	Drawing	1919	$100.00
	'The Numerous Family'	Oil	1926	$250.00
	'The Kiss'	Oil	1927	$500.00
	'The Forest'	Oil	1928	$250.00
	'Sea, Sun, & Earthquake'	Oil	1930	$100.00
	'Vision'	Oil	1931	$100.00
	'The Postman Cheval'	Collage	1931	$100.00
	'Zoomorphic Couple'	Oil	1933	$300.00
	'Barbarians Looking Towards the West'	Oil	1935	$200.00
	'Aeroplane Trap'	Oil	1936	$250.00
	'Endless Town'	Oil	1937	$500.00

ARTIST	NAME	DESCRIPTION	YEAR	COST
	'The Attirement of the Bride'	Oil	1940	$1,500.00
	'Antipope'	Oil	1942	$3,000.00
Ferren, John	'Composition'	Oil	1937	$400.00
	'Oil on Plaster'		1937	$125.00
Fini, Leonor	'The Shepardess of the Sphinxes'	Oil	1941	$50.00
Gabo, Naum	'Model for Fountain'	Construction	1924	$50.00
Giacometti, Alberto	'Woman With a Cut Throat'	Bronze Sculpture	1931	$250.00
	'Model for a Garden'	Wood Sculpture	1932	$300.00
	'Statue of a Headless Woman'	Plaster Sculpture	1934	$475.00
Gleizes, Albert	'Woman with animals'	Oil	1914	$500.00
Gris, Juan	'The Bottle of Martinique Rum'	Papier Collé	1914	$400.00
Haussman, Raoul	Drawing		1919	$11.00
Hayter, William	Engraving		1937	$22.50
	Engraving (on plaster)		1939	$24.00
Hélion, Jean	'The Chimney Sweep'	Oil	1936	$225.00
	'Equilibrium'		1943	$266.66
Hirshfield, Morris	'Nude at the Window'	Oil	1941	$900.00
Howard, Charles	'Discovery'	Gouache	1937	$180.00
	'Prefiguration'	Oil	1940	$200.00
Kandinsky, Wassily	'Landscape with a Red Spot'	Oil	1913	$2,000.00
	'Composition'	Oil	1922	$800.00
	'Upward'	Oil	1929	$500.00
	'Dominant Curb'	Oil	1936	$1,500.00
Klee, Paul	'Male & Female Plant'	Watercolor	1921	$275.00
	'Mrs. P. in the South'	Gouache	1924	$200.00
	'Flat Landscape'	Gouache	1924	$200.00
	'Magic Garden'	Fresco	1926	$400.00
	'Overcultivated Land'	Watercolor on Cloth	1935	$200.00
	'Child of the Mountain'	Oil on Plaster	1936	$100.00
	'Mountain Train'	Watercolor on Cloth	1936	$200.00
	'Rapacious Red Beast'	Cloth	1938	$200.00
Lam, Wilfredo	Gouache		1940	$20.00
Léger, Fernand	'Men in the Town'	Oil	1919	$750.00
Lipchitz, Jacques	'Seated Pierrot'	Lead Sculpture	1921	$75.00
Lissitzky, El	'Composition'	Oil	1921	$400.00

ARTIST	NAME	DESCRIPTION	YEAR	COST
Loringhoven, Elsa von	Object			$25.00
Magritte, René	'Voice of the Winds'	Oil	1930	$50.00
	'The Key of Dreams'	Oil	1936	$75.00
	'Discovery of Fire'	Oil	1936	$175.00
Malevich, Kasimir	'Suprematist Composition'	Oil	1915	$500.00
Marcoussis, Louis	'The Frequenter'	Oil	1920	$275.00
Masson, André	'Armor'	Oil	1925	$125.00
	'The Ladder of Existence'	Gouache	1940	$20.00
	'Two Children'	Bronze Sculpture	1941	$50.00
Matta, Roberto	'Deep Stones'	Oil	1942	$150.00
		Oil	1938	$300.00
		Drawing	1941	$103.00
Miró, Joan	'Two Personages & a Flame'	Oil	1925	$1,000.00
	'Dutch Interior'	Oil	1928	$500.00
	'The Seated Woman'	Oil	1939	$2,000.00
Mondrian, Piet	'Scaffold'	Drawing	1912	$500.00
	'Ocean'	Drawing	1914	$500.00
	'Composition'	Oil	1939	$160.00
Moore, Henry	Drawing		1937	$25.00
	Crayon		1937	$25.00
	'Reclining Figure'	Bronze Sculpture	1938	$150.00
Nicholson, Ben	'Relief'	Wood	1938	$120.00
Oelze, Richard	Drawing		1933	$250.00
	'Archaic Fragment'	Oil	1937	Loaned
Ozenfant, Amédée	'Purist Still Life'	Oil	1920	$500.00
Paelen, Wolfgang	'Totemic Memory of My Childhood'	Oil	1937	$100.00
Pevsner, Antoine	'Construction'	Metal Sculpture	1927	$500.00
	'Relief'	Glass & Metal Sculpture	1934	$500.00
	Surface Developing a Tangency With a Left Curve'	Bronze & Plaster Construction	1939	$500.00
Picabia, Francis	'Very Rare Picture upon Earth'	Painting on Wood	1915	$330.00
	'Infant Carbureter'	Painting On Wood	1916	$200.00
Picasso, Pablo	'The Poet'	Oil	1911	$4,250.00
	'Lacerba'	Papier Collé	1914	$1,500.00
	'The Studio'	Oil	1928	$6,000.00

ARTIST	NAME	DESCRIPTION	YEAR	COST
	'Dreams & Lies of Franco'	Etching	1937	$30.00
	'Dreams & Lies of Franco'	Etching	1937	$30.00
	'Still Life'	Oil	1921	$3,000.00
Ray, Man	'The Rope Dancer Accompanies Herself with Her Shadow'	Oil	1916	$330.00
	'The Rope Dancer Accompanies Herself with Her Shadow'	Drawing	1916	$100.00
	Rayogram			$27.50
	Rayogram			$27.50
	Rayogram			$27.50
	Rayogram			$27.50
Schwitters, Kurt	'Relief Merzbild'	Construction	1915	$200.00
	'Relief Merzbild	Construction	1923	$200.00
	'Blue in Blue'	Collage	1929	$37.00
Seligmann, Kurt	'The Youth of the Count of Gabalis'	Drawing	1941	$210.00
Severini, Gino	'Sea Dancer'	Oil	1914	$300.00
Tanguy, Yves	'Without a Title'	Oil	1929	$300.00
	'Promontory Palace'	Oil	1930	$250.00
	'The Sun in its Casket'	Oil	1937	$400.00
	'If it Were	Oil	1939	$600.00
	'In Oblique Ground'	Oil	1941	$375.00
Taeuber-Arp, Sophie	Drawing		1940	$25.00
Tunnard, John	'P.S.I.'	Oil	1939	$130.00
	Gouache			$102.00
	Gouache			$102.00
Vail, Laurence	Collage on Screen		1940	$1,000.00
	Collage on Bottle		1942	$40.00
	Collage on Bottle		1942	$40.00
	Collage on Bottle		1942	$40.00
	Collage on Bottle		1942	$40.00
	Collage on Bottle		1942	$40.00
	Collage on Bottle		1942	$40.00
	Collage on Bottle		1942	$40.00
	Collage on Bottle		1942	$40.00
	Collage on Bottle		1942	$40.00
	Collage on Bottle		1942	$40.00
Vantongerloo, Georges	'Volume Construction'	Plaster Sculpture	1918	$150.00
Villon, Jacques	'Spaces'	Oil	1920	$100.00
Vordemberge-Gildewart	'Composition'	Oil	1939	$200.00

NOTES

In the following notes, Peggy Guggenheim is referred to as PG, Laurence Vail as LV, Emma Goldman as EG, Emily Coleman as EC, Djuna Barnes as DB, the Solomon R. Guggenheim Foundation as SRGF, and the Archives of American Art, Smithsonian, as AAA. Peggy Guggenheim's book *Out of This Century: Confessions of an Art Addict* (1946; rpt. New York: Universe, 1979) is abbreviated as OTC.

I: FORTUNES AND FAMILY

3   'peculiar, if not mad': OTC, 2.

5   'To sell something': Quoted in Stephen Birmingham, *'Our Crowd': The Great Jewish Families of New York* (1967; rpt. New York: Dell, 1978), 54.

7   'an old gentleman': 'James Seligman, 88, Tells of Early Life,' *New York Times* (April 10, 1912), 12.

7   'James, tell Jim': George S. Hellman, 'The Story of the Seligmans,' unpublished manuscript, 1945, 52, New York Public Library.

7   'When do you think': OTC, 2.

8   'Bearing philosophically': Hellman, 210.

8   James fathered eight: George S. Hellman, *Family Registry of the Descendants of David Seligman* (Baltimore: T. A. Munder, 1913).

8   'an incurable soprano': OTC, 2.

8   'nearly normal': OTC, 3.

8   'I don't see why': Geoffrey T. Hellman, 'Sorting Out the Seligmans or Alas; the Gazebo!' *The New Yorker* (October 30, 1954), 56.

9   'I am tired of being sick': 'W. Seligman Kills Himself in a Hotel,' *New York Times* (February 13, 1912), 7.

9   Eugene was: Geoffrey T. Hellman, 55.

9   'notably miserly': OTC, 3.

9   'More hurt than flustered': Harold Loeb, *The Way It Was* (New York: Criterion, 1959), 97.

9   Very soon, Meyer had: John H. Davis, *The Guggenheims (1848–1988): An American Epic* (1970; rpt. New York: Shapolsky, 1989), 57.

10   'Struck rich ore': Geoffrey T. Hellman, 'Getting the Guggenheims into Focus,' *The New Yorker* (July 25, 1953), 25.

10 'as near a black sheep': Edwin P. Hoyt, *The Guggenheims and the American Dream* (New York: Funk and Wagnalls, 1967), 132.

10 'mésalliance': OTC, 1–2.

11 By the time the First World War: Davis, 117. See also Milton Lomask, *Seed Money: The Guggenheim Story* (New York: Farrar, Straus, 1964).

11 Marguerite Guggenheim was born: Birth certificate no. 33662, New York City Department of Records and Information Services, Municipal Archives; the certificate gives her middle initial as 'S,' as does a *New York Times* account of her first marriage ('Miss Guggenheim Weds,' *New York Times*, March 13, 1922), but no family member knows what it stood for and Peggy never used it again. Perhaps it stood for Seligman.

11 'fiendishly jealous': OTC, 4.

11 'Mama, you lived': OTC, 4.

12 'I don't remember': OTC, 8.

13 'elegant little wax models': OTC, 9.

13 'Never make love': Birmingham, 322.

13 'Of all the brothers': Quoted in Lomask, 40.

13 'looked after by his cook': OTC, 3.

13 'Papa, you must have': OTC, 4.

14 Countess Taverny: Peggy named the woman the Marquise de Cerutti in her memoirs, perhaps her real title.

15 'In 1911 my father': OTC, 6.

15 'If anything should happen': 'Guggenheim, Dying, Sent Wife Message,' *New York Times* (April 20, 1912).

16 'Moi sauvée mais Ben perdu': Quoted at www.encyclopedia-titanica.org/bio/p/1st/aubart_lp.shtml.

16 'when the time came': Quoted in Lomask, 36.

16 'I still inherit': Roberta Brandes Gratz, 'The Art of Being Peggy,' *New York Post* (January 18, 1969).

16 'I suppose, if father had lived': Quoted in Virginia Dortch, ed., *Peggy Guggenheim and Her Friends* (Milan: Berenice Books, 1994), 33.

16 'It took me months': OTC, 12.

2: CHANGES, TAKING LEAVE

18 'gallantly': OTC, 12.

19 'When we got home': Charles Henri Ford to Charles Ford, December 23, 1931, Charles Henri Ford Papers, Harry Ransom Humanities Research Center, University of Texas.

19 'All the girls': Quoted in 'The Calhoun School, 1896–1996,' 16; see www.calhoun.org/history.htm.

20 Ibsen, Hardy, Chekhov: OTC, 15.

20 'gay and really not at all': OTC, 15.

20 'bitter tears': OTC, 9.

20 'insane to save her': OTC, 5.

21 Florette seems to have told Hazel: Interview with John King-Farlow, November 14, 2001; e-mail from Barbara Shukman to the author, December 23, 2001.
22 'I had one teacher': OTC, 16.
22 Kohn later told: Quoted in Virginia Dortch, ed., *Peggy Guggenheim and Her Friends* (Milan: Berenice Books, 1994), 37.
23 'the girls . . . were all': OTC, 17.
23 'This gave me a new': OTC, 16.
24 'The whole thing': OTC, 17.
25 'My mother's one idea': OTC, 18.
25 'My mother was greatly': OTC, 18.
25 'It was ugly': OTC, 19.
26 'actual liberation': OTC, 19.
26 'They did everything': William S. Wilson quoted in Roberta K. Tarbell, *Hugo Robus (1885–1964)* (Washington, D.C.: Smithsonian Institution Press, 1980), 43.
26 'Why doesn't some woman': Madge Jenison, *Sunwise Turn: A Human Comedy of Bookselling* (New York: E. P. Dutton, 1923), 3.
26 The two women hired: Jenison, 46.
27 'Coming under': Harold Loeb, *The Way It Was* (New York: Criterion, 1959), 36.
27 In 1920, the year: See Melvin Paul Lader, 'Peggy Guggenheim's Art of This Century: The Surrealist Milieu and the American Avant-Garde, 1942–1947,' unpublished doctoral dissertation, University of Delaware, 1981, 10.
28 Marjorie Content noted: Quoted in Tarbell, 45.
28 'the long lean eagle': Gorham Munson, *The Awakening Twenties: A Memoir-History of a Literary Period* (Baton Rouge: Louisiana State University Press, 1985), 34.
28 'They were delighted': OTC, 21.
29 'never seemed to care': OTC, 20.
29 Leon had become convinced: Tom Dardis, *Firebrand: The Life of Horace Liveright* (New York: Random House, 1995), 212.

3: THE KING OF BOHEMIA

31 A grandson remembers: Interview with Sandro Rumney, September 7, 2001.
31 The family was also devoted: Interview with Jacqueline Ventadour Hélion, September 8, 2001.
32 'brilliant and versatile': LV, *Piri and I* (New York: Lieber and Lewis, 1923), 56.
32 'learnt to idle': LV, 73.
32 'With his long mane': Matthew Josephson, *Life Among the Surrealists: A Memoir* (New York: Holt, Rinehart, and Winston, 1962), 86.
32 'He was not only': John Glassco, *Memoirs of Montparnasse* (New York: Oxford University Press, 1970), 118.
33 'The thing which had always kept them': William Carlos Williams, *A Voyage*

to Pagany (New York: Macaulay, 1928), 42.

33 'like someone out of': OTC, 20.

33 She sported: Melvin Paul Lader, 'Peggy Guggenheim's Art of This Century: The Surrealist Milieu and the American Avant-Garde, 1942–1947,' unpublished doctoral dissertation, University of Delaware, 1981, 15.

33 painted her lips: Jacqueline Bograd Weld, Peggy: The Wayward Guggenheim (New York: E. P. Dutton, 1986), 46.

34 'a very bourgeois apartment': OTC, 22.

34 'I think Laurence had': OTC, 23.

34 'If I could only be well': William Wiser, The Crazy Years: Paris in the Twenties: (1983; rpt. New York: Thames and Hudson, 1990), 134–35.

34 'bare-legged and be-sandaled': Harold Loeb, The Way It Was (New York: Criterion, 1959), xxx.

35 'As soon as I found': OTC, 27.

35 'I continued in this [hectoring] strain': LV, Murder! Murder! (London: Peter Davies, 1931), 36.

36 'had gone to court': Loeb, 36.

36 'Let's go over': Malcolm Cowley, Exile's Return: A Literary Odyssey of the 1920s (1934; rpt. New York: Viking, 1956), 165.

36 'I can hardly say': OTC, 24.

36 'Whisky is to the imagination': William Carlos Williams, The Autobiography of William Carlos Williams (New York: Random House, 1951), 194.

37 Born in 1892: On Djuna Barnes, see Phillip Herring, Djuna: The Life and Work of Djuna Barnes (1995; rpt. New York: Penguin, 1976). While problematic, this work is far superior to Andrew Field's Djuna: The Formidable Miss Barnes (1983; rpt. Austin: University of Texas Press, 1985); a definitive biography of Barnes does not exist.

37 'the kind of nose': OTC, 24.

37 '[I]t never dawned on me': OTC, 32.

38 '[W]hat I hated most': OTC, 32.

38 'always made [her] feel': OTC, 31.

38 'a new inferiority': OTC, 16.

38 'Maybe if she'd': Interview with Eileen Finletter, April 16, 2002.

38 'Her lack of self-regard': Interview with Anne Dunn, November 20, 2001.

38 When up and about: EC, unpublished diary, EC Papers, University of Delaware Special Collections, 1932, 124.

39 The partygoers had a hand: Kitty Cannell to Bertram Sarason, May 6, 1969, Kitty Cannell Papers, Theatre Collection, Harvard University Library.

39 'The most intelligent': OTC, 35.

39 Her daughter believes: Interview with Giselle Waldman, March 27, 2002.

40 A much-photographed beauty: See Carolyn Burke, Becoming Modern: The Life of Mina Loy (New York: Farrar, Straus and Giroux), 1996.

41 'Laurence and Peggy Vail': Josephson, 315.

41 'we had a suburban sort of party': Williams, The Autobiography of William Carlos Williams, 214.

42 'Shush, Peggy will see': OTC, 43.
43 'standing on a rock': EG to Leon Malmed, March 28, 1928, EG Papers, reel 20.
43 'crossed the still life': Burke, 338.
43 'throwing all the furniture': OTC, 53.
44 They had three luxury cars: Davis, 291.
44 murals by Cocteau: Michael Wishart, High Diver: An Autobiography (London: Quartet Books, 1978), 91.
45 'I found what I wanted': OTC, 56.
45 'You get drunk': LV, 'Here Goes,' unpublished manuscript, 84.
45 'too busy with the laundry': LV, Murder! Murder! (London: Peter Davies, 1931), 261.
45 'Because of my money': OTC, 33.
46 future gallery owner: Julien Levy, Memoir of an Art Gallery (New York: G. P. Putnam's, 1977), 34.
46 Women and Children, in which: OTC, 58.
46 'Never mind': OTC, 58.
47 'Peggy used to observe': Josephson, 316.
47 'lampshades of her own design': Ronald Penrose, Scrap-book 1900–1981 (New York: Rizzoli, 1981), 35.
48 At the party: Burke, 345.
48 'Well now, all we need': Josephson, 320.
48 'Never use the word wife': OTC, 63.
49 'désintoxiquée': Nathalie Blondel, Mary Butts: Scenes from the Life (Kingston, N.Y.: McPherson, 1998), 183.
49 'developed a great love': OTC, 8.

4: THE HEIRESS AND THE ANARCHIST

50 Emma wrote to a friend: EG to Arthur Leonard Ross, March 25, 1925, EG Papers, reel 14.
50 The following summer: Candace S. Falk, Love, Anarchy, and Emma Goldman (New Brunswick, N.J.: Rutgers University Press, 1990), 210.
51 'A woman of your past': Emma Goldman, Living My Life (1931; rpt. Garden City, N.Y.: Garden City Press, 1934), 985.
51 Peggy, however, quickly became: Peggy probably first met Emma through Eleanor Fitzgerald, a Greenwich Village denizen and close friend of Djuna Barnes. Known as Fitzie, she had met Emma while in Chicago, during a free speech campaign, and later worked for Mother Earth and as Emma's secretary. She went on to become the indispensable business manager of the Provincetown Players. Fitzie, whom Emma described as 'a striking girl with red hair, delicate skin, and blue-green eyes,' was known for her generosity and dependability. Emma said of her, '[She] was a most likeable person, with something very fine and large about her' (Goldman, 515). Peggy made Fitzie's acquaintance on one of her visits to New York in the early 1920s, and

immediately recognized a true friend. (Laurence, of course, already knew Fitzie from the production of his play, *What D'You Want*, in 1920 or 1921.)

52   She asked Emma: PG to EG, [May 1928], EG Papers, reel 16. See also PG to EG, [June 26, 1926], EG Papers, reel 16. The EG Papers editors date both letters as [1926?].

52   Fitzie would be one: See M. Eleanor Fitzgerald to Pauline Turkel, April 19, 1954, and PG to Pauline Turkel, April 19, [1955], in the M. Eleanor Fitzgerald Papers, Division of Archives and Special Collections, Golda Meir Library, University of Wisconsin, Milwaukee.

52   'a little villa': Goldman, 985.

53   'But that's what': Quoted in Mary Blume, *Cote d'Azur: Inventing the French Riviera* (London: Thames and Hudson, 1992), 105.

53   'not only thinks': EG to Evelyn Scott, June 1926–July 1928, EG Papers, reel 20.

53   'just like a baby': EC to EG, [between July 1928 and May 1929], EG Papers, reel 20.

54   'produced [John and Dorothy]': OTC, 69.

54   'My melancholy turned': OTC, 71.

54   'more than painful': OTC, 50.

55   'I could not live with': OTC, 72.

55   '[T]hen Laurence slapped me': OTC, 72.

56   'Peggy gave me to understand': EG to Eleanor Fitzgerald, December 8, 1929, EG Papers, reel 20.

56   '[B]ut when I saw': EG to LV, December 7, 1928, EG Papers, reel 20.

57   'It is fair that I should have': LV to EG, [November 1928?], EG Papers, reel 20; in a second letter, he clarified: 'When I mentioned the Guggenheim women, I did not mean that I thought Peggy would appeal to her mother, or let Sindbad live with them. I meant that I would not hurt my son with a certain scatter brain, unstable quality that all the Guggenheim women – even Peggy – possess in some degree.' LV to EG, [November 1928?], EG Papers, reel 20. Florette, Hazel, and Peggy did indeed share this quality, but, especially given the timing, it is unlikely that he was not referring to Hazel and her children's death.

57   'If she nevertheless': EG to LV, Pramousquier, December 7, 1928, EG Papers, reel 20.

57   'to turn Sinbad over': EG to LV, Saint-Tropez, December 7, 1928, EG Papers, reel 20.

58   'growing thinner every day': LV to EG, [November 1928], EG Papers, reel 20.

58   The previous summer: OTC, 64.

58   'Peggy is keeping on her feet': EG to LV, Saint-Tropez, December 7, 1928, EG Papers, reel 20.

58   'not been as careful': LV to EG, [November 1928?], EG Papers, reel 20.

58   'Heaven knows Peggy': EG to Eleanor Fitzgerald, December 8, 1928, EG Papers, reel 20.

59   'developing wonderfully away': PG to EG, EG Papers, reel 20; the EG Papers

editors give the date as [December 1929?], but the date is more likely December 1928.

59   Boyle's biographer: Joan Mellen, Kay Boyle: *Author of Herself* (New York: Farrar, Straus and Giroux, 1994), 134.

59   'Whenever she sensed': Mellen, 137.

59   'too bad he wasn't frightened': OTC, 125.

60   'realized what he could do': OTC, 72.

60   'When I first met John': OTC, 78.

61   'a sour, casual hock': Alec Waugh, *My Brother Evelyn and Other Profiles* (London: Cassell, 1967), 75.

61   A later friend: William Gerhardie, *Memoirs of a Polyglot* (1936; rpt. London: Macdonald, 1970), 325.

61   'John had written only one poem': OTC, 106.

61   'aesthetically worthless': John Holms, review of *Mrs. Dalloway*, *The Calendar of Modern Letters*, vol. 21, no. 5, July 1925 (rpt. London: Frank Cass, 1966) 405.

61   'without aesthetic life': John Holms, review of *The Sailor's Return*, *The Calendar of Modern Letters*, vol. 2, no. 8, October 1925 (rpt. London: Frank Cass, 1966), 141.

62   'obsessive theme': Francis Mulhern, *The Moment of 'Scrutiny'* (London, NLB, 1979), 17.

62   'the most remarkable man': Edwin Muir, *An Autobiography* (1954; rpt. St. Paul, Minn.: Graywolf Press, 1990),177–78.

62   'incapacity to shoulder': EC, unpublished diary, November 9, 1937, EC Papers, University of Delaware Library.

62   Edwin Muir's wife: Willa Muir, *Belonging: A Memoir.* (London: Hogarth Press, 1968), 93.

62   'rather die than sit': Muir, 129.

62   'God come down': EC, unpublished diary, August 9, 1932, to September 9, 1932, 130, EC Papers.

62   'looked like a Spanish': Waugh, 77.

62   'elastic quality': OTC, 69.

62   'tall and lean': Muir, 177.

62   'In his movements': Muir, 177.

63   'was wearing pre-war': Waugh, 77.

63   'a very old soiled mackintosh': Gerhardie, 326.

63   'Peggy told me': EC, unpublished diary, October 2, 1937, EC Papers. DB told a young assistant in her later years that she once said to Peggy, 'How can you say such things about people when your own sister threw her children off the roof?' Hank O'Neal, *'Life is painful, nasty, and short . . . In my case it has only been painful and nasty': Djuna Barnes 1978–1981* (New York: Paragon, 1990), 135.

63   'It was all getting too much': OTC, 72.

63   'The main trouble': EG to EC, January 8 [1929], EG Papers, reel 20.

64   '[Dorothy] will get': EC to EG, [between May 10, 1929, and May 14, 1929],

EG Papers, reel 21.

64 'little shit': EC to EG, [July 1929], EG Papers, reel 21.

64 Once, when Peggy and John: OTC, 80.

64 'Advise you permit': PG to EG, September 14, 1929, EG Papers, reel 21.

64 John finally told: PG to EG, August 5, [1929], EG Papers, reel 21.

64 Another impediment: OTC, 80.

64 they exchanged presents: OTC, 77.

65 'Tiens, tiens': OTC, 85.

65 'The thing in Berlin': PG to EG, August 5, [1929], EG Papers, reel 21.

65 'like ivy to the oak': OTC, 81.

65 'for the children's sake': PG to EG, August 5, [1929], EG Papers, reel 21.

66 'nervy and peculiar': Kay Boyle to Caresse Crosby, [n.d.], Kay Boyle Papers, Special Collections, Morris Library, Southern Illinois University.

5: MR. AND MRS. BONZO

67 'like sardines': PG to EG, September 26, [1929], EG Papers, reel 21.

67 'I feel as though': PG to EG, August 5, [1929], EG Papers, reel 21.

67 'always wanted to do': PG to EG, September 14, 1929, EG Papers, reel 21.

67 a 1932 letter: PG to Hannah Josephson, [n.d. 1932], Matthew Josephson Papers, Beinecke Rare Book and Manuscript Library, Yale University. A letter to the editor from Peggy's teacher, Lucille Kohn, appeared in the New York Times on August 3, 1932, page 14, on the plight of the miners in West Virginia; Kohn, who was organizing in West Virginia at the time, may have sent a clipping to Peggy, or may have described her experiences firsthand.

68 'She is a quick sprite': EC, unpublished diary, November 11, 1929, EC Papers, University of Delaware.

68 'Wendy is a courageous': EC, unpublished diary, November 4, 1929, EC Papers.

68 'Wendy said she could not': EC, unpublished diary, November 11, 1929, EC Papers.

68 'pretensions to inferiority': EC, unpublished diary, November 2, 1937, EC Papers.

68 'Agamemnon has done nothing': EC, unpublished diary, December 4, 1929, EC Papers.

68 'He told her things': EC, unpublished diary, November 16, 1929, EC Papers.

68 'I both loved and hated': OTC, 91.

69 'He is a fool': EC, unpublished diary, December 14, 1929, EC Papers.

69 'as a hostage': EC, unpublished diary, September [n.d.], 1930, EC Papers. 'and by degrees renewed': OTC, 90.

69 'We can't fight her': Kay Boyle to Caresse Crosby, June 30, 1930, Caresse Crosby Papers, Morris Library, Southern Illinois University.

69 'like a little skyscraper': OTC, 91.

69 'Peggy and John': EC to EG, [January 1931?], EG Papers, reel 23.

70 In the winter of 1930 to 1931: The Guggenheims and the Loebs crossed

virtually every path the Joyce family took. Peggy's friend Helen Fleischman, recently divorced from Leon, would seduce and marry Giorgio. Helen's friend Alex Ponisovsky was a close friend to the Guggenheims (and a relative – a Seligman had married into his family), courting Peggy's sister Hazel. He was later active in the Free French and a good friend of Mary Reynolds and Marcel Duchamp. Ponisovsky's sister, Lucia, was married to Joyce's secretary, Paul Leon. Briefly engaged to Lucia Joyce, Ponisovsky gave Joyce Russian lessons, beginning in 1928.

70 'Go ca'canny with the cognac': OTC, 93.

70 'marvelous': OTC, 94.

70 'Djuna and I': Charles Henri Ford to Charles Ford, December 23, 1931, Charles Henri Ford Papers, Harry Ransom Humanities Research Center, University of Texas, Austin.

71 'Not necessary': EG to Alexander Berkman, November 5, 1931, EG Papers, reel 20.

71 'tribute to Peggy': LV to EG, [October 7, 1931], EG Papers, reel 20.

72 'Don't think Peggy': EG to Alexander Berkman, November 5, 1931, EG Papers, reel 20.

72 'But you were so different': EG to PG, November 13, 1931, EG Papers, reel 20.

72 'Speaking of giving up': EG to Alexander Berkman, January 30, 1929, EG Papers, reel 20.

73 'But the friendship': EG to Stella Ballantine, December 7, 1931, EG Papers, reel 20.

73 'all the gay times': EG to PG, September 13, 1933, EG Papers, reel 20.

74 'barbarians, happy German families': LV quoted in Hugh Ford, ed., *This Must Be the Place: Memoirs of Montparnasse by Jimmie 'The Barman' Charters As Told to Morrill Cody* (1934; rpt. New York: Collier, 1989), 199–200.

74 'Awful tales of France': Marian Bouche, unpublished diary, June 11, 1933, AAA, reel 689.

74 Many believe that Hayford Hall: Interview with Malcolm Dunstan, May 18, 2002; Dunstan, the current owner of Hayford Hall, discovered the connection when a busload of Japanese tourists with cameras, members of an Arthur Conan Doyle appreciation society, showed up at his doorstep. Enthusiasts continue to visit.

75 'The house is low': EC, unpublished diary, August 26, 1932, EC Papers.

75 'The beeches': EC, unpublished diary, [n.d.], EC Papers.

75 Djuna, who had weathered: DB resented Peggy's saying that *Nightwood* had been composed at Hayford Hall. 'How could she write such things?' she said. 'You don't write *Nightwood* in a month!' Hank O'Neal, *'Life is painful, nasty, and short . . . In my case it has only been painful and nasty': Djuna Barnes 1978–1981* (New York: Paragon, 1990), 136.

75 'very dreary': OTC, 99.

75 'said she was more conceited': EC, unpublished diary, August 28, 1932, 87, EC Papers.

76 'I might be anything': Quoted in Lyndall Passerini Hopkinson, *Nothing to Forgive: A Daughter's Story of Antonia White* (London: Chatto and Windus, 1988), 95.

76 'But, my dear': EC, unpublished diary, August 28, 1932, 86, EC Papers.

76 'Garter [sic] see': As quoted in Susan Chitty, *Now to My Mother: A Very Personal Memoir of Antonia White* (London: Weidenfeld and Nicolson, 1985), 62.

76 'Our relation is': EC, unpublished diary, August 31, 1932, 106, EC Papers.

76 'talked about Djuna's lack': EC, unpublished diary, August 30, 1932, 100, EC Papers.

76 'I don't want to be': EC, unpublished diary, August 31, 1932, 113, EC Papers.

76 'This is an example': EC, unpublished diary, September 3, 1932, 125, EC Papers.

76 'Djuna said a little truth': Peggy dates these remarks in 1932, though Emily's diary records them in 1933. See EC, unpublished diary, July 23, [1933], EC Papers.

77 'Why, I wouldn't touch': OTC, 101.

77 'I shut my door': EC, unpublished diary, August 9, 1932, 75, EC Papers.

78 black eye: OTC, 96.

78 'Little by little': OTC, 78.

78 'I had been completely': OTC, 114.

79 '[The Bonzos] had rented': William Gerhardie, *Of Mortal Love* (1936; rpt. London: Macdonald, 1970), 82.

79 'an American poetess': Gerhardie, 84.

79 'a shy, sultry': Gerhardie, 74.

80 'a version of Boccaccio': Chitty, 63.

6: ENDINGS AND BEGINNINGS

82 at first $300: Joan Mellen, *Kay Boyle: Author of Herself* (New York: Farrar, Straus and Giroux, 1994), 136.

82 'for consolation': Quoted in Mellen, 151.

83 'You never wash': Mellen, 149.

83 'for some morbid reason': OTC, 96.

83 'gave the impression': OTC, 97.

83 Somehow, after the ceremony: See Mellen, 161.

84 'Peggy's avarice': EC, unpublished diary, December 5, [1932], 215, EC Papers, University of Delaware.

84 'very tight': EC, unpublished diary, December 5, [1932], 217, EC Papers.

84 'We all slept together': EC, unpublished diary, December 13, [1932], 232, EC Papers.

84 'I imagine I felt Garman': OTC, 103.

85 'Djuna lapping and little Tony': EC, unpublished diary, July 21, [1933], EC Papers.

85 'kissing him passionately': EC, unpublished diary, July 23, [1933], EC Papers.

85 'Rather glad we won't': Marian Bouche, unpublished diary, [September 1933], AAA, reel 689. 'Peggy and John moved': All quotations in this paragraph are from Marian Bouche, unpublished diary, [n.p.], AAA, reel 689.

86 'really a *bad* woman': Susan Chitty, *Now to My Mother: A Very Personal Memoir of Antonia White* (London: Weidenfeld and Nicolson, 1985), 109.

86 'very English eighteenth-century': OTC, 107.

86 'I would like to beat': OTC, 107.

87 'a terrible oath': OTC, 109.

87 'What if I never': OTC, 109.

88 'He was so far away': OTC, 110.

88 'let out a terrible scream': OTC, 110.

88 'Whatever your life is': OTC, 111.

88 'Never . . . He is in heaven': OTC, 111.

89 'Now that John is dead': OTC, 110.

89 'and watched my mouth': OTC, 111.

90 Born in 1903 to a wealthy doctor: Stephen Gardiner, *Epstein: Artist against the Establishment* (London: Michael Joseph, 1992), 218.

90 'the gift between your thighs': OTC, 114.

91 'Laurence feels he's': PG to EC, [April 9, 1934], EC Papers.

91 '[T]he house is far nicer': EC, unpublished diary, July 12, [1935], 25, EC Papers.

92 'Anybody can ask': EC, unpublished diary, July 7, [1934], 9, EC Papers.

92 'Very witty conversation': EC, unpublished diary, July 15, 16, 17, [1934], 38, EC Papers.

92 'They are scandalizing': Quoted in Carolyn Burke, *Becoming Modern: The Life of Mina Loy* (New York: Farrar, Straus and Giroux, 1996), 366.

92 'Both her children': EC, unpublished diary, July 12, [1934], EC Papers.

92 'a vulgar Jewish': EC, unpublished diary, August 7, [1934], EC Papers.

92 'like an exhibition': EC, unpublished diary, July 29, [1934], 77, EC Papers.

93 On another occasion: Lyndall Passerini Hopkinson, *Nothing to Forgive: A Daughter's Story of Antonia White* (London: Chatto and Windus, 1988), 97.

93 'Without John to control us': Hopkinson, 103.

93 'three dollars and seventy-five cents': OTC, 119.

93 Their landlady was once: PG to EC, August 28, [1935], EC Papers.

94 Garman would later complain: OTC, 114.

7: AN IDEA

95 'Marxist heated': Michael Wishart, *High Diver: An Autobiography* (London: Quartet Books, 1994), 91.

96 'Having botched': PG to EC, November 26, [1934], EC Papers, University of Delaware.

96 'The latter he got': PG to EC, March 26, [1938], EC Papers.

96 'Let's play the Guggenheim game': EC, unpublished diary, September 6, [1933], 136, EC Papers.

96 'Laurence accepts': PG to EC, [March 2, 1935], EC Papers.

97 'I think one reason': PG to EC, [July 16, 1936], EC Papers.

97 'I have at last found': PG to EC, March 30, [1935], EC Papers.

97 'I seem to be on the verge': PG to EC, [May 9, 1935], EC Papers.

97 It is possible: In a letter dated November 9, 1935, DB asks PG why she doesn't get pregnant, asking, 'Can all those curettages have done the work too well?' DB Papers, University of Maryland.

97 'I like being pregnant': PG to EC, [May 9, 1935], EC Papers.

98 'It was Garman's fault': PG to EC, [February 19, 1936], EC Papers.

98 'speaks for itself': PG to EC, [March 2, 1935], EC Papers.

98 Most impressively: See DB to PG, November 9, 1935, DB Papers. 'How is Proust in French?' asks Djuna.

98 'Proust gives me great joy': PG to EC, [September 1935], EC Papers.

98 'Of course I never write': PG to EC, [May 9, 1935], EC Papers.

98 'This is my first': PG to EC, [May 2, 1935], EC Papers.

99 'I am glad you like': PG to EC, August 28, [1935], EC Papers.

99 'Anyhow it has started': PG to EC, August 8, [1935], EC Papers.

99 'I thus feel': EC to DB, November 9, 1935, DB Papers.

99 '[Peggy] read me': EC, unpublished diary, April 11, 1936, EC Papers.

100 'I still shop': PG to EC, [June 26, 1935], EC Papers.

100 'I think my life': PG to EC, [November 20, 1935], EC Papers.

100 'My life has been': PG to EC, [November 20, 1935], EC Papers.

100 'If I followed': PG to EC, [February 19, 1936], EC Papers. 'Eternal Danger': PG to EC, [July 19, 1936], EC Papers.

100 'It is awful': PG to EC, [May 9, 1935], EC Papers.

101 Kay managed to get under: OTC, 121.

101 'for reminding me': PG to EC, [March 30, 1935], EC Papers.

101 'that she knew': EC, unpublished diary, January 16, 1936, 82, EC Papers.

101 'All my excess energy': PG to EC, [November 20, 1935], EC Papers.

101 'She is madly in love': EC to DB, November 24, 1935, DB Papers.

101 'so passionately connected': PG to EC, [December 3, 1935], EC Papers.

102 'They are not suited': EC, unpublished diary, January 16, 1936, 81, EC Papers.

102 'I think now': PG to EC, [February 19, 1936], EC Papers.

102 Eventually Peggy wrote: The Labor History Archive and Study Centre in Manchester, England, which houses the archives of the GBCP and the papers of Harry Pollitt, contains no reference to PG, though membership records are incomplete. Stephen Bird to author, March 13, 2002. There seems no other evidence that PG fabricated her membership.

103 'Djuna said the English': EC, unpublished diary, June 1, 1936, EC Papers.

103 'Garman has given': PG to EC, [July 1936], EC Papers.

103 'Garman and I': PG to EC, [August 30, 1936], EC Papers.

103 'I was so miserable': PG to EC, [July 1936], EC Papers.

103 'chased her around': PG to EC, [November or December 1936], EC Papers.

104 'Mrs. Simpson's Bed': OTC, 134.

104 'wild night': PG to EC, [early 1937], EC Papers.

104 'I can't bear to think': PG to EC [early 1937], EC Papers.
104 'end this idiotic life': PG to EC and DB, [June 8, 1937], EC Papers.
104 'a marvelous woman': PG to EC, [June 28,1937], EC Papers.
105 'I am so sorry': Letter quoted in Virginia Dortch, ed., *Peggy Guggenheim and Her Friends* (Milan: Berenice Books, 1994), 54.
105 'anti-chi chi gallery': EC to DB, June 21, 1937, DB Papers.
105 'wildly enthusiastic': Folio '65, PG's scrapbooks, reel ITVE 1, AAA.
107 'My life has taken': PG to EC, December 23, [1937], EC Papers.

8: A NEW LIFE

109 'It was a bad blow': PG to EC, [late November 1938], EC Papers, University of Delaware.
109 'he looks like': DB to EC, November 30, 1937, DB Papers, University of Maryland.
110 'Emily was there': OTC, 137.
110 'the angel of anarchy': Roland Penrose, *Scrap Book: 1900–1981* (New York: Rizzoli, 1981), 75.
110 'We were both blasé': OTC, 129.
111 'short, rubicund': George Melly, *Don't Tell Sibyl: An Intimate Memoir of E.L.T Mesens* (London: Heinemann, 1997), 46.
111 he reopened it as: Interview with James Mayor, October 21, 2001.
111 'he looked like a lion': OTC, 138.
111 'art is divine': PG to EC, [July 12, 1937], EC Papers.
111 'got rid of': PG to EC, December 23, [1937], EC Papers.
111 'hoaring': PG to EC, November 1, [1937], EC Papers.
111 'I would have had': PG to EC, December 23, [1937], EC Papers.
112 '[Peggy] has no settled': DB to EC, November 30, [1937], DB Papers.
112 'a fat, very fat': Nancy Cunard to Walter Lowenfels, October 10, 1964, Nancy Cunard Papers, Special Collections, Morris Library, Southern Illinois University.
113 'Marcel, who was a dry type': Quoted in Calvin Tomkins, *Duchamp: A Biography* (New York: Henry Holt, 1996), 137.
113 'a loner': Interview with Calvin Tomkins, November 5, 2000.
113 'Marcel skims ever': DB to PG, December 30, 1965, DB Papers.
114 'I couldn't distinguish': OTC, 139.
115 'fourteen-year occupation': Martica Sawin, *Surrealism in Exile and the Beginning of the New York School* (Cambridge, Mass.: MIT Press, 1997), 7. I have drawn on Sawin's description of this exhibition, 4–12.
115 'the first thing I bought': OTC, 139.
116 'hoaring': PG to EC, December 23, [1937], EC Papers.
116 'I am in Paris': PG to EC, [January 1, 1938], EC Papers.
116 'When you compare': PG to EC, March 26, [1938], EC Papers.
117 Known to be an intimate: For a valuable and much-needed biography of Lucia Joyce, see the recent *Lucia Joyce: To Dance in the Wake* by Carol Loeb

Shloss, New York: Farrar, Straus and Giroux, 2003.

118 'Beckett was a tall': OTC, 140.

118 for over a week: Peggy said they were in bed together for twelve days, but Beckett's biographer Anthony Cronin points out that she met Beckett on December 26 and that Beckett was stabbed on January 6, eleven days later. See Anthony Cronin, Samuel Beckett: The Last Modernist (1997; rpt. New York: Da Capo, 1999), 283.

118 'with great emotion': OTC, 141.

118 There is no reason: Deirdre Bair, Samuel Beckett: A Biography (1978; rpt. New York: Summit Books, 1990), had the advantage of interviewing PG, as well as an unidentified person who wrote his own recollection of the affair; James Knowlson, Damned to Fame: The Life of Samuel Beckett (1996; rpt. New York: Touchstone, 1997), was the authorized biographer. Anthony Cronin's biography is extremely thorough but gets many of the facts of Peggy's life wrong – as the other Beckett biographers do as well. Generally, they don't know what to make of this affair.

118 'one had to accept': OTC, 141.

119 'exciting': OTC, 141.

119 'It seemed ironic': OTC, 141.

120 'She sounded to me': OTC, 150.

9: OUT OF THE GATE

121 'who has been': Evening Standard, [n.d.], PG's scrapbook, reel ITVE 1, AAA.

121 'remarkable feats': Manchester Guardian, [n.d.], PG's scrapbook, reel ITVE 1, AAA.

121 'It is all very lively': The Times, [n.d.], PG's scrapbook, reel ITVE 1, AAA.

121 'though there may be': The Sketch, [n.d.], PG's scrapbook, reel ITVE 1, AAA.

121 'attractively jerky': Unattributed clipping in PG's scrapbook, reel ITVE 1, AAA.

121 'Peggy's influence': Quoted in Angelica Zander Rudenstine, PG Collection, Venice, the Solomon R. Guggenheim Foundation (New York: Harry Abrams, 1985), 99.

122 'Dear Mrs. Guggenheim "jeune"': OTC, 145–46.

122 'good and growing': OTC, 145–46.

123 'I do not seek': PG to Solomon Guggenheim, March 17, 1938, SRGF archives.

123 'It is impossible': Hugh Gordon Proteus, New English Weekly, PG's scrapbook, reel ITVE 1, AAA.

123 dancing a little jig: Anthony Cronin, in Samuel Beckett: The Last Modernist (1997; rpt. New York: Da Capo, 1999), 290, makes much of the fact that Joyce danced a 'slow saraband,' not an 'Irish jig.'

124 'a short affair': PG to EC, [March 26, 1938], EC Papers, University of Delaware.

125 Brancusi had gone: See Brancusi vs. United States: The Historic Trial, 1928

(New York: Adam Biro, 1999).

125 'not art': 'What He Says Goes Back,' *Daily Express* (March 22, 1938), PG's scrapbook, reel ITVE 1, AAA.

125 'I think it is a disgraceful thing': 'Mr. Manson's No,' *Evening News* (March 22, 1938), PG's scrapbook, reel ITVE 1, AAA.

125 'In my opinion': 'Tate Director to Resign,' *Daily Telegraph* (March 23, 1938), PG's scrapbook, reel ITVE 1, AAA.

126 'black-out': 'Black-Outs,' *Time* (April 25, 1938), 36.

126 'wild' drinking: OTC, 149.

127 'a gay little Flamand': OTC, 150.

127 'It was a rather homosexual': OTC, 150.

127 '[b]ecause he is a pederast': PG to EC, [August 12, 1938], EC Papers.

127 'with sorrow': OTC, 151.

128 'He had a lovely': OTC, 155.

128 'Tanguy is completely': PG to EC, [August 12, 1938], EC Papers.

128 'Mr. Tanguy is a most': *The Times* [n.d.], PG's scrapbook, reel ITVE 1, AAA.

131 'I'm not getting married': PG to EC, [November 21, 1938], EC Papers.

131 'The war scares us': PG to EC, [September 23, 1938], EC Papers.

132 'Miss Guggenheim has given': Theodore Goodman, 'The Guggenheim Jeune Gallery,' The Malvern Gazette, [n.d.], PG's scrapbook, reel ITVE 1, AAA.

132 'more and more dully': PG to EC, [September 23, 1938], EC Papers.

133 'I am so rich': DB to EC, July 25, 1938, DB Papers, University of Maryland.

134 'awful autocrat': OTC, 162.

134 'Peggy is over Sam': DB to EC, DB Papers.

135 'Such an assessment': Fred Licht, 'Peggy Guggenheim 1898–1979,' *Art in America* (February 1980), 21. Interview with Fred Licht, April 6, 2001.

10: THE BEGINNINGS OF WAR: THE BEST-LAID PLANS

137 'Who is this John Tunnard': OTC, 159.

137 'I prefer to live alone': EG to EC, [February 21, 1939], EC Papers, University of Delaware.

138 'It cost me a lot': EG to EC, [February 24, 1939], EC Papers.

138 'required more courage': EG to PG, February 22, 1939, EC Papers.

138 'to do her justice': EG to EC, [February 21, 1939], EC Papers.

138 'Once I got': PG to EC, [n.d., early April 1939], EC Papers.

139 'that John [Holms] might': PG to EC, [n.d., early April 1939], EC Papers.

139 'The affair was very': OTC, 162.

140 'I felt that if I': OTC, 164.

141 Centre Guggenheim: See Joan Lukach, *Hilla Rebay: The Search for the Spirit in Art* (New York: George Braziller, 1983), 127–28, for the baroness's European plans.

141 'the best known proponent': James King, *The Last Modern: A Life of Herbert Read* (New York: St. Martin's, 1990), xv.

141 'sensibly withdrew': King, 178.

142 Eliot had of course: Eliot gave Emily the nickname Annie Oakley, not only because of her Oakley Street address, but perhaps because of, a Djuna Barnes biographer speculates, 'her inclination to shoot from the hip.' Phillip Herring, *Djuna: The Life and Work of Djuna Barnes* (1995; rpt. New York: Penguin, 1996), 227.

142 'momentous decision': Herbert Read to Douglas Cooper, May 20, 1939, Getty Research Institute. Cooper seems not to have supported Read's decision, for Read wrote him back on June 15 accusing him of having the viewpoint of a 'snob collector.'

142 'struggle and apprehension': EG to Herbert Read, October 7, 1939, EG Papers, Collection 12, box 1, Tamiment Library, New York University.

142 'was a little nervous': PG to EC, [n.d., May 1939?], EC Papers.

142 'monstrous mathematical': PG to EC, September 1, [1939], EC Papers.

143 'I ask his advice': PG to EC, [n.d., early April 1939], EC Papers.

143 'I assert that all flirting': Michel Remy, *Surrealism in Britain* (London: Ashgate, 1999), 213. Remy, an important contemporary critic, admires Mesens's 'intellectual honesty' and shares in Mesens's thinking that Peggy was 'a sham.'

144 'He treated me the way': OTC, 165.

144 'a sort of twentieth-century': OTC, 167.

144 'very gay & alive': PG to EC, September 1, [1939], EC Papers.

145 'Never in business': Quoted in Sarah Jane Checkland, *Ben Nicholson: The Vicious Circles of His Life and Art* (London: John Murray, 2000), 189.

145 'to try to save': PG to EC, September 1, [1939], EC Papers.

146 'Can't you see': DB to EC, March 22, 1939, DB Papers, University of Maryland.

146 'the thought of P.': DB to EC, March 20, 1939, DB Papers.

146 'little Hitler': DB to EC, November 17, 1939, DB Papers.

146 '[S]he is mad': DB to EC, November 12, 1939, DB Papers.

146 'drunken neurotic': PG to EC, November 3, [1939], EC Papers.

I I: ON THE RUN

148 risqué drawing by Cocteau: PG's grandson, Sandro Rumney, who inherited drawings by Cocteau, his godfather, maintains that she bought other drawings from this show; interview with Sandro Rumney, November 13, 2001.

149 $3,000: Records of what Peggy paid for these early purchases can be deduced from a document her accountant drew up for her New York City gallery (in the Bernard and Rebecca Reis Papers, Getty Research Institute), though because that statement was largely constructed for tax purposes, it may be misleading; however, the prices given are borne out by other sources and are not out of line with contemporary sales, so they are given here. See 'Art of This Century Inventory of Art Works as of December 31, 1942,' page 282.

149 no known photograph: There is a drawing, however, by Charles Seliger, one of Peggy's talented artists in the New York City years. It can be found in

Francis V. O'Connor, *Charles Seliger: Redefining Abstract Expressionism* (Manchester, Vt.: Hudson Hills Press, 2002), 35.

149 Born in Spring Lake: The sketchy information about Putzel that exists comes from the Hermine Benhaim Papers, AAA, reel 3482; 'Howard J. Putzel, Owned 67 Gallery,' *New York Times*, August 7, 1945; interview with Charles Seliger, December 12, 2000.

150 'too cheap': OTC, 180.

150 'At first [Putzel]': OTC, 179.

151 'Everyone knew I was': OTC, 175.

151 'Of everything I own': PG to Henri-Pierre Roche, November 26, 1940, Carlton Lake Collection, Harry Ransom Humanities Research Center, University of Texas, Austin.

152 'sexual enough': OTC, 178.

152 'The day Hitler walked': OTC, 181.

152 'too modern': OTC, 182.

153 when Peggy and Nellie: Nellie van Doesburg in Virginia Dortch, ed., *Peggy Guggenheim and Her Friends* (Milan: Berenice Books, 1994), 65.

153 'Bedales is a joke': DB to EC, March 20, 1939, DB Papers, University of Maryland.

154 'The children are nearly': PG to EC, [early April 1939], EC Papers, University of Delaware.

154 'I admired Peggy': Interview with Jacqueline Ventadour Hélion, September 8, 2001.

154 'Vail's Modern Almanac': The almanacs are in the Kay Boyle Papers, Special Collections, Morris Library, Southern Illinois University.

155 'I am very young': PG to EC, [February 13, 1940], EC Papers.

155 'a Kandinsky, several Klees': OTC, 182.

156 'help rescue and finance': OTC, 189.

157 Marseilles was then: See Varian Fry, *Surrender on Demand* (New York: Random House, 1945); Michèle C. Cone, *Artists under Vichy: A Case of Prejudice and Persecution* (Princeton, N.J.: Princeton University Press, 1992); Andy Marino, *A Quiet American: The Secret War of Varian Fry* (New York: St. Martin's, 1999).

157 'that amazing Scarlet': Mary Jayne Gold, *Crossroads Marseilles,1940* (New York: Doubleday, 1980), x.

157 'I went back to Grenoble': OTC, 190.

157 She gave the committee: Marino, 256.

157 'very romantic wrapped in': OTC, 191.

158 'loplop, bird superior': Martica Sawin, *Surrealism in Exile and the Beginning of the New York School* (1995; rpt. Cambridge, Mass.: MIT Press, 997), 12.

158 'Tomorrow at four': OTC, 192.

159 'Oh, that is nothing': OTC, 195.

160 The Clipper experience: There was even a Clipper cocktail: 1 ½ ounces light or gold rum, ½ ounce vermouth, ½ teaspoon grenadine.

12: THE STATES

161 'One of the women': Jimmy Ernst, A Not-So-Still Life: A Memoir (New York: St. Martin's, 1984),199–200.

162 'The beauties of America': PG to DB, [n.d., 1941], DB Papers, University of Maryland.

163 'a staccato of twists': Ernst, 214.

163 'Darling Kay': Joan Mellen, Kay Boyle: Author of Herself (New York: Farrar, Straus and Giroux, 1994), 265–66.

163 'Oh Kay': Mellen, 247.

164 'His Cubist collection': OTC, 213.

164 'We were shooting': Telephone interview with John King-Farlow, November 14, 2001.

164 'happy reunion': Neil Baldwin, Man Ray: American Artist (1988; rpt. New York: Da Capo, 2001), 239.

165 'kept saying Peggy': EC, unpublished diary, August 14, [1941], EC Papers, University of Delaware.

165 'disappointed': PG to EC, August 3, 1941, EC Papers.

165 'What a pity': PG to EC, [n.d., November 1941], EC Papers.

165 'felt more at home': OTC, 215.

166 'snob debutante': PG to EC, [October 24, 1941], EC Papers.

166 'Our house on the river': PG to EC, [December 12, 1941], EC Papers.

166 'bleeding like a raspberry pie': Charles Henri Ford to Ruth Ford, December 12, 1941.

166 Jimmy Ernst dashed in: Interview with Charles Henri Ford, December 28, 2000

166 '[Hale House] seemed': Milton Gendel quoted in Virginia Dortch, ed., Peggy Guggenheim and Her Friends (Milan: Berenice Books, 1994), 100.

166 'Everyone gathered': 'An Interview with Leonora Carrington,' La Paseanté 17, Cecilia Martinez, trans.; Nadia Van Husselt, ed.

167 'I hope you have forgiven': PG to Gypsy Rose Lee, April 3, 1943, Gypsy Rose Lee Papers, Billy Rose Theatre Papers, New York Public Library.

167 'lack of affectation': Ernst, 211.

167 'need to love someone': Jimmy Ernst, interview with Jeffrey Potter, July 13, 1981, Pollock-Krasner House and Study Center, East Hampton, New York.

167 'a cute little boy': PG to EC, August 12, [1941], EC Papers.

167 'a happily unmarried': PG to EC, July 28, [1941], EC Papers.

167 'a feeling of safety': OTC, 220.

168 'Max Ernst is': John Russell, Max Ernst: Life and Work (New York: Harry Abrams, [1967]), 10.

168 'Normally he was as cold': OTC, 222.

168 'He admitted that he likes': OTC, 221.

168 'It's very strange': PG to EC, August 12, [1941], EC Papers.

169 'It was a horrible marriage': Jimmy Ernst, interview with Jeffrey Potter, July 13, 1981, Pollock-Krasner House and Study Center.

169 Duchamp was still: I have designated acquisitions in 1941 and 1942 with the help of the accounting statements issued by Bernard Reis in the Bernard and Rebecca Reis Papers, Getty Research Institute; and Melvin Paul Lader, 'Peggy Guggenheim's Art of This Century: The Surrealist Milieu and the American Avant-Garde, 1942–1947,' unpublished doctoral dissertation, University of Delaware, 1981, 102–106.

170 'with the amused eyes': John Bernard Myers, Tracking the Marvelous: A Life in the New York Art World (New York: Random House, 1983), 264. For the Reises' background, see Bernard Reis, interview with Paul Cummings, June 3, 1976, AAA.

170 Bernard warned her: Dortch, 11–12.

171 '[A]t that time': David Hare, interview with Dorothy Seckler, January 17, 968, AAA.

171 'It's as if one': Quoted in Sawin, 182.

172 Peggy remarked on how amusing: OTC, 233.

172 'one of the most delightful': See Deborah Solomon, Utopia Parkway: The Life and Work of Joseph Cornell (New York: Farrar, Straus and Giroux, 1997), 135.

172 'people whose names': Quoted in Calvin Tomkins, Duchamp: A Biography (New York: Henry Holt, 1996), 330.

173 'It was Duchamp': Quoted in Tomkins, 331.

173 When she settled down: PG to Frederick Kiesler, March 9, 1942, Frederick Kiesler Center, Vienna.

173 A Vogue survey: All quotations in this roundup of contemporary galleries are from Sallie Faxon Saunders, 'Middle Mean of Art,' Vogue (March 15, 1938). The scholarship of Ingrid Schaffner, 'Alchemy of the Gallery,' in Ingrid Schaffner and Lisa Jacobs, eds., Julien Levy: Portrait of an Art Gallery (Cambridge, Mass.: MIT Press, 1998), 44, led me to this Vogue article.

175 Breton and Howard Putzel: See Cynthia Goodman, 'Frederick Kiesler: Designs for Peggy Guggenheim's Art of This Century Gallery,' Arts (June 1977), 90–95, for Kiesler's background. Most of my information about Kiesler comes from Dieter Bogner, ed., Friedrich Kiesler: Art of This Century (Vienna: Hatje Cantz, 2003) and the curatorial staff of the Peggy Guggenheim Collection's October 10, 2003, exhibit, 'Peggy and Kiesler: The Collector and the Visionary.' For the definitive work on the gallery, see Philip Rylands, Dieter Bogner, Susan Davidson, Donald Quaintance, Valentina Sonzogni, Francis V. O'Connor, and Jasper Sharp, Peggy and Kiesler: The Story of Art of This Century (Venice: Peggy Guggenheim Collection, 2004).

175 'Peggy attracted a good': James Johnson Sweeney, August 10, 1982, 'Inventory of Temporary Exhibits: Art of This Century,' document in Peggy and Kiesler: The Collector and the Visionary, Peggy Guggenheim Collection, [n.p.].

175 '[a]cting alternately': Ernst, 177.

175 'Dear Mr. Kiesler': Letter reproduced as Document 17, 'PG to Frederick Kiesler,' in Bogner, ed.

176 'The exchange of': Frederick Kiesler, 'On Correalism and Biotechnique,'

Architectural Record (September 1939), 60–75.

176 Kiesler believed: Talk by Dieter Bogner, at 'Peggy and Kiesler' opening, October 10, 2003.

176 'Today the framed painting': Frederick Kiesler, 'Brief Note on Designing the Gallery,' unpublished manuscript, reprinted in Bogner, ed., [n.p.].

178 '[The gallery] could': Robert Motherwell, quoted in Angelica Zander Rudenstine, *Peggy Guggenheim Collection, Venice, the Solomon R. Guggenheim Foundation* (New York: Harry Abrams, 1985), 799.

178 wooden 'arms': As distinct from baseball bats; Peggy was the first to make this mistake (in OTC, 229), though photographs clearly show that these 'arms' were triangular pieces of wood.

13: 'WHEN ART WORE A ROSE': HIGHS AND LOWS

179 'Bill, myself': Ethel Baziotes to Clement Greenberg, July 3, 1963, AAA, reel N69–91R.

179 'Miss Guggenheim hopes': 'Peggy Guggenheim to Open Art Gallery,' press release, AAA, reel ITVE.

180 'Mon Bijou de l'Epoque': OTC, 233. Julian Levy, *Memoir of An Art Gallery* (New York: G. P. Putnam's, 1977), 33, says, more prosaically, that she called him 'the jewel of the *Times*.'

180 '[I]t is the last word': Edward Alden Jewell, 'Gallery Premiere Assists Red Cross,' *New York Times* (October 25, 1942), 22.

180 'Frankly, my eyes': Henry McBride, 'New Gallery Ideas,' *New York Sun*, October 23, 1942.

180 Coney Island: 'Inheritors of Chaos,' *Time* (October 24, 1942), 47; *The New Yorker* (October 31, 1942), 73.

180 'Going through the rooms': Emily Genauer, 'Surrealist Paintings Hung Surrealistically,' *New York World-Telegram*, October 24, 1942.

180 'If the Museum': Edgar J. Kauffman, 'The Violent Art of Hanging Pictures,' unattributed clipping, PG Scrapbook, AAA, reel ITVE.

180 'daily attendance': Jimmy Ernst, *A Not-So-Still Life: A Memoir* (New York: St. Martin's, 1984), 234–35.

181 the popular First Lady: The visit was a disaster; Mrs. Roosevelt came to see a photographic show, 'The Negro in American Life,' in June of that year. She could not be induced to look at the permanent collection of abstract and surrealist art, and a visitor made fun of her accent within her hearing. PG describes this visit not in OTC but in a later version of her memoirs, *Confessions of an Art Addict* (New York: Macmillan, 1960),103–104.

181 'a kind of funhouse': Cage quoted in Bruce Altshuler, *The Avant-Garde in Exhibition* (New York: Harry Abrams, 1994), 155.

181 'erratic setting': Grace Glueck, 'Paying Tribute to the Daring of Peggy Guggenheim,' *New York Times*, March 1, 1987.

181 'Admission of Onslow Ford': Ernst, 226–27.

181 'nothing really new': Howard Putzel to Edith Halpert, July 27, 1940, quoted

in Melvin Paul Lader, 'Howard Putzel: Proponent of Surrealism and Early Abstract Expressionism in America,' *Arts Magazine* (March 1982), 88.

182 'a sort of *salon*': Ernst, 227.

182 'I used to throw': PG, ed., *Art of This Century* (New York: Art of This Century, [1942]), 123.

182 'None of the other': James Johnson Sweeney, quoted in Angelica Zander Rudenstine, *Peggy Guggenheim Collection, Venice, the Solomon R. Guggenheim Foundation* (New York: Harry Abrams, 1985), 799.

182 'The works in the permanent collection': Robert Motherwell, quoted in Rudenstine, 799.

183 'woman painter': Ernst, 236.

183 "I made Max work': OTC, 233.

183 'pretty': OTC, 234.

183 'While Max was away': OTC, 230–31.

183 'infatuated': PG to EC, [February 17, 1943], EC Papers, University of Delaware. But Duchamp had a penchant: Calvin Tomkins, *Duchamp: A Biography* (New York: Henry Holt, 1996), 341–42.

184 'He wanted to know': OTC, 236.

184 'vague affair': OTC, 245.

184 'all dolled up': PG to EC, [March 23, 1943], EC Papers.

184 'yields one captivating surprise': Edwin Alden Jewell, '31 Women Artists Show Their Work,' *New York Times*, January 6, 1943.

185 'cool, elegant, and detached': *New York Sun*, February 19, 1943. 'Here is non-objective art': Edwin Alden Jewell, *New York Times*, February 10, 1943.

185 'the quick, succinct transformation': Ingrid Schaffner, 'Alchemy of the Gallery,' in Ingrid Schaffner and Lisa Jacobs, eds., *Julien Levy: Portrait of an Art Gallery* (Cambridge, Mass.: MIT Press, 1998), 51.

186 Jackson Pollock: Pollock worked on his collage in the company of Robert Motherwell, who mentioned burning its edges.

186 'this man was doing': Quoted in Steven Naifeh and Gregory White Smith, *Jackson Pollock: An American Saga* (New York: Clarkson N. Potter, 1989), 442.

186 'both historical and contemporary': 'Art of Collage,' *New York Herald Tribune*, April 25, 1943.

186 'Pretty awful, isn't it?': Ernst, 241–42.

187 'Despite a faint air': *The New Yorker*, May 29, 1943.

187 'a lively, if not': *New York Herald Tribune*, May 29, 1943.

187 '[F]or once the future': *The Nation*, May 29, 1943.

188 'permanent retinue': Michael Wishart, *High Diver: An Autobiography* (London: Quartet Books, 1994), 56.

188 'It won't get me': PG to EC, [March 23, 1943], EC Papers.

188 The son of a Scottish painter: On Macpherson, see Susan Stanford Friedman, ed., *Analyzing Freud: Letters of H.D., Bryher, and Their Circle* (New York: New Directions, 2002), 567–68.

189 'He . . . paints his face': PG to EC, [April 5, 1943], EC Papers.

190 'Mrs. Bowles': Paul Bowles, *Without Stopping: An Autobiography of Paul Bowles* (New York: G. P. Putnam's, 1972), 250.

190 'light, summery dress': Interview with David Loeffler Smith, August 6, 2002.

190 one observer notes: Charles Seliger, unpublished journal, 1969, AAA.

191 'Though her waistline grew': Interview with Anne Dunn, November 20, 2001.

191 'her unfortunate nose': John Bernard Myers, *Tracking the Marvelous: A Life in the New York Art World* (New York: Random House, 1983), 29.

191 'she had style': Interview with Sara Havelock-Allen, September 4, 2001.

191 'not at all ugly': Interview with Yoko Ono, May 30, 2003.

192 Eileen Finletter's comment: Interview with Eileen Finletter, April 16, 2002.

192 Anne Dunn's speculation: Interview with Anne Dunn, November 20, 2001.

192 'I love my independent life': PG to EC, [April 15, 1943], EC Papers.

14: TWO STORIES: POLLOCK AND PEGEEN

193 'You cannot afford to miss': *New York Times*, October 24, 1943.

193 'veristic' surrealism: Werner Haftmann, *Painting in the Twentieth Century* (New York: Praeger, 1966), 267–68.

194 'as a loved son': Quoted in Steven Naifeh and Gregory White Smith, *Jackson Pollock: An American Saga* (New York: Clarkson N. Potter, 1989), 421.

194 'He was the most energetic': Quoted in Calvin Tomkins, *Duchamp: A Biography* (New York: Henry Holt, 1996), 363.

195 'That was more': Quoted in Naifeh and Smith, 427.

195 'For none of the painters': Martica Sawin, *Surrealism in Exile and the Beginning of the New York Scene* (1995; rpt. Cambridge, Mass.: MIT Press, 1997), 242.

195 'saw all her sons': Elizabeth Pollock, quoted in Jeffrey Potter, *To a Violent Grave: An Oral Biography of Jackson Pollock* (New York: G. P. Putnam's, 1985), 23.

196 'Lee was an intense': Michael Loew, quoted in Potter, 64.

196 Pollock's constant attempts: Lee Krasner, unpublished manuscript, [p. 1], wrote, 'You know I have so many myths to fight, I feel I must at last speak up. The drinking was something we faced all the time . . . No one was more conscious of it than he was. Jackson tried everything to stop drinking, all his life – medical treatments, analysis, chemistry, everything.' Jackson Pollock Papers, AAA, reel 3048.

197 'You had to work': Quoted in Naifeh and Smith, 442.

197 Peggy came only gradually: Naifeh and Smith present almost every interaction Peggy had with Pollock and Lee Krasner in a light that is unflattering to Peggy. Most likely, versions of such an event were passed on by Krasner, whose relationship with Peggy was decidedly ambivalent and later openly hostile. But it should be noted that Naifeh and Smith, despite their protestations, did not interview Krasner; they cite as 'interviews' telephone calls to Krasner in which she refused to talk to them. Interview with Francis V. O'Connor, April 25, 2003.

197 Peggy took the gamble: Putzel's relationship with Pollock was cozy. He acted often as a go-between: 'Peggy will buy the *Burning Landscape* for her collection. Do please let it be a surprise when she informs you.' Howard Putzel to Jackson Pollock, [n.d., ca. February 1943], Jackson Pollock Papers, AAA, reel 3046.

197 to celebrate, he went: Interview with Charles Sellger, June 24, 2003.

197 'We were delighted': Interview with Charles Seliger, December 12, 2000.

197 'One day – I think': Interview with Gerome Kamrowsh by Dennis Barrie, January 22, 1976, AAA.

198 'She was very proud': Quoted in Potter, 74.

198 'I consider this exhibition': *Art Digest*, November 1, 1943.

198 'At Art of This Century': Robert Coates, *The New Yorker*, November 20, 1943.

198 'Pollock's talent': 'Jackson Pollock: Paintings and Drawings, November 9–27,' Art of This Century, [1943].

198 'In a way, Sweeney': OTC, 255.

198 'spiritual offspring': OTC, 264.

198 'We like all this': Maude Riley, 'Fifty-Seventh Street in Review,' *Art Digest*, November 15, 1943.

198 '[Pollock] is the first': Clement Greenberg, 'Marc Chagall, Lyonel Feininger, Jackson Pollock,' *The Nation*, November 27, 1943.

199 who would sell just one Pollock: She would, however, sell several paintings from the show in the months to come.

199 'But she could be fun': Interview with Eileen Finletter, April 16, 2002.

199 'an exquisite and delicate': Michael Wishart, *High Diver: An Autobiography* (London: Quartet Books, 1994), 111.

199 'mysterious': Wishart, 111.

199 'This gaiety': Herbert Read, introduction to exhibition catalogue 'Pegeen,' [n.d., ca. 1950], PG Papers, SRGF.

200 She was deeply hurt: Kay Boyle dedicated *Being Geniuses Together* 'To my five daughters and the memory of Pegeen.'

200 'I hardly ever see Kay': Pegeen Vail to EC, October 24, 1941, EC Papers, University of Delaware.

200 Her mother, presumably: Interview with Eileen Finletter, April 16, 2002.

200 'was in the most dangerous': OTC, 253.

200 'responsibility, authority': OTC, 253.

201 Errol Flynn: For material on Flynn's political sympathies and his fondness for under-age girls, see Charles Higham, *Errol Flynn: The Untold Story* (1980; rpt. New York: Dell, 1981).

201 'Life seems so shallow': Pegeen Vail to EC, [December 20, 1943], EC Papers.

201 'I despise myself': Pegeen Vail to EC, [March 9, 1944], EC Papers.

201 'Being bribed': Pegeen Vail to EC, [n.d., 1944], EC Papers.

202 'pathetic': OTC, 258.

202 'so stupid': PG to EC, [November 12, 1943], EC Papers.

202 What Pegeen really needed: PG to EC, April 11, [1944], EC Papers.

202 Peggy, for instance, had asked: Naifeh and Smith, 460. Again, however, the source for this story was Lee Krasner.

202 'It looks pretty good': Jackson Pollock to Charles Pollock, July 29, 1943, quoted in Francis V. O'Connor and Eugene Victor Thaw, *Jackson Pollock: A Catalogue Raisonné of Paintings*, Drawings and Other Works (New Haven: Yale University Press, 1978), vol. 4, 228.

202 The stories around the timing: See Francis V. O'Connor, 'Jackson Pollock's Mural for Peggy Guggenheim: Its Documentation and Its Redefinition of Wall Painting as an Art Form,' in Philip Rylands, Dieter Bogner, Susan Davidson, Donald Quaintance, Valentina Sonzogni, Francis V. O'Connor, and Jasper Sharp, *Peggy and Kiesler: The Story of Art of This Century* (Venice: Peggy Guggenheim Collection, 2004).

203 'I painted quite a large mural': Jackson Pollock to Frank Pollock, January 15, 1944, quoted in Kirk Varnedoe and Pepe Karmel, eds., *Jackson Pollock: New Approaches* (New York: Museum of Modern Art, 1999), 81. Varnedoe writes that the postcard was 'an anomaly in need of further analysis and explanation.' E-mail message from Francis V. O'Connor to the author, August 19, 2002.

203 He would have had: See Carol Mancusi-Ungaro, 'Jackson Pollock: Response as Dialogue,' in Varnedoe and Karmel, 117–52.

203 'We had a party for the new genius': PG to EC, [November 12, 1943], EC Papers.

203 'My relationship with Pollock': OTC, 264.

204 Legend also has it: The details of this episode vary in the tellings. Clement Greenberg not only approved the story but said that the precise word to be used was 'peed.' See Florence Rubenfeld, *Clement Greenberg: A Life* (New York: Scribner, 1997), 309. But Greenberg was not present at the party. He said he first saw *Mural* in January 1944; see Susan Stanford Friedman, ed., *Analyzing Freud: Letters of H.D., Bryher, and Their Circle* (New York: New Directions, 2002), 63.

204 'Pollock was drunk': PG to Francis V. O'Connor, July 25, 1965; letter in O'Connor's private archive.

15: MAKING A MARK

205 'He was in a way': Unpublished manuscript, Hermine Benhaim Papers, AAA, reel 3482.

205 Most attributed the death: He may even have been murdered by someone he picked up on the street; the fact that there were rumors of suicide suggests something was being covered up. On Putzel, see 'Howard J. Putzel, Owned 67 Gallery,' *New York Times*, August 7, 1945; see also Melvin Paul Lader, 'Howard Putzel: Proponent of Surrealism and Early Abstract Art,' *Art in America*, February 1980, 85–96.

206 'To me the whole thing': PG to EC, April 11, [1944], EC Papers, University of Delaware.

206 'an English vicar': John Bernard Myers, *Tracking the Marvelous: A Life in the New York Art World* (New York: Random House, 1983), 24.

206 'flashily beautiful': Interview with Judith Malina and Hanon Reznikov, December 18, 2001.

206 Malina characterizes herself: Interview with Judith Malina and Hanon Reznikov, December 18, 2001.

206 'After careful consideration': PG to Julian Beck, December 3, 1945, private collection.

207 'pretty boys': Interview with Judith Malina and Hanon Reznikov, December 18, 2001.

207 'Going to bed': Interview with Sara Havelock-Allen, May 13, 2003.

207 'Nice tush': Interview with Jock Stockwell, November 3, 2000.

207 'They were the same': Interview with Valery Oisteanu, February 8, 2003.

207 'Nice body': Interview with Charles Henri Ford, December 28, 2000.

207 'bandit-boy': Charles Henri Ford, *Water from a Bucket: A Diary, 1948–1957* (New York: Turtle Point Press, 2001), 227.

208 'wonderful pre-war party': PG to Herbert Read, November 12, 1945.

208 'When Peggy Guggenheim whirled by': Myers, 49.

208 'I only live and breathe': PG to EC, October 15, [1944], EC Papers.

208 'Last night I started': PG to David Porter, January 23, 1945, David Porter Papers, AAA, reel N7–28.

208 'Saroyanesque childhood': Interview with Ethel Baziotes, January 10, 2001.

209 'If many of the canvases': *Art Digest*, October 15, 1944.

209 Peggy bought two: Donald Paneth, 'William Baziotes: A Literary Portrait,' unpublished manuscript, 28, William Baziotes Papers, AAA, reel N7–21.

209 Ethel Baziotes thinks: Interview with Ethel Baziotes, January 10, 2001.

209 'intense enjoyment': Jan Stroup, *Art Digest*, November 1, 1944.

209 'less upsetting': Clement Greenberg, *The Nation* (November 11, 1944), 572.

210 'Marius can't be left': PG to David Porter, [n.d.], David Porter Papers, AAA, reel N70–28.

210 Pegeen, who had recently announced: Pegeen Vail to EC, [n.d., 1944], EC Papers.

210 'I had a wonderful time': PG to David Porter, [n.d., January 1945], David Porter Papers, AAA, reel N70–28.

210 'Can't the women wait': PG to David Porter, February 12, [1945], David Porter Papers, AAA, reel N70–28.

210 number two among her lovers: David Porter to author, October 8, 2002.

210 Bill Davis: Bill Davis and his second wife, Annie, were known, according to Elaine Dundy, *Life Itself!* (London: Virago, 2001), 188, as 'the Gerald Murphys of the fifties, transferred to the new high bohemian playground of the Mediterranean Gold Coast of Spain.' Hemingway gives an account of his sixtieth birthday party at La Consula in *The Dangerous Summer* (New York: Scribner's, 1985), 61–63; a photo of the Davises and Hemingway poolside at La Consula appears on 167. For an extremely negative viewpoint on Bill Davis, see Jeremy Lewis, *Cyril Connolly: A Life* (London: Jonathan Cape,

1997), 461–62.

211 'the best lover': Deirdre Levi to author, January 16, 2002.

211 as Porter decided: Melvin Paul Lader, 'Peggy Guggenheim's Art of This Century,' unpublished doctoral dissertation, University of Delaware, June 1981, 285–87. Porter's foreword was refashioned to serve as an essay accompanying a 'Painting: Prophecy' exhibition in February 1945.

211 'the most important [season]': Lader, 293.

211 'I really don't get': Maude Riley, 'Jackson Pollock,' Art News (April 11, 1945), 59.

211 'nervous, if rough': Parker Tyler, 'Nature and Madness among the Younger Painters,' View (May 1945), 30.

212 'find strong enough words': Clement Greenberg, The Nation, April 7, 1945.

212 'Why are you getting': Quoted in Steven Naifeh and Gregory White Smith, Jackson Pollock: An American Saga (New York: Clarkson N. Potter, 1989), 503.

213 'Things couldn't have turned out': Quoted in Naifeh and Smith, 497.

213 'intense black hair': Charles Seliger, 'A Memory of the Art of This Century Gallery,' unpublished manuscript, 4, private collection.

214 'nearly [having] killed': Paul Cumming, interview with Charles Seliger, May 8, 1968, AAA.

214 'war baby': Interview with Charles Seliger, December 12, 2000.

214 'There was no question': Paul Cumming, interview with Charles Seliger, May 8, 1968, AAA; revised by Charles Seliger, June 24, 2003.

214 'cloak-and-suit' man: Interview with Charles Seliger, December 12, 2000.

214 'There wasn't much money': Charles Seliger, unpublished manuscript, 7, private collection.

214 'There had never been a gallery': Interview with Charles Seliger, December 12, 2000.

215 'She was bright and alert': Charles Seliger, unpublished manuscript, 4, private collection. On Seliger, see Francis V. O'Connor, Charles Seliger: Redefining Abstract Expressionism (Manchester, Vt.: Hudson Hills Press, 2002).

215 'Peggy had great spirit': Interview with Charles Seliger, June 24, 2003.

215 'It was a wonderful': Charles Seliger, unpublished journal, December 24, 1979, AAA.

215 'often mistaken for Max': Charles Seliger, unpublished manuscript, private collection.

215 'bizarre': Edwin Alden Jewell, New York Times, November 4, 1945.

216 'Jackson Pollock is one': 'Reviews and Previews,' Art News (May 1946), 63.

216 'the most important easel-painter': Clement Greenberg, The Nation (April 13, 1946), 445.

216 'The support of': Dore Ashton, The New York School: A Cultural Reckoning (Berkeley: University of California Press, 1972),153.

216 'Five Husbands': PG to EC, [October 27, 1944], EC Papers.

216 'not with the idea': PG to EC, October 15, [1944], EC Papers.

217 'Djuna Barnes was proud': Hank O'Neal, *'Life is painful, nasty, and short . . . In my case it has only been painful and nasty'*: Djuna Barnes, *1978–1981* (New York: Paragon, 1990),135.

217 'Well, I don't care': Jimmy Ernst, *A Not-So-Still Life: A Memoir* (New York: St. Martin's, 1984), 252.

218 An Anglo-American: See Myers, 175.

218 'I like the book': PG to EC, [October 27, 1944], EC Papers.

218 'won't make you hate': PG to Herbert Read, February 2, 1946, Herbert Read Collection, Special Collections, McPherson Library, University of Victoria.

218 'I didn't say anything awful': Quoted in Jacqueline Bograd Weld, *Peggy: The Wayward Guggenheim* (New York: E. P. Dutton, 1986), 347.

219 *Art Digest* commented: *Art Digest*, March 15, 1946.

219 'Stylistically her book': 'Temptations of Peggy,' *Time* (March 25, 1946), 57.

219 'To hide a singular': B. V. Winebaum, *New York Times* (May 26, 1946), section VII, 15.

219 'limited vocabulary': Elizabeth Hardwick, *The Nation* (April 6, 1946), 405.

219 'a gifted literata': Katherine Kuh, *Book Week*, March 31, 1946, 18.

219 '[t]he complete absence': Harry Hansen, 'The First Reader: Art and a Guggenheim,' *New York World-Telegram*, March 26, 1946.

219 'I have read her unspeakable': Aline Saarinen to Bernard Berenson, September 19, 1957, Aline Saarinen Papers, AAA, reel 2069.

220 'She leaves us with': Kuh, 19.

220 'detachment in looking back': Janet Flanner, quoted in Virginia Dortch, ed., *Peggy Guggenheim and Her Friends* (Milan: Berenice Books, 1994), 48.

220 'did not like the idea': OTC, 220.

221 'What I really liked': Gore Vidal, quoted in Dortch, ed., 148.

221 'was like Daisy Miller': Gore Vidal, 'Foreword,' OTC, xii.

221 'It's more fun being a writer': 'Temptations of Peggy,' 58.

16: BECOMING A LEGEND

223 'the magnificent scenery': PG to Herbert Read, February 2, 1946, Herbert Read Papers, Special Collections, McPherson Library, University of Victoria. Before leaving, she lined up: PG to Louise Nevelson, May 26, 1946, Louise Nevelson Papers, AAA, reel D296; see also Laurie Lisle, *Louise Nevelson: A Passionate Life* (New York: Washington Square Press, 1991),143–44.

224 who was in the audience that evening: John Bernard Myers, *Tracking the Marvelous: A Life in the New York Art World* (New York: Random House, 1983), 86–87.

224 They were traveling: The connection among literature, the Cold War, and the CIA has been well established in Frances Stonor Saunders, *The Cultural Cold War: The CIA and the World of Arts and Letters* (New York: The New Press, 2000). The connection between art and politics is far more tenuous: See Serge Guilbaut, trans. Arthur Goldhammer, *How New York Stole the Idea of Modern Art* (Chicago: University of Chicago Press, 1985).

224 'an explorer': Mary McCarthy, 'The Cicerone,' *Cast a Cold Eye* and *The Oasis* (rpt. New York: New American Library, 1972), 71.

224 'She had learned': McCarthy, 74.

225 'Peggy could be a queen': Quoted in Jacqueline Bograd Weld, *Peggy: The Wayward Guggenheim* (New York: E. P. Dutton, 1986), 356.

225 'Sexual intercourse': McCarthy, 73.

226 'The rapid turnover': McCarthy, 73.

226 'An indefatigable Narcissa': McCarthy, 70.

226 'huge gay, forgiving heart': Quoted in Weld, 382.

227 'The only trouble': Max Ernst to Bernard Reis, September 28, 1946, Bernard and Rebecca Reis Papers, Getty Research Institute.

227 In the course of his application: Barbara Seckler interview with Dorothea Tanning, July 11, 1990, to November 5, 1990, AAA, 115–20.

227 Pollock 'begged': Steven Naifeh and Gregory White Smith, *Jackson Pollock: An American Saga* (New York: Clarkson N. Potter, 1989), 528.

228 donate it to the University of Iowa: Edward Ranzal, 'Art Patron Sues Pollock Widow,' *New York Times*, June 9, 1961. Peggy chose the University of Iowa because her sister Benita's husband, Edward B. Mayer, was the son of the postmaster of Iowa City. She also donated to the university Pollock's *Portrait of H.M.* (1945) and two Seligers, including *Homage to Erasmus Darwin* (1945–46).

228 'Pollock has gone beyond': Clement Greenberg, *The Nation* (February 1, 1947), 139.

228 'thoughtfully related': B[en] W[olf], 'Non-Objectives by Pollock,' *Art Digest*, (January 15, 1947), 21.

228 'I never sold a Pollock': Alan Levy, 'Peggy Guggenheim: Venice's Last Duchess,' *Art News* (April 1975), 57.

229 Peggy had not been able: Lader, 321.

229 'I suppose it was the best': Stanley Price, 'The Mrs. Guggenheim Collection,' *New York Times Magazine*, January 17, 1965.

229 'She did some very strange': Charles Seliger interview with Paul Cumming, May 8, 1968, AAA, 39.

229 'I was exhausted': OTC, 267–68.

229 an inventory of which: Perhaps Reis anticipated that his client would like to see the value of her collection on paper at yearly intervals. Interview with Michael Arena, October 30, 2002. The gallery's books are in the Bernard and Rebecca Reis Collection, Getty Research Institute.

230 'With all the museums': Rudi Blesh, *Modern Art: Men, Rebellion, Conquest, 1900–1956* (New York: Knopf, 1956), 208–209.

231 'is in my opinion a serious loss': Clement Greenberg, *The Nation*, May 31, 1947.

231 'I stand by what': Greenberg, February 26, 1980, in 'Inventory of Temporary Exhibits: Art of This Century,' document in *Peggy and Kiesler: The Collector and the Visionary*, Peggy Guggenheim Collection, [n.p.].

232 '[m]uch has been claimed': Martica Sawin, *Surrealism in Exile and the*

Beginnings of the New York School (1995; rpt. Cambridge, Mass.: MIT Press, 1997), vii–ix.

232 'a canny impresario': John Richardson, 'La Dogaressa,' *New York Review of Books* (November 22, 1979), 18.

232 'She was fun': Weld, 278.

232 'absolutely stoned': David Hare, interview with Dorothy Seckler, January 17, 1968, AAA.

233 'Too many male artists': Telephone interview with Yoko Ono, May 30, 2003.

233 'looked like a hag': Quoted in Weld, 310.

17: A LAST STAND

234 'I do not in the least': PG to Clement Greenberg, December 2, [1947], Clement Greenberg Papers, AAA, reel N70–7R.

234 'Isn't it divine?': Mary McCarthy, 'The Cicerone,' *Cast a Cold Eye* and *The Oasis* (rpt. New York: New American Library, 1972), 71.

234 'Don't you think they': PG to Becky Reis, May 10, [1948], Bernard J. Reis Papers, AAA.

234 'bedraggled': PG to Bernard Reis, [July 1947], Bernard and Rebecca Reis Papers, Getty Research Institute.

235 'My husband, Bernard': Becky Reis quoted in James E. B. Breslin, *Mark Rothko: A Biography* (Chicago: University of Chicago Press, 1993), 182.

235 'As a friend and confidante': Lee Seldes, *The Legacy of Mark Rothko* (New York: Holt, Rinehart, and Winston, 1978), 40–41.

237 'a little vaguer': PG to Clement Greenberg, December 2, [1947], Clement Greenberg Papers, AAA, reel N70–7R.

237 'seemed sufficiently normal': PG to DB, Janaury 3, [1948], DB Papers, University of Maryland Library.

237 'as I know what you think': PG to DB, [n.d., 1948], DB Papers.

238 'as though I were': OTC, 275.

238 'rivers' of French champagne: Vittorio Corrain, quoted in Virginia Dortch, ed., *Peggy Guggenheim and Her Friends* (Milan: Berenice Books, 1994), 150.

239 the secretary of Count Zorzi: OTC, 279.

239 Pegeen convinced her to: PG to DB, January 1949, DB Papers, 'Pegeen chose it for me last summer.'

239 'Where is Venetia, who loved to chat so': Michael Wishart, *High Diver: An Autobiography* (London: Quartet Books, 1994), 92. The lyrics are from 'Where Is the Life That Late I Led,' in *Kiss Me, Kate*.

240 'double-decker' seating: Interview with Domingo de la Cueva, May 8, 2001.

240 The interior of the palazzo: Interview with Joan Fitzgerald, May 7, 2001.

240 'some very ignorant': Grace Glueck, 'Paintings Descending a Ramp,' *New York Times Magazine*, January 19, 1969.

241 'It is very strange': PG to Bernard Reis, October 4, [1949], Bernard J. Reis Papers, AAA.

242 'much to Peggy's dismay': Eileen Finletter to author, April 20, 2002.

242 sculptor Joan Fitzgerald: Interview with Joan Fitzgerald, May 7, 2001.

242 'The house was always too cold': Interview with John Hohnsbeen, September 13, 2001.

242 She was known to decant: Interview with Ralph Rumney, September 11, 2001. Rumney made the mistake of pointing this out to her, yet one more black mark against the name of her future son-in-law.

242 an Arthur Rubenstein concert: Telephone interview with Ralph Rumney, July 17, 2001. Rumney confided in Oona Guinness the following day, and she reimbursed him, knowing his straitened circumstances.

242 'an unfair shake': Telephone interview with Yoko Ono, May 30, 2003.

242 She continued to give Laurence: Joan Mellen, Kay Boyle: Author of Herself (New York: Farrar, Straus and Giroux, 1994), 339.

243 Also in the 1950s: Dortch, 50, caption 27.

243 'She was generous with her time': Interview with Anne Dunn, November 20, 2001.

243 'very deft in upsetting': Interview with John Loring, November 8, 2001.

243 'pretty, tanned legs': McCarthy, 71.

243 This habit caused some embarrassment: Paul Bowles, Without Stopping: An Autobiography (New York: G. P. Putnam's, 1972), 319.

243 'brown face [that] had': McCarthy, 71.

244 Seeing some unique slippers: Interview with Kathleen Flanagan, September, 2001; interview with Sandro Rumney, November 13, 2001.

244 'She got much more proper': Telephone interview with Peter Lauritzen, October 20, 2001.

244 'She's looking much better': Marius Bewley to Clement Greenberg, March 2, 1951, Clement Greenberg Papers, AAA, reel N70–7R.

244 Though one detractor: Interview with Joan Fitzgerald, May 7, 2001.

244 'iced vodka': Paolo Barozzi, Con Peggy Guggenheim: Tra storia e memoria (Milan: Christian Marinotti, 2001), 318.

244 'I liked her best': Interview with Charles Henri Ford, December 28, 2000.

244 'Imagine!': Interview with Charles Seliger, December 12, 2000.

244 'It was all quite exciting': PG to Becky Reis, March 9, [1950], Bernard J. Reis Papers, AAA.

245 In the fall of 1950: See Gerald Clarke, Capote: A Biography (New York: Simon and Schuster, 1988), 214.

245 'long-haired Bert Lahr': Truman Capote, Answered Prayers: The Unfinished Novel (New York: Plume, 1988), 69–70.

245 'like Tarzan': Interview with John Hohnsbeen, May 10, 2001.

245 The details are sketchy: For a thorough account, see Barozzi, 133–36.

246 'Raoul was bad news': Quoted in Jacqueline Bograd Weld, Peggy: The Wayward Guggenheim (New York: E. P. Dutton, 1986), 379.

246 'As for me I'm terribly': PG to Becky Reis, October 1, [1951], Bernard J. Reis Papers, AAA.

246 'I'm terribly in love': PG to DB, [July 1952], DB Papers.

246 '[W]e fight like hell': PG to EC, June 23, 1953, EC Paper, University of
Delaware.
246 'beautiful new motor boat': PG to Becky Reis, January 26, [1953], Bernard J.
Reis Papers, AAA.
246 'a lovely little Fiat': PG to Bernard Reis, October 15, [1952], Bernard J. Reis
Papers, AAA.
246 'R left me': PG to EC, August 21, [1954], EC Papers.
247 'I'm terribly sad': PG to DB, October [?], 1954, DB Papers.

18: WHAT REMAINS

248 'Pegeen had a sort of': Interview with Eileen Finletter, April 16, 2002.
249 'Pegeen was in love': Interview with Manina, May 9, 2001.
249 Peggy took her daughter: Interview with Sara Havelock-Allen, September 4,
2001; interviews with Ralph Rumney, September 9, 10, 11, 2001.
249 'It was a *coup de foudre*': Interview with Ralph Rumney, September 10, 2001.
249 'It's Pegeen's': Ralph Rumney, *The Consul*, trans. Malcolm Imbrie,
Contributions to the History of the Situationists International and Its Time,
vol. II (San Francisco: City Lights, 2002), 29.
249 'that awful boy': PG to Bernard Reis, February 12, 1958, and March 21,
1958, Bernard J. Reis Papers, AAA.
249 "She would hide bottles': Interview with Ralph Rumney, September 9, 2001.
249 'This goes beyond Freud': Interview with Eileen Finletter, April 16, 2002.
250 'it was one of the first signs': Interview with Iris Owens, November 28, 2002.
250 'Peggy liked strong people': Interview with Jacqueline Ventadour Hélion,
September 8, 2001.
250 'all the histoires': Sindbad Vail to PG, October 22, 1958, included with
letter from Sindbad Vail to Bernard Reis, October 29, 1958, Bernard J. Reis
Papers, AAA.
250 stealing the Picasso: Interview with Iris Owens, November 28, 2002.
250 Born in 1934 in Newcastle: Douglas Martin, 'Ralph Rumney, Artist and
Avant-Gardist, Is Dead at 67,' *New York Times*, March 31, 2002.
250 'lack of moral rectitude': Interview with Ralph Rumney, September 9, 2001.
'Pegeen wasn't political': Rumney, 36.
251 'He shot FRICK?': Interview with Hanon Reznikov, December 18, 2001.
Ralph demurred: Rumney, 90.
252 'I do not like your list': Thomas M. Messer, 'The History of a Courtship,' in
Karole Vail, *Peggy Guggenheim: A Celebration* (New York: Guggenheim
Museum, 1998), 131.
252 'I've written a book': PG to Bernard Reis, October 12, 1954, Bernard J. Reis
Papers, AAA.
253 'I seem to have written': OTC, 271.
253 'that wonderful painting': PG to Bernard Reis, April 11, [1957], Bernard J.
Reis Papers, AAA.
253 'loathed': Stanley Price, 'The *Mrs*. Guggenheim Collection,' *New York Times*

Magazine, January 17, 1965.

253 'I can't bear': PG to Bernard Reis, March 20, [1968?], Bernard J. Reis Papers, AAA.

254 'It's advertised that Rothko': PG to Bernard Reis, August 22, 1970, Bernard and Rebecca Reis Papers, Getty Research Institute.

254 'I will be glad': Barry Miles, *The Beat Hotel: Ginsberg, Burroughs, and Corso in Paris, 1958–1963* (New York: Grove, 2000), 76.

255 'Disaster!': Rumney, 35.

255 'I've never been': Allen Ginsberg to PG, [July ?, 1957], SRGF.

255 'It was hardly in the cards': Quoted in Miles, 77.

255 'It could be called successful': Gregory Corso to Allen Ginsberg, [February 13,] 1958. Quoted in Bill Morgan, ed., *An Accidental Autobiography: Selected Letters of Gregory Corso* (New York: New Directions, 2003), 88–89.

256 'Good news': Gregory Corso to Allen Ginsberg, [February 13,] 1958. Quoted in Bill Morgan, ed., 84–85.

256 'Very strange, marvelous': Gregory Corso to Allen Ginsberg, [February 13], 1958. Quoted in Bill Morgan, ed., 84–85.

256 'with wry sarcasm': Gregory Corso to Allen Ginsberg, February 6, 1958. Quoted in Bill Morgan, ed., 81.

256 'favorite pet dachshund': Ted Morgan, *Literary Outlaw: The Life and Times of William S. Burroughs* (New York: Henry Holt, 1988), 274.

257 'left a substantial sum': Daniel Farson, *The Gilded Gutter Life of Francis Bacon* (London: Vintage, 1994), 88.

257 After that, the city fathers: Ted Morgan, 259.

257 'Ansen wrote it': David Jackson to Alison Lurie (August 1959), quoted in Alison Lurie, *Familiar Spirits: A Memoir of James Merrill and David Jackson* (New York: Viking, 2001), 32.

257 Peggy's secretary: See Alan Ansen, 'The Return from Greece,' in *Disorderly Houses* (Middletown, Conn.: Wesleyan University Press, 1961), 69–85.

257 'at least twice': Interview with Alan Ansen, June 29, 2001.

257 'now and then between times': PG to Bernard Reis, February 6, 1959, Bernard J. Reis Papers, AAA.

258 'Sounds of Venice': David Revill, *The Roaring Silence: John Cage, A Life* (New York: Arcade, 1992), 194–96.

258 'a great disappointment': PG to Bernard Reis, [n.d., early 1959], Bernard J. Reis Papers, AAA.

258 'open-minded and intelligent': Telephone interview with Yoko Ono, May 30, 2003.

258 'ring-around-the-bed': Telephone interview with Lyle Bongé, October 17, 2001.

259 'a strange confused unhappy woman': Hazel G. McKinley to Kay Boyle, November 8, 1990, Kay Boyle Papers, Special Collections, Morris Library, Southern Illinois University. Hazel would live until 1995. See 'Painter Hazel G. McKinley of Guggenheim Family Dies,' *New Orleans Times Picayune* (June 13, 1995), B4. It is impossible to say just how many times Hazel was married.

259 'dissecting' her: Aline Saarinen to Bernard Berenson, December 15, 1957, Aline Saarinen Papers, AAA, reel 2069.

259 'I am completely convinced': Alfred Barr to Aline Saarinen, March 4, 1958, Aline Saarinen Papers, AAA, reel 2069.

259 'a foul horror': Bernard Berenson to Aline Saarinen, September 23, 1957, Aline Saarinen Papers, AAA, reel 2069.

259 'in her usual good spirit': Herbert Read to Aline Saarinen, June 12, 1958, Aline Saarinen Papers, AAA, reel 2069.

259 'If your puritanical reactions': PG to Aline Saarinen, October 29, 1958, Aline Saarinen Papers, AAA, reel 2069.

259 'long awaited maturity': Aline Saarinen to Bernard Berenson, May 25, 1969, Aline Saarinen Papers, AAA, reel 2069.

260 'poor Sweeney': OTC, 301.

260 Peggy wrote that she also went: Ben Heller says Peggy never attended a cocktail party at his home; telephone interview with Ben Heller, January 27, 2003. See OTC, 302–303.

261 'reasonable market value': Edward Ranzal, 'Art Patron Sues Pollock's Widow,' New York Times, June 9, 1961.

261 apartment of an English friend: Interview with Sara Havelock-Allen, September 4, 2001.

261 A year before, Reis: Bernard Reis to Lee Krasner Pollock, April 5, 1960, Bernard J. Reis Papers, AAA.

261 In the settlement: 'Patron,' New York Times (May 16, 1965), section 2, 21.

261 'perpetual histoires': PG to EC, February 17, 1960, EC Papers, University of Delaware.

261 'I think he has used': PG to EC, April 20, 1960, EC Papers.

261 'once she grew up': PG to EC, April 20, 1960, EC Papers.

261 Ralph would later say: Interview with Ralph Rumney, September 10, 2001. A story was going around: Telephone interview with John Hohnsbeen, February 2, 2003.

262 some Cocteau drawings: Sandro would never see the drawings again after her mother's death; he presumes, as did Ralph Rumney, that Peggy took them. Interview with Sandro Rumney, September 6, 2001.

262 'Her paintings, especially the pastels': Rumney, 90.

263 'However, after thinking': Harry F. Guggenheim to PG, June 4, 1959, SRGF.

264 In any case, Peggy wrote: PG to Bernard Reis, October 30, 1959, Bernard J. Reis Papers, AAA.

264 By the end of 1960: PG to Bernard Reis, December 24, 1960, Bernard J. Reis Papers, AAA.

264 'spiritual home': Joseph X. Dever, 'Peggy Guggenheim Art to Go to England,' New York World-Telegram and Sun, October 26, 1961.

265 'your inquiry concerning': Harry F. Guggenheim to PG, August 6, 1964, SRGF.

265 'I am so very happy': Quoted in Thomas M. Messer, 'The History of a Courtship,' in Karole P. B. Vail, Peggy Guggenheim: A Celebration (New York: Guggenheim Museum, 1998), 128.

19: LAST DAYS

266 Peggy wrote Djuna Barnes: PG to DB, April 26, 1964, DB Papers, University of Maryland.
266 'hospitals, home, property': DB to PG, April 3, 1964, DB Papers.
266 'heavenly': PG to Bill Rose, July 8, 1964, Vassar College Library, Special Collections.
266 'hardly enough energy': PG to DB, April 26, 1964, DB Papers.
266 'We are on the autumn road': DB to PG, October 8, 1964, DB Papers.
267 'a terrific success': PG to DB, October 8, 1964, DB Papers.
267 'He is working': PG to EC, November 5, 1968, EC Papers, University of Delaware.
267 'My friends in Paris': Herbert Gold, Bohemia: Digging the Roots of Cool (New York: Simon and Schuster, 1993), 48–49.
268 'I think Peggy did everything': Ralph Rumney, The Consul, trans. Malcolm Imbrie, Contributions to the History of the Situationists International and Its Time, vol. II (San Francisco: City Lights, 2002), 90.
268 Ralph 'could be mean': Interview with Eileen Finletter, April 16, 2002.
268 '[Ralph] looks more like': PG to Bernard Reis, July 8, 1958, Bernard J. Reis Papers, AAA.
268 'he had a sweet nature': Interview with Eileen Finletter, April 16, 2002.
269 'Life got rather boring': Quoted in Alan Woods, The Map Is Not the Territory (Manchester, Eng.: Manchester University Press, 2000), 50–51.
269 'pudique': Interview with Anne Dunn, November 20, 2001.
269 she and Peggy were not speaking: Interview with Ralph Rumney, September 10, 2001.
269 Peggy would later say: PG to EC, March 28, [1967], EC Papers.
269 'It's still a mystery': Rumney, 92.
270 'I suppose if I'd suspected': Interview with Ralph Rumney, September 10, 2001.
270 'Peggy loved Pegeen': EC to DB, March 8, 1967, DB Papers.
270 'It truly kills': Second ellipsis added in DB to PG, April 14, 1967, DB Papers.
270 she gave each one a gift: Interview with John Hohnsbeen, September 13, 2001.
271 'luckily': PG to Becky Reis, April 1, 1961, Bernard J. Reis Papers, AAA.
271 'I have had a lovely summer': PG to DB, October 10, 1966, DB Papers.
271 'They come here': PG to DB, April 16, 1968, DB Papers.
271 'Go ahead': Interview with John Hohnsbeen, May 9, 2001.
271 'the distinction between a trainee': Thomas M. Messer, 'The History of a Courtship,' in Karole P. B. Vail, Peggy Guggenheim: A Celebration (New York: Guggenheim Museum, 1998), 145.
271 'She drew herself up': Interview with Sandro Rumney, October 4, 2001.
271 'gloomy': Interview with Sandro Rumney, September 13, 2001.
271 'Ralph finished off': LV to DB, March 31, 1967, DB Papers.
272 'so old, so ill': DB to PG, November 21, 1961, DB Papers.

272 'very gallant to the end': PG to DB, May 29, 1968, DB Papers.

272 'Laurence was the greatest': Interview with Sandro Rumney, October 4, 2001.

272 'a Guggenheim Jeune long summer show': Messer, 129.

272 'They're my security': Eugenia Sheppard, 'The Low-Pressure Life of Peggy Guggenheim,' *New York Post*, January 15, 1969.

272 'mellowed': Edmund Wilson, *The Sixties* (New York: Farrar, Straus and Giroux), 760.

272 'like postage stamps': Quoted in Messer, 135.

272 'not only a brilliant': David L. Shirey, 'Peggy's Back in Town,' *Time*, January 27, 1969.

273 'I never dreamt': Grace Glueck, 'Paintings Descending a Ramp,' *New York Times Magazine*, January 19, 1969.

273 'We have some very great cubists': Richard F. Shepard, 'Peggy Guggenheim Entrusts Art Here,' *New York Times* (March 25, 1969), 42.

273 'I'm glad I came': PG to DB, March 17, 1969, DB Papers.

273 '[F]or some time': Messer, 146.

274 'magical': Telephone interview with John Hohnsbeen, February 2, 2003.

274 'the irresistible hour': OTC, 318.

274 'I adore floating': PG to DB, October 3, 1956, DB Papers.

274 Peggy told Djuna she thought it looked better: PG to DB, February 9, 1975, DB Papers.

275 'discerned': Mary McCarthy to Bowden Broadwater, September 28, 1956, quoted in Frances Kiernan, *Seeing Mary Plain: A Biography of Mary McCarthy* (New York: Norton, 2000), 431.

275 'I have never, never forgotten this': Quoted in Jacqueline Bograd Weld, *Peggy: The Wayward Guggenheim* (New York: E. P. Dutton, 1986), 384.

275 'Why is [Peggy] so ostracized?': Mary McCarthy to Bernard Berenson, August 28, 1956, quoted in Kiernan, 328.

275 'Peggy had always bought': Interview with Sandro Rumney, September 4, 2001.

275 John Loring: Interview with John Loring, November 8, 2001.

275 'She never talked about it': Telephone interview with John Hohnsbeen, February 2, 2003.

276 'Also insist': Quoted in Messer, 150.

276 'wide and unseeing': Interview with John Hohnsbeen, May 11, 2001.

276 'no normal taxis': PG to DB, March 10, 1978, DB Papers.

276 'I think life': PG to DB, November 16, 1973, DB Papers.

276 in 1971 conspired: See PG to DB, March 25, 1971; DB to PG, September 3, 1971; PG to DB, September 28, 1971; DB to Bernard Reis, October 20, 1971; DB to PG, December 2, 1971, DB Papers.

277 'no longer received': PG to DB, March 29, 1979, DB Papers.

277 'Being immortal': DB to PG, April 15, 1979, DB Papers.

277 'All of which is long ago': DB to PG, April 15, 1979, DB Papers.

277 'In a sense': OTC, xi–xii.

278 'There's no reason': Telephone interview with John Hohnsbeen, February 2, 2003.

278 December 23: Philip Rylands, e-mail message to author, July 17, 2001.

278 The housekeeper, Isia: Telephone interview with John Hohnsbeen, February 2, 2003.

279 'Big deal': Quoted in Weld, 442.

279 estate turned out: Interview with Sandro Rumney, October 4, 2001.

279 he was severely criticized: Telephone interview with Fred Licht, April 6, 2001.

SELECTED BIBLIOGRAPHY

Agar, Eileen. *A Look at My Life*. London: Methuen, 1988.

Altshuler, Bruce. *The Avant-Garde in Exhibition*. New York: Harry Abrams, 1994.

Ashton, Dore. *The New York School: A Cultural Reckoning*. Berkeley: University of California Press, 1972.

Bair, Deirdre. *Samuel Beckett: A Biography*. 1978; rpt. New York: Summit Books, 1990.

Baldwin, Neil. *Man Ray: American Artist*. 1988; rpt. New York: Da Capo, 2001.

Barozzi, Paolo. *Con Peggy Guggenheim: Tra storia e memoria*. Milan: Christian Marinotti, 2001.

Benstock, Shari. *Women of the Left Bank: Paris, 1900–1940*. Austin: University of Texas, 1986.

Bernier, Olivier. *Fireworks at Dusk: Paris in the Thirties*. New York: Little, Brown, 1993.

Birmingham, Stephen. *'Our Crowd': The Great Jewish Families of New York*. 1967; rpt. New York: Dell, 1978.

Blondel, Nathalie. *Mary Butts: Scenes from the Life*. Kingston, N.Y.: McPherson, 1998.

Bogner, Dieter, ed. *Friedrich Kiesler: Art of This Century*. Vienna: Hatje Cantz, 2003.

Bowles, Paul. *In Touch: The Letters of Paul Bowles*. New York: Farrar, Straus and Giroux, 1994.

——. *Without Stopping: An Autobiography*. New York: G. P. Putnam's, 1972.

Brandon, Ruth. *Surreal Lives: The Surrealists, 1917–1945*. New York: Grove Press, 1999.

Broe, Mary Lynn, and Angela Ingram. *Women's Writing in Exile*. Chapel Hill: University of North Carolina Press, 1989.

Burke, Carolyn. *Becoming Modern: The Life of Mina Loy*. New York: Farrar, Straus and Giroux, 1996.

Butter, Peter. *Edwin Muir: Man and Poet*. New York: Barnes and Noble, 1967.

Caponi, Gena Dagel. *Paul Bowles: Romantic Savage*. Carbondale: Southern Illinois University Press, 1994.

Cardiff, Maurice. *Memories of Lawrence Durrell, Freya Stark, Patrick Leigh-Fermor, Peggy Guggenheim, and Others*. London: Radcliff Press, 1997.

Caws, Mary Ann, Rudolf Kuensli, and Gwen Raaberg. *Surrealism and Women*.

Cambridge, Mass.: MIT Press, 1991.

Chadwick, Whitney. *Women Artists and the Surrealist Movement.* Boston: Little, Brown, 1985.

Checkland, Sarah Jane. *Ben Nicholson: The Vicious Circles of His Life and Art.* London: John Murray, 2000.

Chitty, Susan. *Now to My Mother: A Very Personal Memoir of Antonia White.* London: Weidenfeld and Nicolson, 1985.

Clarke, Gerald. *Capote: A Biography.* New York: Simon and Schuster, 1988.

Cone, Michele C. *Artists under Vichy: A Case of Prejudice and Persecution.* Princeton, N.J.: Princeton University Press, 1992.

Cowley, Malcolm. *A Second Flowering: Works and Days of the Lost Generation.* New York: Viking, 1973.

Cronin, Anthony. *Samuel Beckett: The Last Modernist.* 1997; rpt. New York: Da Capo, 1999.

Crosby, Caresse. *The Passionate Years.* New York: Dial, 1953.

Davis, John H. *The Guggenheims, 1848–1988: An American Epic.* New York: William Morrow, 1978.

De Coppet, Laura, and Alan Jones. *The Art Dealers.* New York: Clarkson N. Potter, 1984.

Dortch, Virginia, ed. *Peggy Guggenheim and Her Friends.* Milan: Berenice Books, 1994.

Dunn, Jane. *Antonia White: A Life.* London: Jonathan Cape, 1998.

Ellmann, Richard. *James Joyce.* New York: Oxford University Press, 1982.

Ernst, Jimmy. *A Not-So-Still Life: A Memoir.* New York: St. Martin's, 1984.

Field, Andrew. *Djuna: The Formidable Miss Barnes.* Austin: University of Texas, 1983.

Ford, Hugh. *Four Lives in Paris.* San Francisco: North Point Press, 1980.

Fry, Varian. *Surrender on Demand.* New York: Random House, 1945.

Gascoyne, David. *Collected Journals, 1936–42.* London: Scoob Books, 1991.

Gere, Charlotte, and Marina Valzey. *Great Women Collectors.* New York: Harry Abrams, 1999.

Gerhardie, William. *Of Mortal Love.* 1936; rpt. London: Macdonald, 1970.

——. *Memoirs of a Polyglot.* 1931; rpt. London: Macdonald, 1973.

Gill, Anton. *Art Lover: A Biography of Peggy Guggenheim.* New York: HarperCollins, 2002.

Glassco, John. *Memoirs of Montparnasse.* New York: Oxford University Press, 1970.

Gold, Mary Jayne. *Crossroads Marseilles, 1940.* New York: Doubleday, 1980.

Hall, Lee. *Betty Parsons: Artist, Dealer, Collector.* New York: Harry Abrams, 1991.

Hansen, Arlen. *Expatriate Paris: A Cultural and Literary Guide to Paris of the 1920s.* New York: Arcade, 1990.

Herring, Phillip. *Djuna: The Life and Work of Djuna Barnes.* 1995; rpt. New York: Penguin, 1996.

Hopkinson, Lyndall Passerini. *Nothing to Forgive: A Daughter's Story of Antonia White.* London: Chatto and Windus, 1988.

Huddleston, Sisley. *Back to Montparnasse: Glimpses of Broadway in Bohemia.* Philadelphia: Lippincott, 1931.

Jenison, Madge. *Sunwise Turn: A Human Comedy of Bookselling.* New York: E. P. Dutton, 1923.

Josephson, Matthew. *Life among the Surrealists.* New York: Holt, Rinehart and Winston, 1962.

Kiernan, Frances. *Seeing Mary Plain: A Life of Mary McCarthy.* New York: Norton, 2000.

King, James. *The Last Modern: A Life of Herbert Read.* New York: St, Martin's, 1990.

Knowlson, James. *Damned to Fame: The Life of Samuel Beckett.* 1996; rpt. New York: Touchstone, 1997.

Lader, Melvin Paul. 'Peggy Guggenheim's Art of This Century: The Surrealist Milieu and the American Avant-Garde, 1942–1947,' unpublished doctoral dissertation, University of Delaware, 1981.

Levy, Julien. *Memoir of an Art Gallery.* New York: G. P. Putnam's, 1977.

Loeb, Harold. *The Way It Was.* New York: Criterion, 1959.

Lord, James. *A Gift For Admiration, Further Memoirs.* New York: Farrar, Straus and Giroux, 1998.

Lukach, Joan M. *Hilla Rebay: In Search of the Spirit in Art.* New York: George Braziller, 1983.

Marino, Andy. *A Quiet American: The Secret War of Varian Fry.* New York: St. Martin's, 1999.

Mellen, Joan. *Kay Boyle: Author of Herself.* New York: Farrar, Straus and Giroux, 1994.

Melly, George. *Don't Tell Sybil: An Intimate Memoir of E.L.T. Mesens.* London: Heinemann, 1997.

Miles, Barry. *The Beat Hotel: Ginsberg, Burroughs, and Corso in Paris,1958–1963.* New York: Grove, 2000.

Morgan, Bill, ed. *An Accidental Autobiography: Selected Letters of Gregory Corso.* New York: New Directions, 2003.

Morgan, Ted. *Literary Outlaw: The Life and Times of William S. Burroughs.* New York: Henry Holt, 1988.

Morris, Jan. *Manhattan '45.* New York: Oxford, 1987.

Mulhern, Francis. *The Moment of 'Scrutiny'.* London: NLB, 1979.

Muir, Edwin. *An Autobiography.* 1954; rpt. St. Paul, Minn.: Graywolf, 1990.

Muir, Willa. *Belonging: A Memoir.* London: Hogarth Press, 1968.

Myers, John Bernard. *Tracking the Marvelous: A Life in the New York Art World.* New York: Random House, 1983.

Naifeh, Steven, and Gregory White Smith. *Jackson Pollock: An American Saga.* New York: Clarkson N. Potter, 1989.

O'Connor, Francis V. *Charles Seliger: Redefining Abstract Expressionism.* Manchester, Vt.: Hudson Hills Press, 2002.

——, and Eugene Victor Thaw. *Jackson Pollock: A Catalogue Raisonné of Paintings, Drawings and Other Works.* New Haven: Yale University Press, 1978.

O'Neal, Hank. *'Life is painful, nasty, and short . . . In my case it has only been painful and nasty'*: Djuna Barnes 1978–1981. New York: Paragon, 1990.

Penrose, Roland. *Scrap Book 1900–1981.* New York: Rizzoli, 1981.

Pollizotti, Mark. *Revolution of the Mind: The Life of André Breton.* New York: Farrar, Straus and Giroux, 1995.

Potter, Jeffrey. *To a Violent Grave: An Oral Biography of Jackson Pollock.* New York: G. P. Putnam's, 1985.

Putnam, Samuel. *Paris Was Our Mistress: Memoirs of a Lost and Found Generation.* Carbondale: Southern Illinois University Press, 1970.

Remy, Michel. *Surrealism in Britain.* London: Ashgate, 1999.

Revill, David. *The Roaring Silence: John Cage, A Life.* New York: Arcade, 1992.

Richardson, John. *Sacred Monsters, Sacred Masters: Beaton, Capote, Dalí, Picasso, Freud, Warhol, and More.* New York: Random House, 2001.

Rubenfeld, Florence. *Clement Greenberg: A Life.* New York: Scribner, 1997.

Rudenstine, Angelica Zander. *Peggy Guggenheim Collection, Venice, the Solomon R. Guggenheim Foundation.* New York: Harry Abrams, 1985.

Rumney, Ralph. *The Consul.* Malcolm Imbrie, trans. Contributions to the History of the Situationists International and Its Time, vol. II. San Francisco: City Lights, 2002.

Rylands, Philip, Dieter Bogner, Susan Davidson, Donald Quaintance, Valentina Sonzogni, Francis V. O'Connor, and Jasper Sharp. *Peggy and Kiesler: The Story of Art of This Century.* Venice: Peggy Guggenheim Collection, 2004.

Sawin, Martica. *Surrealism in Exile and the Beginning of the New York School.* 1995; rpt. Cambridge, Mass.: MIT Press, 1997.

Sawyer-Lauçanno, Christopher. *An Invisible Spectator: A Biography of Paul Bowles.* New York: Weidenfeld and Nicolson, 1989.

Schaffner, Ingrid, and Lisa Jacobs, eds. *Julien Levy: Portrait of an Art Gallery.* Cambridge, Mass.: MIT Press, 1998.

Schenkar, Joan. *Truly Wilde: The Unsettling Story of Dolly Wilde, Oscar's Unusual Niece.* New York: Basic Books, 2000.

Siegel, Jerrold. *Bohemian Paris: Culture, Politics, and the Boundaries of Bourgeois Life, 1830–1930.* New York: Penguin, 1970.

Steegmuller, Francis. *Cocteau: A Biography.* Boston: Little, Brown, 1970.

Suther, Judith D. *A House of Her Own: Kay Sage, Solitary Surrealist.* Lincoln: University of Nebraska Press, 1997.

Tacou-Rumney, Laurence. *Peggy Guggenheim: A Collector's Album.* Ralph Rumney, trans. Paris: Flammarion, 1996.

Tashjian, Dickran. *A Boatload of Madmen: Surrealism and the American Avant-Garde.* 1995; rpt. New York: Thames and Hudson, 2001.

Tomkins, Calvin. *Duchamp: A Biography.* New York: Henry Holt, 1996.

Trevelyan, Julian. *Indigo Days: The Art and Memoirs of Julian Trevelyan.* 1937; rpt. London: Scolar Press, 1996.

Vail, Karole P. B. *Peggy Guggenheim: A Celebration.* New York: Guggenheim Museum, 1998.

Varnedoe, Kirk, and Pepe Karmel. *Jackson Pollock: New Approaches.* New York:

Museum of Modern Art, 1999.

Waugh, Alec. *My Brother Evelyn and Other Profiles*. London: Cassell, 1967.

Weld, Jacqueline Bograd. *Peggy: The Wayward Guggenheim*. New York: E. P. Dutton, 1986.

White, Antonia. *Diaries 1926–1957*. Susan Chitty, ed. New York: Viking, 1992.

Wickes, George. *Americans in Paris*. New York: Doubleday, 1969.

Williams, William Carlos. *The Autobiography of William Carlos Williams*. New York: Random House, 1951.

——. *A Voyage to Pagany*. New York: Macaulay, 1928.

Wiser, William. *The Crazy Years: Paris in the Twenties*. New York: Thames and Hudson, 1983.

Wishart, Michael. *High Diver: An Autobiography*. London: Quartet Books, 1994.

INDEX